Social Democracy in the Global Periphery

Social Democracy in the Global Periphery focuses on social-democratic regimes in the developing world that have, to varying degrees, reconciled the needs of achieving growth through globalized markets with extensions of political, social, and economic rights. The authors show that opportunities exist to achieve significant social progress, despite a global economic order that favors core industrial countries. Their findings derive from a comparative analysis of four exemplary cases: Kerala (India), Costa Rica, Mauritius, and Chile (since 1990). Though unusual, the social and political conditions from which these developing-world social democracies arose are not unique; indeed, pragmatic and proactive social-democratic movements helped create these favorable conditions. The four exemplars have preserved or even improved their social achievements since neoliberalism emerged hegemonic in the 1980s. This demonstrates that certain social-democratic policies and practices – guided by a democratic developmental state – can enhance a national economy's global competitiveness.

RICHARD SANDBROOK is Professor of Political Science at the University of Toronto.

MARC EDELMAN is Professor of Anthropology at Hunter College and the Graduate Center, City University of New York.

PATRICK HELLER is Associate Professor of Sociology at Brown University.

JUDITH TEICHMAN is Professor of Political Science at the University of Toronto.

Social Democracy in the Global Periphery

Origins, Challenges, Prospects

Richard Sandbrook, Marc Edelman, Patrick Heller, and Judith Teichman

CAMBRIDGE
UNIVERSITY PRESS

CAMBRIDGE UNIVERSITY PRESS
Cambridge, New York, Melbourne, Madrid, Cape Town, Singapore,
São Paulo, Delhi, Dubai, Tokyo, Mexico City

Cambridge University Press
The Edinburgh Building, Cambridge CB2 8RU, UK

Published in the United States of America by Cambridge University Press, New York

www.cambridge.org
Information on this title: www.cambridge.org/9780521686877

© Richard Sandbrook, Marc Edelman, Patrick Heller and Judith Teichman 2007

First published 2007

A catalogue record for this publication is available from the British Library

ISBN 978-0-521-86703-0 Hardback
ISBN 978-0-521-68687-7 Paperback

Contents

Tables

Acknowledgments

This book, which emerged from a movable seminar, has received generous intellectual and financial support in the course of its travels. Our first two-day symposium at the University of Toronto's Munk Centre for International Studies, in the winter of 2003, established a pattern: a public forum followed by a private all-day session involving the four authors. We would like to thank Professor Louis Pauly, the director of Toronto's Centre for International Studies, for his consistent financial and personal support for this project.

Richard Sandbrook, a University of Toronto political scientist who has focused his research largely on the political economy of Africa and globalization, had enticed the other three authors to join this project during the summer of 2002. His aim, as he explains it, was to enlist the cooperation of talented area specialists with an interest in distributional issues and diverse disciplinary backgrounds. Judith Teichman is a political scientist at the University of Toronto who has long studied the politics of neoliberal reform in Chile and elsewhere in Latin America. Patrick Heller, a sociologist at Brown University, has written a well-received book on Kerala's political economy of development. And Marc Edelman of Hunter College, City University of New York, has pursued extensive and broad-based anthropological studies of Costa Rica, especially concerning the role of peasants in globalization. Sandbrook's three co-authors would like to acknowledge his leadership role, not only in inspiring this project but also in so effectively pushing it toward completion.

Although this team was well prepared to write an interdisciplinary and transcontinental comparative study, we realized that the process might not be easy. Would we get along? The first movable seminar in Toronto removed that concern; the authors could, indeed, cooperate and even gracefully concede points in heated debates. Other symposia followed, as the authors conducted further field research and resolved methodological and analytical disagreements. Our second two-day symposium, in November 2003 at the Watson Center for International Studies at Brown University, allowed us to gain valuable feedback from Brown's renowned comparativist scholars. Professor Barbara Stallings not only generously provided the funding for this meeting through her Political Economy of Development program, but also contributed valuable ideas in our public seminar. Further symposia took place in Toronto in March 2004, Hunter College of the City University of New York in July 2004, and again at the Munk Centre, University of Toronto, in January 2005. Then the writing of the final draft proceeded in earnest.

The authors have benefited from research grants that have advanced this project. Judith Teichman and Richard Sandbrook gratefully acknowledge their individual research grants from the Social Sciences and Humanities Research Council of Canada. Marc Edelman has received crucial support from Grant #65512-00 34, PSC-CUNY Research Awards Program.

But the book would not have achieved whatever merit it has without the intellectual support and frank criticism of so many friends and colleagues, many of whom participated in our various symposia. A mere listing of names cannot possibly convey the extent of our gratitude and warm regards toward the persons mentioned. Dietrich Rueschemeyer at Brown University and Atul Kohli at Princeton were particularly helpful, the former for ongoing inspiration and feedback, and the latter for organizing a workshop at Princeton to discuss this project and for commenting on selected chapters. Others who have helpfully located relevant sources, shared their views on the issues, or commented on various chapters – and whom we hereby absolve of any responsibility – include Oscar Altimir, Albert Berry, Michael Blim, Sheila Bunwaree, Katrina Burgess, Melani Cammett, Linda Cook, Guillermo Garcia-Huidobro, Lesley Gill, Angelique Haugerud, Paget Henry, José Itzigsohn, Don Kalb, Matthew Lange, James Mahoney, Iván Molina, Stephen Palmer, Lou Pauly, Cranford Pratt, Rajesh Puliyara, Dagmar Raczynski, Ciska Raventós, Don Robotham, Jorge Rovira, Gavin Alderson Smith, and Anil Varughese.

The authors have drawn heavily on the extensive research on Kerala, Costa Rica, Mauritius, and Chile of historians and social scientists who are nationals of the country they study. We wish not only to acknowledge this debt, but also to identify a peculiar interpretive problem to which this debt gives rise. Many of the Keralite, Costa Rican, Mauritian, and Chilean researchers upon whose work we build are, appropriately, social critics. They subject their own political leaders, institutions, and movements to withering criticism, based on an acute awareness of how the reality of their countries diverges from such ideals as equality, solidarity, and participatory democracy. We have certainly been influenced by these critics. Each of the cases we have studied, considered in its own terms, seems to have fallen short of its promise. However, viewed through a comparative lens, the democratic and social achievements of these four cases stand out and demand an explanation. It is this comparative perspective that leads us sometimes to depart from the despairing tone of much contemporary scholarship.

We also wish to acknowledge our resourceful research assistants, all of whom made significant contributions to the final work. Richard Sandbrook wishes to recognize the fine research work carried out in Mauritius by Hansa Munbauhal in 2003–2004, while she was a Masters student at the University of Mauritius. Judith Teichman thanks Sandra Dughman, a political science and law student at the University of Chile, who helped with data collection in Chile during 2003–2004. Marc Edelman gratefully acknowledges the assistance of the staff at the documentation centers of the Instituto de Investigaciones Sociales, University of Costa Rica, and the Consejo Nacional para Investigaciones Científicas y Tecnológicas. And Patrick Heller expresses his appreciation to Rajesh M. Puliyara from the Centre for Development Studies in Trivandrum, who assisted with collecting data for this project.

Last, but far from least, we thank John Haslam of Cambridge University Press, both for his encouragement throughout the writing of this book and for his prompt attention to queries or problems.

Part I

Introduction

1   Social democracy in the periphery

In *A Bias for Hope* (1971, 28), Albert O. Hirschman enjoined social scientists to embrace "a passion for the possible." Our primary task, he noted, is to understand *probabilities*, in the sense of uncovering regularities and uniform sequences. If we limit ourselves to this task, however, we risk fortifying a paralysis of the will by casting situations of backwardness, injustice, or oppression as the inevitable outcome of universal laws. Hopeful cases of social progress will then be dismissed as merely exceptions to the general rule. To avoid this negative tendency, social scientists should also search for *possibilities* – the often hidden opportunities for valued change that lurk in a particular situation. Hirschman's own work sought to widen the limits of what is, or is perceived to be, possible.

This book seeks to do the same thing. It focuses on social-democratic regimes that have, to varying degrees, reconciled the exigencies of achieving growth through globalized markets with extensions of political, social, and economic rights. We show that opportunities exist to achieve significant social progress in the periphery, despite a global economic order that favors the core industrial countries.[1] We explore what has been attained in certain countries, and how and why social-democratic experiments have succeeded, in the hope that this exploration will suggest possibilities for similar achievements elsewhere. Our findings derive primarily from a comparative analysis of four exemplary cases: Kerala (India), Costa Rica, Mauritius, and Chile since 1990. In the global south, where poverty, inequality, illiteracy, hunger, and authoritarian and corrupt governance are widespread, these four cases stand out in contrast.

We arrive at two significant findings. First, the four exemplars cannot be dismissed as inexplicable, historical accidents. Though unusual, the social and political conditions from which these developing-world social democracies arise are not unique; indeed, pragmatic and proactive social-democratic movements help create these favorable conditions. Second, these cases have accommodated, but avoided capitulating to,

---

[1] For a similar viewpoint, refer to Evans 2005; Glatzer and Rueschemeyer 2005.

global neoliberalism (construed as pressures to liberalize markets, reform states, and open economies to cross-border flows of goods, services, and capital). The four exemplars have preserved or even improved their social achievements since neoliberalism emerged hegemonic in the 1980s. Certain social-democratic policies and practices – including the actions of a democratic developmental state – can enhance an economy's global competitiveness.

Context of the study

Both the shortcomings of neoliberal reform and the renewed search for a more desirable alternative warrant a rethinking of the nature and viability of social-democratic models. On the one hand, market-oriented reforms have produced disappointing, and sometimes destructive, results in the global south. On the other hand, the last decade has witnessed a resurgence of interest in more egalitarian and dynamic alternatives to the Washington, or more comprehensive "Post-Washington," Consensus.[2] Implicitly or explicitly, social-democratic principles are central to certain of these alternative visions.

The shortcomings of market reform are widely acknowledged. That neoliberalism's triumph would usher in a more peaceful and prosperous world – an "end of history" – was a popular post-Cold War view. According to this position, the collapse of state socialism in the 1980s allowed all countries to adopt a market orientation and open economies. Free global markets, it was believed, facilitated the free movement of ideas as well as products, thereby opening closed states to the outside world. Free trade and investment, furthermore, could foster the prosperity necessary to defeat poverty and defuse conflicts. Democratization and the development of civil societies would, in time, accompany economic liberalism. All these changes would facilitate a more peaceful world. This optimistic scenario is not being realized, however.

First, even World Bank economists have recently conceded that market reform has not yet delivered on its economic promise. William Easterly, in an article tellingly entitled "The Lost Decades," shows that many developing countries have stagnated despite their adoption of market-friendly reforms. He cites one statistic that dramatically illustrates the lack of success: whereas the median per capita income growth in developing countries in the era of state interventionism (1960–1979) reached

---

[2] The original statement of the Washington Consensus is Williamson 1990. On the controversy surrounding the Washington Consensus and the alleged need to "reform the reforms" in a Post-Washington Consensus, see Santiso 2004.

2.5 percent, it was a disastrous 0.0 percent in 1980–1999 (Easterly 2001, 135). Branko Milanovic (2003) similarly accepts that the development record of 1960–1978 is superior on all measures to that of 1978–1998, noting that the best performers in the second period – for example China and India – did not follow mainstream free-market policies. Disillusionment with the Washington Consensus is especially widespread in Latin America, where "the initial enthusiasm . . . was not matched by results" (Ortiz 2003, 14). Finally, former World Bank Chief Economist Joseph Stiglitz's jeremiads (2002) against "market fundamentalism" in the 1990s are well known. As Milanovic concludes, "something is clearly wrong" (2003, 679).

Second, scholars studying neoliberal reform have identified several destructive trends associated with reform policies:

- High and growing inequalities have accompanied market liberalization.[3] World income inequality has likely been rising, a trend that is incontrovertible if China is removed from the calculation. Within countries, neoliberal policies have also been associated with growing inequality and poverty in most cases. Does growing inequality matter, if the proportion of the global population living in destitution falls? Yes, responds Robert Wade: "Inequality above a moderate level creates a kind of society that even crusty conservatives hate to live in, unsafe and unpleasant," with higher crime and violence and lower levels of interpersonal trust (Wade 2004a, 582).
- Democracy itself is diluted and hollowed out. The scope of democratic decision making shrivels when national governments, through international agreements, surrender their power to regulate in the public interest in such areas as trade, financial flows, investment, and health and environmental standards, and when global financial markets effectively punish governments that deviate from conservative monetary, fiscal, and even social policies. In addition, growing social inequality and atomization lead to lower and less-effective popular participation, as cynicism regarding democratic institutions grows (see chapter 2).
- Market liberalization generates conditions in developing countries that are conducive to instability and conflict. Virtually the entire human population has been drawn into a growing dependence on markets. Where these markets are only lightly regulated, they subject people to rapid and sometimes devastating changes in fortune. Distributional shifts, new forms of economic insecurity, and external shocks demand

---

[3] The literature on income distribution is voluminous and contentious, with different methodologies producing different findings. The following generalizations are supported by these careful studies: Berry and Serieux 2004; Cornia, Addison, and Kushi 2004; Wade 2004a; and Wade 2004b.

strong, coherent states to devise adaptive economic strategies, mediate domestic distributional disputes, and mount social protection. Yet these new tensions, combined with externally influenced austerity programs and anti-state ideologies, challenge the legitimacy and coherence of already weak states. The rise in grievances, coupled with increasingly ineffective and unpopular regimes, provides an opening for violent protest movements drawing on religious fundamentalism, ethnic chauvinism, or charismatic populism.[4]

Social-democratic regimes, in principle, provide an antidote to these destructive tendencies. Not only can their inclusive and well-organized democratic institutions mediate distributional conflicts, but economic security, social cohesion, and equality are also enhanced through such redistributive mechanisms as land reform, job creation, progressive taxation, labor-market regulation, social insurance, and welfare provision. The efficacy of social-democratic regimes, in Europe and elsewhere, explains their resurgent popularity in current debates about development alternatives to neoliberal orthodoxy.

Prominent among these alternatives is neostructuralism. In Latin America, with its long tradition of social-democratic movements (Vellinga 1993), the 1990s saw the elaboration of this policy model by economists associated with the Economic Commission for Latin America and the Caribbean (ECLAC). Neostructuralism, the successor to a structuralist approach whose origins lie in the 1950s, is essentially a technocratic version of social democracy.[5] Neostructuralists claim that their approach can avoid the pitfalls of both protectionist import-substituting industrial strategy and the current free-market doctrine. Neostructuralism, like its predecessor, stresses the historical specificity of the situation of developing countries, in particular the historically derived structural constraints on economic decision making and development. While neostructuralists agree with neoliberals on the centrality of markets and the maintenance of macroeconomic stability, they differ in including equity, as well as growth, as the goals of economic policy. These dual goals require a strong role for the state in economic life as service-provider, manager, and regulator (but not owner). Governments should intervene to promote land redistribution (where warranted), progressive tax reform, technological development, accessible education and health care, a skilled labor force, export markets, and social insurance (Green 1996, 109–22).

Neostructuralism, however, lacks a political analysis. Its economistic focus ignores the empowerment of subordinate classes that is the means

---

[4] For an elaboration of this argument, see Sandbrook and Romano 2004.
[5] For summaries and assessments of neostructuralism, see Lustig 1991, Sunkel 1993, Green 1996, and Gwynne and Kay 2000.

(and also an end) of equitable development. It is unclear how a growth-with-equity strategy can prevail in the face of entrenched and intransigent power elites. This volume, in contrast, emphasizes the politics of experiments in equitable and democratic development.

The recent rise to power of the democratic left in Latin America has further stimulated debates about the viability of egalitarian alternatives. Popular antipathy towards neoliberal policies brought left-of-center governments to office in seven countries that together account for more than three-quarters of the region's population: Brazil (Luiz Inácio "Lula" da Silva), Argentina (Néstor Kirchner), Uruguay (Tabaré Vásquez and the *Frente Amplio*), Ecuador (Lucio Gutiérrez in the early years of his presidency, 2002–2004), Chile (Ricardo Lagos and Michelle Bachelet), Bolivia (Evo Morales), and, less democratically, Venezuela (Hugo Chávez). What united these leaders was not socialist doctrine but a common, if vague, view that neoliberal reform had failed and should be replaced with a development model emphasizing egalitarian policies, social welfare, and a more central role for the state in economic life. With the exception of the radical populist Chávez, all the new leaders might be described as pragmatic social democrats.

The ascent of "Lula" to the Brazilian presidency in October 2002 (with more than 60 percent of the vote) has particularly excited interest in social-democratic approaches. Lula, in his fourth run for president, succeeded the two-time president and professed social democrat, Fernando Henrique Cardoso. The latter's efforts to implement social reforms had been heavily constrained both by domestic power structures – clientelistic politics and the powerful business elite – and by the country's dependence on international financial markets as a result of its huge debt (Smith and Messari 1998). Lula, whose Workers Party (PT) was the largest party in the legislature in 2002, promised a deepening of democracy and redistribution (including land reform) together with renewed growth within a market economy. The PT-led coalition assumed power with impressive credentials for egalitarian reform: it had, after all, already instituted measures to involve ordinary citizens in governmental decision making in the Brazilian states and municipalities it controlled, most famously in the form of participatory budgeting.

Yet Lula, like Cardoso, was constrained in achieving redistributive measures at the national level, especially by a recession in 2003, which reinforced the imperative of attracting private investment and retaining the International Monetary Fund's (IMF) support. Hence, his early response was to combine an orthodox monetary and fiscal policy with limited improvements in pensions and welfare payments and little in the way of land reform. Achieving social reform in a country that is both highly dependent on foreign investment and immensely inegalitarian[6] is fraught with difficulties; nonetheless, we shall contend later that the Workers Party is changing the face of Brazilian politics.

Another locus of social-democratic rethinking is the groups opposed to what they term neoliberal globalization. Actually, the "anti-globalization movement" (as branded by the media) juggles two conflicting visions or development alternatives to neoliberalism. A radical tendency envisages the transformation of global capitalism. One prominent version of this tendency advocates the formation of decentralized, participatory, and ecologically sustainable communities that trade mainly within the community or the region. The limited scale and self-reliance of such a model is thought to enhance solidarity and participatory democracy, as well as environmental sustainability. However, its proponents' reluctance to sketch a plausible strategy of transformation renders this approach utopian.[7]

The alternative, reformist tendency is congruent with social-democratic pragmatism, though its advocates in the global justice movement rarely employ that term. The reformists propose remedies to the destructive tendencies of global capitalism at the national and international level. That the strategy is implicitly social-democratic is clear from its advocates' brief statements of principle. For example, Walden Bello, a prominent figure in the global justice movement and head of the Third World Network, describes the essence of his approach as "a strategy that consciously subordinates the logic of the market and the pursuit of cost efficiency to the values of security, equity, and social solidarity" (Bello 2003, 286). Proposed reforms of the rules governing the global economy, international governance, and new forms of global taxation add up to what may be termed a "social-democratic globalization" (Sandbrook 2003).

However, the dominance of such global institutions as the IMF, World Bank, and WTO (World Trade Organization) by proponents of neoliberal globalization has led globalist reformers to defend national sovereignty as a vehicle for attaining social justice. Not only will effective social democracy at the national level yield security and equity for working people domestically, but such nationally based governments will demand that human rights and social justice apply to global markets as well. As one observer concludes, "the global opposition must pursue a common global program for working people that reinforces their national struggles for

---

[6] In Brazil, the top 10 percent of the population earns half the nation's income; 1.7 percent of landowners own nearly half the arable land (*New York Times Magazine* [June 27, 2004], 33).

[7] This utopian model is assessed in chapter 9.

economic and social equity. Such a program would support national democratic movements and leaders who understand that national social contracts cannot be maintained in a global market that lacks one of its own" (Faux 2004, 49).

Hence, this volume's rethinking of the sustainability and promise of social-democratic approaches derives its significance from both the disappointing record of neoliberalism and a resurgence of interest in egalitarian, democratic, and nationally based alternatives. In principle, social-democratic models are more deeply democratic, proactive, security-enhancing, and inclusive than the orthodox market-oriented model. A brief review of our social-democratic cases indicates that practice is not too distant from principle.

Records of achievement

We selected our cases – Kerala, Costa Rica, Mauritius, and Chile since 1990 – on the grounds of both their celebrated status as social-democratic pioneers and the diversity of their approaches. Many other relevant cases in the global periphery saw their social-democratic path interrupted as a result of ethnically based civil strife (Sri Lanka after 1977), coup d'état (Uruguay in 1973), economic decline (Michael Manley's Jamaica), and/or degeneration into populism and corruption (Venezuela in the 1970s and 1980s). Some of these earlier failed cases, such as Uruguay, have recently resumed their social-democratic path; meanwhile, in other countries, prominently Taiwan and South Korea, democratization has forged some social-democratic features such as redistributive welfare states. Few countries, however, have experienced as lengthy a history of social democracy as the four on which we concentrate.

Although these cases diverge in their circumstances and historical trajectories, they resemble each other in their exemplary socioeconomic development. Each has achieved an exceptional record in comparison to others in its region or country: Kerala in relation to other Indian states, Costa Rica in Central America, Chile in Latin America, and Mauritius in Africa. Chapters 3 to 6 specify these individual achievements. For now, this summary of some of their common successes will suffice:
- They all provide primary health care, including clean drinking water, adequate sanitation, nutrition programs, comprehensive immunization, and access to basic medical services. Not surprisingly, the life expectancy in all cases is over seventy years (compared to an average of sixty-four years for all middle- and low-income countries).
- They have all made considerable progress in education, with (at a minimum) nearly universal access to primary schools and an adult literacy

Table 1.1 *Profiles of the selected cases*

	population (millions) 2001	urban population (%) 1999	GDI per capita 2001 ($US)		GDP growth (% per annum)		Economic structure, 2001 (value added as % of GDP)		
			nominal	PPP	1980–1990	1990–1999	agriculture	industry	services
Chile	15	85	4590	8840	4.2	7.2	8	34	57
Costa Rica	4	48	4060	9260	3.0	4.1	11	37	53
Mauritius	1.2	41	3830	9860	6.0	5.2	6	31	63
Kerala	32	26	304	—	2.2	4.4	29	12	59

Sources: World Bank, *World Development Report, 2003, 2001*; World Bank, *World Development Indicators Databank*, August 2003; India, Census Bureau, National Sample Survey 2002; http://www.indiabudget.nic/es2002–03/esmain.htm.

rate of over 90 percent (compared to an average 75 percent for all middle- and low-income countries).

- They have all dramatically reduced the incidence of poverty, even when their per capita incomes were low or remain low – in low-income Kerala, for instance, only 12 percent of the population falls below the poverty line (compared to 26 percent for India as a whole).
- They have all mounted advanced social-security systems, relative to other countries at the same economic levels, which include protection for all or most people against at least old age and disability (though Chile's bifurcated schemes favor the well-off).
- They all feature consolidated democracies with robust civil societies – a rarity in developing countries – though a defeated military regime not only imposed constitutional constraints on Chile's democracy but also vitiated popular organizations following the coup in 1973.

Clearly, though many problems remain, these societies have made remarkable progress in comparative terms.

This progress, moreover, occurred under diverse demographic, economic, cultural, and political conditions (see Table 1.1). Our cases vary enormously in population, ranging from 32 million in Kerala to only 1.2 million in the island state of Mauritius. They also diverge in the distribution of this population, with Chile a heavily urbanized society, Kerala still largely rural, and Mauritius and Costa Rica clustered between these two extremes. Additionally, the four cases manifest major economic differences, though all are capitalist and have experienced growth in per capita incomes that ranges from average to exceptional.[8] Chile, for example, is an upper-middle-income developing country, whose per capita income is fifteen times that of low-income Kerala. Costa Rica and Mauritius join Chile in the upper-middle-income category. We also find a wide variation in economic structure: whereas industry accounts for more than 30 percent of GDP in Chile, Costa Rica, and Mauritius, Kerala retains a large peasant sector. However, agriculture remains an important generator of export earnings in the remaining three countries.

In terms of cultural composition, our cases fall into two groups. Costa Rica and Chile are quite homogeneous, with a Catholic tradition, a population mainly of European origins, and only a small indigenous or other minority population.[9] Mauritius and Kerala, in contrast, host highly heterogeneous populations. Mauritian diversity features overlapping religious, ethnic, and class cleavages: even the Hindu majority (51 percent)

---

[8] Yet Chile, Costa Rica, and Mauritius have also experienced economic reversals and, as a consequence, structural adjustment programs in the 1970s and/or 1980s.

[9] Costa Rica is also home to small minorities of citizens of African and Chinese origin.

is divided by caste and regional origin. Kerala's population is predominantly Hindu, but significant Muslim and Christian minorities exist. In contrast with other states in India, the Hindus in Kerala have seen their caste divisions diminish, though not disappear. Politically, too, the cases are diverse. Kerala is a state within a federal system – albeit a state with considerable control over social programs – while the others are independent countries. Although all feature democratic governance, democracy in both Chile and Costa Rica has a checkered history that began in the nineteenth century. In contrast, Kerala and Mauritius are more recent offspring of colonial empires, though democracy in both these countries, too, has early origins.

This brief review suggests that even initially poor, heterogeneous, and agrarian-based former colonies can achieve rapid social progress. But in what sense do such diverse cases constitute a general type – social democracy?

Social democracy in the core

What characterizes a social-democratic route is not self-evident. The term has meant different things to different people. Some political parties that would never define themselves as social-democratic (such as the Communist Party of India [Marxist]) pursue what look like social-democratic policies, while certain self-identified social-democratic parties (such as New Zealand's Labour Party) have undertaken typically neoliberal free-market programs. Since social democracy was initially a European movement, a brief review of its development in that continent will bring this ambiguous phenomenon into sharper focus.

Social-democratic thinking rose to prominence in the early twentieth century as some socialists sought to adapt Marxism to what they saw as the new realities of the age.[10] Eduard Bernstein, together with such other revisionists as Jean Jaurès, Benedetto Croce, the Austro-Marxists, and the Swedish Social Democrats, rejected the economistic and deterministic interpretation of Marxism that predominated after the death of Marx in 1883. Popularized in particular by Friedrich Engels, Karl Kautsky, and G. V. Plekhanov, this "orthodox" view treated Marxism as a science of societal evolution. History, from this viewpoint, followed an "inevitable, lawlike progression that leaves little room for conscious human action" (Berman 2003, 117). Bernstein rejected the implicit passivity of this interpretation. In *Evolutionary Socialism*, originally published in German in 1899 and in English in 1909 (Bernstein 1961), he contended that

---

[10] This interpretation draws heavily on Berman 2003.

capitalism would not collapse from its own contradictions, and that therefore socialists would need to rely on determined political action to succeed. Marx had predicted an inevitable polarization and immiseration
as capitalism developed, whereby the middle classes would diminish as
property and power devolved into fewer and fewer hands and the proletariat expanded. Bernstein argued, however, that the middle classes
were expanding, not contracting, in tandem with the expansion of car-
tels. Although capitalism would not spontaneously collapse, socialists
could gain power peacefully by organizing their political activity within
the emergent institutions of parliamentary democracy. People, if given
the choice, would choose socialism (Sassoon 1997, 17). Socialist movements could win power through appeals based both on justice and on
the class interests of workers and intermediate groups suffering from
the social dislocation, corruption, and insecurity of the age. Democratic revisionism, therefore, rejected the passivity and economism of
Marxism (and liberalism) in favor of an active, ethically engaged, cross-
class, and democratically oriented strategy for winning power and transforming capitalism.[11]

Social democracy came into its own only after World War II, following a generation of economic depression and upheaval. The first successful experiment occurred in Sweden in the 1930s and 1940s.[12] Here
we find the prototypical social-democratic features: a class compromise
involving labor and capital, a welfare state predicated on universal entitlements, and full employment policies (Sassoon 1997, 42). The Swedish
Social Democrats, in coalition with bourgeois parties after 1933, fostered
this compromise through a tripartite corporatist structure involving regular negotiations among employers, trade unions, and government. They
introduced progressive labor legislation and progressively extended the
welfare state but avoided major nationalizations. The Swedes led the way
in the postwar world in establishing comprehensive, generous, and universal social programs, based on the idea that citizenship entitles all people to
equal access to important services and a basic living standard, regardless
of their market position. Social democrats conceived of such egalitarian
reforms as elements of socialism introduced within a capitalist society.

---

[11] Lenin, too, rejected a passive stance in developing the theory and practice of the van-
guard party – but he also rejected the possibility that a bourgeois state could be used to
introduce socialist practices.

[12] The depression of the 1930s spurred socialist movements in many countries, including
Chile with its famous "100 days" of a "Socialist Republic" in 1931 under Marmaduque
Grove. Socialist parties of various orientations established themselves in Chile in the
early twentieth century and commanded a fifth of the restricted electorate as early as the
election of 1932.

The standard or "traditional" Western European model of social democracy, then, exhibited the following features by the 1960s (cf. Thomson 2000, 8–9):

- A heavy role for the state in economic life, with an extensive public sector and state regulation underpinning a "mixed" economy.
- The pursuit of equality and justice through high redistributive taxes and a comprehensive and universal welfare state.
- The promotion of full employment, principally by means of Keynesian demand-side management.
- The maintenance of an alliance between the social-democratic party and a centralized labor movement seen as the protector of workers' interests.

This model, however, entered a crisis in the 1970s and 1980s, for several well-known reasons. First, Keynesian policies seemed incapable of countering a combination of high inflation, economic stagnation, and high unemployment ("stagflation"). This failure provided an opening for a resurgence of neoliberal diagnoses and remedies. Second, the consensus around high, progressive taxes crumbled as growing deficits led to even higher taxation to maintain the welfare state. The neoconservative/neoliberal portrayal of the public sector as lethargic and inefficient, in contrast to a lean and efficient private sector, increasingly resonated with electorates. Third, freer trade helped to shrink social democracy's political base: not only did the numbers and power of blue-collar workers fall, but employees associated with the expanding information economy also had little sympathy for state-oriented approaches. Finally, new issues such as feminism and environmental protection emerged in the 1980s to challenge social-democratic commitments to rapid economic growth and top-down social engineering.

To adapt, all European social-democratic parties have, to a greater or lesser extent, undergone strategic and policy shifts in a market direction:

- They have dropped their theoretical commitment to replace capitalism with socialism, accepting that their role was remedial rather than transformational.
- They have become more market-friendly through some combination of avoiding "fiscal irresponsibility," cutting subsidies and selected entitlements, privatizing some state corporations, shifting the delivery of some services to private providers, and supporting freer trade arrangements.
- They have reinterpreted equality as involving more in the way of equality of opportunity and less in the way of equality of outcome through redistribution of income to the poor. On this interpretation, individuals must have an equal opportunity of succeeding in a competitive society, and those who lose their jobs deserve ample retraining opportunities

and assistance in finding a new job. In addition, the state has a responsibility to mitigate, through social policy, the structures that reproduce social exclusion.

• They have loosened their links to organized labor in an effort to appeal to middle-class voters.

Although the degree of adjustment varies, a common core of social-democratic thinking continues to distinguish it from neoliberalism (cf. Garrett 1998, 7, 25; Huber and Stephens 1998, 355–56; Hirst 1999, 87). On the one hand, neoliberals believe that enhancing equality and security by means of generous social welfare, labor-market regulation, steeply progressive taxes, subsidized necessities, and other redistributive measures is self-defeating. Such measures depress profits and investment – reducing growth and employment – and undermine personal responsibility and initiative. Public investments in human capital, however, are justified inasmuch as they augment productivity while advancing well-being. Governments should, in sum, restrict redistributive reform and regulation to a minimum, relying mainly on healthy economic growth induced by liberalized markets and macroeconomic stability to resolve problems of destitution, joblessness, and insecurity. On the other hand, social democrats contend that free-market conditions spawn unacceptable inequalities, economic insecurity, and atomization; therefore, regulatory and redistributive measures to enhance equality, security, and community are needed. A comprehensive, generous, and (largely) universal welfare state, including income transfer programs such as pensions, is a hallmark of this regime. Socioeconomic reform can be achieved without adverse economic repercussions, it is thought, provided that a well-organized party strongly based in the middle and working classes clearly delineates the limits of reform. This implicit or explicit class compromise, its advocates contend, confers competitive advantages on domestic enterprises by generating systemic legitimacy, social cohesion, human capital, and willing workers.

Is it legitimate to extend this general understanding of social-democratic principles to the global periphery?

Social democracy in the periphery

Skeptics might respond that such an extension is irrelevant and ethnocentric because social democracy is closely identified with core capitalist countries. On the one hand, nearly all comparative studies of social democracy refer exclusively to industrial countries. On the other hand, the developing world includes many self-identified adherents to social democracy, together with several countries that have experimented with what appear to be social-democratic routes. The latter considerations surely justify the extension of social-democratic categories to the periphery.

First, the Socialist International, a worldwide organization of social-democratic and labor parties, lists parties from forty-four developing countries as "full" members and parties from fourteen other developing countries as "consultative parties." True, the social-democratic credentials of some of these parties – such as the African National Congress in South Africa – are debatable (De Beuss and Koelble 2001, 189–92). Others play only a minor role in political life. Nevertheless, the list of full members includes some very significant parties active in three of our four cases (Chile, Costa Rica, and Mauritius),[13] together with present or former governing parties from Senegal, Mozambique, Angola, Cape Verde, Uruguay, Venezuela, Brazil, and Jamaica.

Second, social-democratic traditions are entrenched in a number of developing countries, despite the "burdens of history" reviewed in chapter 2. Part II provides detailed studies of the evolution of each of our four exemplars; however, many other experiments, sometimes lengthy though often discontinuous, might also be cited. Social-democratic parties (sometimes identifying themselves as "democratic socialist") have organized in Uruguay and Argentina since the early twentieth century. In Uruguay, for example, the critical juncture occurred in 1904, when President José Batlle y Ordónez used his victory in a civil war to establish the ideological, political, and social foundations of a social democracy. This initiative set the parameters of a policy regime that survived until a coup in 1973 (Weinstein 1975). With redemocratization in 1985, social-democratic principles soon resurfaced, albeit in the changed environment of global neoliberal hegemony (Kaztman, Fligueira, and Furtado 2000). Uruguay's modest "Third Way," buffeted by a deep recession in 1999 and a financial crisis in 2002, came under sharp attack from the left. An election in October 2004 elevated the Frente Amplio ("Broad Front" of Socialists, Communists, and social democrats) to power, buttressed by vague promises to reject the Washington Consensus and institute a more radical social-democratic path.

In Venezuela, too, social-democratic movements trace their roots to the first decades of the twentieth century when Acción Democrática (AD) emerged as a socially reformist opposition during the dictatorship of Juan Vicente Gómez. Chapter 9 picks up the story of the vicissitudes of social

---

[13] Recall that the CPI(M), which governs periodically in Kerala and continuously in West Bengal, claims to be a revolutionary socialist party.

democracy in this country. Suffice it to say now that the enticements of oil revenues, economic crisis, and oligarchical tendencies turned the AD into a corrupt political machine and, finally, a vehicle of neoliberal reform in the 1980s. Popular disillusionment with the social democrats allowed a left-wing populist and erstwhile putchist, Hugo Chávez, to assume power in 1998. Burgeoning oil revenues permitted Chávez to create jobs, generous social programs and health services for workers and the poor – albeit in the context of extreme class polarization and conflict.

Jamaica under Michael Manley's People's National Party (PNP) (1972–1980) also pursued an egalitarian, state-interventionist path that ultimately aborted in a neoliberal reaction (under Edward Seaga in the early 1980s). Although the PNP's rhetoric was more radical than its policies, its government ended in economic crisis and plummeting support as panicked firms exported capital, closed businesses, and reduced bauxite exports (Stephens and Stephens 1983).

Sri Lanka is another case where social-democratic traditions appeared early. Between its independence in 1948 and the late 1970s, it attained the most advanced social indicators of any low-income developing country. The country's political and social achievements date to the 1930s, when Sri Lanka (Ceylon) was still a British colony and social movements and leftist political parties kept pressure on the British. Land reform, progressive labor and social policies, and a heavy reliance on state-owned corporations followed independence. Egalitarian policies, however, were married to sluggish economic growth, which ultimately, together with ethnic conflicts, led to the demise of this state-led experiment in the late 1970s and early 1980s. (The significance of this case, too, is assessed in the final chapter.)

West Bengal, a state in India, has followed a social-democratic path since 1977 (Kohli 1987). Originally casting itself as a revolutionary movement, the Communist Party of India (Marxist) (CPI(M)) has led a Left Front government that has instituted redistributive reforms during its twenty-nine years in power. The extensive land reform of the late 1970s and early 1980s redistributed some land to the poor and secured the tenure of tenant cultivators. As well, a simultaneous decentralization of power to the *panchayats* (local governments), together with the building of local participatory mechanisms, empowered peasants to monitor the land reform and implement local programs. Yet, development indicators in this state today are only marginally superior to nationwide averages – though, significantly, West Bengal's indicators started at notably lower levels than in many other Indian states (West Bengal 2004). Critics claim

that limited electoral competition and clientelistic tendencies have vitiated the CPI(M)'s initially radical vision in West Bengal (Mukhopadhyay
2000).

South Korea and Taiwan have, since their democratic transitions in the
1980s, increasingly resembled social democracies (Wong 2004b, chs. 7
and 8). They have both followed an unusual trajectory, insofar as authoritarian governments forged rapid growth with considerable equality from
the 1960s to the 1980s, while conservative or nationalist democratic governments since 1990 have extended the welfare state. Keenly contested
elections, combined with the insecurities attendant upon economic opening and economic crisis in the late 1990s, have brought welfare issues to
the fore. Well-organized civil associations, rather than labor-dominated
parties, have been at the forefront of the new left. In neither Taiwan nor
South Korea has the party system been organized on a left–right ideological cleavage. Instead, issues of social justice and social protection have
been championed by coalitions of nongovernmental organizations joined,
in the mid- to late 1990s, by labor movements (Wong 2004a, 4–11).
Alliances such as the Taiwan Labor Front, the Taiwan Health Insurance
Coalition, and the Korean Citizens' Coalition for Economic Justice and
Health Solidarity have been instrumental in pressing a social-democratic
agenda, aspects of which have appeared in the electoral platforms of the
mainstream parties. This suggests that while there are diverse routes to
egalitarian development, a robust civil society is likely to be a central
feature.

Although on the grounds of self-identification and actual practice we
can make a case for the relevance of social democracy in the periphery, its
form inevitably deviates from the European prototypes. If the essence of
social democracy is class compromise, a particular model of such compromise characterizes the northern European cases. Adam Przeworski
provides an authoritative dissection of this model (1985, 43, 162; for
another classic statement, see Esping-Andersen 1985). He assumes that
the compromise involves organized workers and capital, with the state as
mediator and enforcer. On the one hand, the unionized workers accept
private ownership of the means of production and the fostering of conditions favorable to the profits of private firms. On the other hand, capitalists
agree to some rate of investment out of these profits (to create jobs), and
some rate of transfer from profits to wages and tax-supported services and
social insurance. Such cooperation between labor and capital normally
augments the material basis of class compromise by raising productivity.
The state orchestrates the compromise and protects profits from undue
demands from below. Radical redistribution is seen as contrary to workers' interests, as it leads to disinvestment, rising inflation, and growing

unemployment. However, the different conditions in developing countries ensure that class compromises, if attained, will be more complicated and fragile than those characteristic of postwar Europe.

Both the peripheral status of developing countries and their divergent developmental sequencing compared to the core industrial countries account for this significant difference. First, we refer to social democracy *in the periphery* to emphasize the particular (though not insurmountable) developmental challenges posed by peripherality within the global capitalist economy. Since we deal at length with the impact of globalization below and in chapter 8, a brief comment will suffice. Not only are these peripheral economies typically dependent on a handful of industrial economies for markets, investment, and imports, but the rules of the global economy (partly owing to this dependency) are, in various respects, disadvantageous to the global south. Joseph Stiglitz (2002, 214) concisely sums up the situation: "Part of the problem lies with the international economic institutions, with the IMF, World Bank, and WTO, which help set the rules of the game. They have done so in ways that, all too often, have served the interest of the more advanced industrialized countries – and particular interests within those countries – rather than those of the developing world." Social-democratic regimes, which try to orchestrate growth and equity through industrial and social policies, thus face major external obstacles.

The second distinctive difference concerns the divergent sequencing of industrialization, democratization, and social citizenship in the core relative to the periphery. In the core, these phases were discrete; in the periphery, they have tended to overlap. This contrast means that, in the contemporary south, social democrats usually pursue class compromises *before* a productive capitalism has generated a strong material base, and in the context of a heterogeneous and differentiated class structure.[14]

A stylized history of northern Europe and North America highlights these stages and dynamics.[15] Agricultural transformation and industrialization were underway in the nineteenth and early twentieth centuries and, throughout most of this period, agricultural and industrial workers labored under appalling conditions. In 1844, Engels penned a moving

---

[14] See Heller 1999, where the sequence argument is developed at length. The early political development theorists also emphasized the special difficulties confronting governments that face simultaneous challenges, though they defined these "crises" in more narrowly political terms. See Verba 1971.

[15] Lipton (1977, esp. 42–43) depicts a similar pattern. T. H. Marshall's famous sequence of rights recognition in western countries overlaps with this schema; Marshall claimed (1950) that the formative period of civil rights occurred in the eighteenth century, while political rights rose to prominence in the nineteenth century, and social rights in the twentieth century.

account of the plight of workers in Manchester in *The Condition of the Working Class in England*. Living conditions only improved as the working class gained political strength (through trade-union organization, extensions of the suffrage in the 1890s and later, and the reliance of the state on citizens' armies in the two world wars) and economic strength (through a shrinking of the "industrial reserve army"). However, full democratic rights and the growth of the political and economic bargaining power of labor happened after capitalism had vastly increased productivity in town and country. The extension of social citizenship in the form of a comprehensive and universal welfare state occurred later still, principally in the 1950s and 1960s. At this stage, Keynesian economics provided an economic rationale for redistributive programs: progressive taxes, good wages, unemployment insurance, and a large public sector transferred resources from the rich to the poor, thereby increasing demand for the products of national industries and avoiding economic instability. Social democracy, from the 1950s to the mid-1970s, was yoked to a dynamic, nationally based capitalism in most core countries.

In the global periphery, however, a compression of these three phases has created a different dynamic. Until the postwar era, the bulk of countries in the periphery participated in the global division of labor as exporters of primary commodities. As well, pre-capitalist forms of production often survived in the countryside and in the burgeoning informal settlements of the cities. These trends, though less pronounced, even applied to the countries of Latin America, which had become politically independent more than a century earlier than Asia and Africa. The Latin American "late-late industrializers" (Hirschman 1968) did not even begin to industrialize until World War I (except Argentina and Brazil, which started earlier), and thereafter produced largely nondurable consumer goods for protected local markets (Kurth 1979, 319). Industrialization accelerated when falling export revenues during the Great Depression curtailed manufactured imports, necessitating local manufacturing. More cohesive and developmental states also played a role in promoting industrialization in this period, as in Brazil under President Getúlio Vargas (Kohli 2004, 164–65). But industries remained stunted, constricted by orientation to limited and protected local markets and by technological and import dependency. Not until the era of "bureaucratic authoritarianism" in the late 1960s and 1970s did some of the larger countries deepen their industrial base.[16] They expanded into capital goods and consumer durables, and several moved into export production.

---

[16] For a discussion of Guillermo O'Donnell's bureaucratic-authoritarian thesis, see Collier 1979. Brazil, however, experienced an earlier period of rapid, and deepening, industrialization from 1945 to the early 1960s (Kohli 2004, 169).

Attempted democratization occurred simultaneously with industrialization in most developing countries. Even in most of Latin America, democracy was an intermittent postwar phenomenon. Where it manifested any vitality, organized labor was well positioned to make demands on governments. Trade unions had emerged in the 1930s in the British colonies, later in the other colonial empires, and several decades earlier in Latin America. Union pressures, however, usually produced only a small "labor aristocracy" or the incorporation of privileged urban workers into narrow populist alliances. As primary-commodity exporters, the competitiveness of developing countries depended on keeping rural labor costs low. Import-substitution industrialization did provide both economic and political rationales for paying urban workers well: these workers could furnish both a market for the goods produced and a political base for populist regimes. Populist alliances were pernicious, however, in that they excluded the rural masses and informal-sector workers, and channeled rents to protected oligopolists. Even more perverse were the state corporatist versions of populism, which often involved an anti-democratic exchange of social benefits to privileged groups at the expense of civil and political rights.

In sum, social-democratic movements voiced demands for equality and social citizenship in an unpropitious postwar context. Public revenues were low while poverty and inequality were usually severe; the heterogeneous poor were found mainly outside the ranks of organized labor in the rural areas and the informal sector, where they enjoyed few, if any, effective rights; economic elites often prospered by extracting rents; and economies depended on a handful of industrial countries for investment, many imports, and export markets.

These circumstances suggest that social-democratic pacts or class compromises, if forged, will be more complicated and fragile in the global periphery. Not only do organized workers play a different role in economic and political life than their counterparts in Europe, but the compromises will also involve more class actors than in the classic European cases (cf. Weyland 1996, 28, 29, 38; Seekings 2004) and may threaten powerful foreign interests. We cannot assume that the labor movement spearheads demands for pro-poor policies; it may instead form a labor aristocracy. Other classes and strata will play a key role in inter-class bargains. The "middle classes" designate heterogeneous groups, some of which will figure centrally in class compromises: these include small farmers/middle peasants, white-collar employees, and small entrepreneurs in the formal and informal sectors. These strata, with the exception of white-collar workers in the public sector, are often (though not necessarily) poorly organized. The "poor" encompass an even more diverse set of classes and strata, with typically even less in the way of organization and political power, and include landless and poor peasants, farm workers, the unemployed and marginally employed, and hawkers, peddlers, and petty producers in the informal (that is, unregulated and small-scale) sector.

Under these conditions, sustainable class compromise falls within definite parameters. Capital will require acceptance of the capitalist system, private property, and a range of macroeconomic policies to aid competitiveness and profitability, especially anti-inflationary policies and moderate taxes. Organized workers and the urban middle classes will demand favorable wages, job security, and good public health and educational services. The poor will expect governmental strategies to create jobs, redistribute land (where landownership is concentrated), and channel public expenditures into accessible public services, subsidies on necessities, and, in middle-income countries, pensions. The least organized strata, however, may well lose out in social pacts, remaining marginalized. Nonetheless, class compromise is an ongoing process; the demands of the poor grow more insistent with keenly fought electoral contests, self-organization, and their representation by nongovernmental organizations. To the extent that political freedoms deepen civil society through self-organization of subordinate groups, social democracies are made, not born.

Yet, social contracts remain fragile because of the conflicting pressures on officials and shifting market conditions. State elites (elected officials and top bureaucrats) respond to redistributive demands from below because (a) they believe that free markets inevitably spawn inequity and inequality, and/or (b) they fear that, if they do not respond, they will be replaced in an electoral contest by the opposition. Elites may respond with clientelism and populist appeals, however, rather than the programmatic measures of social-democratic regimes.

State elites must also maintain business confidence. A sharp decline in business confidence will have dire consequences in dependent countries where economic well-being depends on trade and foreign investment involving just a handful of partners. This decline can lead to capital flight, growing inflation and unemployment, emerging shortages that alienate the middle classes, falling public revenues and, as a final result, a loss of electoral support for the government. Alienation of the business class and growing chaos may even trigger a coup (as in Chile, Uruguay, and Venezuela, for example) (Cardoso 1993; Touraine 1993). The United States and other capitalist powers may exacerbate the situation by employing their military and economic might to destabilize supposedly left-wing experiments.

Moreover, globalization has augmented the structural power of capital worldwide. Whereas, prior to 1980, governments pursuing redistribution could, to some degree, insulate the local economy from global market pressures via control of prices, imports, and exchange transactions, they can no longer employ such measures. Capital flight and the reactions of trading partners now present more daunting challenges than was formerly the case. The power of the IMF, the World Bank, and the major powers to discipline anti-capitalist governments is scarcely disputed, especially in the case of the smaller, less-developed countries. Hence, social-democratic governments are tightly constrained in pursuing their goals insofar as class compromises must reassure capital by establishing strict limits to reform (Stephens and Stephens 1983, 401; Kohli 1987, 102). Shifting global market conditions and miscalculations by party elites, state managers, or popular organizations, however, can overturn these bargains.

To handle these tensions and the developmental challenges arising from the telescoping of progress, a strong and capable state is necessary. *Social democracy in the periphery essentially involves a social-democratic developmental state.*[17] Traditionally, the developmental state entailed an authoritarian or semi-authoritarian regime. Authoritarianism was needed, argued Chalmers Johnson, "to achieve political stability and long-term predictability of the system. Continuity of the government may be achieved by explicit authoritarianism or by a rigged system that nonetheless achieves a monopolization of political power" (1987, 143). Yet there is no inherent reason why developmental states cannot be democratic – provided that the democracy in question is consolidated and not "under-institutionalized."[18] It is disputable that authoritarian governments are any less prone to instability and unpredictability than democratic ones. In addition, while Johnson assumes that an authoritarian "developmental elite" will remain developmental (i.e. oriented to growth with equity), eschewing corrupt and self-serving behavior, mechanisms of accountability in consolidated democracies are probably more likely to achieve this result than mere patriotism in an authoritarian context.

Indeed, democracy and a developmental state may reinforce each other in a virtuous circle. Not only can democratic politics motivate the

---

[17] A similar view is expressed in White 1998.

[18] Kohli (2004, 374) argues that authoritarianism "may . . . be . . . a necessary but not a sufficient condition for rapid industrialization in the developing world"; but this conclusion rests on the assumption that developing-world democracies are generally "underinstitutionalized" – hence, fragmented and ineffective. Yet some developing-world democracies are consolidated and relatively effective, including the four cases discussed in this volume.

state elites to act developmentally, but elite success in achieving growth with equity will further consolidate democratic institutions. Democracy may also augment the capacity of governments by generating legitimacy. Finally, democratic institutions may, paradoxically, enhance the autonomy of political and bureaucratic elites from capital in promoting socioeconomic development.[19] If "consensual autonomy" (White 1998, 30) flows from participatory processes, this agreement not only binds accountable government leaders and bureaucrats to a widely held strategic vision but also provides these leaders with leverage – in the form of broad-based popular support – against private firms and external lenders in obtaining trade-offs. For such autonomy to work in an equitable fashion in a plural society, however, both politicians and bureaucrats must be "inclusively embedded" in society (White 1998, 31). All ethnic or communal groups must be represented in the political and bureaucratic elite to ensure that all groups are, and feel, represented.[20]

A social-democratic developmental state employs many of the same "market-conforming" mechanisms of intervention as the authoritarian variety. State elites manipulate incentives and inputs into the production and distribution processes, so as to realize developmental goals by influencing the decisions of private firms. "The intent of the private system is to maximize profits, limit risks, and achieve stable growth given the political-economical environment in which it must operate, but its decisions on products, markets, and investments are continuously affected by changing costs and availability of capital, export incentives, licensing requirements, and all the other things the government manipulates" (Johnson 1987, 142). Whereas industrial strategies centered mainly on promoting import-substitution industrialization before 1980, the neoliberal revolution, with its emphasis on external openness, has since refocused incentives and subsidies on the fostering of diversified exports and foreign investment. Public ownership of productive assets is no longer a central issue – though, as we shall see, popular attachment to certain nationalized companies runs deep.

State-directed industrial and trade promotion remains feasible today, despite the international agreements and IMF requirements on market orientation. Today, as in the past, "most significant instances of productive diversification are . . . the result of concerted government action and of public–private collaboration" (Rodrik 2004, 8). The policy tools

---

[19] The "secret of the developmental state" is its capacity to discipline capital (Chibber 2003, 74).

[20] This is the form of Peter Evans's "embedded autonomy" (1995) peculiar to multiethnic societies.

available to developmental states have narrowed, however.[21] Under WTO rules, performance requirements cannot be imposed on foreign investors, and export subsidies are illegal (though low-income developing countries can continue to employ them). Bilateral and regional trade agreements also tighten the rules regarding foreign investment, intellectual property rights, and capital-account liberalization (Rodrik 2004, 32–33). Nevertheless, states can still foster exports and private investment in designated areas by orchestrating credit facilities, tax incentives, cheap utility charges, insurance guarantees, appropriate infrastructure, publicly funded research and development, and high-quality education and vocational training. As the developmental state is *social-democratic*, it must also manipulate the distributional outcomes of its initiatives through progressive taxation, side-payments to disadvantaged groups, superior public services and pensions, regulation of labor markets to ensure the fair distribution of productivity gains, and consultation with the groups affected by its policies. Chapters 3 to 6 describe these various mechanisms in specific contexts.

Nonetheless, one finds substantial variation among social-democratic developmental states. One can identify three types of the *regime* we have called social democracy in the periphery:[22] radical, classic, and Third Way. Three criteria distinguish these types from one another (Table 1.2): the conception of *equity* that the state managers seek to realize; the conception of *democratic participation*; and, by implication, the conception of the precise *role of the state* in guiding market forces. Of these three dimensions, equity is the least self-explanatory. Equity promotion, as we use the term, includes those measures that mitigate poverty and injustice by favoring disadvantaged groups and classes at the relative expense of the better-off. The equity enhancement of the more radical regimes, in contrast to the compensatory policies of the Third Way, recognizes that proactive measures must be undertaken to counteract structural inequality. These proactive measures may involve a redistribution of concentrated national assets (especially land) or income shares. In other circumstances, however, sustained growth may also permit reformist governments to

---

[21] For the limitations imposed by trade agreements, see Wade 2003.

[22] A *regime* is not a particular government, but a set of norms, institutions and procedural rules that constrain governmental actions. A *social-democratic* regime is a widely supported set of norms, institutions and rules constraining government to (a) be subject to democratic control, and (b) actively regulate market forces and otherwise intervene to enhance equity, social protection, and social cohesion, in addition to productivity. A social-democratic regime may continue, therefore, despite an election that brings a conservative party or coalition to government. Regimes normally reproduce themselves until a crisis disrupts the institutional arrangements, leading to the emergence of a new regime.

Table 1.2 *Social-democratic regimes in the periphery*

Type	Conception of equity	Conception of democracy	Role of state
radical (modal examples: Kerala since 1960s, West Bengal 1977–early 1990s)	• redistribution of assets to reduce unjust inequalities • empowerment via decentralized participation • universal entitlements to meet basic needs	• organize workers and peasants in own associations • decentralized participation • representative system at center	extensive: emphasizes equity • asset redistribution • universal services, pensions, subsidies • regulation of labor markets • expansive rights
classic (modal examples: Costa Rica, 1950–1980, Mauritius since 1970s)	• universal and comprehensive welfare state • 'good' jobs • growth in wages • limited subsidies of basic needs	• representative system • extensive consultation of all relevant groups in policy innovations	extensive: emphasizes equity and growth • universal services and pensions • regulation of labor markets • targeted industrial strategies
Third Way (modal examples: post-1990 Chile and Uruguay 1985–2004)	• poverty reduction • accessible education and training • safety nets targeted to truly needy	• electoral system in which elites compete for power	moderate: emphasizes market-based growth • adequate training • export promotion • adequate public services

transfer income and services by means of progressive taxes, targeted social programs, and labor-market regulation – with little effect on income distribution.

Radical regimes, exemplified by the experiences of West Bengal (from 1977 to the early 1990s) and Kerala (since 1956) under the CPI(M), adopt a conception of equity that requires a redistribution of assets and resources to reduce unjust inequalities. Such movements typically build support among workers, peasants, and small farmers, and sectors of the urban middle classes over many decades of political activity. When in power, they seek to engineer a redistribution of wealth and income by means of land reform; improving workers' incomes and rights; extensions of health, education, pension, and unemployment benefits; and (in earlier decades) public ownership. Another facet of equity is the empowerment of ordinary people that flows from radical reform of the democratic system. This occurs particularly (as exemplified by Kerala since 1996) through decentralizing responsibilities and resources to local representative institutions. Social democrats in this regime view the self-organization of workers and peasants and the expansion of the cooperative sector as essential political work to ensure the survival of the experiment. Although a parliamentary system operates at the center, often with socialist/communist coalitions in power, a decentralized, participatory system complements this territory-wide representative system. Overall, therefore, the state plays an extensive role in promoting the social, as well as political, rights of citizens in order to provide equal dignity for all.

The classic social-democratic regime, exemplified by Costa Rica (1950–1980) and Mauritius (since the 1970s), equates equity with a universal and comprehensive welfare state and a proactive state that creates good jobs with good wages. This regime rests on a consensual political process in which, despite electoral competition, the major parties agree on the principal economic, social, and political goals. Governments ensure broad popular support for policy initiatives by widely consulting organized groups, including employers. Thus, the consensus tolerates persistent differentials in wealth and accepts the inviolability of private property (perhaps following an initial redistribution) as the price of economic dynamism. The implicit class compromise rests on the premise that everyone wins from economic growth – through profits, side-payments to deprived groups, subsidies on basic goods, labor-market policies, and improvements in public services and benefits. The state is extensively involved in economic life: by regulating labor markets to guarantee that employees benefit from productivity growth; by ownership of utilities, equity stakes, and sector-specific promotional agencies; and by orchestrating incentives to domestic and foreign investors to promote conformity with its industrial strategy. Hence, democratic-developmental states "pick winners" and channel the benefits of economic success to popular constituencies, as well as to business. This finely balanced regime demands a committed leadership and an effective state to balance equity with growth in a competitive political system.

Finally, the Third Way is touted as a modernized social democracy that is adapted to the realities of the global market economy. Although Tony Blair has been its major exponent (Blair 1996; Giddens 2000), it is more accurate to say that this path was pioneered not in Britain, but in Chile under the Concertación since 1990. Uruguay, after exiting from military rule in 1985 to pursue a mildly social-democratic path until radicalization in 2004–2005, is another recent case. A Third-Way regime does not mobilize or broadly consult its citizens; instead, it relies on an elite-driven traditional party politics that largely controls populist tendencies.

The Third Way addresses equity by equipping citizens with the skills, education, and healthful conditions they need to succeed in market competition. Taxes support basic public health and educational systems, along with a basic social safety net to cater for those who cannot fend for themselves in market competition. The state individualizes risks for better-off individuals through tax-supported private insurance schemes that provide benefits superior to those of the public schemes. Meanwhile, labor markets remain largely flexible, though the government presses for basic collective-bargaining rights and adequate minimum wages to assist workers. Third-Way regimes, however, do not entail laissez-faire: state agencies play an extensive role in promoting export industries and economic growth. In sum, this approach works at the margins to enhance equity and promotes poverty-reducing growth but does not confront inherited inequalities. Reflecting skepticism about the relevance of this model for the developing world, Brazilian socialists have derided it as "Tropical Blairism" (Sader 2003).

These social-democratic approaches are often confused with populist and corporatist regimes. But populism, corporatism, and social democracy involve different modes of incorporating the masses into political life. Populism, especially when combined with corporatist structures, superficially resembles the two more egalitarian social-democratic regimes. They are similar in that all these regimes entail an interventionist state and leaders who champion the demands of (at least some) subordinate groups. Populism, however, involves a "personalistic relationship between leaders and masses that tends to be expressed only partially in formal organizations" (Chalmers, Martin, and Piester 1997, 547). The charismatic leader usually couches his appeal to "the people" in opposition to corrupt and supercilious elites. When populist leaders create organizations to attach functionally identified groups to the state in a subordinate position, we speak of populist-corporatist regimes. The groups so organized include workers and sometimes peasants, but rarely capital or the urban poor (Chalmers, Martin, and Piester 1997, 547–48). Typically, populists depend heavily on clientelism, rather than policy appeals, for support among the urban poor, peasants, and workers. Their parties therefore resemble political machines that service extensive patron–client networks. Social-democratic regimes, in contrast, typically involve political movements that mobilize class support on a programmatic basis, depending less than populists on clientelism, personalistic ties, or charismatic leaders. Social-democratic politics are more policy-oriented and institutionalized than populism; equally, they are more genuinely democratic, rights-conscious, and open to autonomous self-organization of constituent groups than state corporatism. There is a danger, however, that social-democratic movements will degenerate into populist-corporatism (as we discuss in chapter 9).

What are the conditions under which these social-democratic regimes emerge in the global periphery? As chapter 7 deals in depth with this issue, we need only to foreshadow the argument in what follows.

Explaining social democracy

The conventional wisdom about the social origins of social democracy lies more in the realm of myth than reality. Consider, for example, this conventional explanation of the unlikelihood of social democracy in Latin America:

Historically, social democracy has been grounded in conditions that are not present in contemporary Latin America and are highly unlikely to develop under an increasingly transnational neoliberal model of capitalist development – namely, centralized and densely organized labor movements that have close political ties to socialist parties, ample fiscal resources to sustain universal norms of social citizenship, and domestic power balances that spawn institutionalized forms of class compromise in which democratic checks are placed on the privileges and functioning of capital. (Roberts 1998, 276)

If these historical conditions are necessary, egalitarian social democracy is destined to remain a marginal tendency in Latin America – and the developing world in general.

Yet the prospects are not as hopeless as this prognosis suggests. Even in the prototypical Scandinavian cases, neither an organized labor movement nor socialist parties account for the initial social reforms in the late nineteenth and early twentieth centuries. Instead, the origins of the social-democratic welfare state can be traced to struggles over who should bear the extensive costs of poor relief that occurred between the ascendant and numerous agrarian middle classes and the traditional, urban-based elites (Baldwin 1990). In Denmark, for example, an emergent Liberal Party, which represented the ascendant small farmers and peasants in this incipient democracy, challenged the hegemony of the urban-based and traditionalist Conservative Party. The agricultural crisis of the late nineteenth century heavily increased the costs of rural poor relief to these rural groups, as poor relief was financed from local land levies. In 1891, moderate free-trading Liberals and protectionist Conservatives arrived at a compromise that included an agreement to create a universal, tax-financed, and noncontributory pension scheme. A universal scheme was devised because of the heterogeneity of the rural workforce; it made little sense to try to distinguish between the self-employed and the dependently employed (Baldwin 1990, 64). This decision to grant all classes a tax-financed benefit shaped later developments – a clear case of path dependency (Baldwin 1990, 290).[23]

Later on, the Social Democratic Party and the union movement, both of which had initially favored a program targeted to the poor, embraced the principle of universality. With their firm backing, social assistance was extended into a universal, comprehensive, and generous welfare state between the 1940s and the 1960s (Esping-Andersen 1999, 78).

The point of this digression is not to suggest that Latin America, or developing countries more generally, will follow the Scandinavian pattern. It is, rather, to cast doubt on the popular notion that a strong, organized working class linked to powerful socialist parties is a necessary or sufficient condition for the *birth* of social democracy. In Europe, it was not a struggle between the "have-nots" and the "have-alls" that led to this outcome; instead, it was the groups in the middle that provided the key to the winning coalitions that shifted tax burdens and established universal social insurance. "Those not among the poorest but nevertheless prone to certain risks had to be convinced that, potentially vulnerable, they too stood to gain" (Baldwin 1990, 299). The peasants, small farmers, and urban middle classes, together with organized labor, may continue to be arbiters of social-democratic routes in developing countries, as they were in northern Europe over a century ago.

There nevertheless remain other preconditions for the emergence and survival of social democracy. For heuristic purposes, we divide the causal variables into three categories, ranging from the most remote or long-term (structural factors) to the more proximate (configurational and conjunctural factors).

A key *structural factor* that our cases share is their early and deep, albeit dependent, integration into the global capitalist economy. Although a large and organized labor movement is not a precondition of social democracy, a largely capitalist social formation is. Social democracy cannot survive in the oppressive environment engendered by the survival of quasi-feudal relations presided over by a traditionalist landlord class or of a large dependent peasantry enmeshed in clientelistic relations. Hence, the pattern of capitalist transformation is crucial. An important associated process is state formation, impelled by either centralizing colonial or postcolonial elites or demands from below (or a combination of the two).

---

[23] The essence of path dependency is that contingent events, such as a political decision to follow one path rather than another, shape institutional arrangements, which then become locked in. Causation therefore flows from contingent historical events to general processes of broader significance, as powerful classes or groups gain a vested interest in the new arrangements. See Mahoney 2000 for elaboration.

A relatively coherent and effective state with some autonomy from dominant classes must emerge, for social-democratic regimes require states that can negotiate equitable social pacts, guide market forces, and administer social programs. Yet, effective and relatively autonomous states are rare.[24] In Part II, we seek to understand why and how such states emerged in our cases.

The second, more proximate, level of analysis involves *a configuration of sociopolitical opportunities*. A major element is the configuration of class forces deriving from capitalist development, the most propitious pattern being one that weakens the landlords while strengthening the working and middle classes (cf. Rueschemeyer, Stephens, and Stephens 1992, 7, 58). Chapter 7 emphasizes the importance of a commercialization of agriculture in which small independent farmers play a significant role. This pattern creates small farmers and market-oriented peasant proprietors whose vulnerability to market forces predisposes them to socializing various risks.[25] As market relations erode the traditional forms of solidarity and reciprocity, social democracy emerges as a modern, national system for subordinating markets to norms of mutual security, trust, and equity. A robust civil society is also critical in understanding the emergence of social-democratic forces. "The growing organizational density of civil society not only constitutes an underpinning for the political organization of subordinate classes, but it also represents a counterweight to an overwhelming power of the state apparatus" (Rueschemeyer, Stephens, and Stephens 1992, 77).

Finally, we arrive at the most immediate – *conjunctural* – factors shaping social-democratic trajectories. A particular pattern of capitalist transformation, process of state formation, reconfiguration of class structure, and civil society does not necessarily produce a social-democratic regime. When this happens, it is the outcome of critical junctures in a country's history, in which organized social actors, through political struggles, propel societies down a particular path. Left-of-center movements, parties, or coalitions commanding substantial policy-based support are usually the central actor. Organization is "the main means of empowering the poor"

---

[24] "Basic features of many poor states exercise a significant and negative effect on their capacity and incentive to provide basic public services to poor citizens" (Moore 2000, 28).

[25] We use the terms "smallholders," "middle peasantry," and "independent family farmers" to denote an agrarian class that owns enough land to produce for the market (though not enough to live off rent) and that relies mostly on family labor. The key relational point is that this class enjoys some independence from landlords. This autonomy derives from either the smallholders' long-standing and secure property rights (as in Costa Rica and Mauritius) or their political leverage rooted in the declining position of landed elites (as in Kerala and, since the 1970s, Chile).

(Rueschemeyer, Stephens, and Stephens 1992, 54). Explaining the lack of redistributive reform in Brazil, Kurt Weyland (1996, 4) focuses on organizational fragmentation, particularly the paucity of encompassing social movements or broad-based and cohesive parties. Such parties or movements must be capable of maintaining control of their mass base; otherwise, redistributive rhetoric or undisciplined asset seizures will panic the capitalist classes, leading to a coup, a debilitating capital flight, or unsustainable populist demands.

Other important conjunctural factors include superpower machinations and international ideological influences. Cold-War rivalries impeded the installation and survival of reformist or left-wing regimes for many years. Moreover, ascendant neoliberal ideas, and their champions in international agencies, have pressured all governments to conform to the new orthodoxy. These themes are elaborated in the next chapter.

Although social democracies emerge from special conditions, social-democratic thinking provides guideposts for political action even where immediate breakthroughs appear improbable. Eduard Bernstein's message a century ago – that leftist parties should not passively wait for the maturing of structural conditions but actively mobilize popular support – remains applicable. To nurture the capacity of subordinate classes and groups to be politically engaged, to encourage policy-based and deliberative forms of demand making, and to press for localized initiatives of popular empowerment will advance the political project. In Jorge Castañeda's words (1993), the left should focus on "democratizing democracy."

Globalization and social democracy

Even if social democracies emerge, will they last? Globalization – the growing integration of national economies into global markets through the increasingly unrestricted flow of trade, investment, finance, and skills – is widely regarded as posing a major threat to their survival. Chapter 8 addresses the controversial impact of global integration, concluding that its implications for developing-world social democracy are mixed. Although the process does limit national economic decision making, equitable development models also offer certain industries competitive advantages in the global economy.

On the one hand, market liberalization restricts a government's autonomy to design its own social-democratic policies at variance with the logic of international competitiveness. Some analysts regard this constraint as spelling the end to social democracy, even in the industrial world (e.g., Teeple 1995; Gray 1998; DeMartino 1999; Rudra 2002). The easier it becomes for investors to shift capital across national boundaries, it is argued, the more credible is their "exit" option. Those governments that fail to adopt anti-inflationary monetary and fiscal policies, provide low taxes, deregulate markets, or remove impediments to the cross-boundary flow of goods, services, investment, finance, and skills risk activating this exit option. Foreign investors are also unlikely to buy the bonds, hold the currency, or invest in the equities of countries with a "restrictive" business environment. Indebted developing countries are subject not only to these private-sector sanctions, but also to the neoliberal policy prescriptions of the IMF and the World Bank. Hence, some scholars contend that an increasingly integrated global economy strips away valuable social programs.

On the other hand, other scholars argue that globalization has not rendered states impotent, at least in the industrial world (e.g., Hirst and Thompson 1996; Garrett 1998; Hay 1998; Weiss 1998; Palan 2000). Geoffrey Garrett (1998, 4) forcefully states this view: "there remains a leftist alternative to free-market capitalism in the era of global markets based on classic 'big government' and corporatist principles that is viable both politically (in terms of winning elections) and economically (by promoting strong macroeconomic performance)." According to this view, many welfare-state programs – medicare, pensions, unemployment insurance, free public education – remain popular among the middle and lower-middle classes, as well as the workers. Indeed, some have argued that free trade only becomes palatable to these classes when welfare states protect their income and employment from their increased exposure to volatile global markets (Rieger and Leibfried 1998). Thus, a political base for a leftist party purportedly still exists in many countries. Moreover, it is argued, social-democratic governments can persuade mobile capital that policies to reduce inequality, employment insecurity, and turbulence are supportive of firms' concern to augment their efficiency, certainty, and profitability. Left-leaning governments can offer certain competitive advantages in exchange for relatively high wages, high taxes, and moderate regulation: orderly industrial relations; wage negotiations geared to productivity; a highly skilled, educated, and healthy labor force; good infrastructure; and relatively low levels of social strife and criminality. Hence, social democracies, far from being antithetical to globalization, may actually complement it.

Christopher Pierson offers a plausible resolution to these conflicting judgments by contending, in relation to industrial countries, that "there is a real globalization effect – but it is much less than is widely assumed" (Pierson 2001b, 87). On the one hand, global integration does limit governments' room for maneuver: enticement of mobile capital leads to increasingly flatter and less progressive tax systems that powerfully constrain redistributive policies; the "exit" option places pressure on corporatist arrangements favoring labor; and the end of preferential trade arrangements restricts employment in certain industries, thus augmenting social strains. On the other hand, many social-democratic policies appeal to the middle classes as well as workers because global integration brings with it increased risks and insecurity. This broad appeal restrains governments from attacking established entitlements (Pierson 2001b, 86).

In the global periphery, the negative "globalization effect" is likely to be more substantial than in industrial countries. An educated workforce, low crime, the peaceful sharing of burdens, legitimate and stable government – these virtues of social-democratic regimes will not appeal to investors in mining, agriculture, and labor-intensive manufacturing, when set against the high taxes and labor costs they entail. Such benefits of social democracy will appeal to high-technology industries whose migration to cheaper sites in the global south represents the latest phase in global capitalism. Competition for the limited investment in such industries is intense, however. In addition, volatile global market forces can wreak havoc on vulnerable developing economies. Economic difficulties not only exacerbate domestic conflicts over the sharing of burdens in social democracies but also push governments into the arms of the IMF, the World Bank, and aid donors – whose leverage to impose a neoliberal agenda is thereby enhanced. Globalization therefore presents new challenges.

Yet, as the case studies of Part II suggest, there are grounds for guarded optimism. Social democracy is a pragmatic and protean movement, constantly adapting to new circumstances amidst charges of opportunism and treachery. Social democracy reinvents itself, safeguarding its essential entitlements, because people are loath to relinquish the security and equity inherent in social citizenship. This versatility provides grounds for optimism, because the alternative to the class solidarity of the left in countries buffeted by global forces is dangerous communal fundamentalisms – whether Muslim, Christian, Jewish, Hindu or ethnically based. Nevertheless, as the next chapter demonstrates, the obstacles to equitable development strategies are often substantial.

2   Burdens of history

History weighs heavily on the global periphery, producing conditions in many countries that are inhospitable to both democracy and social justice. This chapter explores these historical burdens. While in the short term social democracy may not appear possible in many countries, contingent events and human agency can quickly and unexpectedly trigger the emergence of new paths. And although the burdens of history are indeed daunting for some, these challenges are not present in all countries – or at least not to the same degree. Hence, the discussion that follows should be read with a presumption of possibility. It should also be read with a sense of urgency, in view of the failure of neoliberalism and the specter of political and criminal violence in an increasing number of countries.

The pursuit of social democracy usually demands a major departure from past political practices. It requires the creation of a new politics that promotes participatory democracy, challenges the special privileges of powerful groups, and builds a class compromise supportive of social justice. Yet in most southern countries, various forms of authoritarian rule followed the termination of colonial domination, and there was little in the way of demonstrated commitment to improve the lot of the poor. While the advent of the "third wave" of democracy in the 1980s and 1990s represented a substantial improvement over the prevalent military and one-party dictatorships, the inadequacies of new democracies are now widely recognized. Furthermore, the challenge presented by the era of globalization has not been – as is the case for advanced industrial societies – that of protecting the fairly equitable social-welfare arrangements of the Keynesian era. Rather, the majorities in most poor countries stood on the threshold of globalization with little in the way of social protection and, for many, conditions rapidly deteriorated. International circumstances and pressures over the last two decades have often aggravated domestic inequalities of wealth and power, contributing to an environment inhospitable to social-democratic politics and policies.

The social challenge

Poverty has become the key issue in the post-Washington Consensus. Although the extent of world poverty and whether it has been on the decline continue to be hotly debated, its level remains unacceptably high.[1] According to one measure, in South Asia, 78 percent of the population lives in poverty; in sub-Saharan Africa, 76 percent; in East Asia and the Pacific, 48 percent; and in Latin America and the Caribbean the proportion of people living in poverty stands at 21 percent (UN, Department of Economic and Social Affairs 2003).[2] These statistics translate into widespread misery. Although social indicators such as life expectancy, infant-mortality rates, and the incidence of malnutrition improved during the second half of the twentieth century in most countries of the global periphery, these indicators remain well below those of the industrialized nations (Drèze and Sen 1991, 9; World Bank 2001).[3] Moreover, changes in economic structure in the postwar era produced a rapid process of urbanization, resulting in sprawling shantytowns of the urban poor. Policy neglect of peasant agriculture, an emphasis on capital-intensive export agriculture, and a failure to provide adequate services for the rural sector all combined to stimulate migration to cities. Rapid urbanization has created demand for urban public services that many governments have yet to meet. Millions remain without access to safe water and sanitation (Singh 1997, 116–17).

Southern countries (particularly middle-income ones) also have higher levels of inequality than the industrialized nations, and inequality is

[1] Most of this controversy reflects distinct methods of measuring poverty. The most optimistic position is probably the World Bank's (Kieley 2004), which claims that world poverty had fallen in eighteen years from 1.4 billion living in absolute poverty in 1980 to 1.2 billion by 1998, a percentage decline from 28 percent to 24 percent of the world's population. The Bank's measurement is based on monetary income adjusted to take into account local variation in prices (purchasing power parity or PPP). Critics of this form of measurement, including the Economic Commission for Latin America and the Caribbean (ECLAC), argue that it seriously underestimates the extent of poverty because, among other reasons, its basket of goods includes too many goods consumed solely by middle- and upper-income groups. In addition, some experts dispute the Bank's poverty statistics for India and China, the countries that account for most of the poverty decline noted by the Bank (Kieley 2004).

[2] Poverty is often defined as including those who live on less than $2.00 per day (PPP). ECLAC, which bases its measurement on a person's ability to purchase a basic food basket consumed by the less well-off, with the contents of the basket adjusted according to country, estimates poverty in Latin America at 44 percent (CEPAL 2003, 283). There has been growing criticism of income measurements of poverty, however. When measurements include nonmonetary criteria (factors pertaining to vulnerability, for example), levels of poverty tend to be considerably higher.

[3] There continue to be very significant differences between regions. Generally the poorest countries, particularly those of sub-Saharan Africa, show the worst indicators.

increasing in many of them (Betcherman 2002, 13; Cornia, Addison, and Kushi 2004). For a given level of economic development, the higher the income inequality, the greater the proportion of the population who live in poverty. Furthermore, the 2004 *Human Development Report* of the United Nations Development Program (UNDP) reveals that, of sixty-six southern countries for which data was available, more than half have levels of inequality likely to have a detrimental impact on economic growth.[4]

Poverty is closely linked to informal employment. In the periphery, the "informal sector"[5] accounts for 45–85 percent of non-agricultural employment (ILO 2002, 16, 18, 20).[6] Although not all people within the informal sector are poor, there is a statistically high correlation between informality and poverty (ILO 2002, 31). Not only are informal-sector workers poor, but they are also generally not provided for by any formal system of social protection.

Most countries of the global south have failed to develop a welfare state capable of protecting the majority of their people (Gough and Wood 2004, chs. 2 and 3). Whereas in the north the primary gain from the welfare state is the universal reduction in the risk of loss of income, in the global south the need is not just to protect against loss of income, but also to enhance normal living conditions and reduce or eliminate persistent deprivation. This last point is crucial because the persistent deprivation found in the periphery has produced extreme vulnerability to both malnutrition and disease. When combined with inadequate access to medical care, this situation has resulted in the spread of contagious diseases such as the HIV pandemic in Africa and outbreaks of cholera in Latin America and Africa.

Hence, while it is always risky to generalize about regions so enormously diverse as those found in the global periphery, two points are

[4] With the exception of the USA, all of the countries of the OECD have Gini coefficients below .40 (the higher the number, the greater the income inequality). Among sixty-six southern countries, 70 percent have a Gini coefficient above .40 while 52 percent have Gini coefficients above .45 (UNDP 2004, 187–90). Gini coefficients above .45 have been shown to have a detrimental impact on both growth and poverty reduction (Cornia, Addison, and Kuski 2004, 47).

[5] The term "informal sector" refers to own-account workers and irregular and casual employment in very small enterprises. These enterprises are unregulated by the state, do not pay taxes, and workers are not covered by social security. The "modern" (or formal) sector, on the other hand, consists of larger enterprises that (in theory) pay taxes, provide stable employment, and have their wages and working conditions regulated by the state. Despite this distinction, there are important links between the two, and it is increasingly recognized that activities that appear, on the surface, to be self-employment may in fact be linked, through contract arrangements, to the global economy.

[6] In developed countries, the proportion of the labor force in the informal sector is only 10–15 percent (ILO 2002, 15).

abundantly clear: (1) the urgent need for social-democratic politics in the periphery, and (2) the special difficulties impeding its emergence. Equitable social protection is a guiding principle of social democracy, yet it is an attribute that for a variety of historical reasons has been woefully neglected in most peripheral countries. The following section explains why.

Social policy in the global periphery: those who have get more

Social policy in most of the global south is skewed heavily to the benefit of privileged groups and has provided little help to the vast majority of poor.[7] To some extent, this situation is a reflection of weak economies with large informal or subsistence-peasant sectors; such workers lead precarious lives and cannot easily be incorporated into universal social-protection programs requiring participants to make regular monetary contributions. But the absence of social protection for the majority and the regressive distribution of what social protection there is constitute not just a resource issue. It is also a *political* issue. The lives of most people in the global south could be improved substantially with progressive tax collection and more distributive social-welfare measures. As the case of Kerala (with the largest informal sector of our four cases) indicates, low per capita income does not preclude equitable social protection or progressive health and educational programs.

Power structures are the problem. Highly unequal and inadequate social-protection schemes are defended by powerful vested interests, such as the military, top-level civil servants, and organized, formal-sector labor. Where resources are scarce, with privileged groups having access to generous programs, the maintenance of such programs violates social justice while placing a heavy financial burden on the state. Yet the political reality makes it very difficult to redistribute resources.

If the existing social-welfare systems reflect the unequal distribution of power and privilege in postcolonial societies, these inequitable programs have long historical roots. In Africa, for example, the first social-security schemes introduced under colonial rule were discriminatory on racial grounds, benefiting only expatriate Europeans. Rural poverty was ignored and urban poverty barely acknowledged. For the most part, support for the masses of rural dwellers was left to the religious missions

---

[7] Of course, the groups with the greatest assets in the global periphery (landed interests, as well as industrial, commercial, and financial business interests) have not needed, nor benefited from, social-protection policies.

that began to build up their infrastructure in Africa in the nineteenth century. In many countries of Africa, this situation bequeathed a legacy of discrimination against the rural sector and a tradition of dependence on mission-led social welfare (medical care, relief aid, and education). The severely stratified social security systems in Latin America have been traced to the Iberian conquest and colonial rule that established a clear social hierarchy based on race – an arrangement that shaped the socially and racially stratified access to social benefits in the post-independence period. In the immediate post-independence period, the military granted itself and the civil service the first social-security programs (Mesa-Lago 1978, 258). As in Africa, for the masses of rural poor charity work was of central importance, especially in health care, where, until the second half of the twentieth century, church hospitals were the most important providers of medical care.

Noncontributory social assistance schemes, which have the potential to make direct transfers to raise the incomes of the poorest people, have been the *least* common among social-security provisions in the global south. Such schemes, even when they have existed, cover very few of the many needy people. This is, in part, because they invariably contain a variety of restrictive requirements (the incapacity to work, widowhood, dependent children, and the absence of any relative who can help) that effectively exclude a large number of very poor people. In addition to the fact that such payments are too meager to live on, the poor (especially the rural poor) are often unaware of the existence of such schemes, or do not know how to apply (Midgley 1984, 129). But, more than anything, low budgetary allocations have been key in deterring the poor from obtaining social assistance. Very small welfare budgets ensure that only a small proportion of those requiring social assistance actually receives it. Although statistics on the coverage of social assistance are limited, the following gives an idea of how restrictive such programs can be. In late 1970s Zambia, a country of 5 million, a shortage of resources had rendered its social assistance program virtually inoperative. Discouraged by the unlikelihood of receiving benefits, only 5,039 applications had been made for short-term emergency assistance (Midgley 1984, 170, 172, 175).

Historically, while social assistance was conspicuous by its inadequacy, the emphasis has been placed on social insurance programs modeled after those in developed countries. Such schemes involve employee contributions, along with contributions from the employer and the state. Their institution in industrialized nations has provided nearly universal coverage, given that the majority of the labor force is salaried. Not so for southern countries, where most of the labor force is in the rural and/or informal sector. Hence, social insurance programs generally exclude the vast majority of the population (Singh 1997, 2) – precisely those people who are the most vulnerable and whose needs for social protection are the greatest. According to the 1991 Indian census, of a workforce of 320 million barely 7.5 million had social-security coverage (Singh 1994, 1). (Kerala, on the other hand, has introduced both labor protection and social security for informal-sector workers.) Similarly, for Africa, it is estimated that social insurance covers from 1 to 12 percent of the economically active population (Zwanecki 2001, 9). Only a few sub-Saharan African countries (Mauritius, the Republic of South Africa, and Namibia) have managed to introduce a general benefit scheme that covers informal-sector workers. Mauritius has the most advanced social-security system, providing pensions for all, including those unable to contribute to a plan. Among Latin American countries, only Costa Rica has been able to accomplish universalization of social-security coverage, integrating social assistance with social security. Furthermore, Costa Rica is the only Latin American country that has been able to integrate all hospitals into one single system, standardize entitlement, and open the unified system to the dispossessed (Mesa-Lago 2000, 288, 298). The Chilean leadership is currently struggling to achieve a national health plan that will make possible the transfer of resources between its private health-care system, serving the middle and upper classes, and the public system that serves the bulk of the population (see chapter 6).

Domestic politics, as suggested earlier, has shaped the unequal distribution of social benefits and protection. Clientelism, corporatism, and political parties' desire to shore up their popular support, along with the political clout exerted by very powerful groups, have all been factors in determining the hierarchy of beneficiaries (Malloy 1979; Singh 1994, 26; Raczynski 1998, 143; Zwanecki 2001, 4, 9; Haagh 2002). Invariably, at the top in terms of benefits received is the military (with its own hospitals), followed by civil servants – both receive a substantially larger share of state social-security expenditures in countries of the global periphery than in developed countries (Mesa-Lago 1978, 9).[8] Next in the hierarchy are highly organized workers in strategic economic sectors, particularly those working in exporting sectors. Groups receiving the most generous social insurance benefits have successfully opposed reforms that would make possible the introduction of universal systems (for example in health care) since such a reform would likely involve a diminution of their benefits.

---

[8] By the late 1960s, the social-security benefits going to civil servants in southern countries represented one-third of the nation's social-security expenditures, as opposed to one-tenth for developed countries (Mesa-Lago 1978, 313).

Equally discriminatory tax policies are usually regressive, since they are collected from taxes on items used and consumed by the majority of poor people. Progressive taxes, for example those on luxury goods, generally form only a small part of revenues (Mesa-Lago 1978, 16; Midgley 1984, 166). In addition, not only is there large-scale tax avoidance by the wealthy, but also employers pass on the costs of social-security payments to consumers in the higher prices they charge for their goods and services (Malloy 1979). The situation would be redressed if tax revenues were used primarily to benefit the poor but, as we have seen, they are not. Hence, resources are effectively transferred from the poor, who are not covered by social security but who purchase the goods and services that are taxed, to the more prosperous sectors of the population, who receive generous social insurance benefits. And these inequitable arrangements are costly: in some Latin American countries, social insurance expenditures for the privileged accounted for as much as 15 percent of GNP by the 1970s, comparable to many European countries (Mesa-Lago 1978, 3).

Segregated social insurance funds, which provide inordinate benefits to privileged groups, mean that the generous contributions by states, employers, and high-income earners are monies not available for redistribution to lower-income or destitute groups. Critics argue that sub-Saharan African countries would be better advised to improve the health and nutritional needs of the entire population than to spend on social security for the already privileged (von Braun 1991, 397). Hence, despite the expansion of social services in the global south in the postwar period, the result was not an institutionalized social-welfare state, but rather "an incremental model in which existing provisions are expanded in an ad hoc linear fashion and in which existing inequalities and inadequacies are perpetuated, serving the interests of elite groups" (MacPherson 1987, 121; see also, Gough and Wood 2004, ch. 1).

Excluded from social insurance, the vast majority of people, especially those in rural areas, continued to depend on traditional systems of reciprocity and solidarity at the community and kinship level for their survival (Gough and Wood 2004, chs. 2 and 3). Although traditional forms of social security were sometimes highly successful in redistributing toward lower-income groups, with the expansion of HIV/AIDS, especially in Africa, these informal networks are breaking down (Zwanecki 2001, 3, 110). Moreover, traditional self-help organizations are often organized around patron–client networks that represent an obstacle to the kind of political action required for the achievement of more inclusive or universal schemes, even though they may provide a modicum of social protection in the face of extreme vulnerability.

In countries where the majority of poor work the land, the most effective and necessary form of social security is that of securing the rural dweller's control over this land. This is an important aspect of Kerala's success in social protection (chapter 3). But attempts to provide security to rural dwellers through land reform have invariably confronted the resistance of powerful landowners, as the Chilean case so amply demonstrates. Even when land reform becomes law, landowners find ways to circumvent the law, with the consequence that the numbers of families who gain land title may not be large (India, Peru, El Salvador, Bangladesh). Alternatively, the failure to provide support for the reform sector contributes to the return of land concentration (Mexico). Meanwhile, the perpetuation of patron–clientelism in the countryside, in the absence of a politicizing force such as a leftist political party to counteract such ties, inhibits rural dwellers from pressing for redistributive policies. In the absence of state support for rural dwellers in such areas as subsistence insurance and credit, vulnerable rural producers will cling to landowners for security. Handling the issue of land reform within a context of rural political mobilization is probably the trickiest challenge faced by social democracy in the periphery. Two of our cases (Mauritius and Kerala) cleared this hurdle successfully; one (Chile) failed miserably.

In the years prior to the debt crisis of the early 1980s, social policy in the periphery largely bypassed the vast majority of rural poor and vulnerable shantytown dwellers. State subsidies on basics such as food and public transportation were often the lifeline that allowed them to survive. When the debt crisis hit, the ranks of the poor and destitute sharply increased in many countries of the global south, as even these minimal measures of social protection for the poor were dismantled.

The unequal distribution of social protection, characteristic of so many countries, is a situation rooted in politics and, in particular, in the pre-disposition of political elites to maintain themselves in power through measures that discourage programmatic politics. It is to an analysis of these political practices that we now turn.

The origins of authoritarianism and social injustice

The expansion of European trade and colonialism had a profound and lasting impact on the social, political, and economic arrangements of the encountered societies. Between the fifteenth and twentieth centuries various countries, mainly European, divided the globe in their drive for strategic advantage, trade, primary products, labor, and outlets for investment. In some cases, such as the islands of the Caribbean, entire societies disappeared. In all cases, economies were transformed, old social arrangements disrupted, and institutions of colonial political control imposed. While the specific impact of colonial rule varied among countries and regions, that impact would invariably set the stage for the politics of the twentieth century. This was the case even for the countries of the Latin American mainland, where formal independence was achieved a century before Africa and Asia.

A substantial literature argues that the experience of European colonial rule made postcolonial democratic government problematic (Diamond 1988; Abernathy 2000). For instance, the view that British indirect rule fostered democratic governance – owing, among other things, to the opportunities it offered to build on indigenous political institutions (Lipsit, Seong, and Torres 1993) – has been challenged, particularly in relation to Africa. Instead, today's democratic deficit has been linked to the high degree of societal fragmentation associated with indirect rule (Blanton, Mason, and Athow 2001).[9] Countries such as Mauritius and Singapore, on the other hand, with a heritage of *direct* rule, developed effective democratic or semi-democratic states that undertook successful state-led development (Huff 1994; Lange 2003).[10] However, in the more typical case, the former leaders of nationalist independence struggles took over weakly legitimated and autocratic state structures inherited from colonial rule. In the Americas, the struggle for independence in the first quarter of the nineteenth century was an elite affair. American-born Spaniards and Portuguese replaced the Iberians at the helm of the newly independent states and, despite the trappings of democratic institutions, excluded the majority of the population from political participation. In fact, the ascendancy of these new oligarchs meant a worsening of the living standards of the masses of rural dwellers as peasants were divested of their land, which was then turned to production for export markets. In Africa and Asia, independence struggles were led by western-educated indigenous elites, often promising social justice, who crafted nationalist/ populist alliances involving labor and the urban and rural poor. Once in power, however, their taste for democracy and addressing social issues typically waned.

By the second half of the twentieth century, there was a marked trend toward civilian authoritarian and military governments in most regions

---

[9] One study of indirect rule in former British colonies argues that it had a particularly negative impact on various measures of state capacity due to the absence of a large centralized administration and the fostering of local "despotisms" (Lange 2004a).

[10] Other contributory factors were also present in these cases, however, such as their pre-existing economic opportunity structures and small size.

of the global south. In Africa, electoral democracy disintegrated into one-party rule, and then military dictatorships. In Latin America, the military overthrew elected governments between the late 1960s and the mid 1970s, as it did in much of Asia. Whereas in 1970 only one-third of countries of the global periphery had military governments, by 1983, two-thirds of these countries had military or quasi-military governments (Midgley 1987). Even in those countries where electoral democracy survived, the commitment to social justice did not. In India, despite a mass following in the struggle for independence, the Congress Party became a conservative force due to the compromises it made with powerful social interests (Kohli 1987, 57–58).

Another legacy of colonial rule was often fragmented polities – regionally, ethnically, culturally, and in terms of social class. It took Latin America some fifty years of almost incessant civil wars to consolidate its nation-states, and this period was followed by cycles of electoral democracy and military rule in the twentieth century. In much of Africa and Asia, colonial rule contributed to the intensity of sectoral (religious and ethnic) conflict in the post-independence period. The practice of colonial rulers of favoring some indigenous groups over others, the drawing of colonial boundaries without regard to ethnic/cultural identities, and the economic reorganization that disrupted the geographic location of groups,[11] all strengthened communal identities. Ruling these societies would prove to be difficult. The political strategies employed by elites responded to this challenge but, as discussed further below, often served to divide polities further.

One common response was state-led industrialization. The modernizing aspirations of leaders were bolstered by the then current development ideas linking the persistence of poverty to unfair terms of trade and the foreign domination of economies – factors believed to be draining countries of investment capital.[12] One common argument held that, with the absence of a dynamic entrepreneurial class, the state must lead by investing in areas where the private sector was either unwilling or unable

---

[11] The promotion of the production of cash crops involved the institution of private property rights, the acquisition of extensive tracks of land by some, and the expulsion of many who migrated to towns and regions where they came into contact with groups of different ethnic identities (Wallerstein 1982, 413).

[12] The more conservative version of this perspective emerged in the writings of the Economic Commission for Latin America in the 1950s. Much more radical writers, such as Andre Gunder Frank, popularized the notion of the negative impact of "dependency" on Latin American development and influenced development thinking on Africa, as seen in the work of such writers as Samir Amin. Some notable leaders of the day, such as Michael Manley (Jamaica), Julius Nyerere (Tanzania), and Salvador Allende (Chile), also reflected this perspective.

to invest. In the 1960s and the early part of the 1970s, many states took over foreign enterprises, especially in strategic natural-resource sectors. The desire to stimulate industrialization was, in part, responsible for the movement of states into the production of energy and such products as steel, while fear of loss of employment often pushed states to take over failing companies in such areas as sugar production and textiles. The result was usually a chaotic and inefficient state-enterprise sector that was substantially larger than was the case for industrialized nations at the time. By the mid-1970s, the participation of public enterprises in GDP averaged 4 percent for countries of the global south while the comparable figure for the industrialized nations was 1.75 percent (Short 1984, 145). But this expansion of the public sector also followed a political logic: its extension was necessary to hold together highly fragmented polities and maintain tenuous political leaderships in power.

The exchange of material rewards for political loyalty and support, based on personalistic networks of clientelism, is a key feature of most postcolonial political systems. Patron–clientelism has been defined as "a tie between two parties of unequal wealth and influence" that "depends upon the exchange of goods and services" (Powell 1970, 412–13). In this exchange, the lower-status client receives material rewards from the patron in exchange for nonmaterial rewards such as loyalty and deference. The phenomenon was originally and most extensively documented by anthropologists in the rural sector and explained in terms of the desire of highly vulnerable rural dwellers to provide themselves with economic security through establishing a personal relationship with the landlord, thereby obliging him to look after the peasant and his family in case of illness or natural catastrophe. Political scientists have applied the concept of clientelism extensively to all facets and levels of politics.

Clientelism, of course, is not just a feature of politics in the global periphery. It was present in the early histories of now-industrialized nations and has, in fact, persisted in some of them (Hopkin and Mastropaolo 2001, 167). But it is not the main organizing political principle in developed countries, as it is in so many southern countries. In the periphery, the political turmoil faced by southern elites inclines them to the continued use of clientelism, while the persistence of poverty and lack of social protection drives clients to seek out patrons. Political parties have typically used clientelistic methods in order to garner and maintain support. The most successful of these have been mass integrative parties that have used clientelistic methods to unite a heterogeneous (ethnic, regional, and class) support base. Referred to as "populist," such parties have often been headed by charismatic political leaders who have held power by virtue of their ability to garner personal loyalty and distribute material rewards. Mass integrative parties have usually incorporated existing elites (or a fraction of them), and have avoided radical redistributive measures (such as land reform) because they would alienate their powerful supporters. Or, when radical redistributive measures are promised and even initiated, clientelistic mechanisms of political control are typically reestablished with the consequence that the original reform initiative declines.[13] In such cases, apparently radical reform movements abandoned their goals as powerful societal interests increasingly captured them.[14]

Where political authority depends on personalistic relationships and the distribution of material rewards to such an extent that the property of the individual ruler and the state become indistinguishable, we may speak of "neopatrimonialism" or personal rule (Sandbrook 1985). Personal rule, a phenomenon widely observed in Africa, also exists in other regions.[15] Sandbrook's description of the personal rule of Mobutu of Zaire (now the Democratic Republic of the Congo) captures the essence of neopatrimonialism: absolute personal allegiance to the leader is given in exchange for access to power and illegal opportunities to accumulate wealth. The leader's displeasure guarantees personal ruin and even imprisonment, and while thousands of lower-level officials have the opportunity to accumulate some wealth, "the mass of the population is excluded from the spoils and subject to repression" (Sandbrook 1985, 91).

Not only has the politics of most southern countries been dominated by clientelism and, in many cases, neopatrimonialism, but clientelism and neopatrimonialism have been important impulses behind the expansion of the state. Joel Migdal explains how the leaders of fragmented polities attempt to survive politically through allocating government appointments in order to win the loyalty of potential political adversaries. However, this strategy presents the danger of competing power centers (for example from public corporations and their clienteles), making it necessary for the political ruler to create new bureaucratic enclaves, including agencies of state security, that can be filled with loyalists – thereby

---

[13] The aftermath of the Mexican land reform under President Cardenas (1934–1940) and the failure to carry through on land reform in the period following the MNR Revolution (1952) in Bolivia are examples of this.

[14] See Kohli (1987, 60–61) and Stern (2001, 11–12) on this point with regard to the Indian case.

[15] Examples include President Menem of Argentina (1989–1999), President Suharto of Indonesia (1967–1997), and President Anastasio Somoza (Senior) of Nicaragua (1934–1956). The Somoza dynasty lasted under the dictator's two sons until 1979.

producing an ever increasing extension of the state apparatus (Migdal 1988, 288).

Corporatism, which may operate alongside clientelism, is another hierarchical principle that has functioned as a mechanism of political control and containment in much of the global periphery. Corporatism entails formal institutional arrangements for incorporating organized societal groups in a subordinate manner into the party or state apparatus. Such arrangements allow for controlled participation in the political process under the auspices of the state; they are put in place for the explicit purpose of containing actual and potential dissent.[16] Authoritarian Mexico, under the single-party rule of the Institutionalized Revolutionary Party, was a superb example of corporatist rule lasting more than sixty years. In this case, the labor code gave the state the capacity to reward cooperative labor organizations and punish dissident ones through the granting or withdrawal of legal status, while the party apparatus incorporated and controlled the organizations of workers, peasants, and other societal groups. This form of political control has been found throughout the global south, used by patrimonial, populist, and military regimes alike (Bianchi 1986; Nyang'oro 1989; Hadiz 1997). Corporatism and clientelism are particularly effective when they operate together, as when the leaders of privileged (incorporated) organizations are bound to the political leadership through personal loyalty and the material benefits of patron–client ties.

Both clientelism and corporatism are obstacles to social democracy. Clientelist politics are an impediment to democracy because they contravene both equality of access to the state and the resources it dispenses, and political representation based upon a legal order – principles at the core of the democratic notion of citizenship. Clientelism can also thwart the achievement of social justice because, as a practice based on the personal exchange of political support for a material reward, it promotes non-programmatic politics likely to ignore the pressing social needs of the poor as a group. As a personal exchange relationship, clientelism is predisposed by its very nature to avoid policy promises that address broadly defined group or societal needs. Rather, politicians recruit supporters on the prospect of personal, immediate, tangible rewards. As a hierarchical

---

[16] The term "corporatism" is also applied to the arrangements in northern European countries that allow for the participation of societal groups, particularly labor, in the planning and policy process. But the term has a very different meaning in this context in that it signifies active and independent involvement, not subordination. See Schmitter (1974, 93) on the distinction between *societal corporatism* (the corporatism of the advanced liberal democratic welfare state) and *state corporatism* (characteristic of the anti-liberal delayed authoritarian capitalist state).

principle of incorporation, clientelism is highly selective and incorporates in a way that clearly subordinates and divides the poor, thereby further inhibiting lower-class solidarity and political mobilization. Moreover, it leaves out the majority of poor who do not obtain a patron, but who continue to compete for one and who thereby remain politically quiescent in the hope that they will one day be successful. When clientelism permeates the state, as it does in much of the global south, it inhibits the development of a qualified bureaucratic class, since state appointments are given primarily on the basis of personal loyalty to the leadership instead of expertise. Finally, if carried to the extreme of patrimonialism, clientelism is likely to generate extreme inefficiencies and waste.

Corporatism, for its part, by excluding the most radical organizations with the most extensive social demands, ensures that redistributive proposals do not appear on the state or party agenda. By granting privileges of access to some groups while excluding others, corporatism has been an effective method of thwarting political mobilization for policy change.

But neither corporatism nor clientelism is a static arrangement. In some cases, market reform has contributed to the breakdown of corporatist forms of political control (Mexico), while in others (the Middle East) a reinvigorated authoritarianism has been the response of elites who lose this method of political containment (Ehteshami and Murphy 1996). It is probably even more difficult to generalize about the evolutionary direction of clientelism. In many countries, market-oriented reforms in the 1980s and 1990s invigorated cronyism. For example social investment funds made available by the World Bank have been used for clientelist political control. However, there are cases in which the ability of clientelism to control associational activity has diminished in the periphery in response to the strategies of reformist elites. For example, in Porto Alegre, Brazil, traditional clientelism was overcome in large part through the actions of state actors who promoted independent associational formation (Abers 1998), whereas in Mexico, reformist elites have been key in the emergence of pluralist enclaves of associational activity (Fox 1996). Hence, while socioeconomic change has often been instrumental in the erosion of clientelism, elite strategies can accelerate, or even initiate, its decline. Furthermore, a certain amount of clientelism is compatible with any type of democracy, including social democracy (Piattoni 2001, 201). The issue, therefore, is mitigating its pervasiveness, not eliminating it altogether.

Moreover, while weak states, weak civil societies, widespread poverty, the absence of sustained economic growth, and/or economic crises are all important challenges to social democracy, it is their combined interaction that is nefarious. Weak states encourage elites to use methods of political containment that discourage programmatic social-democratic politics, whereas economic vulnerability sustains the demand side of clientelistic arrangements as the poor seek out social protection in the only way available to them. As the case studies in this volume so amply demonstrate, an efficacious state is essential to employment-creating economic growth. Without economic growth, the informal sector will remain substantial, and without regular contributions from a large body of stable, salaried contributors in an expanding formal sector, peripheral states will continue to face financial challenges in the provision of improved educational, health, and welfare programs. Economic growth is key because growth not only provides jobs, and thereby reduces poverty and increases resources available to social programs, but also makes business interests more amenable to increased taxation and the expansion of welfare programs. But a state capable of leading economic growth is not enough – political movements will also have to struggle to reform highly unequal social-protection arrangements if the equity goals of social democracy are to be approached.

The debt crisis and global neoliberalism

The debt crisis of the early 1980s, and the neoliberal reforms arising in response to that crisis, often interacted with preexisting unequal political and social structures to impede social democracy. Policy choices were restricted, and governance reform in the shape of democratization rarely served to empower the poor.

Important changes in the global economy in the 1970s – increased trade competition and advances in information, telecommunications, and transport technologies that made possible the separation of production stages – formed the essential backdrop to the momentous changes of the 1980s. The drive for competitiveness among the multinational corporations, combined with the export-oriented policies of a few countries of the global south, propelled the transfer of industrial operations able to utilize cheap labor to a handful of developing countries.[17] Economic exchanges among industrialized nations increased, with direct foreign investment (DFI) concentrated in those countries that were already the wealthiest. Meanwhile, foreign investment bypassed most low-income countries, with only nine or ten countries of the global south receiving the lion's share of DFI (Schwartz 1994, 243; Hoogvelt 1997, 75;

---

[17] In the electronics industry, for example, US companies moved to Mexico and Southeast Asia and many Japanese firms invested in South Korea, Singapore, and Hong Kong.

Hirst and Thompson 2000, 70; Landau 2001, 109).[18] Some regions, such as sub-Saharan Africa, have been almost entirely bypassed by "global" trade and investment.

These harmful trends were exacerbated when southern-country debt increased dramatically in the late 1970s and early 1980s, as the cost of oil imports and external loans both rose dramatically. Moreover, a sharp rise in interest rates and oil prices coincided with declines in the prices of many southern export commodities (James 1996, 356).[19] Southern countries, facing a sharp rise in their balance of payments deficits, fell into economic crisis. The stage was set for the extensive involvement of the IMF and the World Bank in the economic and social policies of these countries.[20]

With the 1982 crisis, conditional lending, which required recipient countries to agree to prescribed economic measures, increased in importance. Standard IMF Stand-by Agreements (known as Stabilization Programs) became prevalent throughout the 1980s. Such agreements required restrictions in the expansion of money and credit, in public expenditures, and in public-sector wages and employment. Other measures included devaluations of local currencies and measures to encourage foreign capital. By the mid-1980s, with the failure of economies to recover, market-liberalizing reforms came to be seen as the panacea for the economic woes of the global south. The IMF substantially increased its longer-term lending through the Extended Fund Facility (EFF) to correct what it saw as structural maladjustments in production and trade. EFF loans called for trade liberalization, the abolition of price controls, and the restructuring of public-sector enterprises. The World Bank, traditionally a stronger supporter of state intervention and public enterprises than the IMF, now moved to an increasingly anti-statist stance. Its Structural Adjustment Loans (SALs) – loans of three to five years' duration – placed heavy emphasis on trade liberalization, the selling off of public

[18] This group of privileged southern countries is dominated by China where investment is concentrated in the southern coastal provinces. Only 28 percent of the world's population receives 91.5 percent of direct foreign investment (Hirst and Thompson 2000, 71). Large numbers of people, including those in very large countries, and in populous regions within those few countries that do participate in the global system, are left out of the new global order.

[19] One analysis suggests that, even without the oil shocks and high interest rates, the decline in commodity prices was sufficiently serious that many countries would have faced major balance of payments difficulties. Between 1970 and 1992, for a group of ten African countries, the terms of trade plummeted by nearly 60 percent (Osmani 2001, 215).

[20] This role, however, was not envisioned when these institutions were established by the Bretton Woods Agreement (1944). Originally, the IMF was to provide short-term financing for countries with transitory balance of payments problems, while the World Bank was established to provide long-term project-oriented money for the rebuilding of infrastructure in war-torn Europe

companies (including those in core areas such as petroleum and mining), labor "flexibilization" (reforms to the labor code making it easier to hire and fire), and the removal of subsidies. But despite the frequency of such loans, direct pressure from the multilaterals was probably less important in inducing reform than was the continuous policy persuasion (known as "policy dialogue") that occurred among technocrats, bureaucrats, and politicians within the context of the new international market-reform policy culture.

Although there was considerable initial resistance to market-liberalizing reforms, by the late 1980s this policy agenda had taken off. By 1992, for instance, more than eighty countries had privatized some 6,800 public companies, largely in public services such as water, electricity, and telecommunications (Hoogvelt 1997, 138).

Several key features of policy conditionality accounted for its negative impact on living standards in the south. In particular, stabilization and adjustment, though conceptually distinct, were usually implemented more or less simultaneously. Consequently, difficult policy reforms were being carried out in a context of sharp recession involving heavy reductions in public expenditures. This situation stemmed in large part from the fact that the priority of the international financial institutions, in the face of the threat to the stability of the international financial system, was to ensure that countries continued payment on their debts (Aggarwal 1996, 374). Economic growth, consideration of the impact of policies on the poor, and discussions of debt reduction or forgiveness were therefore precluded during the initial years following the debt crisis (Tussie 1988, 294; Griffiths-Jones 1992, 20–21). Hence, as a consequence of payments on the debt, the years between 1984 and 1988 saw countries of the global periphery transferring about US$143 billion to industrialized nations (Nelson 1990, 1). And, between 1986 and 1992, they paid back more to the IMF than they received in loans (Bird 1995, 99). According to one estimate, between 1982 and 1985, the total net transfer of financial resources from Latin America amounted to 5.3 percent of GDP (Kapur, Lewis, and Webb 1997, 627). In Africa and Latin America, the cost of servicing the debt became unsustainable at more than 25 percent of export earnings (Loxley 1986, 82; Havnevik 1987, 13).

Although it is difficult to disentangle the impact of the economic crisis from the policies (stabilization and structural adjustment) that sought to "solve" the crisis, the 1980s clearly witnessed a worsening situation for already struggling citizens.[21] During this decade, per capita GDP fell in sub-Saharan Africa by 1.3 percent per year and distribution became more

[21] A summary of twenty-three investigations shows that the impact of structural adjustment on growth ranged from mildly negative to mildly positive (Stewart 1995, Table 2.2). For conflicting evidence on the impact of structural adjustment on poverty in the Asian

unequal (Osmani 2001, 211). Between 1985 and 1990, the numbers of poor in Africa rose from 198 million to 216 million (Grindle 1996, 19), and extreme poverty increased from 31.7 percent to 33.4 percent (Stewart 2001, 197). Meanwhile, the proportion of the population without adequate access to food also increased (Osmani 2001, 211). During the same period, in Latin America and the Caribbean, the absolute numbers of poor rose from 87 million to 108 million (Grindle 1996, 19) and extreme poverty rose from 13.2 percent of the population to 17.2 percent (Stewart 2001, 197). As unemployment increased due to job losses in the formal sector, increasing numbers of people moved into the informal sector: in Latin America, it is estimated that the informal sector increased by 39 percent between 1980 and 1985 alone (Grindle 1996, 23). Asia, overall, fared considerably better: for one thing, its accumulated debt was substantially lower in relation to exports and GDP. Extreme poverty declined overall in Asia from 36.8 percent to 33.3 percent (Stewart 2001, 197).[22] The plight of the vast numbers of poor was made worse by the fact that while the proportion of budgets spent on servicing the debt sharply increased, social expenditures dropped. In Latin America, for example, real expenditure on health and education fell by 6 percent, while the fall in these sectors for Africa was 10 percent (Grindle 1996, 37; Stewart 2001, 200). Moreover, real expenditures on food subsidies per head fell in nine of the ten southern countries for which information was available (Stewart 1987, 31).

Although all of the cases discussed in this volume faced economic difficulties and were subject to pressures to carry out market-liberalizing reforms, they confronted these pressures with already established universal social programs, unlike the vast majority of countries in the global south. Public resistance in Costa Rica, Kerala, and Mauritius slowed attempts to reduce social programs and carry out privatizations. Even in Chile, where social policy was hit hard and trade liberalization and privatization were fully embraced under military rule, important elements of state intervention to promote exports remained.

cases, see Stewart 2001. The argument was originally made by the multilateral lending institutions that structural adjustment would hurt only/mostly the vested interests in the formal sector who would see their salaries fall and who would lose jobs due to state streamlining, credit restriction, and the like. But reality proved to be considerably more complex, with informal-sector workers hurt by the general decline in the economy, and rural workers confronted with increased prices for inputs and competition from foreign imports.

[22] Poverty did increase in a number of specific regions of some countries during certain years, such as in rural India, until the early 1980s; in urban Nepal, 1984–1985 to 1995–1996; in rural Pakistan, 1984–1985 to 1994–1995; and in urban Philippines, 1971–1985 (Stewart 2001, 193).

Unfortunately, recent changes in the international trading and investment regimes make it more difficult for states to promote export-led growth through developmentally oriented states. The three major agreements coming out of the Uruguay Round (1986–1994) – the Agreement on Trade-Related Investment Measures (TRIMS), the General Agreement on Trade in Services (GATS), and the Agreement on Trade-Related Aspects of Intellectual Property Rights (TRIPS) – constrain the policy choices of southern countries. Indeed, the protection imposed by TRIPS for trademarks and industrial designs impedes the sort of free-wheeling incorporation of foreign processes so important in the early stages of industrialization of the now industrialized nations and the newly industrialized countries (NICs) of Asia. TRIMS bans the imposition of performance requirements on foreign investors regarding, for example, local content or export levels. Although it allows some exemptions for developing countries, it represents a direct challenge to the use of state-directed industrial policy. Finally, GATS, which extends the WTO rules to trade in services (banking, education, health, sanitation), constrains southern countries in protecting their own service industries (Wade 2003).

As for the World Bank and the IMF, their initial lack of concern for the social implications of policy reform gave way by the early 1990s to a renewed interest in poverty alleviation. The social programs supported by the World Bank, however, have been and remain largely programs targeted to the extremely poor, on the assumption that, over the long term, it is the market that will provide the answer to poverty.[23] The Bank continues to see the solution for poverty in the growth generated by ever-increasing integration into global markets. Hence it urges countries to maintain stable macroeconomic policies, reduce trade barriers, and improve the domestic business climate to encourage foreign investment (World Bank 2003a). More recently, the Bank has placed heavy emphasis on the achievement of greater efficiency in the provision of services to the poor (education, health, water, sanitation, and electricity) through privatization and through administrative reforms such as decentralization (World Bank 2004c). The growing recognition by the World Bank of the social burden imposed by debt on the poorest countries – where spending on debt service exceeded that on health and education – is reflected in

---

[23] The highly targeted programs supported by the World Bank have come under considerable criticism. Such programs increasingly involve cash transfers to extremely poor people in exchange for commitments to keep children in school and attend health clinics. In the absence of good and equitable educational and health-care systems, the ability of these programs to transform the lives of the poor is quite limited and such programs do not, of course, address the employment question. Since access is based on questionable assessments of the extent of a family's poverty, these programs also divide communities, thwart social mobilization, and threaten social cohesion.

its Highly Indebted Poor Countries (HIPC) Initiative, launched in 1996. This program explicitly linked debt relief to market-liberalizing reforms, tying debt relief and structural adjustment to the preferred poverty reduction strategy of targeting. Over seventy countries are eligible to benefit from this program. However, while its positive impact has been that poor countries in the program were able to reduce debt payments and increase social expenditures, the scheme committed countries even more firmly to the market-reform agenda.

Multilateral lending agencies and southern political elites have also failed to recognize the importance of equality-enhancing measures in reducing poverty. If growth is to be sustained over time (and if it is to reduce poverty), it must be accompanied by measures to redistribute wealth. But such measures are not a priority for either the international financial institutions or for most domestic policy elites though the World Bank's *World Development Report, 2006* on "Equity and Development" may signal a policy change. Unified social-protection arrangements that are funded by progressive taxation and that redistribute toward the lowest socioeconomic groups are conspicuous by their absence. Indeed, the World Bank's strategy for the establishment of privately provided and contributory social-protection schemes alongside public noncontributory ones makes the transfer of resources from the upper-class contributors to lower-class ones extremely problematic.[24] According to one estimate, the cost of reaching universal coverage without the unification and redistribution that can only occur with a national social-protection scheme would not be feasible in many countries as it would require from 11 percent to 39 percent of GDP in thirteen of them (Mesa-Lago 1994, 38). Nor is labor protection a part of the multilateral formula for poverty reduction. Indeed, both the World Bank and the IMF (and increasingly southern political elites) maintain that labor flexibilization will help solve poverty by attracting private investment. Opponents, however, argue that labor flexibilization has contributed to greater precariousness and inequality. Land-redistribution schemes are also absent, even though land security and support for small agricultural producers are crucial components of social protection for the rural poor.[25]

The current perspective of the international financial institutions on poverty reduction contradicts the premises of social democracy in two important ways. First, whereas the World Bank and the IMF assume

[24] See chapter 6 on Chile for a discussion of the redistributive challenges posed by separate state and private health systems.

[25] The World Bank supports agrarian reform largely in the form of individual property titling programs with the objective of securing property rights to encourage farmer investment.

that market-liberalizing reforms (now with a little help from state investment in "human capital") will generate trade and growth – and hence
prosperity and poverty reduction – social democracy places considerably less faith in the efficacy of global markets and identifies a central
role for both industrial and social policy in diminishing extensive poverty
and inequality. There is no evidence, according to this latter viewpoint,
that market reforms alone will stimulate higher rates of economic growth
and broad-based prosperity. As noted in chapter 1, many southern countries achieved higher growth rates between 1960 and 1980, the period of
heavy state involvement in the economy, than they did subsequently. Second, in contradistinction to the Bank and the IMF, proponents of social
democracy seek to place both economic and social policy at the service of
generalized social welfare. Social democracy recognizes that the plight of
the poor will not be addressed through measures that dismantle the state,
reduce and privatize social services, and then target only the extremely
poor. It therefore advocates state-led industrial policy and equitable universal programs to achieve poverty reduction and greater equality.

Current political impediments to social democracy

Transitions from authoritarian rule to electoral democracy characterized most southern countries during the 1980s and 1990s. The coupling
of political transition with economic reform was initially greeted with
considerable optimism: it was believed that the dismantling of the state
and the sharp reduction in its access to resources would undermine the
clientelistic, corporatist, and manipulative capacities of authoritarian
regimes, thus reinforcing democratization. However, once the glow of
the initial transitions wore off, observers began to express concern about
the quality of these new democracies and about the persistence and even
exaggeration of authoritarian forms. Southern democracies soon came
to be qualified as "hybrid" (Conaghan, Malloy, and Abugattas 1990),
"delegative" (O'Donnell 1994), and "pseudo" democracies (Sandbrook
2000, 2).

The weakness and, in some cases, the deterioration of democracies in
the global periphery are closely related to the debt crisis and its aftermath,
which involved significant changes in domestic power structures. Owing
to the crisis, the influence of international financial institutions in domestic policymaking increased while the need to carry forward unpopular
reforms rapidly necessitated the exclusion of popular organizations and
legislative bodies from policymaking. At the same time, the reform process gave enormously more leverage to domestic business interests and
to multinational corporations. The latter became especially important

in those countries in which the business class lacked sufficient capital to buy the public companies put up for auction. Compounding political and economic inequality, privatization and trade liberalization created opportunities for the enrichment of presidential cronies and the economic elite (Teichman 1995; Tangri 1999, 51). In Mexico and Argentina, for example, a few big domestic businesses (their heads invariably close friends of the president of the day) and their foreign allies bought up public companies – often at bargain prices, or with loans proffered by the state – while at the same time obtaining various state subsidies that allowed them to expand into export markets (Teichman 2002). In South Africa and Zimbabwe, an "alliance of desperation" composed of the state, international financial institutions, and domestic and multinational capital made economic policy in the 1990s (Andreason 2003, 386). Moreover, as the market increases in importance and as the political elite places all of its hopes in global markets and foreign capital investment, the maintenance of an attractive business climate becomes the compelling priority for governments. Sadly, the less leverage a government has vis-à-vis capital, the more the government formulates public policy in ways that send positive signals to economic agents and the less it directly addresses the democratically voiced welfare demands of the broader population.

Domestic economic elites, now with more leverage through market-liberalizing measures, may represent an important obstacle to social democracy. Long resistant to a social-democratic class compromise, they apparently fail to see the possibility of mutual sacrifice for mutual gain. This inflexible mentality responds to a complex of historical and contextual factors characteristic of the periphery. Slow growth and vulnerable economies mean that redistributive political conflict is often perceived as zero-sum. Indeed, in some cases, substantial sacrifices have been demanded of economic elites who lacked alternative economic opportunities to move into. Currently, economic elites and their political allies often continue to resist the expansion of social programs, particularly when such changes involve increases in public expenditures. Hence, they frequently block reform to bring about more progressive tax systems and have lobbied heavily for changes in the labor code that would contribute to greater precariousness and poverty.

Moreover, the failure of market-liberalizing reforms may well undermine state legitimacy, including the legitimacy of democratic institutions. The strong popular support for Venezuelan president Hugo Chávez, for example, stems in part from the vigorous opposition of many Venezuelans to the neoliberal agenda, particularly to the threat of foreign participation in the petroleum industry. As market reform shrinks the state's access to resources for patronage purposes, these measures can just as easily produce authoritarianism or political disorder as democratization (Brumberg 1995, 252). In some African countries, the simultaneous dismantling of the state and destruction of the centralized patronage distribution system has produced what William Reno has termed "the reconfiguration of patrimonial African authority," contributing to a descent into civil war and warlordism.[26] In Sierra Leone, budgetary cutbacks and privatizations benefiting the president and his cronies effectively dissolved the neopatrimonial state, the very glue keeping the polity together. Those regional notables who no longer had access to state patronage acquired private armies and challenged central political authority (Reno 1995, 203; 2003, 56). Foreign firms played a key role in this reconfiguration as they took over collapsing companies and provided security forces used in a failing attempt to keep centrifugal tendencies in check. Rebels, too, employed foreign security companies and paid them with exclusive licenses for the exploitation of valuable resources including diamonds, gold, and timber (Mair 2003, 25–26). The consequence is a practically nonexistent state without even the capacity for minimal territorial control.

Indeed, the sharp deterioration in living standards of the 1980s and 1990s has created fertile ground for a marked increase in violence and organized crime involving such activities as drug trafficking. In Bolivia, structural adjustment and the state streamlining of the 1980s was behind the rapid growth of the drug trade, as former tin miners and others adversely affected by structural adjustment moved into coca growing as a means of survival. Violence increased as the Bolivian state, with the support of the United States, tried to put a stop to drug production and trafficking (García Argañarás 1997). For several decades now, leftist guerrillas in Colombia, who have largely lost sight of their original social objectives, have depended heavily on the drug trade as a source of financing. As the Colombian civil war has become increasingly violent, the deterioration of the economy in the 1990s has propelled more and more of the unemployed into coca production (Kline and Gray 2000). In the worst African cases, the crisis of neopatrimonialism has degenerated into war between rival armed groups whose major objective is looting (Allen 1999, 371). More than one-quarter of African states were faced with armed insurgencies in all or part of the 1990s (Young 2002, 534).

---

[26] It is important to note that market reform was the trigger, not the deeper underlying root, of the rise of violence in the 1990s and the collapse of the state. In a number of notable African cases, state collapse has been traced back to the failure to free the rural sector from the yoke of tribal authorities, and to the particular nature of patronage politics in the African context, especially patronage politics involving the politicization of identity (Allen 1999; Szeftel 2000).

Poverty, food insecurity, and the displacement of large numbers of people have become acute problems in these countries.

Societies in the midst of civil war, existing without even a minimum of state capacity, are far from the possibility of achieving a social-democratic agenda. There is no elite support for social protection and equality-enhancing measures; indeed, there is little interest in a societal compromise of any sort, nor is there a modicum of state capacity to undertake social-democratic reforms. Organized crime, an increasingly important actor in this context, has an especially destructive impact on state and society, brutally eliminating government officials, activists, and journalists who oppose it, thereby extinguishing the possibility of socially and democratically committed political leaderships.

While old forms of popular mobilization have weakened, new forms of mobilization have often been counterproductive to social democracy. In countries where market reforms involved the repression and dismantling of the trade-union movement, the ability of trade unions to effectively make social-democratic demands has been considerably diminished (La Botz 1988; Isamah 1995). Meanwhile, the global religious resurgence, reflecting a desire to establish meaning and order in a rapidly changing world, is probably the most important identity-based phenomenon and has been linked to the fragmentation and insecurity generated by the globalizing process. It is especially strong in the global south where secularism has often come to be perceived as a European imposition. Although social issues are not absent from the demands of such identity-based movements, they are often not their principal goal; such movements, in their extreme manifestations, have shown themselves to be intolerant, undemocratic, and supportive of violence. All these tendencies push any sort of social agenda further from reach, while bringing the issue of ruling-elite survival and its attendant state security (or repressive) measures to the forefront.

Islamism – movements that believe that Islamic doctrine should shape political and social life – is the most powerful opposition force in the Middle East. The reasons for its strength are heavily rooted in history: in the forced eradication of Islamic law by western powers and the imposition of secularism; in the delegitimation of postcolonial rulers due to the Arab defeat in the Six Day War; and in the more general failure of these regimes to bring economic development and social progress to their countries. The fundamentally authoritarian, often brutal, nature of most Middle East regimes, combined with the fact that many have been maintained in power with western support, have, for Muslims, demonstrated the hollowness of western democracy in the Middle East and has spurred a reaction often involving the wholesale rejection of anything western (Tibi 1998, 33, 77; Ghabra 2003, 43–47, 107 119).

For many Muslims, democracy, capitalism, and socialism have all been tried, and they have all failed. Modernity is the problem and Islam, therefore, is the answer. While Islamic liberals or modernists seek a reading of Islam that supports the values of democracy, human rights, pluralism, and a strong civil society, they are still in the minority among Islamists (Fuller 2003, 54). Fundamentalist groups, on the other hand, which seek to rectify the ills of society through adherence to a literal interpretation of sacred texts, through the establishment of an Islamic state, and most importantly, through the implementation of Islamic law or Shari'a, have been rapidly gaining ground. Among fundamentalists, radicals support armed struggle to overthrow the governments of states seen as ruled by the corrupt and unrighteous puppets of western governments. Radical fundamentalists are fiercely intolerant of what they perceive to be deviations from their own particular brand of Islam. Leftist organizations and parties, whose appeal had been based on social class, have largely disappeared from the scene. Leftist ideas, too, are seen as western constructs, and leftist movements are perceived as not having been sufficiently distant from corrupt and repressive secular regimes (Burgat 2003, 49–52).

Islamism is not a movement (or movements) about poverty so much as it is about identity and privilege. It is a movement that pits a non-westernized middle- and lower-class opposition excluded from state patronage against the secular westernized elites in power (Burgat 2003, 21–22). The major impetus to the movement came from the middle, lower-middle and professional classes, as well as university students whose activism spread the movement downward, recruiting from the lower classes, the urban unemployed, and recent migrants to the cities (Yom 2002, 95; Ghabra 2003, 197; Zeidan 2003, 13). Economic and social crises and the subsequent downsizing of government activities were enormously helpful in this mobilizational task. In Egypt, Algeria, Morocco, Turkey, Malaysia, and Indonesia, Islamic organizations have provided a wide range of services (educational assistance, free or low-cost medical clinics, legal assistance, and sports facilities) that the state failed to provide (Fuller 2003, 28). In Egypt and Jordan, for example, the Muslim Brotherhood, an organization of middle-class professionals, extended its influence to the lower classes through a network of social services including clinics, schools, and soup kitchens (Brooks 2002, 613). Nevertheless, a political appeal based on social justice and equity is generally absent even in those countries, such as Pakistan, where social injustice and extreme poverty are the most pervasive. Islamic fundamentalists offer an appeal that channels the general frustrations of poor populations in a way that secular nationalist/socialist ideologies no longer do.

The cases of the Sudan, Iran, and Afghanistan suggest that radical Islamic governments are not supporters of democracy and human rights and that they are likely to make little progress on the social-welfare front. Furthermore, Islamic movements are certainly not the only examples of this type. Recent years have witnessed the rise of Hindu militancy in India, for example, which manifests opposition to modernity and incorporates those left rootless by its encroachment (Varughese 2003). The preoccupation of such movements with issues of cultural purity, and their presumption that a focus on such issues will solve pressing social and economic problems, runs counter to the class and equality orientation of social democracy.

Since the 1980s, social mobilization based on ethnicity has also become a potent force in many countries of the periphery. Like religion, it can be understood only within its historical context, and like religion its move to political center stage is very much related to changes over the last two decades. A growing body of literature, especially on Africa, takes the position that some of the most bloody ethnic struggles may well have been less about identity than about struggles over declining state resources.[27] Political stability has traditionally been maintained by ensuring resources flow to the various ethnic groups via the participation of their elites in the state. While discontent of ethnic groups with their share of resources is at the root of some ethnically based insurgencies, violent insurgency is even more likely if the elite from one or several groups is excluded from state bounty. Maintaining public-sector salaries of civil servants is highly correlated with maintaining ethnic peace (Azam 2001). In this context, then, ethnicity becomes an important element in the language of mobilization and conflict, but not its primary motive. Elites excluded from patronage manipulate populations and situations by making appeals to ethnicity in their mobilizational efforts against the state. At the same time, in an attempt to hold onto power, some states foment ethnic antagonism and carry out ethnic violence against their populations (Allen 1999, 377; Szeftel 2000, 437; Ellis 2003, 35).

Hence, over the last two decades, many states of the global south have been weakened not only from the outside by globalization and pressures from international organizations, but also from within by rising

---

[27] This might also be true for some Islamic movements. Martinez (2000) argues that for much of the rank and file of the rebel Algerian Islamic organization (GIA), the war was a way to accumulate wealth and improve social status. A recent study on Africa found that there was no support for the thesis that cultural factors are significantly associated with African civil wars (Henderson 2000).

ethnically/religiously based movements. Oftentimes the situation has degenerated into criminality and even state collapse – which may further spur identity-based politics. While the poor have often been enthusiastic supporters of identity-based movements, such movements are usually led by disaffected members of the middle and professional classes whose main concerns are not eliminating poverty or fostering equity.

Alongside these disturbing developments, however, there are also hopeful signs of political mobilization with clearly social-democratic goals. Globalization and neoliberal reform, combined with democratic openings, have triggered the emergence of social movements with social-justice and democratization agendas (such as the Landless Workers Movement in Brazil, the Zapatistas in Mexico, and the indigenous movement in Ecuador). Such movements, because they can often count on highly effective international support networks, can achieve important successes (Bob 2001).

Conclusion

The twin political challenges facing social democrats concern a redistribution of domestic political power and a more substantive democracy. These changes would require poor and/or class-based mobilization and participatory politics that address social and equity issues. The process, to be social-democratic, involves a social pact including both the privileged and the currently excluded. Although the objective is to force concessions from powerful vested interests, enormous care is necessary to avoid the political polarization and democratic breakdown that characterized Chile in the early 1970s. Indeed, now more than ever, in an era when private capital has taken center stage, sustained economic growth requires political leaders capable of maintaining business confidence. Rhetoric must, therefore, remain moderate, and a certain amount of trust between the social-democratic leadership and the private sector has to be cultivated. Powerful domestic opposition elites and their middle-sector and professional allies must become convinced that their long-term interests lie in a more democratic, politically stable, and equitable society. Such social-democratic reformism remains a distant prospect in many countries, for reasons we have discussed. But without it, hope for the poor is dim.

The cases examined in subsequent chapters show that it is possible to face and overcome some of the historically rooted obstacles to social democracy. Although Chile experienced retrenchment during the period of military rule in some of its social achievements, all four cases provide examples of the achievement of universal programs of health care, education, and social-security protection. Mauritius, Kerala, and Costa Rica did produce ruling elites committed to democracy who were capable of achieving class compromises. These cases illustrate that a firm elite consensus on democracy can allow a social-democratic agenda to be carried forward through the electoral process. And, as the case of Chile illustrates, military dictatorship, social-policy retrenchment, and sharp political polarization can give way to important social achievements under electoral democracy, even when the class compromise is minimal and fragile.

Part II

Case studies

3   Kerala: deepening a radical social democracy

At first glance, the Indian state of Kerala would hardly seem to be a strong candidate for designation as a social democracy. It is, first, a sub-national state, and even if its population of 31 million surpasses that of many European nations, it does not enjoy the macroeconomic powers that have been the key policy instruments of social-democratic pacts. The state in Kerala cannot control the flow of capital, protect its markets, collect income taxes, or adjust interest rates. Second, whereas social democracy is generally associated with industrialized (or industrializing) societies, Kerala remains a largely rural society, with fully one-quarter of its state domestic product coming from agriculture, and three-quarters of its population living in rural areas. The industrial working class, a key actor in the historical formation of European social democracy, remains small, albeit quite powerful. Indeed, Kerala's economy has all the structural markings of the periphery – a large, small farmer agricultural sector, a small and stagnant industrial sector dominated by agro-processing industries such as coir (coconut fiber) production, and a rapidly growing service sector. At a per capita income of $US500, the material base for social democracy is thin at best. Finally, the dominant political party on the left – the Communist Party of India (Marxist) (CPI(M)) – would most emphatically reject the social-democratic label.[1] For all of these reasons, the class-institutional configuration of social democracy – a centrally managed class compromise between capital and labor – appears to be largely missing. But if we move away from static comparisons of historical forms of social

---

[1] Although the CPI(M) calls itself a Marxist-Leninist party (CPI(M), 2000), it does not espouse a revolutionary line. It defines, as its most important task, the goal of the "establishment of a people's democracy" built on the strength of a worker–peasant alliance, to be achieved through the electoral path. The party program calls only for strengthening the public sector through modernization and regulation of monopolies, and its economic prescriptions are essentially social democratic (some rhetorical flourishes aside). Though the party calls for abolishing landlordism, it also advocates supporting the poor and middle peasantry with subsidies. The only mention of property is in calling for women to have equal inheritance rights. The pragmatism of the CPI(M) has earned it the social-democratic label from many observers (Kohli 1987; Törnquist 1997; Desai 2002).

democracy and instead examine the central social and political dynamics of what distinguishes social democracy from liberal democracy, then Kerala in many respects becomes a prototypical case of social democracy in the periphery – especially when contrasted to the rest of India.

First, as has been argued elsewhere (Heller 2000), democracy in Kerala is more substantive than anywhere else in India. Subordinate classes have been effectively empowered and mobilized and have seen their interests institutionalized in the state. Democratic structures and practices have penetrated deeply into social life, all but displacing traditional forms of social authority. Most notably, the upper-caste landlords who once ruled with absolute social and economic authority over Kerala have disappeared as a social class, and the caste system, though still an important source of identity and social life, no longer mirrors political and economic power hierarchies.

Second, there are probably few examples in the world where the causal link between organized lower-class movements and significant redistributive and social gains is as strong as in Kerala. Repeated spells in power by the CPI(M),[2] combined with an almost continuous process of militant mass mobilization, have exerted unrelenting pressure on the state to expand social programs, regulate labor markets, and implement land reforms. Despite a two-decade period (1970–1990) of virtual economic stagnation, social indicators have continued to climb and poverty rates have continued to fall. No other state in India has been as consistently pro-poor or as successfully redistributive.[3] Large sectors of the working population enjoy a range of social protections, and basic services such as health, education, and food security are provided on a universal basis. Although significant pockets of poverty and social exclusion persist and Kerala's economy remains highly vulnerable to external shocks, in no other major Indian state has the market been so successfully subordinated to social regulation.

Third, iterated cycles of state–society engagement, driven primarily by lower-class movements, have produced a rich set of rational-legal intermediate institutions. Though Kerala lacks the comprehensive peak-level corporatist bargaining structures that characterize European social democracy, it has developed an array of sectoral bargaining structures that play a key role in mediating capital-labor relations (Heller 1999). Those structures have, moreover, penetrated deeply into the countryside, as the

[2] The Communist Party of India (CPI) was unified until 1965 when it split into the CPI and the CPI(M). The CPI(M) has emerged as the dominant communist party in West Bengal and Kerala.
[3] For the most explicit comparative assessments internationally, see Drèze and Sen 1989. For comparisons across Indian states, see Drèze and Sen 1995.

state has implemented wide-ranging land reforms and successfully regulated rural labor markets. State institutions in the form of the most extensive network of cooperative rural banks in the country have crowded out traditional moneylenders while making banking services and loans available to the poor. In every business survey and on all relevant indicators, Kerala consistently ranks first among all states in the rule of law (Debroy, Bhandari, and Banik 2003). In sum, the writ of the modern state is deep and broad, as is its legitimacy.

These characteristics are all the more notable when profiled against the national picture. At the all-India level, the politics of social citizenship, as Mehta (1997) has remarked, are conspicuous by their absence. Subordinate groups are for the most part organized along communal or caste lines, with only the CPI(M) (which is principally confined to Kerala and West Bengal) explicitly addressing class interests. Social programs have been driven more by patronage politics than by programmatic goals; few states have secured significant institutional reforms, and vast swaths of the rural poor have access to only limited public services. The authority of the state, for all its formal Weberian attributes, often stops where the social authority of landed elites, caste leaders, and, increasingly, communal authorities begins (Mahajan 1999). A dominant theme in the political science literature on India over the past two decades has been the criminalization and deinstitutionalization of political life (Kohli 1990). The rise of the Sangh Parivar and its anti-liberal, communalist program is only the most obvious manifestation of India's democratic and social crisis (Hansen 1999).

In explaining why Kerala has traveled such a different path than the rest of the country, three sets of factors are key. First, the early commercialization of Kerala's agriculture transformed the class structure and civil society, producing a configuration of social forces that favored democratization and state intervention. Second, an ideologically cohesive and disciplined communist party fused nationalism, caste reform, and anti-landlord demands into a broad-based lower-class coalition that was able to win elections and initiate redistributive reforms. Third, the sub-national playing field and the configuration of political forces had a moderating impact on how otherwise radical subordinate class demands were formed and ultimately accommodated within the democratic system. As a regional party that was reaching out to a broad spectrum of social groups, the Communists had little choice but to eschew revolutionary tactics and demands, and local elites were constrained by the larger national democratic context from resorting to repression. These favorable initial circumstances for lower-class mobilization in turn gave birth to a virtuous circle of mobilization and state intervention that has driven democratic deepening. A stable but highly competitive balance of left- and right-wing parties that have rotated in power, combined with continuous pressure from social movements, and most notably a labor movement that has reached into the countryside and into informal sectors, have exerted continuous pressure on the state to pursue reforms and provide social services. Since the heyday of land reforms in the 1970s, large-scale mobilization has fallen off, and there have been some tendencies toward organizational degeneration, especially among public-sector unions that have used their political clout to secure significant rents. Nonetheless, political competition has remained acute. A range of civil-society actors have periodically mobilized to trigger new reforms – most notably a wide-ranging initiative for participatory decentralization introduced in 1996.

However, if Kerala's sub-national status has been favorable to lower-class politics, it has made economic management difficult. The state in Kerala enjoys few of the levers of economic power of the national state and has had little success in promoting economic growth (though Kerala's investments in education have paid off economically in the form of remittances). Despite the fact that Kerala's high levels of social development, strong institutions, and good infrastructure make for an attractive investment environment, domestic and foreign capital has shied away and unemployment levels remain high.[4] The liberalization of India's economy in the 1990s has also posed new challenges for Kerala. Fiscal belt-tightening has made it difficult to maintain historical levels of social spending or extend social protection, and the opening of the national economy to global markets has had a particularly disruptive effect on Kerala's agricultural economy. Yet, despite its structural vulnerabilities and a precarious fiscal situation, Kerala's social-democratic gains have been preserved and the social costs of its transition to a more open and competitive economy have been effectively managed.

A record of social progress

If a baseline definition of social democracy is an activist state that can secure basic social rights, provide protection against market forces, and

---

[4] In 2004, 19.2 percent of the labor force was officially unemployed. Many observers argue this figure exaggerates the actual level of involuntary unemployment, pointing to labor shortages in unskilled (and low-caste) jobs such as construction and agriculture. Reviewing the latest data, Zachariah and Rajan observe that, for those aged thirty or older, unemployment is only 6 percent, that many of the unemployed come from well-to-do households, and that they are rarely heads of households (2004, 54). A large portion of the unemployed are highly educated, unmarried youth who prefer waiting to taking a low-status job. Kerala's equitable distribution of income and universal access to basic services reduce the costs of unemployment.

Table 3.1 *Percentage of population below the poverty line*

Year	Kerala	India
1973–1974	59.79	54.88
1977–1978	52.22	51.32
1983–1984	40.42	44.48
1987–1988	31.79	38.86
1993–1994	25.43	35.97
1999–2000	12.72	26.30

Sources: Government of Kerala, *Economic Review*, 2001, 155.

reduce inequality, then Kerala stands out. On all the key social indicators, it has dramatically outperformed all other Indian states and even compares favorably with developed countries. Literacy is 93 percent and life expectancy has reached seventy-two years. A World Bank study found that between 1957–1958 and 1990–1991, of India's fifteen most populous states (including the Punjab, Gujarat, and Haryana – India's market-led growth success stories), Kerala experienced the most rapid decline in poverty (Datt and Ravallion 1996).[5] More recent data paint a similar picture (see Table 3.1). In 1973, with 59.8 percent of its population below the poverty line, Kerala was practically on par with Bihar (61.2 percent) and well above the all-India average of 54.8 percent. By 1999–2000, Kerala's population below the poverty line stood at 12.7 percent, the lowest of any major Indian state, and less than half of the all-India average of 26.3 percent.

Many factors have contributed to these successes, including historically higher levels of literacy and remittances from Kerala's large force of migrant workers. But structural and institutional reforms have been the most important contributory factors. Land reforms in the 1970s virtually abolished landlordism, transformed poor tenants into small property owners, and conferred homestead plots on landless laborers.[6] The introduction of labor legislation in 1975 provided Kerala's 2 million landless laborers, most from "untouchable" castes, with extensive protection in the form of regulated workdays, minimum wages, collective-bargaining

[5] The annual decline was 2.26 percent on the headcount index and 3.93 percent on the poverty gap index (Datt and Ravallion 1996, 30).
[6] By 1993, 2.3 million former tenants had secured ownership rights and 528,000 households had received homestead certificates, providing them land for housing and garden plots (Ramakumar 2004, 19).

rights, and job security.[7] Even the introduction of tractors in the 1970s was carefully phased in to minimize the displacement impact on labor (Heller 1999). Kerala's organized industries, most in the public sector, are heavily unionized, as is the case for most of India. But in sharp contrast to the national pattern, unionization and labor laws have been extended to significant portions of what in the rest of India is classified as the "unorganized" (informal) sector. The resulting bargaining leverage of wage earners in this sector has produced the highest informal-sector wages and the lowest differential with the formal sector in the country. Workers who manually transport goods – called headload workers or "coolies," and historically the most defiled of occupations – now routinely earn wages above those of lower-level white-collar workers, a reversal of fortunes almost unthinkable in India's caste-based division of labor. Social-protection schemes now cover a significant share of the population, and an extensive network of subsidized food shops has practically wiped out malnutrition.[8] Finally, Kerala's extensive health-care and primary education systems, which quite literally reach into every village in the state, have achieved almost universal coverage (Ramachandran 1996; Kannan 2000).

The reach of authoritative state institutions and the extent to which basic social rights of citizenship have been institutionalized and distributed across gender, caste, and class is decisively reflected in basic indicators. Thus, 94 percent of births in Kerala are attended by trained health-care personnel (compared to 34 percent in India), and 91 percent of rural females between the ages of ten and fourteen attend school (compared to 42 percent in India). Only one in four females from scheduled castes are literate in India, whereas three of four in Kerala are. The difference in life chances is starkly captured in Drèze and Gazdar's observation that "a newborn girl can expect to live *20 years longer* if she is born in Kerala rather than Uttar Pradesh" (1996, 40). The achievement of the highest life expectancy, the highest literacy rate, the lowest incidence of child labor, and the lowest infant mortality of any Indian state – and all against the backdrop of relatively poor economic performance – suggest a powerful political and social logic at work.[9]

---

[7] The material impact of these reforms is reflected in rapidly declining rural poverty rates. It is dramatically captured in a recent case study of a Malabar village, where Ramakumar found that, whereas a day's wage in 1955 translated into 0.9 kg of rice, by 2000–2001 a day's wage could buy 10 kg of rice (2004, 228).

[8] The PDS system covers 97 percent of households and accounts for two-thirds of the total rice purchase of the poor (Kannan 2003, 192–93).

[9] Kerala is quite literally two decades ahead of the rest of India. Of fifteen major states, only four in 2001 had surpassed Kerala's Human Development Index (HDI) score of 1981 (Planning Commission, 2001).

Kerala stands in contrast to most of India, where a range of entrenched inequities of social position and capabilities compromise the basic exercise of rights. The extension of both public legality and public services in Kerala has eroded traditional forms of social authority and clientelistic dependencies. Across a wide range of social activities, from accessing primary health services and attending schools to depositing money in banking institutions, citizens have in effect shifted their trust from asymmetrical interpersonal networks to formal public institutions. And this, as Charles Tilly (2000) has argued, is the sine qua non of long-term democratization. Such a shift has not occurred in most of India. Chatterjee argues that most inhabitants of India "are not proper members of civil society and are not regarded as such by the institutions of the state" (2001, 8). Mahajan (1999) similarly makes the case that because most Indians remain deeply embedded in communities, they do not enjoy the full range of civil society freedoms. Their engagement with the state is thus only through political society. In contrast, civil society in Kerala has been differentiated from traditional social structures of control. This is critical in two respects. First, it implies that society itself – that is, the relations between citizens – has to a significant degree been democratized. Second, it points to the fact that individuals engage the state not as members of discrete communities (as Hindus, as Mahars) but as rights-bearing citizens. And this in turn explains two distinctive features of Kerala's politics: (1) the extent to which the politics of social citizenship have commanded center stage, and (2) a relative absence of the caste and sectarian violence that has gripped the rest of the country in the past two decades.[10]

A robust civil society, one that has been critical to sustaining subordinate class organization, is what Kerala, Costa Rica, and Mauritius most clearly have in common and what differentiates them historically from their respective neighbors (see chapter 7). Kerala has the highest levels of unionization in India, and unlike the national pattern, the presence of unions is not limited to the formal sector of the economy. Large numbers of workers in the informal sector – including in the beedi, construction, coir, and cashew industries – are organized. The largest union in the state is the CPI(M)-affiliated Kerala State Karhsaka Thozhilali Union, a 1-million-member union of predominantly lower-caste agricultural workers. Unions in Kerala are almost all tied to political parties, as well as being highly professionalized and characterized by a broader, less militant, and more programmatic outlook than most Indian unions,

---

[10] Varshney (2002) provides a compelling account of how Kerala's civic organizations, by producing dense ties across caste and religious groups, have helped diffuse communal violence.

which tend toward economism and are often little more than vehicles for local powerbrokers.[11] Kerala's mass organizations of women, students, and youth – sponsored by all the political parties – also play an active role in the state's political life. The CPI(M)'s mass organizations alone claim a membership of over 4.7 million. The state's network of worker cooperatives and village-level cooperative banks is the most extensive in the country. And in the political arena, the basic cleavage has been along class lines, opposing a coalition of right-wing parties organized around the Congress against a coalition of left-wing parties organized around the CPI(M).[12] These two coalitions have more or less alternated in power; consistently thin margins of victory point to a relatively stable bipolar distribution of political support.[13]

Kerala also scores high on all measures of democracy. It ranks first among all states in the rule of law, political violence is relatively rare, levels of participation in elections generally run 15–20 percent higher than the national average, and it boasts a vibrant press with the highest per capita circulation of newspapers in India. The effectiveness of Kerala's democratic institutions, however, is best measured by the extent to which they have successfully managed social and economic tensions. During the 1960s and 1970s rural protest was endemic and rates of industrial unrest (as measured in strikes) were the highest in India. In this climate of social unrest, coalition governments were short-lived and often brought down by large-scale mobilization. Kerala's social structure is, moreover, marked by significant cleavages. Historically, its caste system was amongst the most rigidly stratified in India, and it has the largest minority concentrations of Christians and Muslims of any Indian state (roughly 20 percent of the population each). The major caste and communal groups have powerful and active associations, and Christian and Muslim political parties have played active roles in Kerala's coalition politics. Yet, the capacity of

---

[11] In a recent study based on a sample of 100 factories, Teitelbaum (2004) found not only that unions in Kerala were far more likely to be tied to parties than those in Maharashtra, but also that political unions (as opposed to what he terms "parochial unions") are more likely to eschew conflict in favor of long-term cooperation.

[12] In an analysis of survey data collected during the 2004 Lok Sabha elections, the Centre for the Study of Developing Society concluded that the LDF (Left Democratic Front) was supported by "the poorer classes, the less educated and the relatively disadvantaged sections of society" (*The Hindu*, May 20, 2004, AE-3). Though the LDF did receive 71 percent of the dalit vote, that it got less than half the OBC (other backward castes) vote, and only 59 percent of the Ezhava vote (the traditional core constituency of the CPM), suggests that caste has lost much of its political saliency.

[13] The Bharatiya Janata Party (BJP) and its allies have recently made inroads into Kerala, but in comparative terms remain weak. In the 2004 election, the BJP and its allies captured 12.1 percent of the vote, its lowest vote share of any state or territory in India.

the political system to manage these sources of conflict has defied predictions of demand overload. Labor militancy has been on a downward trend for twenty years, the zero-sum logic of caste and sectarian politics has largely been displaced by the positive-sum politics of class coordination, and the bulk of social and economic conflicts are effectively channeled into formal state institutions (Heller 1999). As with the case of Mauritius (chapter 5), Kerala defies the assumption in the literature that diverse and historically fragmented societies are less likely to develop stable political orders and workable social compacts. All of this underscores the extent to which democratic institutions and practices in Kerala have become deeply institutionalized from the bottom up. In contrast to the general Indian picture, in which district and village-level institutions are often in the hands of landed elites or dominant castes, in Kerala a wide range of institutions – including district councils, *panchayats* (local governments), student councils, and cooperative societies – are hotly contested by the major political formations. Representative institutions have also penetrated economic life. Thus, one of the unique features of Kerala's economic scene is the role that voluntary tripartite bodies (industrial relations committees) representing labor, capital, and the state play in actively shaping and coordinating labor relations, industrial policy, and welfare programs across a wide range of industries, including agriculture (Heller 1999).

Finally, there is a clear correspondence between high levels of political participation and government performance. Across virtually every public policy arena, the effectiveness of state intervention in Kerala far surpasses the performance of any other Indian state and can be tied to demand-side pressures (Drèze and Sen 1995). The provision of education, health care, and subsidized food has been characterized by universal coverage and comparatively corruption-free delivery and is a response to broad-based support across all major political parties for the extension of social rights. Redistributive measures, in particular land reforms, labor-market regulation and the extension of social-protection schemes, can all be tied to specific episodes of sustained mobilization (Herring 1983). Most recently, the literacy campaign of 1991 – the most successful in India – as well as a decentralization campaign initiated in 1996 were both the result of pressure exerted by left-leaning mass organizations.

If democracy works well in Kerala, this arises from an active and organized citizenry and from the prevalence of horizontal forms of association over vertical (clientelistic) forms. The resulting patterns of political participation have, in turn, favored the encompassing demands that represent the political essence of social democracy. But how do we explain this pattern?

Historical origins

To understand why and how Kerala has followed a social-democratic trajectory whereas the rest of the nation has largely failed to deepen democracy or promote social development, one has to turn to the watershed historical moment of 1957. That year, when a unified state of Kerala held its first elections, the Communist Party of India (CPI) was voted into power. Though the CPI government was short-lived, its rise to power marked a critical juncture that irreversibly changed the balance of political and social forces in Kerala. The Communists' electoral victory was built on the strength of poor tenants and landless laborers demanding both agrarian reform and social justice; this alliance meant no less than a rupture with the old regime and set into motion path-dependent social and political changes.[14] Thus, even though governments in Kerala have more or less alternated between Communist- and Congress-led coalitions, policies have consistently supported the expansion of the welfare state and the protection of subordinate classes.

The critical juncture of 1957 that locked in a social-democratic trajectory was itself the product of the historical convergence of social, political, and institutional factors. First, the transformation of Kerala's agrarian structure in the nineteenth century sharpened class and community tensions while energizing civil society, particularly in the form of new social justice movements. Second, the independence struggle and the rise of political parties gave further expression to these social conflicts. In particular, the socialists in the Congress Party who would eventually form the CPI were able to meld demands for social justice, agrarian reform, and independence into a coherent program of political mobilization. Finally, Kerala's status as a sub-national state, and the robust procedural playing field that democracy provided, allowed for what were otherwise heightened forms of social and class conflict to play out through electoral politics and the forging of class compromises.

We begin by examining Kerala's agrarian structure which in the nineteenth century consisted of two distinct social formations. The northern part of the state, Malabar, was a remote and often neglected outpost of the Madras presidency under direct colonial rule, in which social and economic power was concentrated in the hands of a notoriously parasitic class of Brahmin landlords, the *jenmies*. Varghese calculates that in 1861 the *jenmies* represented less than 2 percent of the total agricultural population but monopolized "every right and interest connected with land in Malabar" (1970, 39). Backed by the British, the *jenmies* presided over

---

[14] The concepts of critical juncture and path dependency are elaborated in chapter 7.

several layers of tenants, ranging from large, fairly secure upper-caste Nairs, to small and impoverished Muslim tenants. The highly exploitative conditions of tenure produced repeated episodes of peasant rebellion, including the Mappila rebellion in which 3,989 (the official figure) Muslim rebels were killed by the colonial state (Panikkar 1989, 163). By the 1930s, agrarian protest had assumed a broader social base, encompassing prosperous (mostly Nair) tenants and the small tenant-cultivators who constituted the bulk of the peasantry. In much of India at this time, landed elites had rallied to the nationalist cause and were playing a significant role in the Congress Party. But in Malabar, the parasitic nature of landlords and their close ties to the colonial state made them targets rather than allies of the independence movement. This not only, in effect, thrust the peasantry to the political forefront in Malabar, but also ensured that demands for agrarian reform were wedded to anti-colonialism. And as Desai (2001, 2002) has carefully shown, the marginalization of landed elites and the radicalization of the nationalist movement led to the rise to dominance of the socialist wing (and future CPI) in the Congress Party.

The southern half of the state consisted of the two, semi-autonomous princely states of Cochin and Travancore. Both states had successfully centralized power in the eighteenth century by aligning themselves with larger tenants against landlord-barons. This alliance, combined with the export possibilities of the south's abundant cash crops, spurred the royal states to promote agrarian reform, including land reforms in 1865 that created a sizable class of small farmers with secure property rights. The very rapid commercialization of agriculture that followed transformed the south's social structure. As Parayil and Sreekumar cogently remark: "the small peasantry was to a certain extent liberated, land and produce markets expanded, and the incidence of land holding increased to a considerable extent" (2003, 472). Peasant proprietorship became the basis of accumulation and the entire agrarian economy was modernized. Banking and trading activities developed rapidly, especially in the Syrian-Christian community of Travancore, and local capital even began to displace British companies in the rubber plantation sector.

This economic transformation had two notable effects. On the one hand, it triggered an expansion of civil society. In what was otherwise one of the most rigidly hierarchical caste structures in India, commercialization created prosperous segments within all the major religious and caste communities (Tharakan 1998). These elites formed associations dedicated to the social reform and uplift of their communities and invested in community-based schools and hospitals. As early as the 1890s, Nairs, Ezhavas, and Christians were challenging the caste-based traditional order by petitioning the government for access to government jobs (historically reserved for Brahmins) and the expansion of public schools. Even the untouchable Pulayas, whose status as slaves had only been revoked in 1855, organized to demand the right to travel public roads. By the 1920s, these community-based demands had evolved into full-blown socio-religious reform movements (Tharakan 1998) that were directly challenging Brahmanical authority in what was an increasingly pluralistic and politically competitive public arena. Most notably, new middle-class elements from the largest of the lower-caste groups, the Ezhavas, formed a social reform organization (the Sree Narayana Dharma Paripalana) that by 1938 had 200,000 members and 526 branches (Desai 2002, 633). These caste-based movements, however, remained largely reformist, with most of their activities directed toward the "social upliftment" of the community, and toward protest actions driven more by moral indignation than political goals.

On the other hand, commercialization also gave birth to a class of agricultural laborers who, riding on the mobilizational wave of the caste reform movements, began to challenge both the social and material base of dominant classes. As farmers modernized and intensified agricultural operations, the traditional system of "attached" labor (in which lower-caste field laborers were tied to a particular landowner) gave way to a casual labor market. This loosening of traditional clientelism, coupled with demographic growth, produced an agrarian proletariat. Between 1911 and 1951, agricultural laborers increased from 12.6 percent of the rural population to 34.6 percent (Varghese 1970, 128). But while these laborers became increasingly dependent on market forces, working conditions continued to be governed by the social practices of the caste system. In the larger context of the socio-religious movements, political radicalization took the form of a communist-led union movement demanding both higher wages and social reform. This movement of agricultural laborers, which by the 1940s was launching large-scale strikes, received organizational support through close ties to a small but militant communist-organized workforce in the agro-processing sector. In both sectors, the Ezhava caste was predominant, and its associational networks helped bridge the urban–rural divide.

By the time of independence, the agrarian structures of Malabar and Travancore/Cochin were ripe for social transformation. If in Malabar the issue was land, and the movement opposed tenants to landlords, in Travancore/Cochin the issue was labor, opposing lower-caste field laborers to upper-caste and Christian capitalist farmers. If the classic class alliance of Scandinavian social democracy was a green–red alliance of smallholding farmers and an industrial working class, the class alliance in Kerala that triggered a rupture with the pre-capitalist social structure and drove the subsequent social-democratic path might be coded as *green–orange,* orange underscoring the fact that agricultural laborers were a proto-proletariat. If the building blocks of this green–orange alliance emerged from the evolution of Kerala's agrarian economy, two other factors contributed to translating this structural possibility into an actual political trajectory. The first was the political agency of a *social movement party,* the CPI (and later the CPI(M)). The second was the institutional and configurational conditions of a subregional democracy that made this party effective in mobilizing a class alliance.

Classes, in the sense of groups that assume a collective identity on the basis of common economic interests, are not structural givens. They are, in Przeworski's succinct formulation, "formed in the course of struggles" (1985, 69). These struggles take shape on multiple fronts and affect class formation insofar as they come to define new identities. The CPI emerged at the confluence of three distinct movements – the anti-colonial struggle, a caste-reform movement, and an agrarian movement – that brought together issues of sovereignty and democracy, identity and dignity, and exploitation and redistribution. That the CPI was able to exert hegemonic leadership, in the sense of being able to blend these grievances together into an ethical-political movement, was in part made possible by the ideological failure of the Congress Party, which in clinging to its accommodationist line of downplaying agrarian class conflict in the name of national unity, found itself out of step with the social change taking place. Driven more by events and struggles than theoretical insight,[15] the CPI (which was formed by disillusioned socialists from the Congress) built on existing repertoires of contention (strikes, petitions, marches, theatre, temple festivals).[16] It wove together the themes of social dignity and justice of the caste reform movement, economic redress of the agrarian movement, and the democratic aspirations of the nationalist movement, to form a coherent ideological attack against colonialism and the feudal class/caste structure. In sum, it was the Communists' ideological flexibility in capitalizing on popular sources of moral outrage and organizational capacity that underwrote lower-class formation in Kerala.

Desai (2002) has shown just how decisive the political practices of the Kerala communists were by drawing a comparison with colonial Bengal and the Bombay Presidency, the two other regions in India that had been

---

[15] Speaking of the early days of the Kerala Congress Socialist Party in Malabar, K. P. Gopalan noted that, "We had socialist aims without knowing anything about socialism" (cited in Menon 1994, n. 71).

[16] Jeffrey, for example, shows how *jathas* – long, symbolic marches, often the length of the state – evolved from attacks against traditional customs of caste deference, to nationalist opposition, to demands for socialism (1992, 121–22).

the most fully integrated into the world economy. In both Bengal and the Bombay Presidency (now Maharashtra), communist parties in the 1940s did successfully organize industrial workers. In both cases, however, they embraced more orthodox Marxist politics and shied away from working with rural and caste movements. Not only did these communist parties fail to develop a mass base before independence, but their narrow constituency impelled them to the ultra-leftist positions of rejecting the parliamentary route and resorting to insurrectionary tactics. Although the West Bengal CPI(M) would come to power in 1977 (twenty years after the Kerala CPI), Kohli wryly observes that this electoral success came only when the West Bengal CPI(M) "discovered" the peasantry in the late 1960s (1987, 104).

The strategic success with which the Communist Party in Kerala situated itself at the confluence of social movements and the changing agrarian structure was possible only because the communists operated within a favorable institutional and political environment. Agrarian communism has generally resulted either in revolutionary ruptures or violent repression. Kerala's sub-national status precluded either outcome. Although the CPI did not entirely eschew insurrectionary methods, and the state did not entirely resist resorting to violent repression, the rise of agrarian communism in Kerala was a rather peaceful process. It was one that took place largely in the trenches of a British colonial political order that had gradually conceded limited rights of association and opposition to its colonial subjects, and whose repressive reflexes were constrained by its own liberal pretensions. In Mauritius, too, the legal-bureaucratic nature of British colonialism (coupled with the political marginalization of the traditional landed elites) was critical to the success of subordinate class politics (chapter 5). In Kerala, the communists were able to take full advantage of Kerala's vibrant associational life by operating for the most part in public spaces, building a dense network of unions, farmer associations, schools, libraries, cultural organizations, and press organs. Their protest activities ranged from the Gandhian tactics of sit-ins, fasts, boycotts, and civil disobedience to those more typically associated with working-class movements, including strikes, pickets, and marches. If a comparatively favorable balance between civil society and the state expanded the political opportunity structure, it also made possible the "ratchet-effect strategy" of incremental gains that sustained class mobilization (Herring 1996).

With independence, the state–society balance was further tipped in favor of mobilization. A formally democratic state presented an especially attractive object of mobilization, and the process of class formation became inextricably linked with the process of state building. In Malabar, the party pushed for land reforms and won the first district elections; in

Travancore, it organized large-scale strikes of agricultural and industrial workers, demanding state intervention in enforcing minimum wages and regulating work conditions. In 1956, the state was unified along linguistic lines and the following year the CPI captured a majority of seats in the legislative election, becoming the first democratically elected communist government in the world. Though short-lived (the government was deposed by New Delhi in 1959), the CPI's tenure in power represented a threshold in the trajectory of Kerala's mass-based democracy. It marked the ascendancy, through the ballot box, of the poor and propertyless, social groups that in a few short decades had gone from complete social and economic subordination to political power. The 1957 government set into motion a series of reforms that, over the next two decades, would transform the face of Kerala's agrarian social structure. It also set a standard for state intervention and social welfare from which no subsequent government has strayed.[17] Most importantly, the political tide on the agrarian question had turned. The debate on land reform took center stage for the next two decades with all political forces eventually aligning themselves in favor of reform. The fact that land reform was frustrated for two decades by interference from New Delhi paradoxically fueled class mobilization. Because the inequities were acute – Kerala had the highest rates of landlessness and tenancy in the country – and because the communists were effective in keeping the issue on the political frontburner, the delay of land reform provided a source of continuous mobilization.

The birth of democracy in Kerala was indelibly branded with the logic of social transformation. Well into the 1970s, the politics of class struggle occupied center stage. Throughout this period, the conflicts between tenants and landlords, labor and capital, upper caste and lower caste were acrimonious. The communist agenda was one of radical transformation, its methods those of large-scale agitation and labor militancy. Taking its cue from communist organizational successes, the Congress built its own mass organizations. Politics became synonymous with popular mobilization and Kerala often appeared to be teetering on the brink of ungovernability, with hyper-mobilization threatening to overload political institutions.

---

[17] The demand-side dynamic for health and education in Kerala predates the democratic period and can be tied to the comparatively progressive educational and public-health policies of the Princely state of Travancore (Sen 1992). The transition from the Brahmanical paternalism of Travancore, which targeted communities (a paternalism that resembles the contemporary populism of the Indian state), to the social citizenship of Kerala's modern welfare state is, however, the outcome of class politics. Moreover, it is only with the advent of a redistributive state that the gap between Malabar and Travancore, which on all social development indicators was pronounced in the nineteenth century, was dramatically closed in the post-1957 period (Krishnan and Kabir 1992).

Yet class conflicts did not result in breakdown or disintegration because they evolved within a framework of democratic rules of the game that enjoyed a high degree of popular legitimacy and were accepted by all the principal players. The contrast here with Chile before the 1973 coup is striking (see chapter 6). In Kerala, the sub-national character of the playing field checked excesses on either side. Substantively modest but symbolically important successes on the parliamentary front had made "bourgeois democracy" and a reformist line pragmatically, if not ideologically, acceptable to the communists. The weakness of the CPI at the national level ruled out revolutionary tactics. Right-wing mobilization in Kerala, which at times flirted with authoritarian reaction, was curbed by the commitment of Nehru's Congress Party to electoral democracy and by the heterogeneity of the anti-communist coalition.[18] Also, while agrarian communism did produce comprehensive land reform (1970) and agrarian labor legislation (1974) that virtually eradicated the material and social power of landed elites, the process was slowed and defused by constitutional procedures, guarantees of private property, and drawn-out political negotiations. This democratic mediation of class conflicts was significant on two counts. First, in contrast to Chile in 1964–1973, the dominant classes were never threatened with wholesale expropriation, leaving room for negotiated class compromise. Second, though the impetus for agrarian reform came from large-scale peasant mobilizations in the 1960s and 1970s, the fact that reforms wound their way through the public sphere and then into legislation had the effect of embedding the rational-legal state in society. As a result, the institutional capacity for managing class conflicts at the local level was greatly enhanced – as exemplified by Kerala's sophisticated wage-negotiation system for agricultural laborers (Heller 1999).

We can now draw out some broader theoretical lessons. Consonant with the analytical framework developed in Rueschemeyer, Stephens, and Stephens (1992), this account of social-democratization points to the centrality of subordinate actors and highlights the historically contingent and institutionally bounded circumstances of class formation. The centrality of the *process of class formation*, rather than the structural character of the class actor, is underscored by the fact that the historical protagonist was not an industrial working class. Instead it was a broad-based and loosely configured agrarian class forged from the historical convergence of social movements, from the congruence of social domination (caste)

---

[18] The Congress Party in Kerala was essentially an anti-communist front, drawing together upper-caste Hindus, Christian farmers, and Muslims. Though it was able to mobilize a reaction to the first communist ministry, and even succeeded in having the government dismissed by the Center in 1959, it never had either the ideological or organizational cohesion to orchestrate a sustained defense of the traditional social order.

and economic exploitation (class), and from the strategic successes of a communist party born at the intersection of agrarian radicalism and parliamentary politics.

The historic conjunction of social forces and political organization provided the critical wedge that pried open the *ancien régime* and opened up new possibilities for democratic politics. Yet, if this foundational moment transformed the playing field by shifting the balance of power, it did not inexorably set Kerala down the path of social-democratization. Given that class interests and alignments constantly shift, and must compete with other bases of mobilization, the sustained effectiveness of subordinate class politics has to be explained. The temptation here is to follow Atul Kohli's (1987, 1990) seminal work on the CPI(M) in West Bengal and argue that a programmatic and disciplined political party has played the critical role in aggregating and sustaining lower-class interests. Much as in the case of the West Bengal CPI(M), an ideologically cohesive party governed internally by "democratic centralism" has kept factionalism in check, institutionalized lower-class interests, and increased the effectiveness of government policies, especially in the area of poverty alleviation.

Yet a party-centered argument that emphasizes organizational capacity highlights only one side of the equation. In contrast to its twenty-three consecutive years in power in West Bengal, the CPI(M) in Kerala has only ruled intermittently, and never for two consecutive terms. The Kerala CPI(M)'s critical role has been less in its governance capacity than in its mobilizational capacity. Having found itself periodically in the opposition, the CPI(M) has retained much of the social movement dynamic from which it was born. It continually reinvigorates its mobilizational base and reinvents its political agenda. As a *social movement party*, the Communists have thus busied themselves with the task of occupying the trenches of civil society, building mass-based organizations, ratcheting-up demands, and cultivating a noisy but effective politics of contention. This has provided a continuous presence and effectiveness for subordinate groups even when the party is out of power. And much as the party has helped sustain movement politics, conversely, its immersion in civil society has kept oligarchical tendencies in check and has allowed for an uncommon degree of political learning, as witnessed by the party's recent embrace of the "new" social movement project of grass-roots empowerment (as discussed below).

Managing neoliberal globalization

Until 1991, India was one of the most closed economies in the world with tariff barriers that virtually prohibited imports and a state regulatory system that severely restricted the functioning of markets in much of the organized economy. Following a balance of payments crisis in 1991, India adopted a heterodox strategy of liberalization that included significant but gradual tariff reduction, partial currency convertibility, reduced federal expenditures, the dismantling of much of the infamous licensing system and limited privatization. Given the sheer size and diversity of the Indian economy, and the wide range of sub-national political economies, the impact of liberalization has been highly uneven. With respect to Kerala, the impact of liberalization has been mediated by both a high degree of economic vulnerability and a relatively advanced political capacity to manage the disruptions associated with globalization.

Because of its high dependence on primary commodity exports and remittances, Kerala is vulnerable to the vicissitudes of international markets. Dating back to the sixteenth century, its economy has been subjected to repeated boom-and-bust cycles (Parayil and Sreekumar 2003, 476). Today, over 80 percent of Kerala's agricultural crops are traded nationally or internationally and, as such, are subject to global price fluctuations. An estimated 20 percent of all households depend directly on commercial crops (Joseph and Joseph 2005, 45). Kerala also relies heavily on remittances from an emigrant workforce located mostly in the Gulf countries. In 2004, there were an estimated 1.84 million Keralites working abroad whose remittances accounted for 22 percent of the net state domestic product (Zachariah and Rajan 2004). The impact of the remittance economy has had contradictory effects. Remittances have substantially leveraged the local economy, especially in the lean period of 1970–1990. But Harilal and Joseph (2000) point to the "Dutch disease syndrome" of windfalls of external income bidding up the costs of tradeables and negatively impacting growth in the productive sectors of the economy. They also, however, detect evidence that a second generation of remittances appears to be finding its way into more profitable ventures (Harilal and Joseph 2000).

The most obvious and direct social impact of liberalization has been in agriculture. In 1995, New Delhi reduced tariffs and quantitative restrictions on a range of agricultural imports. The immediate result was a dramatic drop in prices as India was flooded with cheaper commodities. Because Kerala is a smallholder agrarian economy, dominated by tree crops that leave farmers limited flexibility in responding to relative price changes,[19] it was especially hard hit. In the case of rubber, which accounted for 32 percent of agricultural domestic product in 1995–1996, prices fell 13.3 percent a year from 1997 to 2000 (Jeromi 2003, 1587). The social impact has been significant, as rubber farmers have been forced

---

[19] In 1995–1996, 93 percent of farm holdings were less than one hectare in size.

to sell rubber at below the cost of production and have reduced wage employment. The fiscal impact on the state has been no less dramatic. Rubber has been a critical source of state revenues, and the collapse of rubber prices aggravated an already serious fiscal crisis. The CPI(M)-led Left Democratic Front (LDF) (1996–2001) was forced to withhold salaries for a few months in 2000 and also suspended a number of development initiatives, including household construction for the poor. Many commentators have attributed the LDF's defeat in the 2001 state legislative election to this fiscal crisis. By 2003, however, commodity prices had recovered, stimulating a rebound in the economy.

Liberalization has also had a deep impact on Kerala's industrial economy. New Delhi has significantly curbed its financial support for public-sector enterprises, which prior to 1991 was the main source of capital investment in Kerala. Kerala has been especially hard hit, since it has the highest proportion of publicly owned enterprises in India. Starved of investment funds, its public enterprises are finding it increasingly difficult to compete both nationally and internationally. Increased investment in the private sector has not compensated for the loss of public investments. Despite ranking high on most infrastructure indicators and having the most literate and disciplined workforce in the country, Kerala continues to have very little success in attracting national and international investors.[20] Much of the problem simply lies with the perception that labor is militant and inflexible (Thampi 2004), a perception belied by consistently declining levels of strike action and the most sophisticated and stable industrial relations system in India (Heller 1999; Teitelbaum 2004).[21] In many respects Kerala is symptomatic of a global trend that has seen nations with highly effective public expenditures being boycotted by capital.[22]

For all its vulnerability to global commodity prices, the fiscal crisis, declining public investment, and sluggish private investment, Kerala has

[20] A 2003 study commissioned by the Confederation of Indian Industry ranked Kerala fifth (out of sixteen) states on a composite measure of attractiveness for investment (Debroy, Bhandari, and Banik 2003), yet Kerala attracted only 1 percent of total investment in India in the 1990s (Jeromi 2003).

[21] Labor militancy has declined dramatically over the past two decades in large part because a more sophisticated labor leadership is acutely aware of the competitive pressures of globalization and the resulting high costs of labor militancy and increasingly better at negotiating long-term agreements with capital.

[22] Moore (2003) has found that countries that do relatively well in addressing social development do poorly in attracting business. Specifically, he found an inverse correlation between his constructed RICE measure (relative income conversion efficiency), which measures the capacity of a government to convert material resources into mass welfare, and the International Country Risk Guide (ICRG), a major international indicator of business confidence.

not fared all that poorly in the post-liberalization period. After a decade of virtual stagnation in the 1980s, Kerala experienced robust growth across all sectors in the 1990s. Between 1992–1993 and 2000–2001, industry grew at an annual average of 7.6 percent, and despite the crash of commodity prices, agriculture maintained a 2.3 percent growth. Overall growth was 6.3 percent, identical to the national average (Jeromi 2003, 1585). In per capita terms, a lower birth rate produced a comparatively better trend rate. In 1990, Kerala's per capita income was 4.6 percent below the all-India average; it had reached 27.7 percent above this average by 2000–2001 (Jeromi 2003, 1584).[23] A comparison with Karnataka, the neighboring state that is home to Bangalore (epicenter of India's software industry and market-globalization poster child), is revealing. In 1994, Kerala's per capita income was virtually the same as Karnataka's, but by 2001, it was 16 percent higher (Government of Kerala, 2003/2004, Table b-23).

Explaining the sources of growth in this period is difficult, largely because of the uneven quality of sectoral data. The factory sector – the one sector for which data is generally good – witnessed respectable growth in the 1990s but attracted little investment capital. The Kerala government often points to the rapid growth in Small Scale Industries (SSI), which nearly doubled both in absolute terms and as a share of the national SSI sector in the 1990s. This could be evidence of new sources of entrepreneurial dynamism, possibly tied to a second-generation shift of remittances from consumption to investment activity. Agriculture, as we have seen, fared poorly because of falling prices, yet this sector in some respects has undergone the most dramatic and market-conforming changes in the past two decades. Thus, the share of commercial crops in net sown area has gone from 57 percent in 1970–1971 to 84 percent in 2001–2002 and crop productivity has climbed steadily, especially for rubber where yield per hectare is now the highest in the world (along with Thailand) (Joseph and Joseph 2005, 50). The three sectors that have witnessed robust growth, and are generally viewed as being the most dynamic, are communications, software, and tourism. What is notable about these sectors is that they all benefit directly from Kerala's significant comparative advantage in human capital and basic infrastructure.

On the social front, liberalization has, in the first instance, had a clearly disruptive effect. Since 1991 New Delhi has imposed increasingly strict budget control measures, severely compromising the fiscal viability of the

---

[23] In an influential article, Ahluwalia concludes that Kerala's growth performance in the 1990s stands out among India's states, having experienced the most pronounced positive changes from the 1980s (2002, 220).

public sector.[24] It has also reduced federal expenditures on key programs, making states that much more dependent on their own revenue sources (mostly highly regressive sales taxes). Most notably, New Delhi has all but stopped subsidizing the price of basic food commodities distributed through the Public Distribution System (PDS). As noted earlier, the PDS in Kerala has been highly successful, reaching into virtually every village and reducing malnutrition to the lowest level in India (Kannan 2003, 201). With the decline of federal price supports for food crops, PDS prices have now almost reached parity with market prices. There are also clear signs that the quality of health and educational services in Kerala is declining, in large part because of an outflow of trained personnel to the private sector.

But the full effect of social austerity programs has been blunted by political and social factors. On the political front, the LDF was in power from 1996–2001 and actively resisted New Delhi's policies. Despite an increasingly tight fiscal situation, social expenditures were maintained and an ambitious program of democratic decentralization was undertaken. Shortfalls in the PDS were initially compensated out of state funds.[25] The Congress-led United Democratic Front (UDF) government that came to power in 2001 has been more open to pro-market reforms, but has also faced significant opposition, including a one-month strike by all labor federations of state employees (including the Congress-affiliated labor federation) to protest cutbacks in the public sector. An effort to cut expenditures by reducing local government budgets was also halted by political opposition. And in the 2004 national parliamentary elections that produced a notable leftward shift overall, Kerala produced the most left-leaning outcome in the country, with the LDF capturing eighteen of twenty seats (including twelve for the CPI(M), by far its best result ever. The Congress failed to capture a single seat in Kerala. This trend was extended when the LDF, running on a platform that criticised the UDF government's neoliberal policies, won the 2006 state legislative elections in a landslide (98 out of 140 seats and 48.6 percent of the vote). The CPI(M) alone secured 65 seats and its highest vote-share ever (33 percent).

[24] Raman (2004, 13) provides evidence that the deterioration of Kerala's fiscal position in the 1990s can be entirely attributed to the dramatic decline of New Delhi transfers, which fell from 10.43 percent of Kerala's net state domestic product in 1991–1992, to 4.09 percent in 1999–2000.

[25] When New Delhi decided in 1997 to limit PDS subsidies to those below the poverty line, the Kerala government maintained its universal coverage by introducing a dual pricing scheme under which 42 percent of households were provided the full subsidy (Kannan 2003, 203).

Most importantly though, baseline conditions in Kerala – a more equitable distribution of income, land security, more effective state services, and high wage floors – have limited the adverse impact of New Delhi's fiscal austerity and the crisis in agriculture. This has especially been true of the most vulnerable segment of the population, rural wage earners. Across India, the biggest impact of liberalization has been the dramatic rise of food prices, which increased 10.8 percent a year in the 1990s and has disproportionately affected agricultural laborers (Pillai 2004). In only three states (Haryana, Himachel Pradesh, and Kerala) have agricultural wage levels grown sufficiently to keep pace with food price inflation. In Kerala, agricultural wages have grown at a rate of 12.5 percent a year from 1989–1990 to 1998–1999, which is well above the rate in any other state. This, in turn, largely explains why poverty levels continued to fall from 1994 to 2001 (Table 3.1).[26] Thus, despite a severe crisis of commodity prices, the wage floor in Kerala has held, especially for the most vulnerable.[27]

Kerala's experience with globalization in the 1990s supports the case – first made by Karl Polanyi – for socially embedded markets. With its more equitable income and asset distribution, more developed and inclusive state services, and strong unions, Kerala has been much better at managing the social costs of global integration than many other nations in the global south. It has done so, moreover, not through specific policies designed to compensate losers, but rather through a self-protective logic, rooted as much in the state as in civil society, of securing and defending basic social rights.

It is less clear, however, how effectively the state in Kerala can manage the challenges of increased competition in a globalized economy. In many respects, Kerala is well positioned to benefit from globalization. Achievements on the social front have provided Kerala with many of the key assets of global competitiveness: a highly educated and mobile workforce, excellent infrastructure (especially communications),[28] robust rational-legal institutions, and established ties to the global economy. The sectors in which Kerala has the greatest comparative advantage are all likely to benefit from globalization, specifically information technology (IT),

[26] Kerala's HDI score improved from 0.591 in 1991 to 0.638 in 2001 (Kannan and Pillai 2004).

[27] Ramakumar (2004, 139) notes that in 2000–2001, female agricultural laborers in Kerala had the highest wages in all states – three times higher than in neighboring Tamil Nadu and Karnataka – and that Kerala was in fact one of only two states where the prevailing wage was higher than the statutory minimum wage.

[28] Kerala has the highest telephone density in India and a 100 percent digital infrastructure that provides abundant and cost-effective bandwidth (reported in an interview posted at http://www.people-on.com, with Aruna Sundararajan, the Secretary, IT, Government of Kerala).

tourism, biotechnology, and medical services, sectors that have already shown some dynamism. Given the shortage of land in Kerala and other structural constraints on attracting manufacturing capital, these sectors are particularly promising, all the more so now that the new capital convertibility has increased Kerala's ability to attract non-resident Keralite deposits.

But seizing such opportunities requires a developmental state, and the evidence of state capacity is mixed. There is no doubting the basic capacity of the state in Kerala, as demonstrated by its achievements on the social development front. It has, moreover – in comparative terms – been highly successful in providing the baseline institutional conditions that market growth requires, most importantly rule-bound governance. But the state in Kerala has not been much of a handmaiden of growth, that is, one capable of providing the selective inputs and nurturing the more dynamic sectors of capital that are the hallmark of the developmental state (Evans 1995; Kohli 2004). It has achieved some notable successes, in particular promoting the IT sector and developing tourism, and has of late been far more aggressive in courting investors. But in contrast to the other cases considered in this book, it faces two severe constraints. First, as a sub-national state, it lacks the full range of policy tools of the nation-state and must, moreover, compete with other sub-national states that have much longer track records of business-friendly relations. Second, Kerala's economy is still underdeveloped, dominated by low-value-added industries, small-scale agricultural production, and poor internal linkages. With such a precarious material base, any reforms in the direction of greater competitiveness necessarily carry high risks. And taking such risks is only further complicated by a political picture in which potential losers are highly organized.

Reinventing the politics of social citizenship

Arguably, the most corrosive effect that neoliberal globalization can have is on the quality, the depth, and the legitimacy of democratic institutions. As Przeworski has argued so forcefully, under conditions of structural adjustment, state downsizing, and increasing marketization of life chances, "people quickly learn that they can vote, but not chose" (1992, 56). And as voice increasingly gives way to loyalty and exit, the inevitable result is an increasing desolidarization of political life and the explosion of "movements of rage." The rise in identity politics and the communalization of the state and civil society in India is only the most obvious example, as is the general decline in support for democratic institutions revealed in surveys in Latin America (chapter 2). Reviewing developments in Kerala over the past decade of liberalization, one is struck by the ambitious-ness of the LDF government's project to reinvent, rather than aban-don, the politics of social citizenship. Upon taking power in 1996 the CPI(M)-led government launched the People's Campaign for Decentral-ized Planning (the "Campaign" for short). The Campaign was designed to basically move the state downwards, not by eviscerating the center (in this case Trivandrum) as in so many other decentralization reforms, but by reasserting public powers by providing local governments with more resources, more authority, and most critically, more participatory structures (Heller 2005). The reforms devolved 35 to 40 percent of the state's planning budget to local governments, gave local governments (municipalities and rural *panchayats*) almost full allocative discretion, and mandated a complex set of nested participatory procedures designed to maximize citizen input in planning, budgeting, and implementation. A wide body of research – including two extensive local-level evaluations – confirms that the Campaign has struck deep roots, and has deepened democracy in various ways (Thomas Isaac and Franke 2002; Chaudhuri, Harilal, and Heller 2004).

First, participation rates have been extremely high. On average, over 1.7 million people have participated in the biannual village assemblies that set budgeting priorities. Equally important has been the spillover effect: the Campaign has witnessed an increase in associational life, as a range of groups have emerged to take advantage of the new opportuni-ties for engaging local government. Most notably, historically marginal-ized groups – specifically *dalits* ("untouchables"), *adivasis* ("tribals"), and women – have taken an active role in the Campaign (Chaudhuri, Harilal, and Heller 2004). And although the Campaign was launched by the CPI(M), it has received support from all parties, especially at the local level where elected officials have seen their responsibilities grow significantly.

Second, the scope of public powers and functions over which ordi-nary citizens have a direct say has increased dramatically. A World Bank report found that Kerala has the greatest degree of local expen-diture autonomy and is the most fiscally decentralized state in India, and second only to Colombia in the developing world (2000: vol. I, 28–29). Local development projects that were once the purview of highly bureaucratic line departments are designed and implemented by popular committees representing a broad range of civil-society actors. Local gov-ernments have built houses and roads, extended water services, pro-moted local agriculture, provided child-care services, and, in sum, taken responsibility for local development. The Campaign, as Kannan and Pillai note, has not only created a "public platform for a vigilant civil society" but has also ensured an "enabling environment for development" (2004, 39).

Third, survey data from seventy-two *panchayats* reveal that public expenditures are now being deployed more effectively than in the past. Greater local input and accountability have reduced corruption (especially in contractor work) and underwritten project development that is much more reflective of local needs (Chaudhuri, Harilal, and Heller 2004). There is also clear evidence that expenditure patterns are now much more favorable to the poor. To give one example, more houses were built for the poor in the first five years of the campaign than in the preceding two decades.

It still remains to be explained, however, why a party that historically has been rhetorically committed to democratic centralism and a fairly orthodox state-led vision of development, has championed decentralization. The explanation is revealing inasmuch as it highlights some of the critical problems and opportunities that social democracies face in the periphery. At the broadest level, the CPI(M) has come to recognize that traditional redistributive politics can only go so far in an increasingly market-oriented world economy. Party leaders have become acutely aware that Kerala needs to be more competitive and that state expenditures have to be more developmentally effective. Democratic decentralization has been viewed by the campaign's architects not only as a means of breaking the hold of inefficient and stifling line-department bureaucracy and rationalizing expenditure patterns, but also as a means of encouraging new forms of local initiative and innovation. The State Planning Board – which was responsible for designing and implementing the Campaign – has tirelessly emphasized that *panchayats* should focus on investing in "commodity-producing sectors." Similarly, there is a very clear recognition that new challenges for providing public goods and social services call for a different kind of state. A strong, centralized, and interventionist state did secure high levels of social development, extensive public infrastructure, and basic institutional reforms. But the second-generation social development challenges Kerala faces (the quality, rather than the quantity, of public services) call for a fundamentally different mode of governance. The fiscal logic of the Campaign is revealing: by reducing rents and leakage through greater accountability, more can be done within existing constraints.

Finally, and perhaps most importantly, the CPI(M) has had to confront the limits of traditional left party politics. Much as is the case for social-democratic parties across the world, the absence or decline of a unified working class and the rise of new organized social actors, including the women's movement and environmentalism, have opened the door to a critique of bureaucratization (and specifically, in Kerala, of Leninism) and a greater openness to civil society. This, in turn, has brought the challenge of deepening democracy into focus, especially the building of local democracy and more participatory forms of citizenship. In many respects, this focus represents a return to the party's social-movement roots, which emphasized building mass organizations and nurturing citizenship over capturing state power. The communist movement's theoretician and first chief minister, E. M. S. Namboodiripad (1957–1959), was a longtime advocate of building local democratic government as the key to sustaining redistributive development. This increased emphasis on local government and local democracy has an interesting historical parallel in Scandinavia, where powerful local governments and associations have long played a central role in social-democratic politics (Rothstein 2001).

Democratic decentralization in Kerala represents a new politics of social citizenship. In marked contrast to conventional, donor-funded decentralization programs that seek to shift allocative authority away from the state and towards the private sector, the Campaign is an effort to refashion public authority in the face of mounting challenges to the state's capacity to promote equitable development and social protection in a global economy. This link between neoliberal globalization and the new vision of social citizenship was clearly articulated by Planning Board Member and CPI(M) leader Shreedharan Namboodiripad (son of the first CPI(M) chief minister):

The state is withdrawing from social sectors – education, health, and other services. Despite advanced educational and health institutions, especially at local level, [we] are facing severe crises because of the resource crunch. This can be overcome only if it is planned at the local level and that all maintenance and other support work is done locally. Thus a major portion of devolved funds are going to the improvement of educational and health services. They [*panchayats*] are also mobilizing voluntary resources in the form of labor and financial contributions. The point is that both rich and poor have a common interest to contribute to improve these institutions. The WB/IMF have committed to the retreat of the state. Here, we are trying to make the state more active at the local level of the economy and social services. Decentralization is our answer to the IMF/World Bank globalization agenda. (Interview, Trivandrum, August 1997)

The Campaign marks both an important rupture as well as a key continuity in Kerala's social-democratic trajectory. There is a rupture with the post-independence redistributive project, which was predicated on building a centralized and top-heavy state apparatus linked to a highly disciplined political party and its mass organizations through quasi-corporatist structures. These structures more or less bypassed civil society; they equated lower-class power with party control of the state. In contrast, the democratic decentralization project seeks not only to devolve bureaucratic and political power, but also to re-embed the state in civil society by promoting participatory democracy. The continuity relates to the dynamics of what has been a steady, if uneven, process of democratic deepening. The process has been driven by iterated engagements between social movements and state institutions. The continuity, therefore, lies in a political project of expanding social citizenship that remains fundamentally concerned with strengthening the state. The rejection of bureaucratic modes of emancipation, and the attendant political emphasis on capturing the commanding heights of the state, has been accompanied by calls for transforming the very nature of the state and of representative politics, and specifically for deepening democracy through greater participation. The "old" social movement logic of redistribution from above has, in other words, been superseded by calls for redistribution from below.

Conclusion

Social democracy requires an activist state that can both manage the delicate trade-offs of class compromises and extend the reach of the public domain without compromising its autonomy. Over the past two decades, however, the faith that was once invested in the state as a progressive agent of transformation has been severely eroded. Given the poor record of many states in the periphery, this loss of faith is understandable. Yet, as all four of our cases demonstrate, despite the severe internal and external obstacles that states in the periphery confront, they can under the right circumstances serve encompassing interests and effectively promote social development and democratization. Kerala provides emphatic evidence of just how transformative a social-democratic state can be. Working with an extremely limited resource base, state reforms and policies have, within less than half a century, lifted Kerala from the status of a quasi-feudal, highly exclusionary, and deeply inegalitarian society to one in which citizens enjoy a range of capabilities comparable to those in industrial countries. The impact of the state was not, moreover, just about providing services, but also about fundamentally transforming social relations both between the state and society, and within society itself. Kerala's achievements in reducing infant mortality and increasing life expectancy are well documented. However, they are no more dramatic than the transformations in class, caste, and gender relations that have also taken place.

The state in Kerala has, moreover, been far more effective in promoting equitable development than any other Indian state, despite having the same constitutional form, institutional structures, and resources as these other states. This highlights the plasticity of state capacity and specifically points to the importance of historical patterns of state–society engagement in shaping institution building. The very different path that Kerala has traveled from the rest of the subcontinent can only be explained by changes in the balance of class forces and how these have played out in a sub-national context. Classes, as we have noted, are the "effects of struggles." In Kerala, the broad-based class coalition that has been the carrier of social democracy was the historical product of three distinct social movements that converged through the leadership of the Communist Party. That such a convergence took place in a sub-national context – the periphery of the periphery – underscores the argument of this book that social democracy is, first and foremost, about political action.

4   Costa Rica: resilience of a classic social democracy

"Costa Rica is not a country. It is a pilot project. It is an experiment." Thus declared José ("Pepe") Figueres in 1982 in the midst of the country's worst economic crisis since the depression of the 1930s (quoted in Cardozo Rodas 1990, 24). Figueres – former Junta Chief, President of the Republic, and founder of the social-democratic PLN (Partido de Liberación Nacional) – was revered by many for his role as the main architect of the Costa Rican welfare state and reviled by others for repressing left-wing labor unions in the aftermath of the 1948 civil war, as well as for later episodes of corruption and friendships with shady characters (such as fugitive financier Robert Vesco). While the claim that "Costa Rica is not a country" would strike most of its citizens as dubious (or as one of don Pepe's characteristic, forgivable exaggerations), the idea that it is – or at least was – a "pilot project" or an exceptional experiment is widely shared, at home and abroad.

Costa Rica's progress in human development and the solidity of its democratic institutions are noteworthy given that other Central American countries have markedly lower levels of well-being and long histories of civil strife and authoritarian rule. The United Nations Development Programme (UNDP) now includes Costa Rica (which ranked forty-seventh worldwide) among those countries with "high human development" (UNDP 2005, 219); in 2001, UNDP recognized that, "Costa Rica and [South] Korea have both made impressive human development gains, reflected in HDIs [Human Development Indexes] of more than 0.800 [on a scale of 0 to 1.0], but Costa Rica has achieved this human outcome with only half the income of Korea" (UNDP 2001, 13). The social indicators that are part of HDI are suggestive of Costa Rica's extraordinary progress. Life expectancy at birth in 2003, for example, was 78.2 years, exceeded in the Western Hemisphere only by Canada, where it was 80.0 years (Chile was third and the United States fourth, with expectancies, respectively, of 77.9 and 77.4 years) (UNDP 2005, 219). The 2003 adult literacy rate of 95.8 percent was slightly lower than that of several English-speaking Caribbean countries, Cuba, and the historically more developed southern cone countries of Argentina and Uruguay (Chile's rate was 95.7 percent). However, Costa Rica's literacy was strikingly higher than those of the other Central American countries: El Salvador (79.7 percent), Honduras (80.0 percent), Guatemala (69.1 percent), and Nicaragua (76.7 percent) (UNDP 2005, 219–20).

The Inter-American Development Bank (IDB) considers Costa Rica a "middle-income" country. This accomplishment is all the more impressive because the most notable advances occurred in just the few decades since the mid-twentieth century. In relation to the rest of Central America in 1920,

Costa Rica was in the penultimate place in terms of Gross Domestic Product, with a GDP slightly greater than Nicaragua's, well below El Salvador's, and only slightly more than one-third of Guatemala's . . . In 1991, however, its GDP was three times that of Nicaragua, nearly twice that of Honduras, 20 percent higher than that of El Salvador, and more than 70 percent that of Guatemala. (BID 1996, 9)

The contrast in per capita GDP is just as striking. In 1940, Costa Rica's per capita GDP was 79 percent of Guatemala's. But in subsequent decades, it pulled rapidly ahead, reaching 1.72 times Guatemala's level in 1980.

This chapter explains why an advanced welfare state emerged in what was – at the mid-twentieth century – a poor, tropical country heavily dependent on just two exports: coffee and bananas.[1] Like Mauritius's sugar-based export economies and Kerala's rubber- and coconut-based ones, this country had, in the era leading up to the developmental state, a typical primary-product dependent economy. The chapter then asks how it was possible to maintain outstanding social indicators even in the aftermath of the early 1980s economic crisis when the developmental state fell into disfavor and was partially dismantled. Part of Costa Rica's continued progress in most areas of human development is clearly attributable to a reorientation toward the global economy in the 1980s and 1990s: new earnings from tourism, financial services, and textile, high-technology, and nontraditional agricultural exports have generated employment and important streams of revenue for the government.

Nevertheless, it would be a mistake to cite Costa Rica simply as a globalization success story. Despite serious and worrisome limitations (including worsening inequality and erosion in the quality and availability of public-sector services), it is also and primarily, even today, a social-democratic success story. Indeed, this chapter argues that Costa

---

[1] In 1951, at the dawn of the welfare state, these two products accounted for 89 percent of Costa Rica's export earnings (Mesa-Lago 2002, 405).

Rica's embrace of the free market has been half-hearted, in large part because of an ongoing political impasse between elites who favor neoliberal reforms and citizens who, to varying degrees, recognize and remain attached to benefits derived from welfare-state institutions. Moreover, the social-democratic legacy included significant subsidies to investors, a literate, healthy workforce, and a well-developed infrastructure, all of which facilitated a new insertion in the global economy (much as occurred in Chile and Mauritius, for similar reasons).

Acknowledging that Costa Rica's embrace of neoliberal reform has been late and half-hearted, or that its insertion in the global economy has been comparatively successful, however, does not necessarily mean that the country's remaining public-sector and social-welfare institutions have survived intact. On the contrary, relentless pressures from Washington in particular (as well as from global markets, the WTO trade regime, and international financial institutions) have led to promises to open the economy further and to privatize important public-sector enterprises. The sustainability of the country's commitment to the well-being of its inhabitants is thus in question. Nevertheless, even after a quarter century of neoliberalism, widespread citizen support for key public-sector institutions has permitted the survival of a reinvented welfare state and, moreover, has made a willingness to adapt, preserve, and extend the model an essential ingredient of political legitimacy for any government.

Origins of Costa Rican exceptionalism

Historians and social scientists have advanced various theses about the origins of Costa Rican democracy and the developmental state.[2] Most interpretations revolve around some combination of structural, institutional, and conjunctural factors, while emphasizing one over the others. In contrast to Chile, Kerala, and Mauritius, Costa Rica began its postcolonial history with relatively widespread access to land, especially in the central part of the country where most of the small population lived and national institutions were based. This structural factor is central to understanding the country's evolution. The Costa Rican coffee elite that emerged in the early nineteenth century depended for its members' superior status less on landownership than on intermediation and other commercial activities. The neutralization of a conservative landowning class – which was key to the emergence of social democracy in Chile,

---

[2] The relevant literature is vast. Significant contributions include: Gudmundson 1986; Molina Jiménez 1991; Williams 1994; Paige 1997; Mahoney 2001; Rovira Mas 2001; and Lehoucq and Molina 2002.

Kerala, and Mauritius – was barely necessary in Costa Rica, where elites early on demonstrated a willingness to extend education and public health to the masses, even if the impetus for doing so initially involved fears of "undesirable" immigration. In Costa Rica the legacy of specific conjunctures, including the role of charismatic leadership (particularly in the period leading up to and following the 1948 civil war), was also central to the emergence of social democracy, as was the case, for example, in Mauritius (where post-independence leaders had embraced Fabian-style socialism while studying in Britain).

The pattern of capitalist development and state formation

Colonial Costa Rica was a backwater in Spain's American empire. With few precious metals and an indigenous population that was not large to begin with and that was decimated early on by European diseases, slaving, and conquest, the region that became Costa Rica attracted only small numbers of Spanish settlers. While the traditional historiography's (Monge Alfaro 1980) portrayal of a society of shared poverty and relative equality is now recognized as exaggerated and ideological, access to land was widespread and, in contrast to the rest of Central America, elites and plebeians shared a common worldview and cultural repertoire (Gudmundson 1986, 1995; Molina Jiménez 1991).

Several factors contributed to forging this shared worldview. First, the small population, availability of land, and near absence of coercive state or landlord institutions meant that income from coffee exports, which commenced in Costa Rica in the 1830s, was more equitably distributed than in countries where exports began later or where large properties accounted for more production. Members of the coffee elite sometimes owned large farms, but most of their wealth derived from processing and exporting. In contrast to other countries, such as Colombia, that contained significant smallholding coffee zones, Costa Rica's coffee region included all of the country's principal urban population centers, giving national-level impact to a system of agrarian relations in which small farms predominated and the influence of a reactionary landlord class was minimal or nonexistent.[3] The early involvement with coffee also made privatization of ecclesiastical and community lands gradual and less contentious, allowing Costa Rica to avoid the violent conflicts between

---

[3] Large cattle haciendas predominated in the northwest and US-owned banana plantations in the southern coastal regions. While the country's overall land distribution pattern was thus quite concentrated, the authoritarianism associated with highly unequal agrarian structures was most pronounced in those regions rather than at the level of the national state or in the central region.

pro-laissez-faire Liberals and pro-clerical Conservatives that wracked other Latin American nations.

Second, beginning in the 1880s, Europhile elites sought to construct a modern state and to invent a Costa Rican nation that was at least nom- inally democratic and distinct from the rest of Central America. They aimed to represent it as racially "white," despite the presence of mixed- origin people, a small indigenous minority, and rising Chinese and Afro- Antillean immigration. Together with high infant-mortality rates, immi- gration became a focus of elite anxieties about the "degeneration" of the white "Costa Rican race" that served as an impetus not just for laws lim- iting "undesirable" immigration, but also for a strong state commitment to education and public health, which, it was thought, would increase the supply of "white" labor and make the importation of Chinese and West Indians unnecessary (Palmer 2003, 145–47). The educational reforms of the mid-1880s, which made available universal primary schooling, con- tributed to consolidating notions of nation, citizenship, entitlement, and rights.

Third, the limited significance in the central part of the country of caste-like forms of oppression favored the early inclusion of most social groups within the concept of the nation.[4] Society was marked by an intimacy between classes that was unusual for Latin America. Relations between small coffee producers and wealthy processors, while intermit- tently conflictual and inherently unequal, were tempered on each side by a strong awareness of mutual necessity and interdependence (Solís 1992, 387). The capital, San José, barely had 90,000 inhabitants in 1950 while the three other provincial capitals in the central valley had only 15,000 each. The residential proximity and interaction of members of differ- ent classes contributed to a greater degree of tolerance and trust between social groups than existed elsewhere in Central America (Molina Jiménez 2002, 10–11, 83, 89). As a final contributing factor to a shared sense of nationhood, in the early twentieth century, Liberal governments founded important public-sector institutions, including the Banco Internacional de Costa Rica (later the Banco Nacional), the Banco de Seguros (later the National Insurance Institute, INS), the National Child Welfare Board, and the National Coffee Office. In the 1930s they intervened in the econ- omy to support cattle, rice, coffee, and sugar prices (Edelman 1999).

The concept of a "social democracy" formed part of a broader dis- course about "the social question" that, after 1900, became a staple of radical intellectuals (Molina Jiménez 2002, 11, 37). The ideological

---

[4] This political construction of inclusion is what underlies Walzer's claim that "the welfare state has had its greatest successes in ethnically homogeneous countries" (2000, 131).

sources of this discourse included anarchosyndicalism, Social Christian doctrine, the populist anti-imperialism of Víctor Raúl Haya de la Torre and his Peru-based but internationalist APRA (Alianza Popular Revolucionaria Americana), socialism, and communism (Cerdas 1978, 153–55; Solís 1992, 146–47). The "social question" and class struggles became more acute during the 1930s depression, when unemployment skyrocketed, living conditions worsened, and the Communist-led banana workers union staged one of the largest strikes ever in Latin America against a US company. But Costa Rican Communism – even before 1935, during the Comintern's ultra-left, pre-popular front period – remained attached to the specificity of the national experience. *Comunismo a la tica* ("Costa Rican-style Communism") promoted a "Minimum Program" in 1932 that coincided in many respects with the aspirations of reformist Liberalism by advocating the creation of a social-security system, abolition of child labor, "hygienization" of the country, and educational reform (Botey and Cisneros 1984, 119–22).

"Social democracy" was not, however, an explicit element in the discourse of smallholding peasants who, in the first six decades of the twentieth century, engaged in intermittent struggles with powerful coffee processors (with whom they also shared ties of mutual dependency, as noted above). Nonetheless, while peasants protested low prices and manifested persistent hostility to new taxes and regulations, they also viewed the state as an essential and usually impartial mediator of social conflicts. Their movements, which were largely independent of political parties and in some ways anticipated later mobilizations of the rural and urban poor, articulated an ideology that identified coffee and smallholding with the nation and that extolled democracy as a protection for small property (Acuña 1987). The way that sectors of the Costa Rican peasantry eventually embraced social democracy was thus comparable to what occurred when Indian peasants in Kerala flocked to Marxism. Both groups viewed the state as a potential ally and democracy as a vehicle for advancing their interests, while the specific ideological content of the movements to which they eventually adhered – social democracy in Costa Rica and communism in Kerala – was less significant than the movements' broader commitment to social justice.

Critical juncture: the civil war and the social-democratic junta

The 1940s in Costa Rica constituted a critical juncture in which the outcome of political struggles, key leadership choices, and institutional changes set the country firmly on a path toward consolidating a social-democratic developmental state. Rafael Angel Calderón Guardia, president in 1940–1944, had developed sensitivity to "the social question" during the crisis of the 1930s and in his medical training at Catholic universities in Belgium. His administration laid the groundwork for a modern welfare state, creating a wide-ranging social-security system (inspired in part by Chile's pioneering reforms in the 1920s), a national health-care system, an expanded pension system, and low-cost housing programs, as well as guaranteeing the right to strike and incorporating into the constitution existing workday and minimum-wage laws (Salazar 1981, 84–85). This top-down reformism entailed an erosion of elite and middle-class support, if only because employers resented the new labor legislation. To shore up his backing, Calderón allied with Catholic archbishop Víctor Sanabria (like him inspired by Social Christian ideas) and with Communist Party secretary general Manuel Mora.[5] In 1944, the *calderonista*-Catholic–Communist alliance backed Teodoro Picado as a presidential candidate; he won the presidency in an election marred by fraud and violence. Picado further irritated anti-government forces by, among other things, managing to pass a mildly progressive income-tax law in 1946.

The opposition to Calderón and Picado brought together disaffected elite interests with middle sectors whose leadership was claimed by a handful of intellectuals and entrepreneurs; this opposition coalesced in 1945 to create the Social Democratic Party. Coffee farmers, concerned about Communist influence in the government and fearful of the eventual extension to the rural sector of the new labor code, often sympathized with the opposition. Over time, both elite and social-democratic factions of the opposition adopted confrontational tactics and some social democrats led by José Figueres, a coffee producer and small-scale industrialist, planned an armed insurrection. The pretext for revolt was the disputed 1948 presidential election, in which a conservative, Otilio Ulate, defeated Calderón's bid to succeed Picado. The *calderonista*-controlled congress refused to certify the results, alleging "irregularities." Figueres began an uprising, starting a five-week civil war that cost some two thousand lives and overthrew Picado's government. The insurgent forces drew heavily on disaffected middle-class urbanites and smallholding coffee producers from the central part of the country (Solís 1992, 284). The most ardent defenders of the government were pro-Communist banana workers from remote coastal regions.

The insurgent victory in 1948 exemplifies how the outcomes of critical junctures, while highly contingent, are shaped by previously existing

---

[5] The Catholics' and Communists' interests in this seemingly peculiar alliance are beyond the scope of this chapter, but Edelman (1999, 53) discusses this issue.

political and class configurations and in turn may shape a path toward social democracy in the periphery. Figueres and the social-democratic opposition had fought the war and controlled the arms of the victorious side. When peace was restored, the traditional elite faction of the opposition was left effectively toothless. In eighteen months of rule by decree, the social-democratic junta repressed the Communists, *calderonistas*, and left-wing labor unions which had been on the losing side, but it also deepened the state's role in the economy and social welfare. Key junta measures included:

• Nationalization of all commercial banks, which received the exclusive right to accept deposits. (This broke the back of the powerful banking interests and permitted channeling loans to sectors of the economy and regions that previously had little access to credit.)
• A temporary 10 percent tax on all capital holdings of over 50,000 colones (approximately US$10,000).
• A 15 percent tax on the profits of the United Fruit Company.
• Founding the public-sector Costa Rican Electricity Institute (ICE), which eventually absorbed most electrical and telecommunications companies and provided subsidized services to industries and consumers.
• Abolition of the army, which social democrats represented as a victory for Costa Ricans' purportedly pacifist vocation that would free up resources for social spending, but which was also intended to thwart any attempt at a conservative restoration.

Figueres's junta called elections (without the participation of the defeated *calderonistas* or Communists) for a Constituent Assembly, which was charged with writing a new constitution. Among the key Constituent Assembly reforms that shaped the country's development model were provisions for the creation of autonomous public-sector institutions outside the control of the executive branch (which was ostensibly intended to insulate them from shifting political winds and personalistic influences) and the creation of a fourth branch of government, the Supreme Electoral Tribunal (intended to insure honest elections).[6] The 1949 constitution – particularly the provisions for autonomous public-sector institutions and for weakening the executive branch – assured that the momentum of the reform process could be maintained even during periods when the social-democratic forces did not control the presidency. In yet another example of how decisions at critical moments produce path-dependent processes,

---

[6] Other key measures were suffrage for women and full citizenship rights for the Costa Rican-born descendants of black West Indian immigrants on the Atlantic coast.

these constitutional protections for public-sector enterprises proved difficult to reverse, thus greatly complicating neoliberal campaigns for privatization in the 1980s and after.

Enthusiasts of the democratic developmental state picture 1948 as a unique conjuncture, a break with the past propelled by Figueres's visionary leadership. Their critics stress continuities with previous reformist traditions and suggest that the post-civil war era was less a clearly conceived utopian experiment than a period in which antagonistic social forces stalemated each other – conceived either as the populist *calderonismo* versus the authoritarian corporatist (but nominally social-democratic) movement of Figueres (Schifter 1978, 209), or as the Figueres junta against its erstwhile conservative allies (Lehoucq and Molina 2002, 225). This sort of interpretation suggests that opposing groups viewed a democratic system as a lesser evil, a more acceptable form of competition than violent conflict. In particular, proportional voting, which compensated parties that lost presidential contests with representation in the legislative branch, reduced the stakes of any given election and thus the potential for institutional breakdown (Lehoucq 1990). In any case, most of the post-civil war junta's reforms – in nationalized banking (Brenes 1990), expansion of the public sector (Masís Iverson 1999, 50), electoral oversight (Lehoucq and Molina 2002, 7–8), and abolition of the military (Muñoz Guillén 1990, 115–56) – had important institutional and legal antecedents, sometimes dating to the early twentieth century.

The evolution of social democracy

The "golden age"

The "golden age" of the Costa Rican developmental state – the era of classic social democracy – was 1949 to 1979. Three sub-periods may be distinguished, each corresponding approximately to one of the post-civil war, pre-economic crisis decades: (1) during the 1950s, the state – sometimes termed an *Estado gestor* or "managerial state" – became involved in planning, encouraging economic diversification, and providing favorable conditions for private capital; (2) this emphasis continued in the 1960s, but, especially after Costa Rica's 1963 entrance into the Central American Common Market (CACM), the state focused more on attracting private capital for import-substitution industrialization (ISI) aimed at regional markets; and (3) during the 1970s, the state increasingly assumed the role of entrepreneur (*Estado empresario*), acquiring ownership of, or founding enterprises in diverse sectors of the economy. Even though social democratic and opposition governments usually alternated in power, over the entire three-decade period that preceded the 1980–1982 economic crisis, the state deepened its commitment to investing in human capital and social welfare. Social policies that accompanied growing state intervention in the economy had a progressive redistributive impact (see below).

During the first post-civil war decade, framed by the eighteen-month junta in 1948–1949 and by Figueres's first elected term as president in 1953–1958, the state deepened its involvement in the economy and social welfare. The existing National Production Council became a semi-autonomous commodities board which acquired grain from farmers at guaranteed prices and established retail outlets that sold staples to consumers at subsidized prices (eventually generating a gigantic deficit). The Ministry of Economy, Industry, and Commerce further intervened in the grain market by fixing permissible profit levels at each stage of production, processing, and marketing. Public-sector agencies set prices for staple foods, petroleum products, alcohol, and transportation. The National Wage Council – composed of equal numbers of labor, employer, and government representatives – established minimum wages for different categories of private-sector employment. The nationalized banks began to make loans to promising new sectors, including livestock, sugar, rice, cotton, and light industry; smallholders received credit at preferential rates. A Central Bank was founded to oversee the four nationalized banks and to give the state greater control over monetary policy; in effect, this began a three-decades-long tendency to overvalue the Costa Rican currency, the colón, in the interests of encouraging capital goods imports (but also fueling rampant consumerism and persistent trade deficits). Highway construction programs doubled the length of the road network between 1950 and 1962 and the founding in 1953 of the Autonomous Pacific Electrical Railway Institute gave the public sector a strategic presence in transportation. The creation of a National Water and Sewer Service completed the public sector's control of the main utilities (electricity, telecommunications, and potable water).

In the area of social policy, this decade saw the founding in 1954 of the National Housing and Planning Institute, which provided construction services and subsidized mortgages to low- and middle-income home buyers. The number of high schools tripled between 1949 and 1954 and primary enrollments covered 90 percent of the school-age population by 1960 (Barahona Montero 1999, 160–61). In 1957, free and obligatory schooling was extended through the ninth grade. A modest agrarian reform program initiated in the 1960s titled or redistributed over 1 million hectares of land for some 60,000 beneficiaries (Román Vega and

Rivera Araya 1990, 17). The state encouraged development of production, credit, purchasing, marketing, and savings cooperatives in the coffee sector, thus reducing the power of the traditional elite. The health-care system modernized and grew rapidly, as did the proportion of the population covered by the social-security system, which in the 1970s expanded to cover the entire population. A National Planning Office opened in 1963 and designed multi-year, inter-agency development efforts. In 1975, a family assistance program began to provide meals to schoolchildren, allowances to needy families, and infrastructure construction to rural communities.

A cycle of industrial expansion commenced with the 1959 Industrial Protection Law and accelerated four years later with Costa Rica's entrance into the Central American Common Market. Initially, the CACM was modeled on the protectionist ISI strategy of the United Nations Economic Commission for Latin America (ECLA), though US corporate interests seeking a presence in the region rapidly became its most enthusiastic supporters and beneficiaries.[7] Central American countries, united behind a common regional external tariff system, provided investors with exemptions from income taxes and customs duties on imports of raw materials and capital goods. Because the most dynamic zone of the CACM, in terms of purchasing power and investment volume, was the corridor between San Salvador and Guatemala City, Costa Rica, located at the other end of the isthmus, had to provide additional incentives to attract capital. In addition to tax breaks that were not unlike those provided by neighboring countries, the Costa Rican public sector assured the following: the availability of inexpensive credit (sometimes at negative real interest rates); cut-rate electric power, telecommunications, and water;[8] and artificially low prices for key industrial inputs, such as sugar for food and beverage manufacturers. Another attractive feature was that while Costa Rica generated less overall demand than the San Salvador–Guatemala City corridor, its citizens' per capita purchasing power was significantly greater than that of other Central American countries. Also, beginning in 1972, Costa Rica-based exporters who exported nontraditional products containing 35 percent or more local raw materials to non-Central American markets received tax credit certificates (CATS) that were worth up to US$200,000 for each US$1 million in exports. Eventually CATS became negotiable instruments and both a

---

[7] In Costa Rica's first decade in the CACM, three-quarters of all investment came from abroad, largely from US companies (Molina and Palmer 1997, 23).

[8] ICE's electrical rates were the lowest in Central America and they remained unchanged between 1959 and 1973 at about US$0.02 per kilowatt-hour (Sojo 1984, 46). Its telephone rates remain today among the lowest in the world (Fumero Paniagua 2004, 209).

major drain on the Costa Rican treasury and an insufficiently acknowledged source of the export dynamism that characterized the post-1982 period of supposed free-market reform (see below).

The 1960s ISI model, while fostering production of finished goods previously purchased abroad, did not really involve an overall substitution of imports. Between 1966 and 1972, imports of raw materials and industrial equipment exceeded manufactured exports by US$250 million (Molina and Palmer 1997, 24). By the early 1970s, after a decade of ISI, Costa Rica imported approximately US$80 of machinery and raw materials for every US$100 of industrial output (González-Vega 1984, 356). This, along with repatriation of profits by foreign firms, contributed to growing current account deficits (as did the overvalued currency and the 1970s oil shocks).

Signs of diminishing dynamism in the ISI model led the Costa Rican state to assume a more active role in the economy in the 1970s. This was facilitated by the election of José Figueres to a second presidential term in 1970 and his succession by fellow PLN leader Daniel Oduber in 1974 – the first time since the 1948 civil war that the PLN and the generally more conservative, less statist Social Christian opposition had not alternated presidential periods. Social Christian governments had dampened the growth of the state. The PLN's control of the executive branch for eight years in the 1970s, however, brought an unprecedented expansion of the public sector and, eventually, new vulnerabilities. Between 1974 and 1977, public investment in productive activities grew at an astonishing annual rate of 183 percent. This expansion, though, was funded almost entirely through borrowing, with the foreign debt rising from US$164 million to US$1.061 billion in 1970–1978 (Molina and Palmer 1997, 24–25).

Most emblematic of the "entrepreneurial state" was the formation in 1972 of the Costa Rican Development Corporation (CODESA), a public-sector holding company that eventually included subsidiaries involved in transportation, petroleum refining, aluminum smelting, sugar refining, cotton production and ginning, fruit packing, fertilizer, and cement. In contrast to Chile's CORFO, founded more than three decades earlier and with an emphasis on providing credit rather than assuming direct control, Costa Rica's CODESA specialized in activities that private capital was reluctant to enter into because of high start-up costs or unusual risks. Not surprisingly, most CODESA subsidiaries manifested lackluster economic performance, which required them to absorb ever-greater shares of the available public-sector credit.

Between 1948 and 1980, about 100 new public-sector institutions were founded, many with diverse and sometimes overlapping mandates in job training, education, health and nutrition, poverty reduction, and related areas of social welfare. By 1980, the public sector accounted for nearly one-quarter of GDP and almost one-fifth of the workforce. Public employees formed a significant proportion of the large middle class and were also a bastion of support for the state-centered development model. The state's intervention in the economy was perhaps greater than its proportion of GDP or the labor force might suggest, since it closely regulated many activities and had monopolistic control over provision of key goods and services (Vargas Solís 2002, 87; Hidalgo Capitán 2003, 54–55).

The country's overall economic performance in this period was dynamic and its social progress exceptional. From the early 1950s until 1979, Costa Rica's growth rates were among the highest in Latin America. It achieved impressive reductions in poverty and income inequality. Health indicators improved markedly. From schools and health clinics to ICE telephones, the reach of state and public-sector institutions into even the most remote areas contributed to diminishing the urban–rural gap and to creating a nearly universal sense of shared national identity among the citizenry.[9]

Crisis and economic reform

Costa Rica's three-decade-long experiment in building an advanced welfare state in a relatively underdeveloped tropical country benefited from favorable conditions during 1949–1979 but nonetheless suffered from underlying vulnerabilities. The 1949–1979 period was, for the most part, a time of expanding markets and good prices for the country's exports. Productivity advances in key sectors, especially coffee and bananas, contributed to Costa Rica's economic dynamism (though they also discouraged diversification). Annual flows of foreign investment rose from less than US$1 million in 1958 to over US$400 million in 1978, making it possible to finance both social spending and the sophisticated sorts of consumption to which the middle and upper classes had become accustomed (Garnier and Hidalgo 1998, 40). In the 1970s, when the rhythm of foreign investment gradually diminished as a result of the broader world economic crisis, Costa Rica increasingly relied on foreign borrowing, primarily commercial bank loans with variable interest rates.

---

[9] This increase in institutional capacity at the national level was not matched in the municipalities, which were originally created to administer rural cantons or small cities. Post-1950 urbanization often had a chaotic quality, since municipalities, which lacked budgetary resources and trained personnel, frequently failed to provide adequate regulation and services (e.g., zoning, garbage collection).

The country's vulnerabilities were evident by 1980. The petroleum price shocks of 1973 and 1979 constituted a major blow to a country that imported all of its oil. The Costa Rican government responded by completing the nationalization of the country's one oil refinery (in which it previously had minority ownership). This had little impact on the persistently negative balance of payments or on rising inflation, which was soon reflected in the growing cost of servicing variable-rate loans from foreign banks. Moreover, the Central American Common Market, the country's main customer for manufactured goods, had been in disarray since the 1969 "soccer war" between Honduras and El Salvador and also suffered from unanticipated, persistent trade imbalances between its members (Bulmer-Thomas 1987, 177). Moreover, as the Sandinistas intensified their war against the Somoza regime in Nicaragua in 1977–1979, Costa Rica was physically cut off from its CACM trading partners to the north. Coffee prices, which reached an unprecedented peak in 1977, plummeted soon after. In 1979, Eurodollar interest rates (on which much Costa Rican borrowing was based) skyrocketed from 6 to 19 percent (Fox 1998, 24).

The Costa Rican model of development had, in addition, accumulated a series of internal contradictions that were difficult, if not impossible, to resolve in the absence of a favorable external environment or a robust system of taxation. Many sectors – food, for example – received public subsidies at both the production and consumption ends, thus fueling gaping deficits. Public-sector industries, particularly those in the CODESA conglomerate, were hemorrhaging money. Some actuaries warned that the generous system of retirement pensions for public employees might be unsustainable. The foreign debt rose rapidly, growing from 1.5 times export earnings in 1979, to a ratio of 2.3 in 1981 and 3.5 in 1983; by 1983, interest obligations alone were equivalent to 44 percent of the country's export earnings (Vargas Solís 2002, 87).

Rising inflation and trade deficits put pressure on the colón, which had long been fixed at an artificially high value (thus contributing to the trade deficits in the first place). In 1980, the government responded by establishing a system of multiple exchange rates governing different types of transactions. This stop-gap solution proved unwieldy and, in a two-year period from late 1980 to late 1982, Costa Rica's currency suffered a devaluation of approximately 500 percent. The social impact of the crisis was severe, with unemployment levels not seen since the 1930s depression, a sudden impoverishment of the middle and lower classes, and an unraveling of the social safety net that had, until then, cushioned the downwardly mobile from absolute pauperization.

Despite this grim panorama, Costa Rica in the early 1980s was in an unusually advantageous position. As a small debtor, even modest infusions of aid could have beneficial effects. In addition, geopolitically, Costa Rica was sandwiched between two of Washington's *bêtes noires*, Sandinista Nicaragua and General Manuel Antonio Noriega's Panama. As the bearer of an enviable democratic tradition without equal in the region, the country became a privileged recipient of US largesse and a favored client of the international financial institutions. Indeed, between 1982 and 1995, the United States provided Costa Rica with nearly US$1.8 billion in aid (in 1994 dollars), most of it "economic support funds" intended to shore up the balance of payments (Fox 1998, 17). In the immediate post-crisis years of 1983–1985, US aid was equivalent to 35.7 percent of the Costa Rican government's budget, one-fifth of export earnings, and about 10 percent of GDP (Edelman 1999, 76–78). One US Agency for International Development (USAID) report refers to this support as Costa Rica's "Sandinista windfall" (Fox 1998, 3). In return for the windfall, USAID insisted on measures to auction off CODESA companies; to foster currency reforms, private-sector banks, and nontraditional export enterprises; and to create private institutions – from agricultural schools to export promotion offices – that competed with (and frequently undermined) state and public-sector agencies. Washington further sought to enlist Costa Rica as an ally in its war against the Sandinistas in Nicaragua (Honey 1994). The scale of this US aid, as well as the way disbursements were tied to the fulfillment of specific reforms, greatly strengthened those sectors of the elite sympathetic to neoliberalism and hostile to the social-democratic model.

International financial institutions also played an important role. The IMF provided Costa Rica with an emergency stand-by loan in 1982 (as well as several subsequent stabilization loans). The IMF's main role was to set macroeconomic targets, especially reducing inflation and the fiscal deficit. The methods included raising utility rates, reducing public-sector employment, and removing remaining obstacles to liberating interest rates and floating the colón. IMF targets became benchmarks for a system of cross-conditionality that governed negotiations with the World Bank, private creditors, and USAID. Importantly, however, the IMF's recommended austerity measures and the USAID windfall contributed to renewed growth and dramatic reductions in inflation and the fiscal deficit in 1983–1985.

Popular reactions to austerity and adjustment measures have, since the early 1980s, constituted a check on the efforts of international financial institutions (IFIs) and others to liberalize the economy and undermine the welfare state. In marked contrast to Kerala, in particular, grass-roots mobilizations have occurred without encouragement or direction from left-wing or other political parties, but have instead typically arisen from ad hoc community or sectorial organizations. In 1983, for example, huge electricity rate hikes sparked widespread indignation and massive protests that commenced in poor neighborhoods of San José. Eventually local committees joined in a national coordinating body and won temporary rate reductions and promises that customers who had refused to pay their bills would not have service cut off (Valverde, Marenco, and Soto 1985).

In 1985 and 1988, the World Bank made structural adjustment loans to Costa Rica.[10] These were contingent on being in compliance with IMF agreements and on a range of reforms, including measures to reorient industrial and agricultural production to non-Central American markets, tariff reductions, eventual elimination of subsidies for basic grains producers and for consumer prices of staple foods, continued mini-devaluations of the colón, reductions in the public sector's budget and workforce, and restructuring of the foreign debt. Grass-roots reactions were again intense, albeit short-lived, as large and small grain farmers staged demonstrations against cuts in agricultural support prices and credit programs (Edelman 1999).

As in other countries (e.g., Chile) where structural adjustment programs contributed to impoverishing significant sectors of the population, the World Bank in the late 1980s adopted an anti-poverty strategy based on short-term "social compensation" programs targeted at the poorest zones and social groups. With support from the Bank and other external sources, Costa Rican governments in the late 1980s and early 1990s established special housing construction and food-bond programs aimed at the poorest of the poor (Trejos París 1993). The proportion of poor households peaked at nearly one-third in 1991 before declining over the next three years to approximately one-fifth, a percentage that remained largely unchanged into 2003 (Proyecto Estado de la Nación 2005). When growth and redistribution effects are disaggregated, however, it is clear that reductions in poverty rates in the 1990s resulted more from the former than from the latter (Trejos Solórzano 2000, 544–45).

By the late 1980s and early 1990s, Costa Rica's economy and society had experienced a profound shift. As in Chile and Mauritius,

---

[10] A third structural adjustment agreement, the first to focus mainly on state reform rather than opening markets, called for dismissing 25,000 state employees and generated enormous controversy in the early and mid-1990s. Costa Rica's Legislative Assembly rejected the accord and the World Bank withdrew its support. The IDB, also a party to the agreement, eventually disbursed its part of the loan, but without the requirement that the public employees be fired (Clark 2001, 74–75; Raventós Vorst 2001, 373–74; Hidalgo Capitán 2003, 145–46).

nontraditional exports expanded at an impressive rate; taken as a whole, garments, seafood, ornamental plants, and food crops such as tubers, pineapples, melons, and macadamia and cashew nuts overtook the historical mainstays, coffee and bananas, as a source of foreign earnings. Tourism, much of it based on the country's successful effort to place approximately one-quarter of its territory in protected reserves and to sell itself as a "green republic," became the largest source of hard currency by 1993, topping coffee and bananas and even the fast-growing nontraditional export sector (Evans 1999; Honey 2003). This diversification of exports lessened Costa Rica's historical vulnerability to fluctuations in world coffee prices. It also generated large numbers of mostly low-wage jobs, while contributing to a feminization of the workforce, especially in the garment and tourism sectors (Tardanico and Lungo 1995, 240–44). Labor unions, particularly in the private sector, rapidly lost ground to employer-sponsored *solidarista* associations that, though they did provide workers with some benefits (e.g., housing loans, subsidized lunches, severance payments), also reorganized the labor market around individual, rather than collective, contracts. Nonetheless, continued state labor-market regulation made the situation of the working poor considerably less precarious than in Chile.

Other shifts contributed to reshaping social relations. Adjustment-related budget pressures on public institutions, in health care and education in particular, brought difficulties in service delivery and increasing reliance by middle-class and elite families on private medicine, primary and secondary schools, and universities. This deepened the cultural divide between the affluent and the working class and further eroded the broad support that public health care and education – and, more generally, the classic social-democratic model – had long enjoyed (Molina Jiménez 2002, 122–24). Opportunities in the tourist sector, as well as the arrival of cable television in the early 1980s, generated widespread interest in learning English, which intensified the allure of private bilingual schools and further opened the society to transnational cultural influences and consumption aspirations. The urban landscape, once heterogeneous in terms of class and zoning, increasingly assumed the geographically stratified pattern found elsewhere in the Americas, with gated communities and garish malls for the well-to-do and supermarkets and large chain businesses with ample parking lots replacing the small stores that earlier anchored the commercial and social life of towns and cities.

Nevertheless, the informal economy of impoverished street vendors and "microentrepreneurs" expanded less than in most Latin American countries – primarily because the number of low-wage jobs grew after the 1980–1982 crisis and state regulation of labor markets continued to discipline employers, albeit to a lesser degree (Tardanico and Lungo 1995; Itzigsohn 2000). A broader process of informalization, however, affected professionals and employees of small businesses, many of whom were reported as "self-employed" so as to avoid the higher payroll taxes employers pay for formal employees (Itzigsohn 2000, 80–81). Income distribution fluctuated within a narrow range for most of the 1990s and then worsened significantly in 1998–2001 (Proyecto Estado de la Nación 2002, 54, 93). In relative terms, the middle class lost ground during the 1990s, while the upper and lower classes gained income shares (Hidalgo Capitán 2003, 318).

Finally, the post-crisis period saw the emergence of a large immigrant underclass that carried out menial tasks that most Costa Ricans had become reluctant or unwilling to perform. Composed primarily of Nicaraguans, who came to constitute at least 7 percent and perhaps as much as 10 percent of the national population in 2000 (and a much larger proportion of the economically active population), this substantial group of low-wage, frequently undocumented, workers provided a subsidy for the living standards of the better-off Costa Ricans who hired them as farm and construction laborers, domestics, parking attendants, and guards (Morales and Castro 2002; Sandoval García 2002; Hidalgo Capitán 2003, 286). On the one hand, the Costa Rican economy's absorption of this large immigrant workforce was an indication of very considerable dynamism. The Nicaraguan presence also suggests, however, as is the case with the Afro-Creole minority in Mauritius or the large immigrant communities in western Europe, that the high living standards associated with the welfare state are sustained partly on the backs of those not participating fully in it.

Coping with globalization

By the early 1990s, within a decade of the crisis, Costa Rica was widely considered a neoliberal success story – misleadingly, as much of its "success" was a legacy of thirty years of social democracy (Edelman 1999, 3, 81–84). This section examines the ways in which the Costa Rican state's historical and ongoing involvement in social welfare and its half-hearted embrace of neoliberalism facilitated a new type of insertion in the global economy. It suggests that some aspects of both the social-democratic legacy and the more recent "reformed" welfare state were not only strikingly similar to one another but also provided significant advantages for success within a globalizing economy.

Half-hearted neoliberalism

Costa Rica moved quickly in the area of trade liberalization, but reform of the state has been gradual and remarkably piecemeal in comparison with the experiences of other Latin American countries (Rovira Mas 2000; Clark 2001; Hidalgo Capitán 2003). While traditional neoliberal prescriptions (including lowered tariffs, interest-rate liberalization, privatization, and public spending cuts) played some role in stabilizing and then reshaping the economy, a variety of non-market elements have arguably been of greater importance. These include massive US aid in the 1980s, preferential market access under the US Caribbean Basin Initiative, and continuing mini-devaluations of the colón. Some of the dynamism of the new model may be attributed to legacies of the social-democratic welfare state, notably the huge subsidies for exporters granted (until 2000) under the CATS tax credit program and the decision of many foreign investors to locate in Costa Rica because of its well-developed infrastructure and highly educated, healthy workforce. Beginning in the mid-1980s, exporters also received exemptions from taxes on raw materials, semi-processed goods, and machinery and equipment, as well as from those on income generated in export activities. Export-Processing Zones (*zonas francas*) provided export enterprises with these and other benefits, as well as streamlined customs inspections and complete exemption from taxes on assets and capital repatriation, and municipal assessments and licenses.

Thus, even in the period of neoliberal reform, state action continued to play a major role in Costa Rica's adaptation to the globalized economy. Yet, certain characteristics of the state and society also explain why the country's transformation has been so slow and incomplete. Some of the key reforms of the 1980s – such as the elimination of basic grains subsidies and the reduction of tariffs – only required executive decrees. Others – such as ending the monopoly of public-sector banks and the privatization of CODESA – were accomplished with enabling legislation. None of these "easy reforms" involved major budgetary outlays or new institutional structures. Moreover, during this period, Costa Rica's geopolitical position contributed to marked leniency on the part of the international financial institutions when, as frequently happened, the country missed macroeconomic targets (Clark 2001, 63, 70).

The situation in the 1990s and after was different. With the resolution of the wars in Central America, the stance of Washington and the financial institutions toward Costa Rica became less generous and forgiving. A succession of pro-neoliberal administrations made concerted efforts to deepen the privatization process, retrench large numbers of state employees, and "rationalize" other aspects of public administration. The results of these campaigns have not been very dramatic, however. A small number of public-sector enterprises underwent privatization, some agencies and government ministries were consolidated, private firms were permitted to generate (but not distribute) electrical energy, employees of the state insurance monopoly were allowed to sell policies as independent agents, and reforms of the pension, health, and education systems introduced new, market-like efficiency criteria (Clark 2001, 78–82; Hidalgo Capitán 2003, 274–83). Attempts to radically shrink the public payroll, however, met with little success; indeed, the number of public employees grew by 31.1 percent during 1980–2000, although public-sector employment as a proportion of total employment fell from 19.6 to 14.1 percent. In contrast to Chile, with its highly flexible employment regime, virtually nothing has occurred in Costa Rica in the area of labor-market reform (Hidalgo Capitán 2003, 203, 225–31). Meanwhile, public expenditures on key aspects of social welfare, including health and education, maintained or increased their size in relation to GDP and on a per capita basis.

Indeed, the most successful reforms of the second half of the 1990s, while often represented as being consonant with neoliberal doctrine, actually served to solidify welfare gains initiated during the "golden age" of 1949–1979. Pensions, education, and health care have been, in Costa Rica and elsewhere, central pillars of the developmental state. Recent reforms in these areas are notable in that they mix market, quasi-market, and state-directed modalities while maintaining or even increasing levels of public investment. Nevertheless, the impetus for the reforms has grown more out of elite concerns about efficiency, competitiveness, and macroeconomic balance than from the values of justice and equity that were fundamental to the social-democratic project and that underlie popular support for the developmental state.

Consider the reforms made to the social-security system (CCSS). It provides insurance for medical services, maternity, disability, old-age pensions, and death benefits for survivors. Since its founding in 1941, and especially after 1970, the proportion of the population covered under its programs has risen dramatically. However, as late as 2001, only slightly more than one-half of the economically active population was covered by the core CCSS insurance for disability, old age, and death (IVM); those excluded from IVM coverage are primarily independent and low-income informal-sector workers (Proyecto Estado de la Nación 2002, 105). Still, those not covered by IVM were nonetheless eligible for minimal support under the state-funded noncontributors' regime (Régimen No

Contributivo de Pensiones por Monto Básico). The reform of the social-security system that began in 1990 reaffirmed, at least formally, the principles of universality, equity, solidarity, and obligatory participation inscribed in the Costa Rican constitution and the CCSS charter (Martínez Franzoni and Mesa-Lago 2003). Real and anticipated financial imbalances, however, were more immediate concerns. Among the problems were an aging population (with a projected worker–retiree ratio of 3:1 in 2040 as compared with nearly 6:1 in 2001), employers' failure to make contributions to the system promptly and accurately, insufficient yields on CCSS investments (almost all of which were in Costa Rican government bonds), and a disproportion between the generosity of benefits and the small size of employee and employer contributions.

Post-1990 reforms rested on three pillars: (1) continued protection for the entire population under existing CCSS programs, with the state subsidizing the cost; (2) continued obligatory coverage for salaried workers, with the cost paid by employees, employers, and the state; and (3) additional pension coverage for the individual through voluntary – and private – plans to be regulated by a new supervisory agency. In addition, independent workers' payments for IVM coverage, which were voluntary until 2005, became obligatory. This change, the fruit of a broad societal consensus that followed a remarkably widespread consultation with diverse interest-group organizations, strengthened the system in a context of an aging population and increasing labor-force informalization.

Educational reforms of the late 1980s and 1990s obeyed a different dynamic. The crisis and subsequent adjustment programs of the 1980s caused a grave deterioration in the public-school system. By the end of the decade, President Oscar Arias, who had promised during his 1986 campaign to provide a computer for every school, initiated a series of measures, continued by his successors, to place public education on a sounder footing. A grant from USAID in 1988 and a World Bank–IDB loan package in 1993 permitted extensive investments in teacher training, school buildings, and equipment (Clark 2001, 98–99). A new education law in 1996 established a range of pedagogical and organizational objectives, such as limits on class size, two years of obligatory preschool, foreign-language and computer instruction for all students from preschool on, and a minimum of six hours of daily instruction. In 1997, a constitutional amendment required the government to allocate the equivalent of 6 percent of GDP to education, and while this target has not yet been met, education spending per capita did begin to climb significantly the year after the amendment.

The renewed emphasis on education reflected an awareness of the possibilities of a development model based on human capital investment and advanced technology (as well as foreign tourism). Preschool programs expanded enrollments, more than one-half of primary students received English instruction, and in-school computer access grew to 52 percent of primary students and 42 percent of secondary students by 1999 (Proyecto Estado de la Nación 2000, 80). A strategic alliance with Microsoft gained free Internet access for all schools (over lines provided by the state-run ICE) (Buitelaar, Padilla, and Urrutia-Álvarez 2000, 302). These improvements, however, did little to stem the flow of middle- and upper-class children into private schools.

The crisis and the adjustment programs of the 1980s also had a negative impact on health-care budgets and delivery, and led to reforms in this sector as well (Castro Valverde 1998, 16; Sáenz 1998, 83–87). Diseases such as dengue, malaria, cholera, and measles – which had been practically eliminated in the previous two decades – suddenly reappeared; infant-mortality rates climbed in outlying cantons (though not overall). In addition, long lines, deteriorating equipment, and complaints about errors in diagnosis and treatment in public clinics drove more affluent patients to private doctors who, unlike those in the public clinics, often provided them rapid admission to public hospitals.[11] The absence of a system of primary-care physicians (*médicos de cabecera*) to coordinate the growing use of specialists increased the burden on the hospital system (Sáenz 1998, 85). The reforms approved in the early to mid-1990s, with financial backing from the World Bank, involved a reorganization of the health-care system but continued, and in some respects deepened, the involvement of the state in this sector (Sojo 1998, 75).

In 2002, 86.8 percent of the population contributed, directly or indirectly through household members, to the CCSS health insurance fund, although the entire population was entitled to benefits (CCSS 2004). The reform initiated in the early 1990s involved: the transfer of local clinics and functionaries from the Health Ministry to the CCSS, a measure intended to eliminate redundancies in service provision and planning; new investments in equipment and personnel; and, most importantly, the division of the country into ninety health areas, each consisting of "segments" of 4,000–8,000 inhabitants attended by "integral care teams" (EBAIS). The EBAIS, which were first established in the poorest rural zones, delivered primary care but also implemented programs for disease

---

[11] The critical health-care situation led to the declaration of a national emergency in 1994, which permitted urgent actions to control dengue and malaria, develop vaccination campaigns, and strengthen primary care (Castro Valverde 1998, 18). In 1991–2000, private health-care expenditures grew from 26.4 percent to 31.5 percent of total health-care expenditures. The recent rise of private hospitals has reduced affluent Costa Ricans' stake in the public system (Martínez Franzoni and Mesa-Lago 2003).

prevention, health education, and community participation in the design and evaluation of services. Integral care programs focused on the specific issues of children, adolescents, women, adults, and the elderly, as well as health-related environmental and occupational safety concerns. Resources that used to be allocated only according to previous years' spending levels were now assigned according to a formula that takes into account past demand for services as well as productivity measures and a series of health and demographic indicators and delivery targets specific to each area (Carrera 1997, 210; Sojo 1998, 77–91).

The CCSS's new "quasi-market" reorganization sought to create contractual relationships or management commitments with explicit performance and productivity criteria that determined the allocation of resources to CCSS units; this involves a bureaucratic separation of the functions of collecting premiums, financing the system, and purchasing and providing services. In 1997, the state's payment of its longstanding debt to the CCSS contributed to placing the entire system on a firmer financial footing (Sojo 1998, 75–80). The "quasi-market" organization is, however, quite distinct from a pure market model in that the CCSS still accords priority to universal coverage and equitable distribution of resources, defined as "equal opportunities to access health services for users with equal needs" (Sojo 1998, 76).

Rather than a substitution of the state by the market, the pension, education, and health reforms of the 1990s suggest a complicated and evolving interrelationship of both modalities. This mix of state and market mechanisms is also central to what some have termed the "national innovation system" – that complex of public- and private-sector institutions that aims at the incorporation into the economy of new technologies, processes, and forms of organization (Buitelaar, Padilla, and Urrutia-Álvarez 2000). Beginning in the mid-1980s, numerous institutions – public and private – were founded to promote exports (for example, the USAID-supported Coalition for Development Initiatives, CINDE), to regulate technical and quality norms (the Technical Standards Institute, INTECO), to furnish technical support to industry (the Industrial Technical Assistance Unit, UATI), to provide managerial training (the Integrated Business Services System), and to encourage the use of the latest informatics advances in industry (the Center for Technical and Industrial Informatics Management, CEGESTI). Units and individual faculty at the four public universities, moreover, are increasingly involved in applied research and development, enterprise incubation, and private-sector consulting.

One high-profile achievement of this effort to enter the knowledge-based economy was the 1996 decision of microchip producer INTEL to locate a major production facility in Costa Rica. The country bested Brazil, Chile, Indonesia, Mexico, the Philippines, and Thailand in the competition to site the new US$300 million plant. According to the World Bank, while Costa Rica had various attractive features, the decisive factor was its educated labor force (World Bank 2003b, 5). Other studies indicate that the presence of high technology manufacturing and software firms not only attracted INTEL but provided the basis for a "cluster" of advanced components enterprises (Saca 1999, 64–68). CINDE played a key role in persuading INTEL to come to Costa Rica; the World Bank's Foreign Investment Advisory Service provided expertise on creating comparative advantage and representing it abroad, as well as suggestions for revising intellectual property laws and lists of companies to target for siting high-tech manufacturing and call-center facilities (FIAS 1996, B1–C2). Shortly after INTEL decided to come to Costa Rica, other high-tech and medical equipment firms, notably Microsoft and Abbot Laboratories, also opened production facilities; Procter and Gamble established a major global business center; and numerous call centers, some providing technical support and others Internet gambling, serviced customers from throughout the Americas (Rodríguez-Clare, 2001; Sánchez-Acochea, 2006).

INTEL's impact illustrates the advantages and the limitations of the high-tech strategy. In 1999, the last year of the high-tech boom, Costa Rica's GDP grew by 8.4 percent. If INTEL's output is excluded, however, GDP rose by barely 3 percent; more than half of the increased production that year was due to INTEL. In the same year, of the US$6.6 billion in exports, two-fifths were from INTEL (in most recent years, the proportion has been closer to one-fifth). For the first time in years, the country ran a trade surplus. Of INTEL's net commercial surplus of US$1.5 billion, approximately US$1.3 billion were repatriated. Thus the real "INTEL effect" on the economy consisted of about US$200 million in salaries, electricity, and locally purchased goods and services. Coffee, in contrast, generated US$300 million in local GDP, despite low international prices (Brenes 2001, 54–55). The company's high salaries have created upward pressure on wages for highly skilled employees, a plus for those who directly benefit but also a perversely negative impact in terms of Costa Rica's attraction to foreign investors.

With the end of the 1990s technology boom, INTEL's exports declined. The size of INTEL's investment in Costa Rica means that it is unlikely to depart, as a number of the more footloose garment *maquilas* have in recent years. However the expiration of certain tax concessions and looming bottlenecks in the supply of electricity and telephone lines have created uneasiness among some Costa Rican planners and the company's executives. INTEL's venture capital division has invested in a small number of Costa Rican high-technology firms (Cordero Pérez 2003), and the company has participated in a joint training program with one of the public universities and the public-sector vocational training institute (Instituto Nacional de Aprendizaje). Its production facility, however, has generated few horizontal or vertical linkages with local high-tech companies (Buitelaar, Padilla, and Urrutia-Álvarez 2000, 365–67).

Popular resistance to market-based reforms

Costa Rica's half-hearted embrace of neoliberal reform may be understood as part of a "political logic of social policy" deeply rooted in the political system and society (Rovira Mas 2000, 567). During the crisis of the early 1980s and the subsequent restructuring, the PLN (the traditional social-democratic party) adopted heterodox policies that included many elements of the neoliberal agenda. While severe divisions between social-democratic traditionalists and neoliberal "pragmatists" continued to divide the PLN, party ideologies and platforms manifested a marked sympathy with the "Third Way," understood in the Costa Rican context as something between the pre-1980 welfare state and the Chilean model. In 1995, for example, the PLN changed its charter to allow for privatization of public-sector monopolies (Clark 2001, 71).

The PLN's move toward the political center narrowed its differences with the Social Christian Unity Party (PUSC). Although the PUSC generally favored faster and more thoroughgoing economic liberalization, its roots in the Social Christian reformist tradition gave it continuing support among sectors of the working class and poor, as well as among some members of the political class who had been skeptical of the rush to the free market. This doctrinal convergence between the PLN and the PUSC, in a political system with a two-party tradition and a recent history of extremely close presidential elections, meant that neither party could afford to take measures that would alienate any significant sector of the electorate. Given the country's four-year electoral cycle, newly elected presidents have only a very brief window of opportunity to try to ram reforms through the Legislative Assembly before the onset of the next election campaign. In addition to the difficulties of having the assembly approve radical reforms, other checks in the political system, notably the Comptroller's Office and the constitutional court, sometimes blocked efforts to reform public-sector institutions along neoliberal lines.

In addition to these structural constraints, deep-seated opposition to the neoliberal agenda has stymied reform efforts and brought growing disillusionment with the political system. The public mood is evident in:

- Widespread backing for continuing public ownership of the telecommunications, electricity, insurance, and oil-refining monopolies, all of which have functioned with reasonable levels of efficiency and profitability, despite being targeted for privatization (Clark 2001; Seligson 2002).
- Continued public support for the nationalized banks which, despite increasing competition from private financial institutions and a scandal that closed one of the banks, actually have higher profitability levels than their private counterparts (Micco and Parizza 2005, 149).
- Anger at the frequent, costly corruption scandals, which have involved the plundering of public-sector enterprises and banks, kickbacks and influence peddling, drug trafficking, tax evasion, and fraudulent invoicing designed to capture export subsidies (Molina and Palmer 1998; González Ortega and Solís Avendaño 2001).
- Growing street crime and violence that threatens average citizens and is only infrequently dealt with effectively by the police and courts.
- A generalized, profound aversion to conflict (and an affinity for negotiation and compromise) and a continuing acceptance of the official pre-neoliberal statist discourse (Alvarenga Venutolo 2003, 175).

Although Costa Ricans do not live in a genuinely egalitarian society, many still express a visceral rejection of exaggerated social distance between individuals and strata (Rovira Mas 2000).

The erosion of the two-party system since the mid-1990s is one indication of this disillusionment with the direction the country has taken and has implications as well for the feasibility of approving neoliberal reforms. The number of parties fielding candidates in presidential elections rose from seven in 1994 to fifteen in 2002 and fourteen in 2006. While minor parties received 8 percent of the vote in 1998, they garnered 30 percent in 2002 (Ryan 2004, 88). In 2002, for the first time, the major party presidential candidates failed to receive sufficient votes to avoid a run-off election. Abstention has risen markedly, while public-opinion polls during the 1990s indicate significant declines in various aspects of overall system support (including national pride, trust in institutions, and belief that rights are protected). Costa Ricans, however, continue to express higher degrees of support for democracy than in other Latin American countries affected by crime, violence, and corruption (Seligson 2002).

This fragmentation of the two-party system is one manifestation of a political impasse between neoliberal elites and the statist citizenry that has also been evident in the strong, albeit sporadic, opposition to some of the reforms proposed during the past decade. Protests, which in the 1980s drew mainly on specific sectors affected by economic adjustment (public employees, small farmers), have grown since the mid-1990s to include a broader range of constituencies. In 1995, for example, a month-long strike and major protests occurred when the government of José María Figueres Olsen (son of former president José Figueres) attempted to close the teachers' pension fund, which provided more generous benefits (at greater cost to the state) than the social-security system. While Figueres Olsen ultimately succeeded in reforming the fund and moving most of its administration to the social-security system, the mobilization served notice that any related moves could have a high political cost (Clark 2001, 84; Alvarenga Venutolo 2003, 173–74). The following year, labor groups occupied the headquarters of the social-security system to protest projected changes in pension systems. This resulted in the suspension of the proposed reforms, the initiation of a broad process of public consultation culminating in the creation of a National Reconciliation Forum, and a series of ninety-six agreements that were incorporated into a new worker protection law (Martínez Franzoni and Mesa-Lago 2003). In 2000, weeks of road blockades and even larger demonstrations erupted throughout the country when the Legislative Assembly approved (in the first of three required debates) a measure to privatize the Costa Rican Electrical Institute (ICE) that distributes electricity and runs the telephone system (ICE's monopoly status is guaranteed in the constitution). Public fears included the possibility of higher electricity and telephone rates and corruption during the privatization process. But the movement, which enjoyed broad support and effectively stalled the privatization campaign, also invoked nationalist struggles dating to the early twentieth century, the identification of ICE with the nation, and the idea of an "authentic social democracy" (Solís 2002, 44; Alvarenga Venutolo 2003, 175).

More recently, in 2004, thousands of demonstrators marched to protest political corruption, the proposed Dominican Republic–Central American Free Trade Agreement (CAFTA), and the privatization of motor vehicle inspections – which aroused particular ire among truckers, who used their rigs to block major highways. Late in the year, two ex-presidents were in prison for receiving bribes related to CCSS medical equipment contracts or the privatization of the ICE's cellular telephone service (another ex-president living abroad was subpoenaed in the latter case). As has occurred elsewhere, the direct connection between corruption and privatization intensified skepticism about the sale of public-sector enterprises.

CAFTA represents the latest critical conjuncture, as yet unresolved, in the ongoing contention over Costa Rica's development path. Opposition to the accord built on earlier protests against the ICE privatization and resentment about high-level corruption. In negotiations leading up to this 2004 Agreement with the United States, Costa Rica acceded to US demands and promised to open its public-sector insurance and telecommunications monopolies to foreign competition. It also secured from US negotiators eleven side agreements intended to place specific agricultural and manufacturing sectors outside the treaty framework; this was nearly twice as many as any other Central American country and is indicative of the overall sophistication and doggedness of the Costa Rican negotiating team. Nonetheless, by late 2005, with CAFTA scheduled to enter into effect in 2006, Costa Rica had not yet ratified the agreement. If Costa Rica ratifies the accord, cellular and Internet services will have to permit foreign investment by 2006–2007, while some kinds of insurance will open immediately (with others being phased in between 2008–2011).

The Legislative Assembly received CAFTA for consideration as part of a package with a major fiscal reform act, a bill to make the ICE more competitive once the telecommunications sector is opened to foreign investors, and a US$370 million IDB Trade, Integration, and Competitiveness loan. Negotiated largely in secret by the executive branch, which represents it as providing a cushion for further opening the economy, the loan is contingent on the fiscal, customs, and spending reforms. The assembly may not amend the trade agreement and it also requires a two-thirds majority to ratify loans or constitutional changes, something increasingly complicated given the presence of more minority-party deputies in the legislature. These stringent ratification requirements, consistent public opposition, and constitutional protections for public-sector monopolies are all likely to slow approval of CAFTA and other neoliberal reforms, even though the IDB package contains ample resources for "consultations" intended to influence the outcome of the process (McElhinny et al. 2004, 21–22, 37). In the 2006 presidential election, former president and Nobel Peace Prizewinner Oscar Arias, running for the PLN on a pro-free-market platform, defeated a left-leaning anti-CAFTA opponent by just over 1 percent of the vote, suggesting that Costa Rica remains polarized and in a political impasse.

Conclusion

During the golden age of the social-democratic developmental state, Costa Rica was strongly identified with the Second International and, in years when the PLN controlled the executive, was an obligatory stop for European social democrats visiting Latin America. During the economic crisis of 1980–1982 and the subsequent restructuring, the PLN abandoned its defense of the large state and assumed elements of the Third-Way model. Costa Rica adopted an increasingly hybrid development model based on a major opening to world markets and a minimal degree of privatization and reform of its large state apparatus. The privatizations of the 1980s mainly involved jettisoning money-losing corporations. The reforms of the 1990s in many respects continued the country's tradition of state involvement in social welfare and contributed to maintaining its extraordinarily high levels of health and literacy.

The prospects for the Costa Rican welfare state are nonetheless worrisome. First, inequality has risen since the late 1990s, for two reasons: the benefits of the knowledge-based economy accrue disproportionately to a small number of high-income earners, and the market opening and piecemeal privatizations have provided unprecedented opportunities for illicit income of all kinds. Second, the fiscal basis of the state is weak, as a result of tax concessions to investors and widespread tax fraud (Lehoucq 1997, 8; González Ortega and Solís Avendaño 2001, 62). Taxes accounted for only 10.1 percent of GDP in 1980 and 13 percent in 2005, one of the lowest levels in Latin America, while in OECD countries they typically equal one-third of GDP. In Costa Rica, much of the fiscal burden consists of indirect taxes that fall disproportionately on lower-income sectors. The "fiscal pact" demanded by IDB would, if approved, generate more revenue, but it is unclear if this would compensate for reduced tariff income after CAFTA. While foreign debt restructuring during the 1980s and 1990s relieved much of the pressure from the international financial institutions, the ballooning internal debt and capital flight constitute additional sources of macroeconomic vulnerability. The public debt has reached US$9.8 billion or US$2,450 per capita – equivalent to about 60 percent of GDP and 250 percent of exports. Fifty percent of the government and public-sector budget is now borrowed, and debt service consumes 15 percent of exports (McElhinny et al. 2004, 21).

Yet Costa Rica's reformed welfare state has survived diverse neoliberal challenges for a generation, in an ongoing, arduous process of adaptation. This is no small achievement. It has required reinventing institutions and lives, compromising with cherished principles, and modifying expectations. The reformed welfare state exists in constant tension with political and market forces that erode public-sector institutions and the social solidarity on which they are based. Political contention shapes this tension and decides the outcomes at least as much as market forces, as the struggle against privatization of ICE in 2000 and against CAFTA in 2004 suggest.

Despite concerns about widespread symptoms of social malaise, Costa Rica clearly benefits from some unusual historical strengths, most of which derive in large measure from its social-democratic past and its contemporary reformed, yet still activist state.[12] Its high levels of human capital, dynamic export sectors, and demonstrated capacity to adapt effectively to rapidly changing circumstances will provide advantages even if public-sector enterprises face new levels of foreign competition. The solidity of democratic institutions and the rule of law are such that influential ex-presidents of the republic and other powerful figures have, in recent years, been charged with wrongdoing and successfully prosecuted. Even the political stalemate around further state reform and trade and investment liberalization, an impasse much decried by media commentators and elites, will likely assure that the cruelest aspects of market society are kept at bay and that changes in Costa Rica's admirable social system are piecemeal, incremental, and partial, giving the society ample time to adjust and defend itself.

---

[12] Worrisome symptoms of malaise include crime and violence, the emergence of a pervasive individualistic consumerism, differentiated "class cultures" (Molina Jiménez 2002, 121–30), and widespread clinical depression (González Ortega and Solís Avendaño 2001, 134).

5   Mauritius: evolution of a classic social democracy

In a region beset by ineffectual or predatory neopatrimonial rule, Mauritius stands out in contrast. Its postcolonial governments have pursued similar goals to those proclaimed in most African countries: economic growth, equity, national autonomy, and freedom. Its governments have also designed typical policies since 1968 to achieve these goals: a heavily interventionist state involving a myriad of regulations and controls, protected import-substitution industrialization, the establishment of an Export-Processing Zone, and gradual market liberalization (starting in the 1980s). However, in contrast to nearly all sub-Saharan countries, Mauritius has made steady progress in attaining its ambitious goals. This underdeveloped and racially stratified country has achieved not only sustained growth, but a degree of equity, a remarkable welfare state, and a consolidated democracy. Although the reasons for this success are diverse and contested (Subramanian and Roy 2003), that Mauritius has avoided economically debilitating neopatrimonial rule (see Sandbrook 2000, 17–19 and ch. 5) is of key importance. Instead, a social-democratic developmental state has boldly orchestrated strategic responses by private firms to changing market conditions for more than twenty years, in the process defying free-market orthodoxy.

Why has this activist state succeeded whereas others, attempting the same sort of strategy, have dismally failed? To promote equity with growth in a largely market economy, governments require not only a relatively substantial degree of autonomy from capital, but also sufficient bureaucratic capacity to design and implement market-conforming industrial and social policies. In addition, strong democratic institutions based on a vibrant civil society must develop. These institutions play a pivotal role, in motivating politicians to seek equitable socioeconomic development, providing the mechanisms for managing societal conflicts, and building consensus on a broad socioeconomic strategy. Unusual historical/structural conditions in Mauritius provided the foundations for this conjunction of democracy with a developmental state. Astute policy and farsighted leadership took advantage of these historical benefits, especially in the design of appropriate political institutions, the successful identification of niches within global markets, and the negotiation of favorable preferential trade arrangements. The current phasing out of preferential trade arrangements, in tandem with WTO agreements constraining a state's ability to pursue an industrial strategy, challenges this development model.

Mauritius has achieved remarkable economic, social, and political progress since the early 1980s. It is, however, an improbable success story. The next section sketches this story, before turning to the explanation and evolution of this classic social democracy.

An improbable success story

Mauritius in the 1970s shared several of the problems and trends that characterized most African countries. It did not seem predestined for the unusual achievements that followed. First, like others in this region, this small country of 1.2 million endured a history of servile labor, extreme racial inequality, and a monocultural economy. France, which controlled the island until 1810, forged a colonial society in which a small French oligarchy exploited African slaves on their extensive landholdings. When the British took over, they employed incentives to convert these mixed estates into sugar plantations. The new colonial power abolished slavery in 1835 but replaced the slaves with indentured laborers from South Asia, a system that continued until 1910. In the 1860s, Mauritius briefly emerged as the leading cane producer in the British Empire. At independence in 1968, sugar production occupied 94 percent of all cultivated land, and accounted for 93 percent of the country's exports. Nineteen large plantations dominated the sugar industry.

Second, Mauritius at independence suffered the rapid population growth and high unemployment that bedeviled other countries in the region. At an annual rate of 3 percent in the 1960s and 1970s, the country's population grew at about the norm. Unemployment ranged as high as 20 percent between independence and 1982 (Darga 1996, 80). While the expanded educational system generated increasing numbers of graduates in the 1970s and early 1980s, many of the jobs that were available were unskilled, poorly paid, and seasonal. Unemployed, well-educated young people rallied to the militantly socialist, class-oriented Mouvement Militant Mauricien (MMM), formed in the revolutionary atmosphere of the late 1960s. In desperation, the government created an agency in the 1970s to facilitate emigration (Gulhati and Nallari 1990, 95).

Third, Mauritius was typical in its reliance on extensive state intervention into economic life, and in its need to undertake structural adjustment to deal with an economic crisis in the early 1980s. The first postcolonial government controlled the exchange rate and capital exports, set nominal interest rates, established parastatals to promote its social and economic goals, imposed an export tax on sugar, subsidized basic foods, mounted public works projects to absorb the unemployed, invested in free public health and education facilities, and provided substantial protection for firms producing for the home market (Gulhati and Nallari 1990, 11–17). Where the government diverged from the African norm was in its promotion of manufactured exports – by means of a set of incentives and astute management of the exchange rate – at the same time that it encouraged import-substitution industrialization. It established an Export-Processing Zone in 1970. Revenues from sugar exports were used to diversify and industrialize the economy, as well as support an expanding welfare state.

Mauritius, like most other African and Latin American countries, suffered an economic crisis in the 1970s. Although the government addressed the crisis before it became as acute as elsewhere, the economy nonetheless exhibited these common symptoms: a decline in the terms of trade, a worsening of the balance of payments, a tripling of the external debt throughout the 1970s, a reduction in output, high unemployment, and persistent inflation. The roots of the crisis are also familiar. The government was unable or unwilling to reduce entitlements – subsidies, pensions, free schooling and medical care – to balance the decline in revenues resulting from two hikes in the price of oil, a world recession, a drop in sugar prices, and a series of cyclones and droughts that devastated sugar harvests. Unremitting pressure exerted by trade unions and a radical opposition party (the MMM) dissuaded the government from adopting an early austerity program.

Between 1979 and 1985, Mauritius carried through a series of stabilization and adjustment programs with loans from the IMF and the World Bank. These programs combined orthodox measures (devaluation, demand reduction, cuts in subsidies, reduction in government spending) with some unorthodox (non-market) policies, such as continued import controls and job security provisions, food subsidies, export taxes, and a refusal to end free education and health care.[1] These measures were unusually successful: by 1983, Mauritius was well on the way to recovery.

Fourth, Mauritius is similar to many African countries in its extreme cultural diversity (Miles 1999). Hindus comprise just over half of the population (52 percent). Most Hindus are the progeny of 294,000 indentured

---

[1] It is likely that the international financial institutions countenanced these heterodox measures as a way of defusing the radical threat from the MMM.

laborers who were recruited from the Indian subcontinent to work on the sugar plantations, and then remained on the island (see Allen 1999, 16–28). But Hindus do not constitute a unified voting bloc; they are divided by caste and regional/linguistic origins. Hindus predominate in the public service and some professions, and are heavily engaged in agriculture as laborers and small planters. Muslims, also the descendants of indentured laborers, form about a sixth of the population. They are mainly involved in commerce in the towns and cities. Descendants of slaves, the Creoles account for 27 percent of Mauritians. Darker-skinned Creoles (often referred to as Afro-Creoles) constitute the bulk of this category. Afro-Creoles are disproportionately represented in low-paid, low-status employment, especially in the towns, and reside disproportionately in impoverished neighborhoods (Laville 2000). A small minority of light-skinned Creoles form an educated and prosperous elite. Having embraced the language, religion, and culture of the white property owners, these Creoles have succeeded in the professions and private firms. The Chinese, though few in number (2–3 percent of the population), are economically influential as entrepreneurs and shopkeepers. Finally, Franco-Mauritians, a tiny but wealthy minority, have diversified from sugar-cane production into manufacturing, tourism, and financial and business services.

Mauritians, like others in Africa, tend to divide politically by ethnicity and religion, though in this country ethnicity, religion, and class overlap. Several instances of communal violence marred the transition to the island's independence, just as "tribalism" marred decolonization in many mainland African countries. British troops intervened to quell Hindu–Creole clashes and Creole rioting in 1964–1965 and Creole–Muslim riots just six weeks before independence in 1968. The emergent country seemed headed for communal disaster. Confounding expectations, however, the country maintained social harmony for twenty-one years – until three days of unnerving riots and looting spearheaded by the Afro-Creole underclass in February 1999.

Yet, despite these all-too-familiar circumstances, Mauritius has made rapid advances while other countries have languished. From 1982 to 2004, the economy expanded by an average of almost 6 percent per annum – albeit with periodic downturns instigated by severe cyclones or droughts. Mauritius experienced a downturn in 2002, with real GDP growth of only 1.8 percent, though the rate rebounded to between 4 and 5 percent in 2003 and 2004 (Mauritius Chamber of Commerce and Industry, 2006). With annual population growth at a low 1.2 percent, the average annual increase of real per capita GDP has been over 4 percent. Real income in Mauritius more than doubled in twenty years – to almost

$3,900 per capita in 2002, whereas the comparable figure for sub-Saharan Africa as a whole was $451 (purchasing power parity figures are much higher in both cases – World Bank 2004a). Moreover, growth has been accompanied by considerable diversification, especially into manufacturing industries and high-end tourism, offshore banking and business services, including freeport services, and information and communications technology. Mauritian firms have even begun to invest in other African countries – textile and clothing manufacturing in Madagascar, sugar estates and factories in Mozambique, and joint ventures in information technology in Namibia and elsewhere. Although Mauritius has not matched East Asia's performance, its record has surpassed those of all other African countries except Botswana.

Substantial social equity has accompanied this economic success. One indicator of the relative well-being of national populations is the United Nations Development Programme's annual ranking of countries according to a composite score, the Human Development Index. Mauritius in recent years has ranked first or second among African countries on this index, thanks to its extensive welfare state. Life expectancy, adult literacy, school enrollment, and infant mortality rates approach those of the industrial countries, and place Mauritius at or near the top in sub-Saharan Africa. Also, income inequality has diminished since independence. The Gini coefficient (where 1 signifies perfect inequality in income distribution, and 0 perfect equality) fell from 0.5 in 1962 to 0.37 in the mid-1980s, where it has remained, with minor oscillations, ever since.[2] Nonetheless, wealth remains concentrated, with 1 percent of the population, mostly whites, owning just over half of the land under cane cultivation and about 65 percent of the stock of productive assets (Mistry 1999, 554). Were it not for the tax-supported welfare state – with social spending accounting for 40 percent of public expenditures – this concentration of wealth might well have sabotaged democracy.[3]

Indeed, the welfare state commands such overwhelming public support that politicians tamper with entitlements at their electoral peril.[4] Public pensions, originating in the 1950s, were expanded into a comprehensive scheme on the eve of the hard-fought 1976 election. This scheme included a universal Basic Retirement Pension (BRP) at age

---

[2] For example, a household budget survey (2001/2002) records the Gini at 0.371, down from 0.387 in 1996/97. See Mauritius Central Statistical Office 2002b.

[3] That the state has actually been able to collect taxes from the wealthy distinguishes Mauritius from most other countries in the region.

[4] A massive opinion poll in 2002 discovered that 88 percent of respondents proposed that government spend more on social security, and 78 percent recommended that government raise taxes on the rich to redistribute income to the poor (Centre for Applied Social Research 2003, 109).

sixty (the equivalent of about \$70 per month in early 2005), together with pensions for widows, invalids, and orphans. For workers, a National Pension Scheme, based on compulsory contributions from employers and employees, complements the basic pension. When the government announced in late 2004 its intention to restrict the Basic Retirement Pension to those whose regular pension was less than Rupees 17,333 (\$630) per month, it was widely denounced as a stooge of the IMF (*L'Express* [Port-Louis] September 23, 2004). Primary schooling, which has been free since colonial days, became compulsory in 1993. Governments extended free schooling to the secondary level in 1976, and to the tertiary level in 1988. The University of Mauritius, built just before independence, features a modern and well-maintained campus and an enviable student–teacher ratio.

Comprehensive and free medical care is a major and cherished legacy of the country's first prime minister (and medical doctor), Sir Seewoosegur Ramgoolam. In the 1970s and 1980s, government built health centers so that no citizen would be more than three miles from primary health care. Currently, 63 percent of medical doctors work in the public sector, with the remainder in private clinics where the price of services is publicly regulated (Mauritius, Ministry of Health and Quality of Life 2001). The state has achieved remarkable success in controlling communicable diseases – through the provision of clean water to all, the extension of a sewerage system begun in 1959, immunization campaigns, and the continuation of an anti-malaria campaign introduced by the colonial government in the 1940s. Continuing subsidies of basic foodstuffs (white rice and flour) further improve overall health statistics by reducing malnutrition.

Other effectively administered public programs target particular disadvantaged groups. A Central Housing Authority started to build housing estates following a devastating cyclone in 1960. The Mauritius Housing Corporation (MHC) has extended housing loans to middle-class families since 1963. Since the 1980s, the MHC has assisted low-income families in purchasing a house by means of subsidized loans and grants. Widespread house ownership provides most people with a stake in the system.

There are also several targeted anti-poverty programs that respond, in some measure, to the needs of those bypassed by the miracle.[5] A Presidential Educational Trust provides financial help to children in "deprived" areas from the age of three. A Trust Fund for the Social Integration of

---

[5] Because there is not an official or widely accepted poverty line in Mauritius, one cannot accurately estimate the poverty rate. Scattered shantytowns, especially on the outskirts of Port-Louis, attest to the persistence of poverty, however. Informed Mauritian academics suggest that about one-fifth of the population would be considered poor according to any realistic measure.

Vulnerable Groups, established in 1998, finances community development projects, micro-credit schemes, loans to needy students, and free school meals. It had disbursed Rupees 107 million (US$3.7 million) by early 2003. The European Union has provided the bulk of the funding (US$4 million) to A Nou Diboute Ensam (ANDE) since 1999, which acts as a funding agency to support microenterprises and community projects run by local NGOs. The state also provides social assistance to households whose income falls below a basic level as a result of natural disaster, loss of employment, or abandonment by the breadwinner. Although critics charge that applying for this benefit is complex and humiliating, such schemes do not even exist elsewhere in the region.

Finally, the government mounts employment and training schemes – schemes whose importance has grown along with the unemployment rate (close to 10 percent by 2002) (see Mauritius, Central Statistics Office 2003, Table 5). These schemes upgrade skills, train people for employment in specific industries, and provide paid job experience to unemployed university and college graduates. Various subsidies and services also promote small and medium enterprises, which employ about 30 percent of the labor force.

In addition, governments have used a centralized and highly regulated industrial relations system both to enhance the security and well-being of most employees and to control labor. Alarmed by wildcat strikes instigated by the Marxist-Leninist Mouvement Militant Mauricien in 1974, a moderately social-democratic Labour government enacted a draconian Industrial Relations Act (IRA) in the midst of a state of emergency. This act has made it difficult for unions to stage a legal strike, a situation that the amended IRA of 2003 did not change. The prime minister can declare even a legal strike unlawful for sixty days if, in his opinion, the work stoppage "will imperil the national economy" (article 92). The labor minister may also submit disputes to conciliation and arbitration tribunals under various circumstances. The decisions of such tribunals are supposed to take into account national competitiveness and productivity, as well as the issues in dispute. Various acts also exempt employers in the Export-Processing Zone (EPZ) from regulations concerning overtime, maternity allowance, holiday work, night work for women, and termination of employment.[6] Nevertheless, the industrial relations machinery has delivered important benefits to labor. This machinery, through union–employer–government deliberations (in a Tripartite Committee) and various labor tribunals, balances remuneration to workers with such considerations as improving productivity and checking inflation. A National

[6] At its height in the early 1990s, the EPZ employed almost one-third of the labor force.

Remuneration Board recommends minimum wages and minimum terms and conditions of service for various private industries. A Permanent Arbitration Tribunal imposes settlements where the parties to a dispute are not engaged in serious negotiations. Within the public sector, another arbitration tribunal resolves disputes and a National Remuneration Board recommends periodic salary increases. Finally, non-EPZ employers are legally required to justify layoffs to a Termination of Contracts and Services Board on economic grounds – and compensate laid-off workers – before they can declare workers redundant. The IMF regularly condemns this job protection as counterproductive "rigidities" in labor markets (see, e.g., IMF 2002, 19).

The Mauritian model comprises political, as well as economic and social, facets. True, the early years were not propitious: a state of emergency in 1971 and postponement of the first postcolonial election (by four years). Nevertheless, Mauritius has not deviated from the democratic path since the delayed election in 1976 (in which a chastened MMM adopted the "electoral road" to power).[7] The country has experienced seven hotly contested national elections, all of which observers deemed free, fair, and orderly, and four of which led to peaceful changes of government. Despite flaws (periodic corruption and nepotism, occasionally unstable coalitions), democracy in Mauritius has consolidated itself to a degree that is unique in Africa.

However, two darker aspects of the record must also be mentioned. First, Afro-Creoles, about a quarter of the population, have not shared equally in the rising prosperity. Stereotypes depict them "as a present-oriented people, who cannot save money and have a natural propensity for alcohol" (Laville 2000, 281). A range of subtle biases in the educational system, especially the importance placed on a mastery of English, impede Afro-Creoles in attaining the higher education and training needed to escape the unskilled and semi-skilled positions they predominantly hold (Bunwaree 2001). Politically, too, Afro-Creoles face hurdles in making their voices heard. Whereas other ethnic groups field their own associations to press their interests, Creoles have historically joined Roman Catholic associations – and rarely fill leadership positions (Laville 2000, 286). In addition, few black Creoles have sat in Parliament, where they might voice the aspirations and frustrations of this group. The result has been growing ethnic/class tensions, which exploded in three days of rioting in 1999.

Second, gender inequality persists in Mauritius (see Thacoor-Sidaya 1998; Bunwaree 1999). Until recently, the country harbored a traditional,

---

[7] For a historical review, see Srebrnik 2002.

patriarchal society (or congeries of societies). Much has changed in the past twenty years, especially as a result of the academic success of women within a free educational system based on competitive examinations. However, women are still found disproportionately in the lowest paid, least skilled, most insecure jobs. At least two-thirds of those employed in the EPZ, whose firms are exempt from many of the country's labor protections and wage requirements, are women (Liang Lung Chong 1998; Uppiah 2000). With the decline of many EPZ firms since the mid-1990s, female unemployment has soared.[8] And if Mauritian female employees are disadvantaged, female guest workers suffer even more. To reduce costs, EPZ firms have replaced local employees with 17,000 guest workers, overwhelmingly female, from China and South Asia. Periodic reports deplore the working and living conditions endured by these guest workers (Mauritius Research Council 1999, ch. 6).

So Mauritius is not a paradise. It has, however, attained notable social achievements: a broadly based (albeit not inclusive) prosperity, a wide range of free public services and benefits, safety nets targeting vulnerable groups, the rule of law, and a vibrant and democratic political system. These rare accomplishments derive, in large measure, from an effective developmental state.

Explaining success

Although conjunctural factors such as astute policy, good leadership, and preferential trade arrangements contributed to Mauritius's success, historical/structural ones created the foundations for a democratic developmental state able to take advantage of opportunities. In particular, three unusual structural conditions have facilitated the emergence of such a state.

First, Mauritius emerged at the beginning of colonial rule as a capitalist social formation, in which land and labor were treated as commodities. That Mauritius was uninhabited when the Dutch occupied it in the seventeenth century is key to understanding its unusual class structure. No potentially reactionary pre-capitalist classes – a landed aristocracy or poor peasantry – survived into the nineteenth and twentieth centuries, as they did elsewhere. Whereas other countries of the region comprised largely peasant societies that were inclined to clientelism and personal rule, Mauritius developed a powerful mercantile and agrarian bourgeoisie, a large class of small landowners and merchants, and a rural and urban

---

[8] In 2002, overall unemployment approached 9 percent, whereas female unemployment exceeded 13 percent.

proletariat. This class structure facilitated the formation of a disciplined capitalist state, while opening the possibility of an eventual social-democratic class compromise.

An independent bourgeoisie emerged under French rule, with its roots in commerce and estate agriculture (see Allen 1999). This class transformed itself into a plantocracy when the British promoted Mauritius as a sugar colony following its takeover; its members depended largely on local resources to expand their holdings and productivity (Allen 1999). (Foreign-owned plantations were few in this remote colony.) Local capital accumulation continued in the postcolonial era, when state incentives channeled the plantocracy's surplus into the EPZ and, to a lesser degree, tourism and business services.[9] Its cohesion enhanced by French culture, Catholic religion, and intermarriage, the business class remains well organized and powerful.

Labor, in contrast, has rarely acted as a united force. From the start, labor in the form of slaves and indentured workers was treated as a commodity. But a class-in-itself did not become a class-for-itself. With the end of the indentured labor system in the 1920s, unions emerged to cater to the interests of a rural and urban proletariat (dockworkers and transport workers were particularly well organized). However, only in the late 1930s and early 1940s, in the context of general strikes and the formation of militant unions, and again in 1971–1974 at the height of MMM's radical class appeal, did unions unite across ethnic lines to advance common interests (Oodiah 1991; Gokhool 1999). Otherwise, ethnic rivalries and suspicions pitted the largely Hindu agricultural workers against the largely Afro-Creole urban workers. Labor legislation, by encouraging the proliferation of small, weak unions and restricting labor's right to strike, further undercut labor's power.[10] Ironically, the weakness of the working class has allowed moderate social-democratic governments to reassure capital, an important configurational factor that facilitated class compromise.

A variegated petty bourgeoisie also emerged in the nineteenth century. One fraction was composed of an educated and mainly Creole commercial and bureaucratic class ("les gens de couleur") that remains prominent today. Another, much larger, fraction was a Hindu yeomanry who purchased cane land, beginning in the 1870s, from Franco-Mauritian plantation-owners forced to retrench in hard times. By 2002, almost

---

[9] About half of the total equity of firms in the EPZ is owned by Mauritians – which is a high level of local ownership even in comparison with South Korea and Malaysia. See Subramanian and Roy 2003.

[10] More than 300 registered unions existed in the 1990s, some with as few as ten to fifteen members (Khoodabux 2000, 99).

90 percent of the arable land was devoted to sugar cultivation, and small planters owned nearly half of this total. (Seventeen large firms own the remaining cane fields, together with the sugar mills.) The 35,000 independent growers – whose families account for about 15 percent of the population – own plots as large as 400 hectares, though 90 percent of the holdings are two hectares or less.[11] The larger of these independent farmers, by investing in their children's education, had engendered by the 1940s (together with government scholarships) a substantial Hindu professional and bureaucratic class that competed with the Creole elite for jobs in the colonial bureaucracy.[12] Muslim store-owners and Chinese entrepreneurs formed further ethnic fragments of the small-scale, and later, large-scale business class.

Second, the complex overlap of class and ethnic divisions facilitated a social-democratic compromise by separating economic from political power. At independence, economic power resided in the hands of a small Franco-Mauritian and Creole elite who owned and ran the sugar plantations. The colonial state depended upon sugar revenues, yet British governors had rarely identified with the French-speaking elite who held them at arm's length. Meanwhile, the educated offspring of the predominantly Hindu small planters, facing exclusion from the upper echelons of the sugar industry, sought advancement through the colonial state and independence movements, especially the Mauritius Labour Party (MLP – formed in 1936). Politics and the state provided the majority Hindus with a way of countering the economic power of the plantocracy. Democratic politics would empower the Hindus in particular, for leaders could tap the support of the majority whose hostility to the plantocracy ran deep – a hostility deriving from a harsh history, from the fact that most small planters had family members who worked seasonally on the large plantations, and from an exclusionary and stratified racial system. The state, through its top posts and control of contracts, offered an alternative route to economic success. Although the plantocracy and Creole elite opposed independence and majority rule for fear of Hindu domination, the British nonetheless transferred power to a largely Hindu leadership in 1968.

The local capitalists who chose to remain in Mauritius (at least half) accepted an implicit bargain in the early 1970s. They yielded their political dominance and accepted some redistribution from growth in exchange

---

[11] These statistics on landownership are drawn from Mauritius, Ministry of Environment 2002. Tea cultivation, with 680 hectares under cultivation in 2002, is overwhelmingly a smallholder crop, with only one of 1,350 planters cultivating more than 100 hectares. See the *Digest of Agricultural Statistics* at http://www.statsmauritius.gov.mu/report/natacc/agric02.

[12] This interpretation draws on Houbert 1982–1983; Darga 1996; and Allen 1999.

for the legitimacy that a modest social-democracy would generate – provided social reform excluded exorbitant taxes or asset redistribution. Just as the 1948 civil war in Costa Rica laid the basis for social democracy through the defeat of left-wing radicalism, so the Labour government's defeat of radical tendencies in the early 1970s – through the state of emergency, detaining of militants, and Industrial Relations Act – constituted the same sort of critical juncture. This era's tacit compromise has prevailed ever since; even the militant MMM accepted the consensus in 1982 when it entered a coalition government.[13] Fabian-socialist ideas, imbibed during lengthy stays in Britain, have united the leaders of the major parties, providing the ideological basis for a classic social democracy that drew support from the descendants of slaves and indentured laborers.

Third, the patterns of governance established under British rule built the foundations of a postcolonial democratic-developmental state. Actually, the directive, developmental stance of this postcolonial state traces its origins to the first decades of British rule in the nineteenth century. Although the colonial state never pre-empted market forces, it did forcefully intervene to mold these forces in accordance with a plan. The British orchestrated the transformation of Mauritius from the middle of the nineteenth century into a plantation economy based on sugar. The colonial power provided a range of incentives to planters, mobilized investment capital as needed, built the infrastructure of roads, railway, and port facilities, amended the legal code to establish limited-liability companies, and created a reliable labor force through the indentured labor system (Reddi 1997, 2–6). The strategy succeeded, establishing a tradition of an activist capitalist state.

But a developmental state, to be developmental, must be effective. Effective states are those whose executive commands broad political authority, as well as a disciplined and expert bureaucracy. Whereas other African states have disintegrated since independence, the Mauritian state has remained coherent and strong. Its authority and administrative capacity derive from an unusual colonial experience.[14] Political conditions in the colony pushed the British authorities to extend political rights, establish direct rule through an extensive bureaucracy, and open this bureaucracy to local talent at a much earlier stage than in other colonies.

---

[13] This interpretation draws on Seegobin and Collen 1977; Houbert 1982–1983; Meisenhelder 1999.

[14] Kohli (2004), in a major comparative study, contends that the colonial experience is generally crucial in the formation of developmental states ("cohesive capitalist states") in late developers.

In particular, tensions between the French plantocracy and British colonial officials motivated the latter to secure the support of local allies through legal and constitutional reform. The British legal system, introduced in the 1830s, accorded a "technical equality" to all people, regardless of race. On many occasions in the nineteenth century, British judges ruled in favor of Indian indentured laborers in disputes with their employers (Reddi 1997, 9). Also, the colonial authorities tried to limit the Franco-Mauritian oligarchy's influence and maximize their own, by extending political rights, first to educated Creoles ("Coloureds") and, in 1885, to literate Indians. The oligarchy's demand for retrocession to France, following World War I, accelerated this process. Although the era of mass politics dates only from the formation of the MLP in 1936 and the extensions of representative government in 1948 and 1959, the Indian vote had become significant in Legislative Council elections as early as 1921. Indians already formed 31 percent of the electorate (Reddi 1989, 10). Even those denied the franchise avidly followed political debates and attended campaign rallies from this early date (interview, S. Reddi, Réduit, May 16, 2003).

Equally conducive to democratic consolidation was the development of a robust, if ethnically fragmented, civil society during colonial rule. British rule accustomed people to a free press, in addition to regular elections and the rule of law (Reddi 1989; Dukhira 2002, 42). General strikes in 1937, 1938, and 1943, and the organization of trade unions, announced the arrival of the working class upon the historical stage. It was to play an important role in pushing politics to the left in the revolutionary era of the early 1970s. In addition, the hardy cooperative movement that exists today traces its roots to 1913–1915. Fifteen cooperative credit societies emerged in that period under the tutelage of an expert contracted by the colonial government. By 1932, 2,100 members belonged to twenty-eight of these credit societies, most catering to small planters. The postwar period saw an upsurge in cooperatives and their extension to workers, civil servants, entrepreneurs, consumers, and fishermen, as both the colonial and postcolonial governments fostered their growth through advisors, training, and conducive legislation. By the year 2000, more than one-tenth of the population (156,000 people) belonged to 563 cooperative societies.[15] The island's tightly knit communities have also spawned a variety of other civil associations over the years. The umbrella body of NGOs, the Mauritius Council of Social Services, estimated that 5,000 voluntary organizations operated in the country in 2000, though only

---

[15] This information is drawn from Mauritius, Ministry of Commerce and Co-operatives 2003.

about 300 were well-structured and permanent organizations (interview, Ram Nookadee, Mauritius Council of Social Services, 2003). These trends help explain the unusual vitality of democracy in Mauritius. And, with governments based on consent, political rulers have eschewed a standing army – thereby avoiding the debilitating military coups afflicting other African countries.

Bureaucratic independence, discipline, and élan – without which a developmental state would collapse into ineffectiveness and corruption – also emerged from unusual colonial circumstances.[16] Not only was this colonial state exceptionally well articulated, but also it employed a much higher proportion of indigenous personnel than elsewhere in the region. The absence of traditional political institutions left the British with no choice except direct rule through its own employees. The extensive nature of the colonial state prepared the ground for its developmental role; it had "four times the per capita state revenues, three times the number of police officers per capita, and ten times the number of magistrates and cases per capita" than other British colonial states in Africa (Lange 2003, 404). It also relied heavily on local employees. Even in the 1920s, Mauritians accounted for 93 per cent of employees in the civil service, police, and judiciary, though Britons still filled the top positions. However, by 1932, 65 percent of officer-level positions were held by Mauritians (Lange 2003, 404). Indians entered the civil service as clerks in the 1920s, but discriminatory practices limited their rise into the higher posts However, after 1936, the colonial authorities had to compete for the support of Creoles ("Coloureds") and Indians against the militant MLP. It did so partly by opening up opportunities for them in the public sector. The British fostered a local intelligentsia by awarding university scholarships to the top secondary school graduates – the number of annual scholarships eventually rising to twenty. The Indians and Creoles who won most of these scholarships would typically join the civil service or judiciary upon their return from Britain. It was members of this meritocratic elite who moved ahead as the public sector expanded after 1948 with the extensions of public education, health care, and welfare services. Hence, career bureaucrats developed an *esprit de corps* and managerial tradition decades before independence.

Meritocracy has continued, as the public service has resisted the politicization plaguing other countries in the region (Carroll and Joypaul 1993, 434). An independent Public Service Commission, whose five members are appointed by the figurehead president of the republic in consultation

---

[16] This paragraph draws on the extensive historical research of S. Reddi, interview, May 19, 2003 and M. Lange 2003.

with both the prime minister and the leader of the opposition, retains its constitutionally prescribed independence. The commission oversees recruitment, promotion, and disciplinary action within the public service. Although informed Mauritians acknowledge that civil servants are not immune to ethnic biases and corruption, the service retains considerable integrity. Public-sector employment continues to attract well-qualified applicants. In a country with limited secure employment, jobs that offer guaranteed employment with good benefits remain highly valued. Hence, as two informed analysts conclude: "Mauritius has a senior public service which seems to be as competent, as ethical, and as committed to the goal of service to the public, as any public bureaucracy in the developed countries" (Carroll and Carroll 1999a, 187–88).

This brief historical excursion answers the conundrum of why Mauritius has developed an effective democratic developmental state whereas most other African countries have not. Mauritius has benefited from unusually favorable historical conditions. In addition, small size may facilitate the developmental state's task of micro-managing the economy.

But the Mauritian success is not simply the inevitable outcome of structural factors. Mauritians made history, though not under circumstances of their own choosing. In particular, political leaders designed postcolonial institutions that fostered social cohesion and consensus on broad policy directions.[17] The first prime minister, Sir Seewoosegur Ramgoolam (1968–1982), adopted a conciliatory, non-communalistic, and issue-oriented approach to politics. He rejected a communal appeal to the Hindu majority (52 percent of the population), partly because his Labour Party had originated as a trans-ethnic, anti-colonial movement and partly because the Hindus were too riven by caste and regional loyalties to respond readily to such an appeal (see Teelock 2001, 378–82, 391–96). Consensus also rested on the leaders' social-democratic outlook – an outlook that resonated with the popular yearning for equity in this racially stratified former sugar colony. Mauritius thus avoided the familiar cul-de-sac of many African countries: authoritarian leadership and acute ethnic conflict.

Institutional arrangements systematically undercut communalism. First, the independence constitution mandates an electoral system that encourages all major parties to nominate candidates from minority as well as majority communities. The main island is divided into twenty constituencies of three members each, while Rodrigues (the second island of Mauritius) encompasses a single two-member constituency. These multi-member constituencies penalize parties that appeal exclusively to a

---

[17] A fine study emphasizing the importance of institutional design is Brautigam 1999.

single ethnic group; other ethnic communities will respond by boycotting the latter's candidates to elect their own favorite son in one of the three slots. Second, the so-called "best losers" system reassured all communities, when this was important during the first decade of independence, that they would not be deprived of representation (Mathur 1997). An independent electoral commission appoints up to eight losing candidates to each new National Assembly to represent "underrepresented" ethnic groups.

A third innovation is an inclusive party system. Before independence, most parties had a distinct ethnic basis: Creoles, Muslims, and Hindus each dominated their own party or parties. However, caste, regional, and personal divisions among Hindus undercut their ability to use their majority status to impose Hindu domination of political life. Ramgoolam, after assuming leadership in 1956, continued to recruit candidates for the Labour Party[18] from all communities. Other parties, sooner or later, followed suit. Communal appeals became rare after independence. Also, governing has required the formation of coalitions, and this practice has further blurred ethnic divisions (Carroll and Carroll 2000, 136). Cabinets now routinely include ministers drawn from all communities. No ethnic group, with the major exception of the Afro-Creoles, need fear that democratic processes will ignore their interests.

The "civic network," as it was originally called, is another institution that political leaders use to accommodate diverse interests and build policy consensus. This consultative tool originated in 1979, just prior to the adoption of a stringent structural adjustment program. To foster acquiescence to painful economic reforms, the government consulted a wide range of voluntary associations about the choices to be made. Since then, successive governments have regularized this consultative process. In the months leading up to a budget, the finance minister "makes the rounds of the country's major stakeholders, listening to their views, exchanging comments, accepting their written analyses. Each evening, these consultations are reported on the state-run television news: union members meet the minister one day; business associations another; and major social welfare NGOs and other groups have their days" (Brautigam 2004, 662). When the budget is presented, its details are widely disseminated by newspapers and the finance minister's website. Lively debate, both in and outside parliament, ensues. Each ministry has also developed a "consultations list" of organizations to be consulted on major policy issues. In 2002, the government formalized this innovation in the National

---

[18] The MLP was formed during the labor unrest in 1936 by Maurice Curé, a member of the Creole middle class. Only in the 1950s did Hindus assume leadership.

Economic and Social Council, which brings together representatives from employers, unions, youth organizations, women's groups, senior citizens, NGOs, the universities, and experts in various fields. Although it is difficult to gauge the degree to which these consultations influence the budget and other legislation, they are apparently effective in building public support for policies and public trust in government (Carroll and Carroll 1999b).

An effective and social-democratic developmental state is, therefore, an outcome of long-term historical processes, a certain configuration of class and ethnic forces, and conjunctural factors such as astute leadership and institutional design. This state has succeeded in promoting industrial and social policies whereas others, pursuing similar approaches, have failed.

Adapting to globalization

The Mauritian state has deftly balanced developmental and distributional imperatives in responding to the challenges of global competition. When growth falters or unemployment grows, pressure mounts on the elected government to launch a new development initiative. Government leaders speak of building another "pillar" of the economy, a new activity that exploits some niche within global markets. They forge an agency to foster the new activity, they craft incentives to redirect resources from declining industries and attract foreign investors, and they provide the necessary infrastructure, training, and education. Yet equity, not just growth, remains a prime consideration. This priority arises from the ethnic/religious tensions that simmer just beneath the surface of this well-established democracy. Of particular importance is the latent hostility of the descendants of indentured laborers and slaves toward the tiny white and mulatto minority that dominates the capitalist class. Non-Hindus also remain wary of the Hindus who predominate in government employment. *No government can survive in an election, and no industrial strategy can succeed, unless the benefits of growth are seen to be shared.* Redistribution from growth, principally in the form of good jobs and an expansive welfare state, assuages the underlying tensions, maintains social peace, and retains a government's electoral support.

Three phases in the evolution of industrial strategy reveal bold and deliberate policy responses to economic problems. Parties disagree on specific policies and issues of probity and strong leadership, but not on fundamental visions. This consensus allows the bureaucrats consistently to implement industrial strategies, irrespective of election campaigns and changes of government. In this respect, Mauritius is strikingly similar to Costa Rica. Both countries have pursued the same trajectory of diversification: from primary exports to tourism, textiles, and clothing, to financial and business services, and, finally, to information and communications technology.

Phase 1. Survival in the face of severe economic and political challenges drove Ramgoolam's MLP government to develop tourism and manufactured exports as two new pillars of the economy. The high unemployment after 1968, the prospect of growing numbers of educated jobseekers, and the evident popular appeal of the Marxist-inspired MMM in the early 1970s forced the government to act. It did not neglect sugar (the primary "pillar"). In the African, Caribbean, and Pacific (ACP) sugar protocol of the Lomé Convention of 1975, Mauritius capitalized on its close ties to both Britain and France to negotiate the largest single sugar quota within the EEC/EU at a guaranteed price that has averaged 90 percent above the market price (Subramanian and Roy 2003). This success justified the levying of an export tax, heaviest (24 percent) for the largest plantations, to finance an expanding welfare state and economic diversification. (Under heavy pressure from the planters and the IMF, the government progressively reduced this tax and then abolished it in 1994.)

Tourism was an attractive option, in light of the country's natural beauty and the falling cost of long-haul jet transport. So the government promoted tourism by providing financial and fiscal incentives to (mainly foreign) investors, creating a Mauritius Tourism Promotion Authority, and building the requisite infrastructure and training facilities. Tourism has grown from 1,000 visits per year in the late 1960s to 660,000 in 2001. This sector now generates direct and indirect employment of about 50,000 jobs (one-ninth of the total), and a fifth of the country's foreign exchange (Arunasalon 1997, 32; Mauritius, CSO 2002a, 119).

Concurrently, the MLP (until 1982) and successor governments fostered a third pillar, clothing and textile exports, beginning with legislation in 1970 to create an Export-Processing Zone. This initiative capitalized on the country's assets – well-educated and (initially) low-cost labor, a wealthy business class flush with investible surplus from lucrative sugar exports, the rule of law and good governance, preferential access to the European market, and generous import quotas in the US market under the Multifibre Agreement (allowing firms from Hong Kong, in particular, to circumvent its own quotas by investing in Mauritius). The proactive state encouraged foreign and local investors to invest in the EPZ through a variety of incentives and institutional support from an Export Development and Investment Authority (Darga 1998, 11–13; Meisenhelder 1999, 287–89). Incentives included tax concessions (no corporate income tax for ten years; no taxes on dividends for five years; a partial tax exemption on reinvested profits; tax rebates for foreign technicians); duty-free import of inputs; guarantee of free repatriation of profits, dividends, and capital; loans at subsidized rates; subsidized water, electricity, and telecommunications rates; and looser labor regulations for the EPZ, as detailed earlier. Despite these concessions, manufacturing exports did not take off until the 1980s. Between 1982 and 1988, employment in the EPZ nearly quadrupled (Gibbon 2000, 17). Almost full employment obtained in the early 1990s, a situation which led to substantial wage increases and, subsequently, to the industry's fading competitiveness. By the late 1990s, however, the export-oriented clothing industry still accounted for 15 percent of employment and about a quarter of GDP (Gibbon 2000, 3, 19).

The boom created by tourism and garment exports not only generated much-needed employment in the 1980s and early 1990s but also permitted the extension of the welfare state. Governments really had no alternative on the latter score, if they hoped to win re-election. The electorate would not look favorably on an administration that simply augmented the wealth of an already privileged economic elite, extending the latter's sway from sugar plantations to manufacturing and tourism. Income and corporate taxes, though reduced over time, remained progressive and were used to extend free education to the secondary and tertiary levels, to expand public pensions and safety nets, and to subsidize basic foodstuffs and fertilizer to the small (Hindu) planters. Such actions fortified the belief that all segments of the population benefited from international trade.

Phase 2. However, the developmental state did not rest on its laurels. Rising wages and inflation beginning in 1988 cast doubt on the future competitiveness of EPZ exporters. Having emulated Taiwan's model of export-oriented industrialization in the 1970s and 1980s, the state moved in the 1990s to make Mauritius the Singapore (financial and business hub) of southern Africa. Mauritius could create many lucrative jobs and local business opportunities, it was believed, if it developed into a regional financial and business center – a fourth pillar of the economy. The liberalization of interest rates in 1988, the creation of a stock exchange in 1989, and the abolition of exchange controls in 1992 laid the groundwork for such a role. Thereafter, the edifice was completed with an Offshore Business Activities Act and an Offshore Trust Act, the creation of a freeport in Port-Louis, and the establishment of an Offshore Business Activities Authority and tough legislation to check money-laundering and other unsavory practices. (The authority advertises itself as a "one-stop agency" to deal with all matters pertaining to the development of the offshore sector.) Investors are enticed with a zero tax on profits from offshore operations, free repatriation of profits, exemption from duties on imported equipment, income-tax holidays for eligible expatriates, and a series of double taxation avoidance treaties.

This sector has achieved moderate success, fueled by the negotiation of the double taxation agreements with more than thirty countries by 2000.[19] Offshore banking and management companies alone employed 1,185 people and generated about 3 percent of GDP in 2000, according to the Offshore Business Activities Authority. Of course, many of the people working in this sector are well-paid accountants, lawyers, managers, economics graduates, and executive assistants who, in turn, create employment in the service sector. Also, offshore activities generate more intangible economic benefits. The promotion of this sector has encouraged Mauritian entrepreneurs to develop business links with, and invest in, the countries of the Southern African Development Community, the Common Market of East and Southern Africa, and the Indian Ocean. As a report from the United Nations conference on Trade and Development notes, "the 'flying geese' pattern . . . is finally in the making in Africa, with tiny Mauritius as the hub" (UNCTAD 2001, 1). "Business tourism" also helps to fill the high-end hotels and restaurants. And, finally, local professionals have gained expertise by working with expatriates.

Liberalization of India's trade and foreign investment regimes since 1991 has boosted Mauritius's offshore business sector. Owing to a double taxation avoidance agreement between the island and India, much foreign investment in that country is now routed through Mauritius. British, American, East Asian, and even Indian investors in India thereby avoid capital gains taxes on their investments (United Press International, May 30, 2000 and July 6, 2001). In 2000, tiny Mauritius became the largest source of foreign direct investment in India (*Mauritius News*, June 2001)! Nonetheless, southern Africa is not as economically dynamic a region as Asia, and therefore Mauritius's chances of replaying the Singapore experience remain slim (Anker, Paration, and Torres 2001, 95–97).

Phase 3. Mauritian governments do not lack boldness. Having learned from Taiwan and Singapore in the two earlier phases, the developmental state now seeks to emulate the Bangalore experience in India. The plan is to transform Mauritius into a "Cyber Island".

---

[19] Interviews with Professor Shyam Nath and Mr. K. Junglee, economists at the University of Mauritius, Réduit, May 22, 2003. This strategy has drawbacks for social democracies, in that it entails catering to wealthy individuals and firms that seek to evade taxation and it can enhance income inequality through the salaries paid to high-priced financial professionals.

By 1999, the old economic strategies had reached their limits, inasmuch as economic growth had slowed after 1994 while the fiscal situation had worsened (Mistry 1999; Anker, Paration, and Torres 2001, 88–92). Most disturbingly, the country had moved from a position of almost full employment in the early 1990s to an unemployment rate of 5 percent in 1995 and nearly 10 percent in 2001. Mauritius's vulnerability to changing market conditions was starkly revealed.

The ongoing loss of non-reciprocal trade preferences for exports accounting for nearly two-thirds of the total is forcing employers to raise productivity. The ACP sugar protocol with the EU expires in 2007. To increase their competitiveness, plantation owners have further mechanized field operations and centralized milling in six capital-intensive factories. Consequently, employment in the sugar sector has recently declined by 8,000 jobs to a total of 21,000 in 2005 (Economist Intelligence Unit, *Country Briefing*, September 6, 2005). Employment in the EPZ, the country's largest employer, has also fallen. Substantial wage increases in the early 1990s made many clothing firms unprofitable at existing export prices (Gibbon 2000, 19). In addition, quotas granted under the Multifibre Agreement are being phased out between 2005 and 2008. Output in Mauritius is expected to drop by 20 percent in 2005, and by a total of 50 percent by 2008 (Economist Intelligence Unit, *Country Briefing*, September 6, 2005). This move to freer trade pits Mauritian manufacturers against lower-cost Asian competitors. Some firms, to survive, are relocating their more labor-intensive processes to nearby Madagascar, where wage costs are only a fifth of those in Mauritius, or are upgrading their equipment. Most remaining firms have replaced some of their Mauritian workers with cheaper foreign Asian workers. And a few firms have moved upmarket into more lucrative, high-quality clothing lines.

In tourism, too, the prospects of employment growth are bleak. The industry by 1999 had nearly reached its ecologically and socially sustainable limit of 700,000 arrivals per year. Finally, offshore financial and business services had not yet taken off by the century's turn, and the relative poverty of the southern Africa region, together with competition from South Africa, did not augur well for the sector's future. New employment would require a new economic initiative.

Following two years of consultations and debate, the government opted in 2001 to reinvent the country as a regional hub of information and communications technology (ICT).[20] Mauritius could thereby capitalize on its relatively well-educated and bilingual (French-English) workforce, its well-developed telecommunications network (including a connection

---

[20] The plan is neatly summarized in IMF 2002, 12 and Tolnay 2002.

to an underwater fibre-optic cable), its attractive environment, and its historical ties to India. Construction of the Ebene Cyber-City began in mid-2002 at a site 15 kms from Port-Louis, supported by a concessionary line of credit of US$100 million from the Indian government. The sixty-hectare business includes a high-rise office tower, fifty plots that have been leased to private companies (mostly Indian), residences, the requisite technological infrastructure, and recreational facilities. Mauritians have initially been employed in technologically simple call centers, mainly targeting France, and back-office services for large corporations. It is also expected that the cyber-city will become a hub of software development, employing ICT professionals from India and South Africa at first, and an incubator for Internet and software start-up companies. Plans underway include a new university campus dedicated to information technology, co-sponsored by the University of Mauritius and an Indian institute.

Besides providing the physical infrastructure at enormous expense, the state is promoting this initiative in several other ways. It offers a package of tax and immigration concessions to attract investors. It has undertaken various programs to augment computer literacy and understanding of ICT among all Mauritians. Two state agencies – the National Productivity and Competitiveness Council and the National Computer Board – mount training programs, organize workshops and exhibitions to diffuse knowledge, and facilitate local ICT start-up companies. Computers and computer instruction have been introduced in all schools from the primary level upwards. Large buses ("Cyber Caravans") containing ten computers each roam the island offering courses in basic computing, word processing, and the Internet to people from all walks of life. Government promotes home computer use by subsidizing the purchase of one computer per household. The latter program has succeeded: by October 2000, 24 percent of urban households and 18 percent of rural households already owned a computer, while 12 percent of all households had Internet access (Mauritius, *National Computer Board News* No. 6, October 2001) – a remarkable record for a middle-income developing country. To further encourage Internet usage, the government provides free access to the Internet from designated post offices throughout the island.

This daring plan to make ICT the fifth pillar of the economy may falter, of course. Few local firms or citizens yet possess the needed high-technology skills, and the global competition in this sector is intense. Yet the initial indications are positive. When the Ebene complex opened in July 2004, 65 percent of the office space had been rented by twenty-two call centers, fifteen business-process outsourcing companies, and ten software firms. The prime minister forecast a 90 percent occupancy rate by year's end, with 2,000 Mauritians employed.[21] This forecast proved accurate: by mid-2005, the Cyber Tower had achieved 98 percent occupancy (*L'Express* [Port-Louis], May 20, 2005). Call centers and back-office services still accounted for the bulk of firms, but companies involved in more complex activities – software development, website development, on-line education, multimedia and disaster recovery (for banks) – were also represented (Mauritius, Bureau of Investment: http://www.boimauritius.com).

Whether the initiative succeeds or not, it demonstrates that Mauritius's democratic developmental state survives, despite globalization. This activist state has selectively and gradually implemented market opening, negotiated preferential trade arrangements, built a social-democratic welfare state, coordinated incentives and infrastructure behind job-creating industrial strategies, and eased exporters' adjustment to freer trade.

Prospects

Although only a speck in the Indian Ocean, Mauritius inspires interest owing to its success in avoiding the bleak fate of many plantation societies. Such societies often evolve political and economic institutions that are antithetical to democracy, let alone social democracy. The institutions protect the small but powerful landed oligarchy from the laboring poor majority, thereby inhibiting not only democracy and equality, but also the innovation and entrepreneurship on which economic growth depends (Easterly and Levine 2002, 3–4, 9–11). In contrast, Mauritius has diversified its economy and sustained an equitable pattern of development, under the aegis of a social-democratic developmental state.

Yet this attractive model has emerged from an unusual history and is thus unlikely to be widely emulated. On the one hand, admirers will be encouraged that even a multiethnic, racially stratified plantation society can build a successful democratic developmental state. They will identify, as critical determinants of success, this tiny country's astute leadership, policy and institutional design, together with its robust civil society. These are elements that others can aspire to replicate in their own countries. On the other hand, they must confront the deeper truth that Mauritius only superficially resembles other African countries. Several peculiar historical conditions underpinned its success: a thoroughly capitalist society with a cohesive and powerful bourgeoisie, an overlap of class and ethnicity that permitted a separation of political from economic power, political

---

[21] Reported in the Ministry of Finance, "Speech Introducing the 2004–2005 Budget", Port-Louis, June 11, 2004. See also *L'Express* (Port-Louis), July 2 and 6, 2004.

processes that generated a hardy democratic culture and "consensual autonomy," and an effective process of state building. Although Costa Rica, Kerala, and Chile met several of these conditions, not many other countries do.

Globalization poses further challenges. Mauritius has succeeded, so far, in finding new niches to fill in the world economy. It has taken advantage of the benefits provided by its democratic welfare state – industrial policies, political stability, social cohesion, and an educated and healthy labor force – to diversify its economy and attract investment. It has extensively benefited from preferential market access to the European and US markets. Mauritius has directed the bulk of its sugar exports to the EU to fill its substantial quota at a price that is generally 90 percent above the market price, and it has gained duty-free access for its clothing exports to the EU under the Multifibre Agreement and the USA under the African Growth Opportunity Act. Looming free trade, however, will pit Mauritius against low-cost Asian producers of sugar and garments, as already is the case in business services and software. The country's relatively high wages raise costs of the more labour-intensive exports.

To compete, the Mauritian state seeks to nudge firms into upmarket garment exports, to foster lower costs of sugar production through voluntary retirements, mechanization, irrigation, and the concentration of sugar mills, to upgrade tourist facilities, and to galvanize Mauritius as a financial and ICT center. But the state has progressively fewer tools at its disposal to realize this agenda, owing to growing pressures from the IMF, WTO agreements, and donors. The government is pressed to liberalize trade, investment, banking and labor markets; privatize state corporations, and cut taxes and subsidies. Even so, this highly pragmatic and social-democratic developmental state has met many challenges before, and will probably continue to do so in the future.

6   Chile: the tumultuous path to the Third Way

Of our four cases, Chile is the most difficult to classify as a regime type. In contrast to the relatively clear paths that Costa Rica, Kerala, and Mauritius have traveled, Chile's history has been discontinuous and contorted. During the radical-mobilizational period that culminated in the Allende government (1970–1973), Chile moved much further to the left than any of our cases and was arguably the most radical experiment in democratic socialism ever undertaken in the periphery. Yet, during the Pinochet dictatorship (1973–1990), not only did Chile embrace market reform with the fervor that only a highly disciplined, authoritarian regime can muster, but it did so while aggressively repressing the popular sectors. The ambiguous character of the post-Pinochet center-left Concertación (1990 to present) reflects this tumultuous history of successive class polarization and lower-class demobilization. On the one hand, Concertación governments have implemented neoliberal reforms with a consistency that has no counterpart in the region. On the other hand, class-based demands have remained central to the political process and Concertación governments[1] have embraced the language of social democracy. Moreover, these governments have been more effective in expanding social benefits and tackling poverty than other states in Latin America (aside from Costa Rica and Cuba). Although Chile's lower classes have yet to regain the political influence they enjoyed in the Allende period, the current configuration of power does make some degree of social regulation of the market a political necessity. For reasons explored in this chapter, Chile since 1990 represents something of a hybrid of neoliberal economics and social democracy – the original "Third Way."

Chile's status as a social democracy is a controversial issue: as one of the most unequal countries in the world, Chile stands apart from Kerala,

---

[1] The most important parties in the Concertación alliance are the Christian Democratic Party (PDC) and two socialist parties: the Socialist Party (PS) and the Popular Party for Democracy (PPD).

Costa Rica, and Mauritius.[2] But we argue that the country's substantial achievements in poverty reduction and social development since redemocratization in 1990,[3] combined with ongoing state-directed efforts to reduce inequality, expand social services, and promote economic development, qualify Chile as a social democracy, albeit a diluted, Third-Way variant. Chile has departed from the regional norm both in the effectiveness of its developmental state and in its post-1990 sensitivity to lower-class demands. Although the state's relationship to lower classes clearly falls short of the institutionalized linkages of our other cases, it is also a far cry from the disorganized populism and rampant clientelism that is the norm of intermediation in Latin America. The class-based nature of state–society interactions in Chile can, moreover, be traced to patterns of class mobilization that have characterized the country's modern history.

Chile's journey toward its current minimal and grudging social pact, combining the protection of private property and an open, market economy with increased social spending and poverty reduction, has been orchestrated and dominated by its political elite.[4] This elite has pursued market-based growth with vigor, but has also had to respond to a relatively well-organized labor constituency. The resulting class compromise is both fragile and constantly subject to the renegotiation of specific social and economic aspects. Political leaders face, on the one hand, criticism from below of the economic model and pressure to improve labor protection and equality in social services, and, on the other, fierce opposition to such reforms from a powerful private sector. On a number of the most contentious issues, such as reform of the labor code and the health-care system, the Chilean state has been unable to mediate a broadly acceptable class compromise. Labor thus remains restive.

Let us sketch Chile's evolving social record – one of both important achievements and notable inadequacies – before turning to the tumultuous origins of the current Third Way.

---

[2] In 1997, its Gini coefficient, the standard measurement for inequality, stood at .55 (Morley 2001, 166–69).

[3] Between 1990 and 2000 poverty was reduced from 38.6 percent of households to 20.7 percent (CEPAL, 2003, 282).

[4] The term "political elite" will be used to refer to the top leadership of Concertación: the president, his Cabinet, and their advisors. In 1990, labor and business signed an agreement in which labor recognized the right of private property and declared its support for the continued pursuit of export markets and foreign investment. Business agreed to recognize the right of trade union organizations to exist and operate. It was also agreed that the state must guarantee equality of opportunity, provide protection to the weakest members of society, ensure full employment, and eradicate poverty (Ruiz-Tagle 1991, 155–57).

The social record

Chile's social progress can be divided into four historical phases: (1) an initial stage from the 1920s to the mid-1960s during which social programs were steadily expanded; (2) a radical redistributive phase from the mid-1960s to 1973; (3) a phase of retrenchment in social protection during military rule (1973–1989); and (4) the years from 1990 to the present, involving expanded social programs geared to the reduction of poverty. Each of these phases witnessed the dominance of a distinct economic and social vision, and each reflected a particular constellation of political forces and circumstances. Chile's current brand of social democracy, therefore, emerges from a historical process characterized by profound discontinuities.

The adoption of the first genuinely redistributive measures occurred in the 1920s with the creation of the country's first social-security programs (old-age pensions, health benefits, maternity benefits, and family allowances) for white- and blue-collar workers. Although state involvement in public education began in the nineteenth century, in 1920 primary education was made mandatory and from the 1930s onward the system expanded rapidly (Olivarria-Gambi 2003, 112). The establishment of preventive health care in 1938 played a key role in the reduction of infant-mortality rates and higher life expectancy while bringing under control a number of infectious diseases (Borzutsky 2002, 51, 62). Overall, social-welfare spending rose from 27 percent to 37 percent of public expenditures between 1940 and 1961 (Sunkel 1965, 124). The beneficiaries of most of these social initiatives, however, were largely the organized urban working and middle classes. Social-security programs neglected unorganized workers, the self-employed, rural-sector tenant farmers, rural wage earners, and *minifundistas* (very small landowners); rural poverty was deep and widespread. Moreover, social-security provisions became increasingly unequal and enormously costly, reflecting the pattern of selective incorporation. Inordinate benefits were allotted to privileged groups, most pensions were extremely low, and the cost of Chilean social security in relation to GDP became one of the highest in the world (Borzutsky 2002, 61).

The 1964–1973 period, encompassing the administrations of Eduardo Frei (1964–1970) and Salvador Allende (1970–1973), marked the years of the greatest redistribution in the country's history. Programs targeted those groups – the urban poor and peasants – who had hitherto been excluded from social improvement. Asset redistribution, through the massive expropriation of industrial enterprises and large landholdings, was a key part of the strategy to improve living standards. Wages increased in both the urban and rural sectors and employment expanded rapidly in the new land-reform sector and in newly acquired state companies (Foxley, Aninat, and Arellano 1979, 205, 211, 218). Legislation in 1965 raised the rural wage to the level of the minimum urban wage. Spending also increased in education and social-security protection expanded considerably. But only permanent workers on the largest landed estates benefited from land reform, leaving out *minifundistas* and temporary rural workers, while resistance from landowners made minimum-wage legislation difficult to enforce. So, though social-security protection was expanded during the period, the goal of providing a universal program that would include *minifundistas*, small farmers, temporary rural labor, and independent urban workers was blocked by the stiff political resistance of the highly organized current beneficiaries (Borzutsky 2002, 99, 149).

Nevertheless, the poor benefited from the expansion of a wide variety of social programs, such as a literacy program and a milk-distribution program. Despite certain inadequacies in social protection, by the early 1970s Chile had made significant social progress in comparison with other Latin American countries. Social security covered 68 percent of the population, primary school enrollment was at 97 percent, literacy rates reached 90 percent, and infant mortality stood at 82 deaths per 1,000 live births – down from 217 in 1940 (Foxley, Aninat, and Arellano 1979, 176; Olivarria-Gambi 2003, 109).[5]

While all of these indicators, except social-security protection, were either maintained or continued to improve in the following decades, there was nevertheless a marked retrenchment in social policy and a sharp increase in poverty and inequality during the subsequent period of military rule (1973–1989). Whereas the percentage of poor families stood at 28.5 percent in 1970, that figure reached 56.9 percent in 1980 and 48.7 percent in 1987 (Montecinos 1997, 225). Income distribution also became more unequal (Edwards and Cox Edwards 1987, 162) and private consumption dropped (Ortega 1988, 44). Rural areas were especially hard hit: poverty persisted and even increased in some rural areas as the rural labor force became overwhelmingly seasonal and strongly segmented by gender (Kay 1997, 16). Everywhere, wages declined sharply and unemployment rose to record levels, skyrocketing to 22 percent by 1982. The military suspended the right to strike and to bargain collectively, withdrew legal recognition from the umbrella labor confederation, closed unions, and confiscated union goods. The 1979 labor code severely restricted union activities, leaving labor almost no recourse

---

[5] This last figure continued to improve in the following decades reaching 33 by 1980, 14 by 1990 and 10 in 2002 (Olivarria-Gambi 2003, 109; UNDP 2004, 168).

against arbitrary and numerous layoffs and unsafe working conditions. Repression and the "disappearances" of union activists and leaders were also frequent.

In addition, under military rule per capita spending on education and health declined. By 1986, government expenditure per capita on social welfare was 14 percent less than in 1970 (Aguilera Reyes 1994, 32). Moreover, privatization reforms undertaken by the military government to the health-care and educational systems generated sharp inequalities. The establishment of a two-tier system in health care – involving a private system for the well-off and a public system for the remaining 85 percent of the population – produced a sharp deterioration of health services as both government and upper-class financial contributions to public health care dropped. New inequalities emerged as the health-care companies discriminated against women and the elderly. At the same time, a sharp distinction arose in quality between publicly subsidized schools attended by the lower classes, which did not charge tuition, and the private tuition-charging schools used by the upper classes. Finally, not only was the newly privatized social-security scheme extremely costly, but it also failed to generate adequate pensions. And there was still no social support for the self-employed – those in the informal sector and small farmers.

On the positive side, military rule eliminated some of the most blatant inequalities within the social-security system. A noncontributory means-tested pension for indigents over age sixty-five, the physically disabled over age seventeen, and (after 1987) the mentally ill was established (Castiglioni 2001, 41). Temporary work programs were also established to address the severe unemployment problem. Indeed, the military regime's social policy targeted the most desperately poor, establishing means-tested mother–infant programs and feeding programs for the lowest income groups. Still, the proliferation of soup kitchens during the period reflects the inability of families to meet nutritional needs (Montecinos 1997, 227). The increased attention in social policy given to the poorest 10 percent of the population, moreover, was at the expense of the less and medium poor who saw their access to social expenditure drop and their living standards decline (Tironi 1988, 177). However, it is likely that the military regime's highly targeted approach in the midst of increasing misery allowed basic social indicators, such as the infant-mortality rate, to continue to improve. The military also benefited from a comparatively high-capacity state with a long record of delivering services.

The first three civilian Concertación governments (1990–2006), led by Presidents Aylwin, Frei, and Lagos, have grappled with the social legacy of military rule – poverty and inequality. Adopting the slogan of "growth with equity," Concertación sought to rectify the social deficit primarily through economic growth and the pursuit of new international market opportunities but complemented this strategy with substantial increases in social spending and programs targeted to the poor. In this sense, its approach is a variant of the "Third Way."[6] Some analysts contend that as much as 73–80 percent of the decline in poverty since the early 1990s has been due to economic growth (job creation and wage increases), and that the remaining 20–27 percent of the decline is attributable to increased social expenditures (Beyer 1995, 21; Meller 2000; World Bank 2002, 8). Social spending has certainly risen dramatically since 1990. Of particular note was the increased spending on Chile's universal programs (health and education) with the objective of upgrading public services.[7] Social expenditures as a proportion of total expenditures rose from 61 percent in 1990 to 69 percent in 2000 (de Mesa and Benavides Salazar 2003, 21). Education spending increased at an average annual rate of 10.6 percent and health spending at 9.4 percent (de Mesa and Benavides Salazar 2003, 38). By 1999, social expenditures represented 16 percent of GDP, placing Chile at the upper end, though not at the top, among Latin American countries (CEPAL 2002, 269–70).

While there was broad targeting within social programs (for example, education expenditure emphasized the rehabilitation of primary education in poor areas), highly focused targeting of the social investment type also occurred. The latter, however, represented a small percentage of social expenditures. Programs targeted women, youth, and indigenous groups. The best-known targeted program was administered by FOSIS (Solidarity and Investment Fund), established in 1990. FOSIS provides matching funding for projects generated by NGOs, social organizations, and municipalities to address the needs of marginalized groups. In 2003, the government put into place a new, highly targeted program (*Chile Solidario*), aimed at the indigent, or extremely poor (6 percent of the population).

Although social services and protection have expanded significantly, the lower classes in Chile remain highly vulnerable. The labor regime is

[6] There are important differences in the experiences of the European Third Way and the Chilean case. Chile's Third Way did not emerge as a consequence of a negotiated attempt to balance the demands of capital and labor, but, rather, as a consequence of seventeen years of military rule which imposed an economic and social transformation. Nor have tripartite negotiations between government, business, and labor been an important part of the Chilean experience.

[7] The largest portion of social expenditures throughout the period was pension contributions (40 percent in 1993) (Scott 1996, 165). The enormous cost of pensions is a continuing legacy of the country's inefficient and unequal social-security arrangements, further exacerbated by the military's reform of the system, which placed an enormous financial burden on the state with clear implications for the state's ability to address other social needs into the future.

still highly flexible, making it difficult for workers to protect their conditions of employment. This is especially true for temporary female workers, who endure very low incomes and harsh working conditions (Petras and Leiva 1994, 153; Barrientos 1997). Indeed, critics argue that the high degree of labor flexibility in Chile produces such precariousness in employment that poverty reduction may not be sustainable (Escobar 2003, 70). In contrast to Chile, Mauritius, and Kerala, where the rural sector was fully incorporated in the transition to social democracy, the rural sector was long excluded in Chile and rural poverty has proven highly resilient. *Minifundistas*, smallholders, seasonal wage laborers, and independent informal-sector workers have very low incomes and are still without adequate social protection. Poverty, though greatly reduced overall, has increased in some regions of the country[8] and extreme poverty has not improved (de Mesa and Benavides Salazar 2003, 22). Chile's growth trajectory is also precarious: dependence for economic growth on natural resource-based exports is limited by land availability, the imminence of resource exhaustion, and new competitors in international markets (Kurtz 2001, 9; Cademartori 2003, 79).

On the political front, there is the additional problem of the weak legitimacy accorded to democratic institutions by the public. According to a UNDP survey of Chilean public opinion, only 45 percent of Chileans see democracy as preferable to any other form of government (UNDP 2002, 269). Moreover, the majority of Chileans have been unhappy with their government's performance on the social front despite its widely hailed success in poverty reduction: in one opinion survey, a majority of respondents identified poverty, reform of the health-care system, and unemployment as the most important political issues (*El Mercurio*, "Encuesta CEP de diciembre," December 30, 2000).

The following sections tell the story of how Chile's Third-Way regime came to be. Class politics has a lengthy history in this country, leading to the polarization and hyper-mobilization of 1964–1973. The Pinochet-led authoritarian reaction in 1973–1990 involved a determined effort to expunge class-based politics through a demobilization of popular sectors. Yet, despite all the repression, class politics still matters. Although business is powerful and recalcitrant and governments pro-market, issues such as labor reform, inequality, and social protection are still central to political debates. Another constant throughout Chile's tumultuous history is the directive role of the state. While the state expanded dramatically during the popular-mobilization phase, it retained an important

---

[8] Between 1998 and 2000, poverty declined in seven regions but increased in five (Feres 2001, 10).

role even during the free-market heyday of military rule. Today, under the Concertación, the state's role in guiding and/or prodding the private sector into new markets has accelerated while social-justice issues have been resurrected. These, then, are the ingredients of the Chilean Third Way: a political leadership committed to growth with equity within an open, market economy, a strong and directive state, a powerful capitalist class, and the continued articulation of class-based interests.

The historical context (1925–1964)

Chile's state-led industrialization and efforts at social protection during these years were shaped by the structural transformation triggered by the country's integration into the world economy as a nitrate and, later, copper producer. This integration led to the emergence, by the late nineteenth century, of a militant and well-organized working class in northern, isolated mining communities. These communities would become fertile ground for the Marxist appeals of the socialist and communist parties. At the same time, the very weakness of that mining export economy – as evidenced by its virtual collapse during the Great Depression – was an essential ingredient both in the process of Chilean state formation (as the state became the leader in industrial development) and in the growing radicalization of left-party appeals and their recruitment of industrial working-class support.

In addition, a key configurational factor – an institutionalized competitive-party system through which a coalition of capitalists and big landowners exercised control – nurtured left radicalization but also ensured the political exclusion of the rural poor.[9] The electoral victory of the center-left Popular Front (Frente Popular) over the political right in 1938 at first raised the specter of a significant diminution of the power of landed conservative interests – a powerful force given that 9.7 percent of landowners owned 86 percent of the arable land (Drake 1978, 36). But the country's economic elite, including its big landed interests, was itself undergoing change: as a consequence of the collapse of the country's mining export economy in the early 1930s, the economic elite abandoned its long-standing opposition to industrialization. The Popular Front, which included the Socialist Party along with members of the landowning class, brokered a deal in which large landowners agreed to support state-led

---

[9] The well-institutionalized party system that emerged between 1891 and 1924 has been described as a "quasi parliamentary oligarchic system" (Loveman 1988, 149) in which the country's landed elite, through its clientelistic manipulation of the rural vote, was able to obtain controlling representation in Congress (Remmer 1984, 81).

industrial expansion in return for the prohibition of peasant unioniza-tion and strikes,[10] increased public credit, and substantial subsidies to improve irrigation and transportation for agriculture (Drake 1978, 222–23; Zeitlin and Ratcliff 1988, 213).

Hence, the ascension of the Popular Front to power did not signifi-cantly diminish the power of landed interests as originally hoped by the left members of the coalition. The consequent failure to bring about sig-nificant social improvements in the rural sector combined with the grow-ing belief that the social gains made during the years of Popular Front rule had not been sufficient, spurred, in the case of the Socialist Party, a turn to revolutionary Marxism and the abandonment of the use of clien-telism (Drake 1978, 39). At the same time, a legal framework (the 1931 labor code) that kept the trade-union movement divided and politically weak encouraged radicals to work through the left political parties.

The Popular Front years were also important in the construction of a state apparatus that would lead development in the years to come. The government initiated a program of import-substitution industrialization (ISI) and oversaw a rapid expansion of the state. The key organization charged with leading Chile's industrial development was CORFO (Pro-duction Development Corporation), established in 1939. CORFO super-vised the development of infrastructure, provided financing to the private sector, and created enterprises in a variety of important economic sec-tors.[11] ISI and its concomitant government expansion generated a rapid increase in the working and middle classes. Industry's share of GDP rose from 13 percent in 1940 to 21 percent by 1950, while industrial employ-ment and real wages rose (Velasco 1994, 386; Silva 1996, 37). With the expansion of the state, employment in the central administration of the public sector more than tripled between 1925 and 1965. Unionization in the urban sector proceeded rapidly: by 1969, close to 34 percent of the labor force was unionized (Angell 1972, 47).

This state-led industrial transformation gave rise to new urban working-class segments that would become politically mobilized. Orga-nizations representing new working- and middle-class groups became closely tied to political parties, which championed their social-welfare demands. The rural sector, where mobilizational activities were restricted, was neglected not only in terms of improved social policy,

---

[10] Peasant unions were outlawed on paper until 1947, and in practice until 1967 (Drake 1978, 36).

[11] Between 1940 and 1946, it created thirty-two enterprises including enterprises in elec-tricity (National Electricity Company, ENDESA), in steel (Pacific Steel Company, CAP), and petroleum (National Petroleum Company, ENAP). Many of these com-panies provided cheap inputs to the private sector.

but also in terms of investment and modernization. Landownership was highly concentrated in a small number of wealthy families; however, the overwhelming majority of fortunes derived from mining, commerce, industry, and finance. The most powerful landholders were not dependent upon the income they earned from land and were, as a consequence, not motivated to modernize agriculture (Valenzuela 2001, 258).[12] The political power of these big landowners ensured that the rural poor lacked the organizational strength to make the gains that were made in other sectors. During the Popular Front years, real incomes of agricultural workers declined such that by 1952, industrial wages were three times agricultural wages (Mamalakis 1976, 102).

Although popular resistance in the rural sector was not absent prior to the 1950s, changes from the mid-1950s paved the way for more concerted efforts to organize the rural poor. Several interrelated factors contributed to the declining clientelist grip of the landed elites and their parties on the rural poor. First, stagnation in the agricultural sector (a reflection of the heavy emphasis of public policy on industry and the urban sector, and of landowners' neglect of agricultural modernization) had stimulated increased rural–urban migration. Second, the extension of communication networks into the countryside, the expansion of the monetary economy into remote rural areas, growing corporate ownership of agricultural enterprises, and an increase in landless workers all contributed to the breakdown of patron–client ties and opened the possibility for the radicalization of the peasantry as political parties began to compete for their vote (Petras 1970, 256–57, 262). A third essential ingredient was the electoral law of 1958, which increased penalties for electoral fraud and bribery, thereby making it increasingly difficult for landlords to control the votes of peasants on haciendas. These changes took place in the context of highly militant trade union movements and left political parties. After 1958, the socialist and communist parties spread their ideology into the countryside where they competed for votes with the Christian Democratic Party. By the early 1960s, the parties of the old elite (the liberals and conservatives) began to see a drop in their seats in Congress (Loveman 1988, 265).

Under pressure from the political left, the country's political center had begun to crumble as the Christian Democrats and Radicals moved leftward and the economic elite became increasingly fearful of threats to property interests. While the rural sector was a new and important site

---

[12] Those who owned large tracts of land did not regard their estates as agricultural enterprises but held them for reasons of social prestige, as collateral for loans, and for their potential for mineral deposits.

of political mobilization from the late 1950s onward, support for the left parties still centered in the working class. Leftist parties capitalized on workers' discontent. Of particular importance in this regard was the anti-labor regime of President Carlos Ibañez (1952–1958), whose policies produced a calamitous decline in workers' income (Mamalakis 1976, 197) and solidified labor solidarity and leftist unity.

Class polarization and conflict (1964–1973)

By the mid-1960s, a configuration of sociopolitical forces had emerged that underpinned both an attempt at social transformation and the mobilization of sharp resistance to that project. As the country's political center disintegrated, a coalition of left political parties, supported by a well-organized and militant working class, faced off against a political right, dominated by the country's economic elite that also engaged in political mobilization. Chile's marginalized rural poor experienced a rapid political awakening that, precisely because it had been so long delayed, proved to be explosive. This pattern stands in stark contrast to that in Costa Rica, Kerala, and Mauritius, where peasantries attained basic political and civil rights at a much earlier stage.

The regime, during this phase, is perhaps best described as radical-mobilizational, given the goal of securing redistribution (particularly asset redistribution) through mobilization from below. Both the Christian Democratic administration of Eduardo Frei (1964–1970) and the left Popular Unity (UP) government of Salvador Allende (1970–1973) pursued this redistributional goal. The parties of the UP (the socialist and communist parties) and an important fraction of the Christian Democratic Party called for the elimination of capitalism within the context of the democratic constitutional order. The UP rejected the legitimacy of private property and sought socialist transformation in which the private sector would play a subordinate role; to this end, it planned expropriations in agricultural land and in a wide range of industrial activities. The landed/business elite, the right-wing National Party, and, eventually, the remaining portion of the Christian Democratic Party fiercely rejected these plans. The absence of even the most minimal of class compromises guaranteeing the protection of private property blocked the emergence of social democracy. As the left gained in electoral strength, the gulf in fundamental principles became increasingly apparent, as did the unwillingness to find common ground.

Political polarization reached its apogee with the UP government. President Frei had initiated agrarian reform in 1965, but expropriations of private property peaked under Allende.[13] State takeovers in the urban industrial sector reached unprecedented levels: the number of industrial enterprises in the hands of the state jumped from 61 in 1970 to 362 by 1973, resulting in increases in the state's participation in industry from 28.4 percent of assets to 69.4 percent and in employment from 9.1 percent to 23.7 percent (Foxley, Aninat, and Arellano 1979, 204–05). In this process, the upper and middle classes saw their way of life being overturned, while the left and its supporters feared the defeat of their dream of a socialist transformation. Chilean politics were at an impasse. Rapid political mobilization by political parties was the central component of this process.

Both the Popular Action Front (FRAP – the precursor left alliance to the UP) and the Christian Democratic Party campaigned hard in the countryside from 1958 onward (Petras 1970, 260). The 1964 election featured a marked upsurge in rural political organizing. The left (with Salvador Allende as its presidential candidate) gained support in rural areas where workers received wages and in rural communities close to mining areas; the Christian Democratic Party was able to garner support from isolated tenant farmers still subject to pressure from landlords and from farmers of medium-sized holdings (Petras 1970, 205). The election of a Christian Democrat, Eduardo Frei, to the presidency in 1964 was an important turning point. Frei had received support from the political right, fearful of the growing strength of the militant left. From 1964, Chilean politics became increasingly polarized.

As Frei attempted to meet his election promises regarding agrarian reform, rural unionization, and the enforcement of labor laws, he alienated his rightist supporters. The 1967 law that made possible rural unions stimulated accelerated unionization activity, to the chagrin of the right. Now in control of the state, the Christian Democratic government used state agencies, particularly INDAP (Agricultural Development Institute), to organize peasants, concentrating its efforts (like the left) on farm workers dependent on wages as they proved easiest to organize. Although the share of rural dwellers organized into unions rose sharply, the movement remained severely divided. By 1971, there were five different nationwide organizations: one linked to the left parties, two to the Christian Democratic Party, one to MAPU (a radical breakaway from the Christian Democratic Party), and one linked to the rightist National Party. Not until MAPU's defection from the Christian Democratic peasant

---

[13] Allende expropriated 76 percent of the total number of landholdings expropriated between 1964 and 1973 and 64 percent of the agricultural land expropriated (Martner 1988, 155).

organization in 1971 (that is, after the election of the UP in 1970) did the political left command a majority of organized peasant support (Castells 1974, 344). As the land-reform process accelerated, large landowners organized in defence of their interests. While the left encouraged peasants to take over large landholdings, the National Society of Agriculture, headed by the large landowners, engaged in a massive incorporation of *minifundistas* (Hernández 1973, 137). The UP's peasant support remained lodged among wage earners residing on the large landholdings (the major beneficiaries of the land-reform process); the only *minifundistas* to support the UP were the Mapuche (Castells 1974, 247).

Although the left battled to increase its electoral support in the countryside, its most important electoral base continued to be in the urban centers (particularly the industrial working class) and among workers in the mining centers.[14] The FRAP and then the UP benefited electorally from the fact that Chile had become an industrialized and highly urbanized society. By the early 1970s, 28 percent of the country's GDP was accounted for by manufacturing (Thorp 1998, 162), 78 percent of the population lived in urban centres (UNDP 2004, 168), and only 19.7 percent of the economically active population remained in agriculture (Martínez and Tironi 1985, 118). Growing support from urban workers for the left was spurred both by the country's slow economic growth – at 1.7 percent per capita, per annum, it was the lowest in Latin America (Edwards 1985, 11) – and by chronic inflation fueled by expanding budget deficits and redistributive pressures.[15] The country's ISI strategy could not provide the economic growth that might have mitigated political polarization.

Despite the growing economic and political chaos, however, the 1964–1973 years were important in Chile's later economic success. The economic model depended heavily on state direction and some of the state activities during these years would lay the groundwork for later success. In the late 1960s, the Frei administration advanced the idea of developing an internationally competitive agro-industry. CORFO then began to research the best foreign and local business practices and to promote the creation of "leader processing firms" that would assist in the adoption and diffusion of modern processing industries. Another objective was the improvement of agricultural practices among small producers through the spread of new technology (Pérez-Alemán 2000, 147). In

---

[14] In the 1964 election, 60 to 72 percent of the vote in northern mining communities went to the FRAP while it won 67 to 100 percent of the vote in industrial centers (Petras 1969, 195).

[15] By 1973, the public-sector deficit had skyrocketed to 30.5 percent of GDP and inflation hit 438 percent (Larrañaga 1992, 2).

1967, CORFO established a Plan for Fruit Development, which provided a variety of measures essential for export success: market analysis,
technology, credit, and tariff drawback (Kurtz 2001, 5). CORFO also
laid the basis for a new export infrastructure in such sectors as fishing,
chemicals, and pulp. In line with the goal of agricultural improvement,
a semi-autonomous institute of agricultural research was established in
1964, the National Institute for Agrarian Research (INIA), with the goal
of building capacity in agricultural technology (Kurtz 2001, 5). In 1965,
the University of Chile, in partnership with the University of California at
Davis, embarked on a ten-year program to train agricultural economists
and agronomists (Agosín 1999, 94). The state was also directly involved
in a variety of productive activities, which would pay off after the mid-
1980s. The 1965 National Forestry Plan established goals for government
plantings and in 1970 the state directly planted 46 percent of total forestry
plantings; by 1973, this figure was 96 percent (Wisecarver 1992, 485).
Hence, despite the economic difficulties associated with state direction,
state expansion in this period contributed to future achievements.

   Chile's radical-mobilizational phase, in triggering intense class polarization and fear among the middle and upper classes, set the stage for
the coup and the imposition of policies that reversed many of its accomplishments in social welfare. The threat to propertied interests went well
beyond the agricultural sector; indeed, had the threat remained confined
to large, unproductive landholdings, a military coup might have been
avoided.[16] But while the coup signaled a decisive defeat of the left, the
expansion of the educational system and some of the programs set into
motion by CORFO would have a lasting positive impact. Even agrarian
redistributive reform, only partially reversed, created the conditions for
a dynamic export-oriented entrepreneurial class by the mid-1980s.

Critical juncture: military rule and the new economic model (1973–1989)

The 1973 military coup constituted a critical juncture that would transform the Chilean economy, its social structure, and, eventually, the thinking of its left political elite. These changes explain the demise of left
militancy and the post-1990 political leadership's willingness to maintain
a market-oriented model with a more pro-business orientation than in our
other three cases. The coup was enthusiastically supported by the Chilean
business class, including small and medium business where conflicts over
wages and working conditions had been especially acute (Martínez and

---

[16] Concern for increasing the level of agricultural production had prompted right-wing
President Alessandri's 1962 land-reform proposal affecting large idle properties.

Díaz 1996, 77). It was also supported by the United States, which had contributed to the destabilization of the Chilean economy through financial assistance to the opposition (notably in support of the famous truckers' strike) and through backing a credit embargo (Petras and Morley 1975, 79–118, 134). The military government quickly instituted trade liberalization, privatization, and state streamlining. It also adopted a flexible exchange rate and a variety of export-promotion measures.

This combination of policies triggered the reconstitution of the business class – the emergence of a new and dynamic group involved in the export of a new set of products. At the same time, bankruptcies precipitated the demise of the older ISI entrepreneurs and weakened the working class which, in addition to high levels of unemployment and reduced wages, saw its trade unions disbanded and their leaders murdered or jailed. But the labor group most devastated by the experience of military rule worked in the rural sector. Here the new dynamic agro-export sectors depended upon temporary (largely female) labor. The dramatic increase in seasonal employment fragmented communities and produced new forms of dependence on agricultural capitalists (Kurtz 2004, 81, 90). Effective trade union representation was almost entirely absent for these workers and continues to be so today (Kay 1997, 15; Haagh 2002, 99, 198). The military ensured quiescence in the countryside by excluding former rural activists from purchasing land and by denying them rural employment. While the working class and rural labor lost power, military rule also left a legacy of extreme power concentration along with a set of authoritarian institutional arrangements designed to keep the new economic model in place long after the return to civilian rule.

The period of military rule falls into two distinct phases (1974–1981 and 1985–1990), punctuated by the economic collapse of 1981–1983. The first period can be distinguished by the presence of a ruling alliance of the military, a group of technocrats known as the "Chicago Boys,"[17] and the executives/owners of the country's major conglomerates (Silva 1996). This initial period of military rule involved the implementation of a draconian stabilization program ("shock treatment"), an inflexible adherence to certain market principles, and relations of cronyism between economic policymakers and the executives of the country's three largest conglomerates. The 1985–1989 period, on the other hand, saw a broadening of the ruling alliance to include a wider cross-section of entrepreneurial interests and a more pragmatic approach to economic policy. Across the two periods, however, there was a common emphasis

---

[17] The Chicago Boys were named for their education in economics at the University of Chicago, an experience that occurred as a consequence of an exchange program established between the Catholic University and the University of Chicago in the 1950s.

on export-led growth and a role for the state in the new economic model.

The military government's 1975 economic program stipulated that by 1978 all import tariffs were to be reduced to a uniform 10 percent and that all quantitative restrictions be removed. This eliminated the discriminatory arrangements that had prevented some sectors (such as lumber) from exporting. High tariffs on machinery and equipment had discouraged such businesses from attempting to enter export markets since high costs rendered their products uncompetitive (Ossa S. 1992, 384; Agosín 1999, 96). Other factors were also important in encouraging entrepreneurs to seek out export markets: the restriction of domestic demand (a consequence of both the economic crisis and economic policy), labor repression (which lowered labor costs dramatically), and exchange-rate depreciation (which until 1979 contributed to export competitiveness) (Edwards and Cox Edwards 1987, 124; Agosín 1999, 85).

As agricultural exports expanded 68 percent between 1976 and 1977, trade liberalization also produced high levels of bankruptcy in sectors that had been highly protected, such as textiles and leather goods (Edwards and Cox Edwards 1987, 23). So while many import-substitution businesses disappeared, and the production of traditional crops (such as wheat) declined, investments expanded into new areas, such as fruit production (Mujica Ateaga 1992, 344). Investments in forestry also increased. Industrial exports (largely those based on natural resources) increased their participation in total exports from 14.5 percent in 1974 to 33 percent by 1981 (Griffiths-Jones 1991, 24).

Despite the anti-state rhetoric of the regime, export-promotion policies were part of the story. Forestry, for example, received massive state subsidies and promotion prior to 1983, with a new program providing for subsidies of up to 75 percent of the costs for timber planting along with inexpensive credits provided through the Central Bank to the Banco del Estado to finance forestry development projects (Wisecarver 1992, 498; Agosín 1999, 94–95; Kurtz 2001, 7). In addition, ProChile (Chilean Trade Commission), established in 1974, played an increasingly important role in stimulating exports. Under the authority of the Ministry of External Relations from 1979, ProChile organized firms into sector-specific export committees that then defined export projects and provided the specialized services firms needed to develop exports (Pérez-Alemán 2000, 47). Other export-promotion measures included a 1974 decree allowing exporters to recover taxes paid on the inputs of exported products, and the establishment of trade offices abroad.

Counter-reform in the countryside was also an important aspect of the new economic model. Between 1974 and 1981, 28 percent of the land in state hands was returned to its original owners, 52 percent was sold to workers and *campesinos*, and the rest was sold at public auction. Despite the fact that many new smaller landowners were later forced to sell their land, land concentration did not return to the level of the pre-1964 period (Scott 1996, 156). Moreover, the process now gave rise to the emergence of a more dynamic agro-livestock entrepreneurial sector (Scott 1996, 157; Díaz 1997, 181). While large holdings were important, there were also some 10,000 industrialized farmers tied to trading companies that exported (Martínez and Díaz 1996, 2).

The government's decision to peg the country's currency to the US dollar from 1979, followed by the economic crisis of 1981–1983, almost produced the demise of the new economic strategy.[18] But by 1985, with the support of the World Bank, the model was back on track. Now, however, a much broader cross-section of the private business sector was given access to the state policymaking apparatus, and economic policy became more pragmatic. The exchange-rate policy now became flexible with a floating band and daily devaluations. The government also reduced tariffs – raised in 1983 in response to the economic crisis – and reinitiated privatization, which now moved into areas such as electricity and telecommunications.

One of the most important aspects of economic policy after 1985 was the increased state support for nontraditional exports. *Fundación Chile*, a semi-public agency providing support for the export sector, initiated the cultivation of salmon in 1982 and engaged in the first commercial production of salmon in 1986–1987. By the 1990s, salmon had become one of Chile's major exports (Ffrench-Davis 2002, 148). In the second half of the 1980s, ProChile stepped up its promotion of the establishment of export-oriented business associations. Such an association of firms was key in the tomato industry (Pérez-Alemán 2000, 50) and in the wine industry where a state-inspired winemakers' association allowed specialized medium-sized wine growers to find an export niche in an industry dominated by large producers. Deferred taxes on imported inputs and loan programs from the Inter-American Development Bank and CORFO further supported export expansion.

Employment generated by the growth and expansion of export activities would become key to poverty reduction. The labor force in the agro-livestock sector grew from 447,000 in 1975 to more than 880,000 by 1988

---

[18] The economic crisis stemmed from a variety of exogenous factors including a decline in the terms of trade, the increase in interest rates, and the Mexican crisis, which brought to a halt the flow of funds from abroad. But the economic collapse was also exacerbated by the reckless lending by the financial institutions belonging to the country's big conglomerates and by the delay in devaluation.

(Mujica Ateaga 1993, 254). The fruit and vegetable industry became one of the most dynamic employment generators, accounting for 18.6 percent of industrial employment in 1985–1992 (Mujica Ateaga 1993, 42). Benefiting from the investment made in the 1970s, fresh fruit exports increased at an average annual rate of 15.8 percent between 1983 and 1987, and by 1987 constituted 80 percent of agro-livestock exports (Mujica Ateaga 1993, 253). Export-led growth also had important spin-offs. By 1990, there were 4,102 enterprises tied directly to export activities; by 1992 this figure was 5,432 (Aguilera Reyes 1994, 62). Networks of small producers as suppliers to large firms also became predominant in agro-industrial production. Although economic-policy changes under military rule contributed to the model's success, it is important to bear in mind that Chile's export drive also rested, in part, on the accomplishments of the period prior to military rule.

The new economic model, with its dependence on fiscal equilibrium, a streamlined state, and a highly flexible and quiescent labor force, required political institutions that would discourage "populist" pressures after the return to civilian rule. The 1980 constitution, as amended in 1988, provided a variety of institutional mechanisms that would encumber any newly elected civilian government, and thus sustain the new economic model. One of the most important of these mechanisms was the provision for nine appointed senators; this was key because President Pinochet appointed nine loyalists in 1988 who, in alliance with representatives from the right-wing parties, were able to block constitutional reform following the return of civilian rule.[19] In addition, the presence of the appointed senators forced the Concertación government to negotiate with the political right for the passage of ordinary bills. Another important change was the 1975 law giving the finance minister ultimate authority over all decisions with financial implications, a measure that weakened the policy strength of other ministries and agencies within the state and bolstered fiscal conservativism. Finally, one of the most important legacies was the inequality of political power bequeathed by the military regime, which had given the private sector privileged access to the state while excluding other societal groups.

Concertación and the Third Way

These legacies of military rule have constrained Chile's post-1990 brand of social democracy, a case of path dependency. Two principal features distinguish Chile's Third-Way regime from our other cases of social

---

[19] A bill passed in August 2005 eliminated all unelected senators by March 2006.

democracy: its unwavering commitment to trade liberalization and privatization despite considerable public opposition; and its predisposition to a policy process that discourages participation by civil society and rank-and-file party members, while affording business access to the highest reaches of government.

Initially, the civilian leadership appeared strongly committed to the reversal of those military-instituted policies that its supporters found most reprehensible. Though declaring that poverty was most effectively addressed by sustained export-led growth, the Concertación promised "profound changes" in the labor code, a new universal unemployment system, tax reform, and expansion in social programs. It was soon to face an uphill struggle against opposition parties and the private sector in pursuing its promises. Confronted with a recalcitrant private sector, whose confidence it viewed as essential for the success of its economic program, Concertación, between 1990 and 2000, clearly opted for a strategy that privileged export-led growth and the maintenance of business confidence over a more concerted effort to reduce inequality.

Concertación's behavior must be viewed within the context of the country's "pacted" transition. That transition involved the commitment of incoming political elites not to tamper with the major features of the neoliberal economic model. Various institutional features were put in place to ensure that the model remained intact. But the leadership of the Concertación did not need to be coerced into acquiescence; many leaders, including individuals closely associated with the UP experiment, came to strongly support the new economic model – provided it incorporated measures to address the social deficit. Several factors contributed to this changed mindset: a reassessment of the UP years, the influence of new market ideas, criticism of the Eastern European socialist experience by those who spent their exile there, and the improvement of the Chilean economy after 1985 (Silva 1991, 400; Puryear, 1996). The resistance to labor and wider civil-society involvement in the policy process also sprung, in part, from this reassessment of the UP experience – from the belief that "excessive" social mobilization is destabilizing and would, in the long run, worsen conditions for workers and the poor. Left party leaders now maintained that changes should not be made unless accepted by capitalists (Petras and Leiva 1994, 92). The Argentine political transition, in which pressures for improved living standards produced a disastrous level of inflation and severe economic crisis, further reinforced the belief that "populist pressures" must be contained.

Hence, business, under the Concertación government, retained privileged access to the policy process, and power remained concentrated in the hands of the Finance Ministry (Teichman 2001, 84, 92). An array of

institutionalized channels, in addition to easy personal access to top policymakers, has provided the business community with the opportunity
to influence policy. Business people participated in working commissions
on economic policy, in consultative bodies, in monthly meetings with the
head of the Central Bank, and in the negotiation of trade agreements.

The new civilian government was keen to demonstrate its commitment to the market. One of its first moves after coming to power was
further trade liberalization. The administration also pursued privatization of airlines, mining, electricity, and ports, and sought to loosen foreign investment restrictions on the state-owned copper company.[20] In
addition, the Concertación added some new ingredients to the export-
led model. The signing of many bilateral trade agreements, especially
with Latin American countries, opened up new markets for manufactured goods. It also explicitly used the state in the promotion of economic
expansion, augmenting official support for small and medium enterprises,
including support for their participation in foreign markets. These policies help account for Chile's continuing (albeit slowed) export growth
despite appreciation in the peso before 1999, for the continued reduction in poverty in the late 1990s, and for the country's comparatively good
track record in employment-creation.

Concertación paid increasing attention to export opportunities for
small and medium enterprises, owing to their important job-creation
role. In addition to ProChile, a new program, "Projects of Promotion"
(PROFOS), promoted exports in sectors such as textiles and footwear
that had been adversely affected by the economic model of the past
decades. By 1997, there were 305 PROFOS involving 3,400 small and
medium enterprises in these sectors (Pérez-Alemán 2000, 49, 50). Similarly, the National Fund for Technological and Productive Development
(FONTEC), established in 1991 to provide funding and subsidies to
promote research and technological development, has supported a significant number of small and medium enterprises (Alarcón and Stumpo
2001, 180–83).

Some of these policies appear to have shaped further changes in the
country's export profile and its continued dynamism. By the end of the
1990s exports of manufactured products produced from local natural
resources accounted for less than 30 percent of exports, whereas the
export of manufactures not based on natural resources – as well as manufactures based on new types of local natural resources (such as, textiles,
apparel, plastic products, paper, and household furniture) – became more
dynamic, reaching 35 percent of exports by the second half of the 1990s

---

[20] The major purpose of these privatizations was to increase business confidence.

(Ffrench-Davis 2002, 154). Diversification into Latin American markets has also occurred. Whereas Chile's exports to industrialized countries tend to be processed natural-resource products, its exports to Latin American countries are, increasingly and in the majority, manufactured goods.

Yet, Chile's export model remains a highly concentrated affair. Only eighteen firms generate an estimated 60 percent of Chilean exports. Indeed, economic power remains highly concentrated: fifty private conglomerates exercise horizontally diversified control over large segments of the economy (Díaz 1997, 160, 162).

The support given by the state to the business community in matters of industrial policy, however, was not matched by the business community's cooperation in achieving some of the administration's pressing social objectives. Business proved to be an intractable obstacle in the state's struggle to rectify the inequalities bequeathed by the military regime. This is evident in efforts at equitable reforms of the tax system and the labor code, where the institutional legacy of military rule helped to strengthen business policy preferences. The desire to increase social spending required additional fiscal resources, which the government wished to finance through increased taxes. But business strongly opposed tax increases and was supported in this opposition by the political right in Congress. Hence, in order to institute tax reform, the executive was forced to negotiate with the congressional right wing: the consequence was a tax reform that fell well short of the original objectives. Instead of a permanent 10–20 percent increase in the corporate tax on profits, the Concertación government settled for an increase of 15 percent for a limited four-year period and a regressive increase in the value-added tax from 16 to 18 percent (Boylan 1996, 9; Muñoz Gomá and Celedón 1996, 197).

With respect to the labor code, labor's representatives argued that its key features undermined the unions' ability to improve the living standards of workers, a particularly pressing problem in the rural sector. In 1990, no more than 10 percent of workers were covered by collective contracts, and unionization stood at only 12.5 percent. One of the main demands made by labor, originally supported by Concertación, was collective bargaining above the firm level. The 1991 labor reform made this possible only if management agreed.[21] Another reform attempt was mounted in 1995; but it was blocked by opposition from the business

---

[21] It did eliminate dismissal without cause, the sixty-day strike limit, and the prohibition of trade unions for seasonal workers, a measure essential to an improvement in rural working conditions. But union affiliation and union activities remained extremely weak in the rural sector due to the pressures exerted by management.

community and the political right in the Senate, including the appointed senators.[22] Failure to satisfy labor on the issue of reforming the labor code led to increasing tension between Concertación's leadership and the union movement.

In addition to backing down from one of its original labor-reform goals and compromising on tax reform, the two Concertación administrations prior to 2000 failed to introduce measures to address the dual nature of the health-care system.[23] This challenge would be taken up by the next administration, which would meet similar obstacles.

As a consequence of its policy exclusion, labor became increasingly restive. Strikes and demonstrations against various aspects of the government's neoliberal program increased through the 1990s. Rank-and-file members of the Concertación, particularly members of the Socialist Party, were critical of the government's failure to reform the labor code and of its commitment to further privatization.[24] Unrest among socialist rank-and-file militants within Concertación was reflected in the growing demand that the next Concertación presidential candidate be a socialist.

The force of society's demands was, however, blunted by two factors. First, though labor protest among urban workers and miners was on the upswing, the once highly mobilized rural masses remained politically quiescent for the reasons explained in the previous section. Second, civil-society organizations, though very active in the struggle for democratic transition, were largely absent from the political scene following the return to civilian rule. There have been a variety of explanations for this. Most observers point to the subordination of civil-society organizations to the political parties, beginning in 1986 when the political parties took leadership of the democratic transition (Oxhorn 1995). The "culture of fear" arising from the prolonged period of military rule is cited as an additional ingredient discouraging political involvement (Petras and Leiva 1994, 92). Moreover, the transition has involved the institutionalization

---

[22] While the private sector and many Concertación leaders argue that reforming the labor code so as to grant workers greater protection (that is, making the code more rigid) will generate more unemployment because it becomes more expensive to lay off workers, the trade unions and other members of Concertación argue that more flexible labor markets generate poorly paid and precarious employment.

[23] Although a reform of the educational system was introduced in 1996, the system continues to display significant inequalities. The reforms introduced have not significantly reduced the high proportion of functional illiteracy that characterizes lower-income groups in Chile. See Schiefelbein 2003.

[24] In the 1996 municipal elections, the two socialist parties increased their support at the expense of the Christian Democrats, and in that same year, the Communist candidates won three presidencies: of the Professors' Association, the Students' Federation, and the health workers' union, while the coal workers' union began to replace socialist leaders identified with the government by Communist Party members (Teichman 2001, 188).

of many grass-roots organizations that have been contracted by the government (through FOSIS) to carry out training programs and establish microenterprises. The attempt to transform local solidarity organizations into market-competitive enterprises has often had the impact of breaking down community solidarity, as individuals and organizations compete over access to government resources (Paley 2001).

Despite these mitigating factors, social issues played an important role in the 2000 electoral campaign. Concertación's presidential candidate, the Socialist Party's Ricardo Lagos, used the defeat of the 1999 labor reform – Concertación's third attempt – as evidence that the opposition center-right candidate was not as concerned about social issues as he claimed (*La Tercera*, December 2, 1999). The 2000 election, which saw a narrow win for the Concertación presidential candidate, set the stage for a more concerted governmental effort to address equity, for a change in government attitude toward labor and civil-society involvement in policy, and for increasing disharmony between the government and the private sector. But, though tensions between business and government have increased, resistance on the part of the government to broader public participation in policy has remained.

Current challenges: maintaining the delicate balance

For a decade, the Concertación leadership had ensured business confidence through a combination of policies geared to winning business support. Nevertheless, it succeeded in substantially reducing poverty, though changes to the labor law fell considerably short of labor demands, and inequality has remained unacceptably high. The first two Concertación administrations had made some effort to placate labor and address public concerns, but by the turn of the century, it was apparent to many that the scales had been tipping in the direction of the powerful business lobby.

Shortly after taking office in 2000, President Lagos acknowledged that many Chileans were dissatisfied with the current neoliberal economic model (*Global News Bank*, March 8, 2000). He also announced a reform of the labor code, equality-enhancing reforms to the health system, and a new program to end extreme poverty, known as *Chile Solidario*. In addition, in what appeared to be an acknowledgment of the closed nature of the policy process, he also promised that his government would be "in permanent contact with the people" (*Global News Bank*, March 8, 2000). He set up a "Council of Social Dialogue" (a tripartite bargaining council involving government, business, and labor) to reach a consensus on a new labor bill. He also established a new civil-society consultative mechanism, the Citizens' Council, as part of his "Program for

Strengthening the Alliances between Civil Society and the State."
Although the new administration pledged, again, that integration into
the international market continued to be its "strategic project," it now
linked the development of human capital with efforts to provide high-
quality jobs by attracting foreign investment (Lagos 2001).

More has been achieved on the export-promotion front than on the
social-reform or public-participation issues. The Lagos administration
continued the strategy of seeking new international markets. It signed
trade agreements with the United States, the European Union, and South
Korea; in 2003, it opened negotiations for trade agreements with New
Zealand and Singapore. It also introduced a new strategy, similar to that of
Costa Rica and Mauritius, of seeking high-technology investors with the
objective of establishing Chile as the Latin American hub for back-office
business services (such as accounting and financing), call and customer-
service centers, and software development. The program, administered
by CORFO, aims to encourage competitiveness, new investment, better
jobs, and equal opportunities for Chileans (CORFO 2003). By 2001,
it claimed to have attracted fifteen new investment projects (CORFO
2001).

The central concern of business confidence – seen as essential to investment, economic growth, and job creation – has remained paramount.
Hence, the Lagos administration backed down when faced with stiff resistance from the private sector to its labor- and health-reform proposals. In
an attempt to equalize the quality of health care, the government proposal
called for the establishment of a "Solidarity Fund," to support guaranteed
coverage for an expanded basket of health-care services for all Chileans.
It was to be funded by contributions from both the public and private
health-care systems. However, as this proposal entailed a reduction in the
inflow of funds to private health-care providers, it incurred the wrath of
not just the private health-care companies, but also of the private sector more generally (*La Tercera*, November 15, 2001; *Estrategia*, April 10,
2002). Business and the political right eventually succeeded in having
the Solidarity Fund removed from the legislation (*La Tercera*, August 30,
2004). Although the socialist parties continue to campaign for its rein-
sertion, the polarization on the issue is reflected in the views expressed by
some party members who have questioned the very principle of health-
care provision by profit-making companies (*La Tercera*, November 16,
2001).[25]

---

[25] Divisions over the labor- and health-reform proposals also occurred within the Concertación itself with some members supporting the position of the private sector. The
government's proposal that the program be financed by new taxes on alcohol, tobacco,

Similar difficulties afflicted the government's reform of the labor code. Its difficult passage reflected the lack of consensus among the ruling Concertación elite on the issue, the dissatisfaction of the labor movement with the status quo, and the influence that the private sector exerts on policy. While the government again entertained the idea of making collective bargaining above the firm level obligatory, it quickly abandoned the idea in the face of stiff business resistance (Haagh 2002, 102). Two attempts to arrive at a consensus on reform through tripartite discussions within the newly established Council of Social Dialogue failed. When labor secured some provisions it viewed as representing a significant advance, business demanded the resignation of the labor minister (*La Tercera*, September 21, 2001; November 15, 2001).[26] Government–business relations remained tense for many months thereafter.

Subsequent labor-reform initiatives have alternated between an attempt to placate business and an effort to improve labor protection. A bill to ease regulations restricting the length of the working day produced a hostile labor reaction in the form of a general strike in 2003 – a strike that coupled its opposition to the proposed legislation with a rejection of the country's neoliberal model that, it charged, was producing poor-quality, precarious employment and a small number of very wealthy people. Then, in 2004, as economic growth returned and business profits shot up, the government introduced a new labor bill which, it claimed, would distribute the benefits of economic growth more equitably by reducing the working day and regulating overtime pay (*La Tercera*, September 5, 2004). This initiative, negotiated only with labor representatives, angered business.

Although the return of economic growth has seemingly opened the policy door to labor, little progress has been made in the area of civil-society involvement in social policy.[27] This administration, like the previous two Concertación administrations, appeared to prefer an acquiescent and passive civil society. Political leaders took the position that it is the elected representatives who should make policy, not civil-society organizations and especially not NGOs that, from their perspective, can have very

and fuel satisfied no one. At the time of writing it appeared that the reform would be financed by the increase in the value added tax (IVA) – once again, a regressive solution.

[26] Fines on businesses for unjustified dismissals were increased as was compensation to workers for such dismissals; employers now had to specify reasons for layoffs and workers could appeal to a tribunal; the number of workers required to constitute a union was reduced; severance pay for years of service was increased, and workers fired due to union activities had to be rehired (*La Tercera*, August 31, 2001).

[27] The information in this paragraph draws from personal interviews carried out in September/October 2003 of three senior level government officials and four leaders of NGOs. Since anonymity was promised, interviewee names are omitted.

particular interests not necessarily congruent with broader societal needs. Civil-society consultations remain confined to the social investment fund agency, FOSIS, which, as the organization that grants funding to NGOs for specific programs, listens to NGOs' viewpoints on administrative aspects of those programs. Moreover, FOSIS programs have become increasingly targeted, moving from investment in community projects to the targeting of aid to individual families. Critics argue that while the former promoted community involvement and action, the latter discourages it and even divides communities. One of the most telling cases of the state's rejection of civil-society involvement in policy relates to the new anti-poverty program, *Chile Solidario*. In this case, senior officials in the Ministries of Finance and Social Planning developed policy – after close consultation with the World Bank. Senior officials flatly rejected the policy participation of societal organizations, even when World Bank funding for such consultations appeared to be forthcoming. By 2003, the work of the Citizens Council had ground to a halt when its recommendations for measures to strengthen civil society went unheeded and it failed to receive most of the funds that had been promised. By 2003, civil-society leaders claimed to be virtually excluded from social policy.

Political pressures for redistributive measures became particularly pressing when economic growth slowed following the 1998 Asian crisis. It is during economic downturns that the inadequacies of social protection stand starkly revealed.[28] However, the room for political maneuver in such circumstances is limited when a government accords highest priority to macroeconomic stability and business confidence. While the political opposition resists tax increases, the public demands rectification of inequalities and increased social protection – all of which requires increased expenditures. The return of good economic times has recently emboldened the government to propose increased taxes on the private sector (e.g., a new tax on mining operations); but it continues to confront stiff resistance from business.

For the Concertación, continued social gains are tied to new export opportunities, especially ones that provide higher-quality employment. Chile's economic model, to date, has reduced poverty largely by generating employment of the low-skill, low-pay variety. Improving living standards for workers in these sectors is an uphill struggle when improved wages and working conditions are believed to reduce global competitiveness, and therefore, ultimately, employment as well. Continued improvement in living standards will likely require a significant alteration in the

---

[28] Chile has yet to provide social security protection to its independent and informal-sector workers, most of whom do not belong to any social-security program.

type of employment generated. But success in securing export niches that create well-paying jobs involves increasingly intense competition with firms in other countries with similar strategies; success will depend on factors that lie beyond the government's control.

Chile's most pressing challenges, however, are political. It is vital to secure a social pact that allows for measures to reduce inequality while opening channels for policy input from labor and civil society. Achieving these objectives will be a difficult struggle in the face of a powerful business class and a political right accustomed to getting their own way. Although a recent bill eliminating appointed senators removed one of the institutional obstacles to a more inclusive policy process, a powerful business community will continue to be influential. Yet, the failure to achieve a class compromise that emphasizes equality issues risks political unrest and a further erosion of the legitimacy of democratic institutions.

Conclusion

Chile's journey toward the Third Way has been tumultuous. Well-organized class interests have scripted a history of political polarization and sharp swings in policy experiments from Marxist/socialist to radically neoliberal. These extreme policy experiments each contributed, in its own way, to the current scenario.

Chile's struggle for social justice originated in a militant labor movement and in leftist political parties. These parties spread socialist ideology to the shantytowns and the countryside, propelling forward the land reform of the radical-mobilizational phase – a reform crucial to the dynamic export-led growth of subsequent years. The goals of equity and social justice, purged of the earlier Marxist rhetoric, survive in the current Concertación leadership. Purer versions of the old ideology live on among the rank and file of the left parties and trade unions. It is the growing pressure from these sectors for more concerted efforts to reduce inequality, combined with the strong resistance to such efforts on the part of the economic elite, which accounts for the tenuousness and fragility of the country's class compromise.

The Pinochet dictatorship, for its part, has shaped the country's market society in profound ways, locking in fundamental institutional features. The alliance backing the military included the country's most powerful conglomerates, a considerable portion of the middle class, and the orthodox economists known as the Chicago Boys. This new ruling alliance dismantled the old ISI model. The new incentive system that this dismantling entailed (tariff reductions and the weakening of labor protections, in particular) did more than stimulate agro-livestock exports: it triggered a transformation in the country's economic and social structure, along with the expansion of an entirely new export profile. It was this new package of exports that led to economic growth and stimulated employment opportunities. But the success of this economic model depended upon a restrictive labor regime.

Despite the swings in policy experiments, the involvement of the state in economic promotion has remained constant. The state has supported technological innovation and new entrepreneurial activities, and has pursued new export markets. This state activism had its origin in the activities of CORFO and continued even during military rule.

The Chilean path to the Third Way, involving political chaos, traumatic policy reversals, and military dictatorship, is not one any country would wish to replicate. Its experience does, however, offer some worthwhile lessons. It highlights the importance of the state in the promotion of export-led growth, the impact of programmatic political parties and movements, the lingering problems associated with the failed incorporation of the rural poor, and the possibility of constructing a social pact (albeit fragile) in a country with a history of political polarization and class conflict. Indeed, it was the very extent of political polarization and the trauma of military rule that laid the basis for the current frail compromise, combining the neoliberal economic model with social-justice goals. The result is a diluted form of social democracy that has dramatically reduced poverty through an effective collaboration between the state and the private sector, but has been unable to lessen income and wealth inequalities. The private sector and the political right, viewing measures in this direction as incompatible with their neoliberal vision, remain powerful enough to block many egalitarian measures. Yet, a dissatisfied labor movement and a restive civil society continue to press for equality-enhancing measures. The story of Chilean social democracy is, therefore, far from over.

Part III

Patterns and prospects

7 Social and political origins

Each of our four cases evokes claims of exceptionalism. Mauritius is often described as a "miracle," Kerala as a "model," Costa Rica as the "Switzerland of Central America," and Chile as the "tiger" of Latin America. When examined individually, the contingencies of history, social or cultural particularities, and visionary leadership naturally carry much of the explanatory weight. But when viewed comparatively, a general type emerges. In all four cases democratic institutions have allowed for the effective expression of subordinate-class interests and resulted in patterns of development that are remarkably equitable by regional standards – albeit with a more discontinuous and inegalitarian pattern in Chile. The fact that our cases (and others) share such a strong resemblance to each other while being so different from their neighbors points to something more than just accident or idiosyncrasy at work. These are, in effect, *exceptionalisms of a general type* and suggest a homology – a common causal history.[1] This chapter explores this homology by teasing out the necessary historical conditions and processes that underwrite trajectories of social-democratic development.

To make sense of these *exceptionalisms of a general type*, they need to be grasped from different levels of analysis that move from the most general causal variables to the most proximate. We develop our analysis and argument at three levels. We first demonstrate that all of our cases share the same long-term *structural* properties of having been integrated early and deeply into the global capitalist economy. The terms of this integration helped shape a *configuration of sociopolitical opportunities*, specifically a set of class relationships, organizational spaces (civil society), and institutional conditions that were preconditions for the emergence of social-democratic forces. We find that agrarian class relations, and in particular the role of independent peasants, are particularly important in molding social-democratic outcomes. Finally, we briefly refer to the *critical*

---

[1] For a discussion of why homology has far greater scientific explanatory power than analogy, see Elster 1999, 7–8.

junctures that led to the establishment of these regimes – in particular, we focus on the organized social actors (parties, movements, leaders) who decisively shaped these junctures.[2] The explanatory leverage of each of these levels of analysis – the structural, the configurational, and the conjunctural – is spelled out in general terms in the following three sections.

In the second half of the chapter, we explain the origins of social democracy in our cases by means of this analytical framework. The Chilean path has been distinct from that of Kerala, Costa Rica, and Mauritius in several respects. In Chile, demands for inclusive and equitable development came principally from a militant, largely urban, working class. In Kerala, Mauritius, and Costa Rica, social democracy had significant agrarian roots. The defeat of democratic socialism in Chile in 1973 – in contrast to the more continuous path of social-democratic development in the other cases – can be attributed partly to the relative lateness and explosive nature of the political incorporation of rural underclasses. The authoritarian reaction of 1974–1989, in turn, explains Chile's more limited, Third-Way version of social democracy since 1990.

Structural origins: capitalism and the global economy

Social democracy is a response to capitalism: no capitalism, no social democracy. A stunted or undynamic capitalism, such as has prevailed in most countries of the global periphery, inhibits the emergence of social democracy in three ways. It restricts the material resources available for distribution, leads to weak subordinate-class formation, and is associated with weak states.

The path to social democracy in our four cases begins with capitalism – the early development of an enclave mining economy in Chile, and the deep commercialization of agriculture in Kerala, Mauritius, and Costa Rica. The impact of capitalism on democracy and social democracy is mediated through the particular patterns of class formation it triggers. The different terms of integration into the global economy of Chile, on the one hand, and Kerala, Mauritius, and Costa Rica, on the other, explain in part why Chile's path to social democracy has been more discontinuous and less complete. In Chile, the mining economy led to the formation of a militant, ideologically cohesive, and well-organized working class represented by programmatic parties. This class has been strongly associated with the success of social democracy in Europe, but in Chile the specific configurational dynamics that evolved out of the enclave mining economy

---

[2] Collier and Collier define a critical juncture as "a period of significant change, which typically occurs in distinct ways in different countries (or in other units of analysis) and which is hypothesized to produce distinct legacies" (1991, 29).

proved much less favorable to social democracy. The Chilean path differs from the European one not only in the comparatively small size of the working class in Chile, but also in the fact that the agrarian sector was slow to modernize. In contrast, in Kerala, Mauritius, and Costa Rica the deep commercialization of agriculture precipitated the formation of organized subordinate classes in the rural sector that in turn underwrote the political success of social democracy. Why and how the increasing orientation of rural society to markets is important to our specific cases will be addressed later, but the general point here is that the commercialization of agriculture matters for political trajectories because of the ways in which it transforms agrarian class relations.

In the most influential version of this argument, Barrington Moore (1966) identifies three possible trajectories. Where landed elites make a gradual transition to commercial activities and align themselves with the bourgeoisie, the stage is set for democracy. Where landed elites fail to adapt but remain politically strong, they react by using the state to reassert their power, leading to right-wing authoritarianism. Finally, where landed elites fail to adapt to the market and are politically weak, they are defeated by a revolutionary peasantry resulting in left-wing authoritarianism. Although Moore's argument continues to provide powerful analytic insight into the social origins of democracy, it has, for our purposes, three shortcomings. First, Moore's focus on the bourgeoisie as the carrier of democracy ("no bourgeoisie, no democracy") obscures the fact that its role in promoting political representation in Europe only went so far – enfranchising men of property – and that it took the working class to push the process further to universal male suffrage (Rueschemeyer, Stephens, and Stephens 1992). Moreover, those countries where the middle class emerged as a powerful political actor in its own right produced a form of liberal democracy that has more or less precluded the formation of social democracy (Luebbert 1991). Second, commercialization matters not only because it creates new actors (who may or may not be good for social democracy), but also because it promotes the rise of civil society. The creation of new markets stimulates new channels of communication outside those controlled by the royal court or the aristocracy, as well as demands for protection of property through the rule of law. This is the dual sense in which Habermas (1989) links the rise of the market to the creation of the classical public sphere of the seventeenth and eighteenth centuries.[3] The creation of protected public spaces also

---

[3] Brenner (1985) has argued that under certain prevailing property relations, commercialization can result in a deepening of labor-repressive institutions, as in the Second Serfdom of Eastern Germany. Much the same could be argued for many plantation economies. But in the absence of extremely effective mechanisms of landlord control, commercialization does erode traditional dependencies.

increases the opportunities for independent subordinate-class organization. Third, Moore failed to recognize the possibility of a fourth road
to modernity, one in which the period of commercialization is marked
by consolidation of a market-oriented smallholding rural class. And this
class, as we shall see, has played a key role in the social-democratic trajectory.

Aside from the impact of capitalism on internal class relations, integration into the global economy has important consequences in its own right.
Indeed, the link between global exposure and the dependence on trade,
on the one hand, and social democracy, on the other, is well established
in the European context (see chapter 8): the more a national economy
depends on imports and exports, the more likely it is to invest in social protection. Katzenstein (1984) and Cameron (1984) specifically locate the
mechanism for this in the logic of class compromise. To be competitive in
export markets, capital demands a particularly productive and quiescent
labor force, but in exchange, labor demands that it be protected from the
greater risk of recession and dislocation that an outward-oriented economy entails. The compromise then takes the form of the welfare state.
More recently, Rodrik has shown that there is a robust statistical correlation between the degree of economic openness and the level of public
expenditure in OECD countries (1997, 52). He also shows that the relationship holds even when extended to a larger sample of 115 countries,
and concludes that "the social welfare state is the flip side of the open
economy" (1997, 53). Rodrik's findings, however, raise as many questions as they answer. The measure of welfare in his 115-country sample
is government consumption, which excludes income transfers and public
investment, but includes military expenditure. It is not at all obvious that
government consumption can be treated as welfare – a wasteful populist
regime could spend as much as an effective social-democratic regime.
The decisive factor lies, as in the version of this argument presented by
Katzenstein (1984), in the make-up of the social forces that mediate the
effects of this otherwise robust structural relationship.

In sum, exposure to new market forces matters, but only as this exposure is mediated by class relations, and more specifically by the balance
or configuration of class power. This has been powerfully demonstrated
by Luebbert's (1991) analysis of interwar politics in Europe. In what
he labels "aliberal" societies – those that went toward either fascism or
social democracy – the middle peasantry emerged as the pivotal class.
Where it aligned itself with the urban middle class, the result was fascism, most clearly in the case of Germany; where it was coupled with the
working class (the Scandinavian red–green alliance), the outcome was
social democracy. But, in both cases, the middle peasantry was politically

mobilized owing to the failure of liberal solutions to economic crisis. As Luebbert notes, in aliberal societies: "liberals' reluctance to stabilize commodity markets at prices peasants found acceptable, their fixation with a return to the gold standard and the consequent deflations, their embrace of urban, secular, sometimes anticlerical, cultures, and the liberal ineffectiveness that derived from division within the urban liberal community all alienated peasants" (1991, 282).

Hence, when independent smallholders were exposed to the market without being protected, they rebelled and asserted their political interests. Depending on the configuration of class alliances, they either opposed liberal economics but embraced liberal politics (social democracy)[4] or rejected both liberal economics and liberal politics (fascism). Either way, what the peasants did was critical to the political outcomes of interwar Europe.

Configurations: class power, civil society, and the state

Although theorists of industrial society as well as some neo-Marxists have provided functionalist explanations for the rise of social democracy, the comparative literature on the welfare state makes a compelling case that the rise of different kinds of welfare states can be ascribed largely to the variable strength of working-class organizations. This theory points both to the size, organizational coherence, and encompassing nature of the working class, and to the willingness of working-class parties to forge cross-class political alliances in gaining electoral power (Evans and Stephens 1988). In its emphasis on the relational and historically contingent nature of working-class power, this is in fact a balance-of-class-power model much in the tradition of Barrington Moore. Outside of Europe, the explanatory leverage of this model loses some of its precision, but overall still holds. Thus, both Collier and Collier (1991) and Rueschemeyer, Stephens, and Stephens (1992) provide powerful accounts of the trajectory of democracy and social inclusion in Latin America that draw on the idea of a balance of class power.

Although this model takes on added complexity in the context of the global south – owing to the more uneven dynamic of class formation and to the critical significance of the timing and modalities of working-class incorporation (Collier and Collier 1991) – it nonetheless underscores two critical findings. First, following once again in the footsteps of Moore,

---

[4] All three of the foundational social pacts struck in the 1930s in Norway, Sweden, and Denmark provided protections for small farmers against the market. These included agricultural price support, interest-rate reductions, debt restructuring, and protective tariffs (Luebbert 1991, 268).

the thesis that the resilience of landlords and of labor-repressive agriculture represents a major hurdle to democracy holds firm, if with interesting modifications (Huber and Safford 1995; Paige 1997). Second, the size and the encompassing nature of the working class is also critical to explaining pressures for social and redistributive reforms. Thus, the short-lived democratic-socialist regime in Chile (1970–1973) rose to power on the strength of a working class that was highly unionized and represented by programmatic parties. The Southern Cone countries in general have had stronger labor movements and more generous welfare states than others on the continent. In South Africa – the only southern African country with a significant industrial working class – the African National Congress (ANC) came to power in large part on the strength of a highly solidaristic labor movement (Adler and Webster 1995) and championed a social-democratic agenda.[5] In South Korea, a militant working class was not only instrumental in pushing for democracy, but has successfully bid up wages and secured new collective-bargaining structures since the democratic opening (Koo 2001).

Within the analytical parameters of the balance-of-class-forces argument, we need to make two qualifications to adapt the model to the circumstances of late developers. First, the historical protagonist is no longer exclusively the industrial working class (Chile excepted), but rather rural lower classes, albeit often aligned with the working class. This modification is crucial because, among other things, it explains why social democracy in the periphery consists mostly of social insurance schemes and accelerated social development but has only very limited instances of the formal state-orchestrated tripartite class compromise that defines European social democracy. Second, a key element of the viability of social democracy in the periphery is the autonomy of lower classes. In European social democracy, organized working classes have aligned themselves with the state without compromising their autonomy. In contrast, because of the nature of the "overdeveloped" state (Alavi 1982) in much of the developing world, lower-class mobilization often results in either state-led corporatism or repression. In Latin America and India, selective incorporation has generally been the rule, while in East Asia, sustained growth was in large part made possible by the repressive subordination of labor (Deyo 1987). In either scenario, the continuous and constant demand-side logic of social-democratic politics is thwarted. The possibilities of

---

[5] That South Africa has subsequently traveled a very different path underscores that a favorable balance of class forces is a necessary but not sufficient condition. Explaining the ANC's embrace of neoliberal orthodoxy calls for also considering the role of civil society and of the political party system.

preserving lower-class political autonomy are in turn tied to the quality and depth of civil society.

Civil society looms large in any explanation of social democracy in the periphery because it is the terrain on which social classes are formed. As Rueschemeyer, Stephens, and Stephens (1992) have shown, the presence of a robust civil society has been a determining factor in the democratic trajectories of South America, Central America, and the Caribbean. But, in contrast to neo-Tocquevillian views of civil society that simply equate associationalism with democratization, Rueschemeyer, Stephens, and Stephens argue that it "is not the density of civil society per se, but the empowerment of previously excluded classes aided by this density that improves the chances of democratization" (1992, 50). Developing an argument first formulated by Therborn (1977), they show that the self-organization of the working class is critical to the prospects of democratization. In turn, the existence of a robust civil society is important because it creates the spaces in which subordinate groups can associate and self-organize, increasing the likelihood that these groups will become coherent political actors capable of independently articulating their interests. Rueschemeyer, Stephens, and Stephens emphasize this point specifically in reference to *the state* (as is the norm in treatments of civil society), arguing that a strong civil society is one in which state repression or direct control of social activity is limited. But the existence of public spaces also means that subordinate actors can organize *free of a range of social dependencies*, most notably direct material dependencies (debt bondage, manor-based tenancy, guilds) as well as pre-democratic authority structures (chiefs, castes, caciques, rural bosses).

It is important, therefore, to analytically disentangle two dimensions of civil society that are often conflated. If the existence of *robust public spaces* increases the probability of subordinate-class mobilization, *associationalism* itself has a far more contingent impact on democracy. Associational life may promote horizontal ties; but it can also become the conduit through which reactionary elites or authoritarian regimes mobilize support. The latter occurred, for example, in the fall of democracy in Weimar Germany (Berman 1997), and the building of authoritarian regimes in Italy and Spain (Riley 2005). The rise of Hindu nationalism in India, which is by definition antithetical to secular plural democracy, is only the most recent example of how associational practices can breed anti-democratic ideologies (Jaffrelot 1996; Hansen 1999). In all of these cases, reactionary elites nurtured mass bases of support by tapping into paternalistic, hierarchical, and militarist traditions and social structures.

If the relationship between civil society, working-class formation, and democratization is well established, it takes on even greater analytic precision when we turn to the question of social democracy. That most observers and comparative studies have found Scandinavian countries to have the highest levels of associational life in advanced democracies suggests an affinity between civil society and social democracy. The affinity exists through two mechanisms. First, the nature of civil society shapes the form of subordinate-class self-organization. In Sweden, a vibrant mass-based civil society emerged in the nineteenth century, including popular movements (*folksrorelser*) such as the temperance movement, the free churches, the labor movement, and cooperatives. Because voluntary associations predated mass organizations (such as parties and labor confederations), the working class and the middle peasantry in Sweden were self-organized and independent actors before the advent of electoral politics. In general, social-democratic parties emerged in European countries where the working class was already well organized at the turn of the century. In contrast, those countries in which liberalism took hold in the interwar period (most notably France, England, and Switzerland) were marked by early labor movements whose organizational power was limited by craft forms of association (France and Switzerland) or splintered trade unions (England). This, in turn, allowed liberal parties to incorporate sections of the working class at an early stage of electoral politics

Second, civil society can also pave the way for social democracy by facilitating inter-class coordination. Antonio Gramsci (1972) saw the importance of civil society in this light, though he emphasized its ideological function. Contemporary interpretations have pointed to the role that cross-cutting civic structures can play in managing social conflict (Varshney 2002). If social democracy requires a continuous negotiation and renegotiation of distributional conflicts, it follows that dense, horizontally linked civil-society structures can greatly facilitate that process. This is obviously true in an organizational sense, namely that the presence of robust and legitimate intermediary bodies reduces the transaction costs of coordinating interests. But it is also true because of the way in which it shapes the political behavior of actors. Where civil society has emerged as a key arena for debating and reconciling differences, organized actors are much less likely to resort to power politics or even coercion. In Habermas's terms (1996), the existence of robust public spheres increases the chances that the "better argument," rather than force or sheer bargaining power, will prevail.

The final piece of the configurational analysis is the state, both because of the direct way in which it shapes political life and because of its key role in promoting social and economic development. States play a central role not only in regulating relations between society and the state, but also in regulating relations within civil society (Skocpol 1985). By defining the institutional rules of political life and mediating relations between social groups, states help determine which interests are represented and how they are coordinated. The state is thus critical to any process of class compromise. But favorable structural conditions and class configurations will come to very little if social reformers inherit state apparatuses that lack the technical capacity, the infrastructural reach, and the legitimacy to secure and allocate resources. Because social democracy essentially involves "scaling up" from community-based solidarity (the moral economy) to societal solidarity (the public moral economy), it requires a high-capacity state. At a minimum, any social-democratic state must enjoy the authority and capacity to secure revenues. The social-democratic state must also be capable of intervening in many areas of social and economic activity, without provoking exit by key economic actors.

Such fine-tuned intervention requires both the autonomy and bureaucratic efficiency of the Weberian state, and the embeddedness of Evans's developmental state (1995). As we saw in chapter 2, the history of state formation in the periphery has generally not been favorable to social democracy. European states were the product of a long history of state formation that included the gradual development of jurisprudence, administrative techniques, and the infrastructural and authoritative powers to mobilize revenues and citizens. State building took place through a long process of extending state authority (particularly the right to tax and conscript) in exchange for citizens' rights. However, the external origins of state power in much of the developing world preempted this positive-sum internal bargain between states and social forces. Colonialism not only bequeathed state machineries largely geared to extraction rather than development, but also left behind ruling oligarchies whose power rested on their ability to privatize or patrimonialize state powers. In sum, history in the global periphery has conspired to impede the formation of the differentiated, professionalized, rule-bound, and autonomous institutions of the modern state.

Nevertheless, specific colonial legacies and the modalities of integration into the world economy have, in practice, produced a wide range of state-building trajectories in the periphery. For example, Japanese colonialism generally had a salutary effect on state formation in East Asia (Kohli 2004). Where the British imposed direct, rather than indirect rule, colonial societies generally inherited more robust and rational-legal institutions (Lange 2004). Also, mineral-based enclave economies often provided the material basis for strong states that was lacking in other circumstances. Indeed, in all four of our cases, historical circumstances either created comparatively strong states by the standards of the region, or the possibility for rapidly increasing state capacity (Kerala). In each case, when social reformers or subordinate groups came to power, they could work through state institutions that had been to a considerable degree differentiated from oligarchic or patrimonial control and were able to implement broad-based reforms.

Critical junctures and actors: political parties and ideology

To understand how the rise of capitalism, processes of state building, the reconfiguration of class relations, and the contours of civil society shaped social-democratic trajectories, we have to pay attention to the role of organized actors, in particular political parties. High levels of lower-class mobilization do not necessarily produce social-democratic politics. Indeed, populism is the more common outcome. The role of parties is critical in aggregating interests and providing a consistent and programmatic outlook. Kohli (1987) has made a compelling case that the Communist Party of India (Marxist) in West Bengal has been able to tackle poverty much more effectively than any other party in India because of its organizational discipline, ideological coherence, and class base. But electorally dominant, left-of-center political parties are quite rare in the developing world; where they do emerge they are often subject to oligarchical tendencies.[6]

A close look at our cases reveals intense competition between comparatively moderate parties producing left-of-center outcomes owing to the ratcheting-up effect of competitive mobilization. This effect is triggered only if lower classes are well organized and oriented toward distributive gains. In Kerala, Costa Rica, and Mauritius, left-of-center parties played a crucial role in articulating lower-class interests in a coherent and policy-relevant manner, without threatening dominant interests to the point of triggering a reaction. Under these conditions, political elites concerned with short-term electoral gains will often make small distributive concessions that, because of party competition, trigger further rounds of demand making. In contrast, the revolutionary militancy of the Socialist

---

[6] It would be hard to imagine a more disciplined and programmatic party than the African National Congress. But its dominant party status has produced autocratic tendencies, allowing a technocratic elite to capture the party, jettison its historical social-democratic mandate, and embrace neoliberal orthodoxy. Similarly, the twenty-two-year rule of the CPI(M) in West Bengal has been marked by increasing patronage, organizational sclerosis, and rampant corruption.

Party and its allies in Chile in 1970–1973 produced a zero-sum confrontation with the dominant class and, consequently, an authoritarian reaction. In the post-Pinochet period of restored competitive politics, the comparative weakness of subordinate-class organizations – that have yet to recover from the repressive demobilization of the authoritarian period – and the relative autonomy of political parties from lower-class interests, have dulled the redistributive possibilities of democratic politics.

Finally, geopolitical factors can play a central role. Even when all the above domestic factors are favorably aligned for social democracy, they can be trumped by external interference. The intervention of superpowers in the developing world has generally not been kind to the fortunes of democracy. Social democracy would be a more common phenomenon in the global periphery had it not been for the bipolar logic of the Cold War, in which social democracy challenged both liberal capitalism and authoritarian communism. Social-democratic experiments in Eastern Europe were cut short by the Soviet Union. US intervention has had similar effects on emergent social democracy in the Americas, most notably in Guatemala, Jamaica, and Chile. Conversely, our three more successful social-democratic experiments have all slipped under the radar screen of geopolitical power plays.

The cases: capitalism and the global economy

All our cases share the common structural characteristic of having agricultural systems that experienced comparatively early commercialization driven by export orientation. This is dramatically the case for Kerala, which has been a major trading center since 3000 BC (trading cardamon and cinnamon with ancient Babylonia), and which was a nodal point in colonial spice routes as Europe's main supplier of black pepper and other spices. By the end of the nineteenth century, Kerala was also exporting large quantities of coir (coconut fiber) and a range of semi-processed agricultural commodities. It was, by far, the most export-oriented region of India. The only comparable case in South Asia was Sri Lanka, with its heavy dependence on tea exports. The fact that Sri Lanka has also traveled a social-democratic path (until at least 1977), achieving levels of development comparable to Kerala, underscores the link between early commercialization and social democracy.

In the postcolonial period, Costa Rica's economy was dominated by coffee exports. To this day, its political elites have deep roots in the coffee economy. Of course, most of the economies of Central America developed as coffee-exporters, but the impact of this cash crop was arguably more pronounced in Costa Rica than in Guatemala, Honduras, El Salvador, or Nicaragua. Costa Rica was unusual in that the early displacement of the relatively smaller indigenous population all but eliminated vestiges of subsistence-based peasant agriculture, and the country was therefore more dependent on coffee than the other coffee-exporters. Coffee remained the dominant export throughout the nineteenth and well into the twentieth century. Even as new crops (sugar and cotton) and meat exports grew in importance in the other Central American economies in the 1940s, coffee remained the most important crop in Costa Rica. Just as importantly, it is the country's early emergence as an exporter that led to the dominance of market-based relations. In contrast to the rest of Central America, Costa Rica's entire coffee commodity chain was integrated by market forces from an early stage, with a distinct separation of labor, land, and processing markets.

Sugarcane has been just as central to the Mauritius economy. The capacity to produce sugar, among other crops, initially attracted French planters to this uninhabited island. The French relied on African slaves for labor but were followed by the British who abolished slavery and instead imported Indian indentured laborers. Following their acquisition of Mauritius in 1810, the British aggressively expanded sugar production by reducing tariffs, providing credit, and building an extensive road infrastructure. In the first two decades of British rule, the area under sugarcane increased fivefold, and Mauritius was briefly the largest sugar exporter in the world (Lange 2003, 406).

Chile resembles Kerala insofar as both had a settled agrarian structure well before agriculture was commercialized. As with Kerala, Chile stood out regionally as being the most globally integrated, having developed the strongest export economy (based on nitrate, copper, and silver) of all the Spanish-American countries in the 1830–1860 period (Bergquist 1986, 21). Agriculture was first commercialized in response to demand for cheap food from the mining sector. Commercialization further accelerated when global demand for wheat increased in the mid-nineteenth century. Chilean landlords responded by dispossessing smallholders and expanding their estates. Between 1850 and 1875, wheat exports increased fourfold (Kay 1981). As in the case of Kerala, however, commercialization of agriculture did not imply modernization, and the traditional, landlord-dominated social order remained largely intact

All of our cases were therefore integrated into the global economy earlier and more deeply than their neighbors, with Mauritius being in effect created by global commercial markets, and Costa Rica, Kerala, and Chile witnessing significant changes in their economies and social structures as a result of global exposure. Commercialization had a range of effects. First, it accelerated state building. Taxes on export earnings provided the state with significant resources, and export-orientation required a more active role by the state in providing infrastructure and marketing. Compared to their neighbors, all of these countries had much earlier and more active state involvement in providing social services, which in large part explains why they continue to achieve the highest levels of social development in their regions. An important difference is that the state in Chile largely neglected rural areas until the 1960s, whereas the state in Costa Rica, Mauritius, and Kerala (at least the Southern Princely states before India's independence) penetrated and organized rural areas early on. The second, but somewhat less causally direct, effect is that the commercialization of agriculture triggered a certain social effervescence, including migration, new urban–rural linkages, and a loosening-up of traditional relations that produced new patterns of association. This is clearly the case in the highly segmented societies of nineteenth-century Kerala and Mauritius where new economic opportunities stimulated inter-group competition and eventually led to demands for social reform. In Costa Rica, the increased market orientation of coffee elites paved the way for the influence of liberalism. In Chile, however, the effect was largely contained to urban areas where the mining-based working class developed a vibrant associational culture. The commercialization of agriculture, passing as it did through the social power of the landed elite, resulted in the displacement of the small peasantry and the introduction of new forms of labor control, including the institution of *inquilinos* (explained below).

The most important effect of commercialization was on class relations. Although this dynamic (examined in the next section) unfolded over the course of decades, it was punctuated by politically decisive critical junctures. Rather than reiterate the historical narratives presented in chapters 3 to 6, we focus here on explaining the transitional periods that propelled each of our cases down its particular social-democratic path. During the interwar period, all of the cases experienced significant economic crises that triggered political reconfigurations. In Europe, the interwar mobilization of workers against the ravages of liberalism signaled the dawn of a new era of mass politics. In our cases, the Depression and the spread of political liberalism produced a different problem, namely the problem of how to incorporate the agrarian sector. Costa Rica's critical juncture begins gradually with demands made by smallholders for protection from the market and the social reforms in the 1920s and 1930s but reaches a watershed with the civil war of 1948. In Kerala, the transitional juncture begins with the caste reform movements in the south and the agrarian reform movements in the north in the 1930s and culminates politically with the electoral victory of the Communist Party of India (CPI) in 1957.

In Mauritius, the critical period begins with an agrarian crisis marked by labor militancy in the 1930s which triggered a cycle of continuous pressure for social and political change that lasted until independence (1968). Finally, in Chile, the agrarian problem was contained, but not resolved, until the 1960s by a landed elite that exerted tight social and political control over the countryside; it would explode politically after 1964, producing a rapid decompression of agrarian relations and political hyper-mobilization. This produced two inextricably and tragically linked critical junctures: the radical-mobilizational period (1964–1973) that ushered in an abortive but dramatic socialist experiment, and the author-itarian reaction (1974–1990) that set the stage for a labor-repressive vari-ant of neoliberal reform. While the radical-mobilization period extended social and political incorporation beyond the urban working and middle classes to the rural population and swept away the landlord-dominated agricultural system, the authoritarian period reversed mass incorpora-tion but completed the process of agrarian capitalist transformation. The Pinochet legacy of exclusion and demobilization explains the limits of social democracy in contemporary Chile.

Agrarian class relations before the critical junctures

Of all our cases, the agrarian class structure in Chile was the one most clearly dominated by an estate-based landed elite in the mid-twentieth century. What is striking about the pattern of landholdings in Chile is not simply the concentration of landed power, but the economic insignif-icance of smallholders. Thus, in 1955, *minifundistas* (very small landown-ers) accounted for 37 percent of the farms but possessed only 1 percent of the arable land, whereas *latifundistas* (estate owners) had only 7 percent of farms but owned 65 percent of the arable land (Kay 1981). The high concentration of land, an abundance of labor, and the absolute political domination of landlords were more than sufficient to secure cheap and dependent forms of labor. The highly unequal distribution of land and the extra-market control of labor "resulted in an inefficient allocation of resources as well as encouraging a rent-seeking attitude among land-lords with negative consequences for agricultural investment" (Kay 2002, 467). In this respect, Chile was a classic illustration of how pre-capitalist class relations can fetter capitalist development.

Yet Chile's landed elite differed from many other landlord classes of Latin America and South Asia in two principal ways. First, it accepted a quasi-parliamentary system within which a competitive polit-ical party system had emerged. There was, therefore, a space for chal-lengers to the power of traditional elites. Second, the landlord class had demonstrated – in contrast to the parasitic landlords of Kerala – some responsiveness to markets by responding to the global demand for wheat in the nineteenth century with expanded production, and by developing interlocking relations with Chile's industrial and financial elites. Indeed, by the mid-twentieth century through extensive inter-familial ties and overlapping material holdings, landed and industrial elites had "thoroughly . . . coalesced into a single, indissoluble, dominant class" (Zeitlin and Ratcliff 1988, 10).

Compared, however, to the Costa Rican coffee elite, which by the 1930s had little extra-market power in rural areas, the Chilean landed elite retained a firm grip over the peasantry well into the 1960s. What was unique to Chile's agrarian structure in this respect is that it was neither capitalist nor feudal, but "a specific historical form of seignorial commodity production" (Zeitlin and Ratcliff 1988, 153). The institution of *inquilinaje* (labor-service tenancy) – which was at the heart of the Chilean agrarian system – involved production by tenants on the land with the inputs of estate owners in exchange for a dwelling and minimal subsistence.[7] As Bauer has shown, the *inquilinaje* system was first introduced largely through the dispossession of a relatively independent smallholding peasantry in response to the new demand for wheat in the 1870s (1995, 26), a process that included violently repressing two revolts in the 1850s. It was, in other words, the commercialization of agriculture that ushered in semi-feudal relations of dependency. The significance of these agrarian relations for Chile's political development is neatly summed up by Zeitlin and Ratcliff:

To maintain and reinforce this system has been an unavoidable and enduring social objective of the great landed families and their allies ever since. They successfully maintained the social and political isolation of agrarian labor, secured state financial subsides for agriculture, exempted their resident tenants and other workers from labor legislation and prevented them from securing the right to organize, even after the labor movement had become a major political force in mining and industry, and above all, stymied all efforts at agrarian reform. (1988, 154)

The resulting balance of class forces was clearly revealed when the Chilean working class first flexed its electoral muscle in 1938 to join the Popular Front government. The incorporation of labor was made possible by a dominant-class pact based on the support of landed elites for accelerated industrialization policies in exchange for new subsidies and public resources for agriculture, as well as prohibitions against peasant

---

[7] Despite the harsh and degrading conditions of *inquilinos*, landless peasants preferred tenancy to wage labor because of the greater security, and the higher status and better living conditions that came with it (Kay 1981, 492).

unionization and strikes that effectively guaranteed the landed elite's political domination of the rural sector (chapter 6). This class configuration – a declining but still powerful landed elite allied with an emerging but dependent bourgeoisie and a politically and socially supine rural population – is, in Barrington Moore's model, a tailor-made prescription for right-wing authoritarianism. Specifically, the fact that landlord control over the countryside survived well into the 1960s was consequential on three counts. First, in Moore's sense, it prevented the consolidation of a strong, modernizing liberal bourgeoisie, the classic path to democracy. Second, for all its strength, militancy, and autonomy, the Chilean working class could not mobilize rural workers to build an encompassing social-democratic coalition. And third, it strengthened the hand of the military. As Collier and Collier have argued, "the strength of the oligarchy – due in part to is clientelistic control of the countryside and thus to the 'unavailability' of the peasantry – meant that mobilization would not be adequate to overcome oligarchic power. In these cases, the military became a more decisive actor" (1991, 170–71). Chile was, therefore, ripe for authoritarianism, but not before a period of lower-class mobilization that does not neatly fit the Moorian model.

The radical-mobilizational period (1964–1973) rapidly transformed the traditional agrarian structure. It did this both by eroding labor dependency through unionization and new legislation, and through land redistribution that weakened the traditional elite. This period marked the political awakening of the rural poor, and the resulting decompression of agrarian relations contributed to the political destabilization that ended with the Pinochet coup. Although the military period (1974–1990) was marked by significant reversals in redistributive gains and the repression of the peasant movement (Kurtz and Houtzager 2000), economic transformation continued apace. By the 1980s, a once moribund traditional agrarian economy had been transformed into a dynamic nontraditional agricultural export sector. Chile's agrarian transition, long postponed by an entrenched and powerful landed elite, was complete – but largely on terms that favored property and profits at the expense of labor and wages, and that produced a rise in rural poverty.

Costa Rica's exceptional trajectory of social-democratic development is often attributed to an egalitarian social structure rooted in yeoman smallholders. But if characterizations of Costa Rica as the Switzerland of Central America are more national myth than reality – glossing over the power of the coffee oligarchy and the impoverished status of nineteenth-century smallholders – the myth has some *comparative* basis in reality (chapter 4). In his analysis of landholding data from the mid-twentieth century for all four central American coffee-exporting countries (Costa Rica, El Salvador, Honduras, and Guatemala), Paige (1997) finds Costa Rica has the smallest estate class and the largest peasant proprietor class (subfamily and family). Large estates (more than fifty *manzanas*) account for 83.7 percent of total coffee area in Guatemala, and over 50 percent in Nicaragua and El Salvador, but such estates cover only 30.6 percent in Costa Rica. And whereas peasant proprietors are negligible in Guatemala (11.6 percent of holdings) and of middling size in Nicaragua and El Salvador (24.5 and 18.9 percent, respectively), they represent the largest rural class in Costa Rica, with 47.8 percent of the total coffee area. If one adds the category of small employer farms (22.1 percent of area), then predominantly family-based farms in Costa Rica account for 69.9 percent of the coffee area. With this class producing 62.5 percent of the total coffee crop, its economic significance is undeniable (Paige 1997, 60–61).

If the broad contours of agrarian classes in Central America are congruent with a class-based theory of social democracy, the specific nature of the coffee elite in Costa Rica is just as telling. The agro-industrial fraction has been far more powerful than the agrarian landed fraction, whereas the latter has predominated to varying degrees in Nicaragua, Guatemala, and El Salvador. Agrarian landed elites have a stake in repressive labor regimes, and have historically opposed democracy. The power of the agro-industrial elites derives from the market, in particular its control over processing, finance, and exports. As a quasi-bourgeoisie, it is more likely to support formal democracy. This predisposition is reinforced by its relation to rural producers. Owing to the prevalence and tenacity of small property owners in Costa Rica, expropriation or direct extraction was ruled out. Market exchanges became the dominant economic relation. As a result, "politics revolved around the gentlemanly disagreements between large and small property owners, and the elite soon found that such conflicts could be easily managed by the gradual extension of the franchise to rural property owners and the establishment of democratic institutions" (Paige 1997, 87).

As Mauritius was uninhabited before the seventeenth century, its social structure was entirely the product of colonialism and devoid of the patrimonial dependencies of European feudalism and sub-Saharan kinship-based orders. During the French period, Mauritius was dominated by a plantocracy that relied on slave labor and might well have continued along this course (Haiti comes to mind) had not European history in the form of the Napoleonic Wars intervened. The arrival of the British heralded not only a transition from slavery (abolished in 1835) to indentured labor, but also the transformation of rural class relations. On the one hand, the bifurcation of power between British rulers and the Franco-Mauritian plantation owners separated political from economic power and created the basis for the subsequent rise of a developmental state. On the other hand, the extension of direct rule into rural areas, combined with market-based land distribution that began in the 1870s, loosened ties of dependency to the Franco-Mauritian elite and underwrote the formation of a smallholding Hindu peasantry (Lange 2004, 84). When these producers and agricultural workers were granted full rights by the colonial state, this newfound liberty led to a rapid expansion of local associational life (chapter 5). The tight correspondence of economic position and ethnic identity fueled a powerful social identity, rooted in a resentment by indentured laborers against an exclusivist white plantocracy, and fed directly into political activism. But subordinate classes were not as united as in Kerala. The divisions between the largely Hindu agricultural workers and the largely Afro-Creole urban workers prevented the consolidation of an urban-rural lower-class alliance that could have broadened support for the radical-socialist Mouvement Militant Mauricien (MMM) in the 1970s. At the other end of the class order, the Franco-Mauritian landed class quickly adapted to its new circumstances, redirecting its surpluses – with significant encouragement from the state – to new commercial and industrial ventures.

Overall, the evolution of class relations and patterns of ethnicity paved the way for a gradual, and largely non-violent, agrarian transition. A landed elite that might well have been the basis for authoritarianism was neutralized, a process facilitated by its weak political position, the lucrative opportunities it discovered in the postcolonial economy, and the absence of a potentially sympathetic military force. And a Hindu yeomanry that would become a key social base for democratization not only took root but prospered. Today, independent and mostly small growers control 45 percent of land in sugar and have done well enough that their educated children have become part of the professional and bureaucratic class. This class configuration produced a social-democratic outcome as moderate center-left parties used the state to mitigate a steeply stratified racial order.

In Kerala, the early commercialization of agriculture led the Maharaja's state of Travancore to implement the first land reforms in the subcontinent. The reforms abolished royal land monopolies, introduced private property, and empowered a market-oriented class of Syrian-Christian farmers. As these farmers modernized operations, they increasingly replaced tied-labor arrangements with wage labor, creating the first full-blown capitalist sector in Kerala.

While in the south (Travancore and Cochin), commercialization of agriculture accelerated proletarianization of the peasantry and the breakdown of what were otherwise feudal caste-based relationships, in the north (Malabar) commercialization and increasing pressure on land made complex tenancy arrangements increasingly unviable. The Brahmin (*Namboodiripad*) class of overlords was proscribed by caste codes of ritual purity from directly engaging in agriculture. The *Namboodiripads* extracted rents but did not manage their lands carefully and failed to respond to new commercial challenges. As they became increasingly obsolete, they were also politically marginalized by the nationalist movement because of their collaboration with the British. In the 1930s, tenants were emboldened to demand tenancy reform ("land to the tiller") and join forces with the proletarianized agricultural laborers and agro-processing sector workers of central and southern Kerala.

The resulting grand agrarian alliance brought the Communist Party of India (CPI) to power in Kerala in 1957 and spelled the demise of Kerala's landlords. It also marked the ascendancy of small property owners. Although the Syrian-Christian farmers aligned against the CPI because of its anti-clericalism, the CPI had the full support of the sizable tenant class. Through the agrarian agitations of the 1930–1940s, many of these tenants had acquired *de facto* proprietary rights. They would gain *de jure* rights with the land reforms of the 1970s, and subsequently form Kerala's largest social class. By 1976–1977, large holdings (over 10 hectares) accounted for only 8 percent of holdings (Prakash 2004, 126).

Paradoxically, the power of this smallholding class was amplified by its political divisions. After the 1970 reforms, many tenants-turned-proprietors, in a classic case of embourgeoisement, abandoned the CPI(M) in favor of the Congress (Herring 1983). But many remained loyal to the party, and active in its farmer's wing, the KSS (Kerala Karshaka Sangham). As a result, both major political formations in Kerala, the Congress-led UDF and the CPM-led LDF, vie for the support of this class. Generous welfare programs that have benefited rural areas, significant subsidies for agriculture, and the highest rates of per capita loans for agriculture in all of India are reflections of this political logic.

Agricultural laborers also made significant gains with the passage of the Kerala Agricultural Workers Act in 1975. Coupled with a high rate of unionization, the act – which includes minimum wages, security of employment, collective bargaining, and a pension scheme – has provided agricultural laborers with social protection and the highest wages in India. The act, in effect, marked the institutionalization of an agrarian class compromise. In exchange for property rights, landowners (mostly smallholders who hire some labor) conceded labor's right to a share of the social surplus (Herring 1983; Heller 1999).

In sum, Kerala's agrarian transition has been marked by a double movement. On the one hand, commercialization and the attendant transformation in the class structure ushered in a capitalist economy. Labor was freed from the clutches of the caste system, land was commodified, the wage form was universalized, and production has been modernized, most notably with a dramatic shift beginning in the 1970s from food crops (primarily rice) to cash crops (rubber and coconut). On the other hand, a reformist communist movement eschewed collectivization in favor of secure property rights for a smallholding peasantry and significant protection and bargaining rights for agricultural laborers. Both classes remain organized and politically powerful, and enjoy effective social services. Land and labor have been embedded in the regulatory and social institutions of a social-democratic state. Capitalist transformation has thus been accompanied by a broad-based incorporation of the rural sector.

Reviewing our four cases, we find that two key developments in the evolution of the agrarian class structure set the historical stage for subsequent political transitions. The first was the containment or even marginalization of traditional agrarian elites. In Mauritius, the plantocracy was socially isolated by its ethnicity and religion from the Hindu peasantry, and politically at odds with the British colonial state. It could not effectively resist pressures from below or from the state; instead, it diversified into new economic activities after independence. In Kerala, the *Namboodiripads* were so invested in their caste-based social status that they failed to respond to new economic opportunities. And because of their collaboration with the British colonial state, they were quickly swept aside by the left-controlled nationalist movement. In Costa Rica, immigration patterns and the evolution of the coffee economy created a market-oriented agro-processing elite that had different political reflexes than the landed agrarian coffee elites typical of other Central American countries. In Chile, a powerful landed elite transformed itself enough to survive into the 1960s, but not enough to break with its authoritarian reflexes. When threatened from below, it proved reactionary. Ironically, however, traditional agrarian relations were not restored during the Pinochet dictatorship.

Independent smallholders and middle peasants, too, have played a significant role in shaping political outcomes. Smallholders were of minor significance in highly urbanized Chile. The landed elite enjoyed almost absolute political control over the peasantry, arresting the process of agrarian transition and the political incorporation of the rural population until the 1960s. In contrast, in Kerala, Mauritius, and Costa Rica, patterns of commercialization and state intervention conspired to create a strong, resilient, and politically decisive middle peasantry. In Costa Rica, coffee elites had little choice but to coordinate their interests with an entrenched smallholding peasantry. In Mauritius, the British state, the Hindu peasantry, and their educated offspring created an alliance of convenience against the Franco-Mauritian plantocracy. In Kerala, a vast and well-organized peasantry which included tenants and agricultural laborers politically outmaneuvered landed elites in the decisive period of the 1940s. Barrington Moore (1966) has famously remarked that modernization inevitably comes at the expense of the peasantry. Not so in Costa Rica, Kerala, and Mauritius, where a class balance of weak or nontraditional landed elites and a strong and organized peasantry ensured that the agrarian transition – propelled by commercialization – was based on the social and political incorporation of the rural sector. To paraphrase what E. P. Thompson (1964) said of the English working class, these smallholders were present and active in their own transformations. Broad-based incorporation of the rural sector could avert the social dislocation and political conflict that otherwise accompanies agrarian transitions (as in Chile).

Although the role of landed elites in political change is well documented, the role of smallholders or middle peasants in securing social democracy in the periphery has received little attention. Danish and Swedish social democracy can be traced to farmers demanding that urban middle classes bear some of the cost of rural poor relief in the late nineteenth century. A similar logic appears to have been at work in our agrarian cases. In all three, the self-organization of smallholders and their links to other social classes paved the way for both broadening democracy and state intervention. In Costa Rica, organized subordinate groups, including smallholders, made democracy and social reform the most pragmatic choice for political elites (Mahoney, 2001). In Mauritius and Kerala, smallholders led the drive for democratization. Research on agrarian democracies (the United States, Switzerland, and Norway) has pointed to the historical affinity between smallholders and democracy; but how does one explain this class's affinity with social democracy? We believe that the reason can be found in the ambiguous relationship of rural middle classes to capitalist development. As property owners, they share interests in common with the bourgeoisie and are fiercely protective of their independence (hence the central role small peasants have played in peasant revolutions). But, as smallholders, they have limited economies of scale; they must, therefore, rely heavily on state support for inputs, infrastructure, and marketing. They are, moreover, extremely vulnerable to market fluctuations. Hence, smallholders are drawn to an activist state that can supply important inputs and social protection.

Mobilization and transformation

Having explored the *class configurations* that underpinned actual or abortive social democracy in our cases, we now examine the dynamics of *critical junctures* and how these, in turn, shaped historical trajectories.

Hyper-mobilization and elite reaction in Chile

A comparative scholar in the early 1960s might be excused if, taking the case of Europe as a point of reference, she had arrived at the conclusion that Chile's class structure was conducive to democratic stability. Chile's landlord class had diversified its economic interests and had supported a representative (though limited) democracy for decades. Its middle class was growing and, though workers were mobilized and often radical, they had already wrested significant concessions from capital. The countryside was quiet, and a well-developed party system was seemingly more than capable of handling the conflicts that all democracies generate. Indeed, in terms of the three key ingredients for social democracy – a sufficient material base, a high-capacity state, and a well-organized working class led by cohesive political parties – Chile was certainly more favorably positioned at this stage of its history than any of our cases to follow a social-democratic trajectory. Except, of course, for the unresolved agrarian question.

The immediate cause of the Pinochet coup is clear, as chapter 6 reveals. The authoritarian reaction was a response to irreconcilable class antagonisms precipitated by the radical actions and redistributive demands of the left. In the decade preceding the coup, the political situation had polarized as electoral competition was extended into the countryside, and as centrist and leftist parties made rapid electoral gains. Revolutionary demands by elements of Allende's Popular Unity coalition, combined with seizures of factories and land, represented unacceptable threats to dominant class interests. Civil-society institutions seemed incapable of mediating these tensions.

If we extend our gaze beyond the explosive decade of the 1960s, however, what stands out is the pattern of repression, mobilization, and incorporation that characterized subordinate-class politics, a pattern that derived from Chile's arrested agrarian transition. From 1880 to 1920, the Chilean working class, located primarily in the mining sector, grew into a militant and politically organized force. As worker militancy was met with repression, the left parties agreed to an incorporation pact in the 1920s that was enforced by the military.[8] By 1928, the left's organizational capacity had been dismantled. It was resurrected a decade later – a testament to the strength of its social base – to enter the Popular Front government. Again, a pact was formed, with organized labor receiving generous benefits, but at the expense of its organizational autonomy and on the premise "that social relations in the traditional rural sector would remain unchanged" (Collier and Collier 1991, 163). With the rise of Cold War anti-communism, the Communist Party was violently repressed in 1949, and after 1952 the Socialist Party, increasingly disillusioned with the Popular Front rule, took a sharp turn toward revolutionary Marxism. The left, having learned from two failed episodes of limited incorporation, was now no longer willing to compromise: "the left retained its commitment to industrialization and an electoral road to socialism, but it eschewed fundamental compromise with the dominant sectors of the capitalist system. It moved vigorously to organize the rural working class and began to stress the importance of agricultural transformation to achieve its developmentalist and redistributive goals" (Bergquist 1986, 73–74).

The rural sector was ripe for transformation. As early as the 1920s, Chile's export economy had begun to disrupt the landlord-dominated agrarian structure as "militant workers, impatient bureaucrats, and urban middle groups, began to intrude into the countryside" (Bauer 1995, 34). The rural social structure underwent important changes from the 1930s onward. The *inquilino* system of obtaining labor became unprofitable compared to wage labor, and disappeared (Kay 1981, 495). In the absence of social protection and labor organizations (unionization was banned), the resulting proletarianization meant that rural poverty and insecurity deepened (chapter 6). When the Marxists and Christian Democrats began mobilizing in rural areas, the political equation suddenly shifted. The Christian Democratic victory of 1964 opened the floodgates to radical reform and mobilization. The class pact that had left the countryside in the hands of the dominant class was dead. The Christian Democratic government introduced legislation facilitating unionization and even organized peasants directly: the number of rural workers organized in unions exploded from 2,000 to 140,000, and Kay estimates that by 1970 roughly 40 percent of peasants were organized (1981, 501). The expropriation of one-third of *latifundios* and new wage legislation

---

[8] Collier and Collier define this period of incorporation which includes the Alessandri (1920–1924) and the Ibáñez (1927–1931) presidencies as the critical juncture in Chilean history (1991, 164).

directly attacked the material interests of landlords. Class conflict further escalated under the Popular Unity government (1970–1973), especially as the leftist parties become more directly involved in mobilizing peasants, including confrontational activities such as strikes and land seizures (*tomas*). If, by 1973, the rural population was much better off, elite interests had been dramatically undermined. Indeed, the very existence of Chile's landed elites was under threat.

The politicization of rural workers and tenants, combined with the modernization of landed elites, presented, if only for a fleeting moment, a path that might have carried Chile down the road of deepening democratization. That this path was suddenly cut off is perfectly in keeping with a nuanced version of the balance-of-class-forces model. On the one hand, agricultural relations were never dominated by the extra-economic coercion of plantation economies or hacienda relations (characterized instead by semi-coercive ties of paternalism and land–person ratios that favored landlords), leaving open the possibility of the classical English road to capitalist farming based on wage labor. Landed elites in Chile were inclined to adapt to market opportunities, increasingly favoring wage labor over *inquilinos* and extending their economic activities into the industrial and financial sectors. On the other hand, this situation condemned the peasantry to economic vulnerability. When the left tapped this insecurity and resentment – in effect bringing the peasantry into politics – it set the stage for precisely the kind of class confrontation that Luebbert (1991) has shown led to the rise of fascism in Germany.[9]

In Chile, the alliance of the urban working class and the rural poor threatened the position of the dominant class. The bourgeois/landed elite reactionary alliance was a highly organized and cohesive dominant class that enjoyed significant political and media clout. In the crisis conditions of late 1972, the right-wing parties that represented this class were able to cast the Popular Unity government as a threat to private property in general – not just the property of large landholders and monopolists – and rally the support of small business, including smaller landed interests, and other sections of the middle class. When one adds a military establishment with a history of political intervention, the precedents of authoritarianism in the Southern Cone, the strident revolutionary rhetoric of some

---

[9] Luebbert (1991) argues that it was not so much the hegemonic power of Junkers that set the stage for the rise of Hitler as the alliance of urban and agricultural workers that triggered an authoritarian response. Beginning in 1920, agrarian workers were mobilized in Germany by the Social Democratic Party, and by the end of the decade, two-thirds were covered by collective agreements and all were covered by generous welfare measures. This alienated rural households (especially Protestant farmers in the west) who depended on hiring labor and felt that their property was being threatened, pushing them into the electoral alliances that brought Hitler to power.

elements of the left, the general climate of the Cold War, and covert US interventions, the situation was ripe for reaction. What this highlights, above all, is that small shifts in the balance of class power – which in this case tilted the balance from workers and peasants to the dominant class – can have significant path-changing effects.

Pressure from below and elite-led reforms in Costa Rica

In Costa Rica, the absence of a feudal past, a frontier economy, relative ethnic homogeneity, and the easy availability of land for smallholders all but precluded the rise of a socially distinct traditional landed elite. Indeed, Costa Rica's coffee elite derived its economic power less from landholdings (which were smaller than the regional standard), and more from processing and marketing activities (chapter 4). As control of the market and not control of labor was the basis of its economic power, the coffee elite had little interest in a labor-repressive state. It was more attuned to a state-interventionist version of liberalism than to the socially exclusionary doctrines and practices of most landed elites in Latin America. This pattern may largely explain the notable degree of social solidarity that has been a mainstay of national politics. One might even be tempted to ascribe Costa Rica's successes to an enlightened elite, but this would hardly mesh with the significant resistance of the coffee elite to the reforms of the 1940s. It would also fail to account for the significant role played by pressure from below.

The reforms that culminated in the 1948 civil war began in the 1930s. In response to the Depression and the precipitous decline of coffee prices, small coffee producers organized the National Association of Coffee Producers, demanding price regulation and putting them into direct conflict with coffee processors. In contrast to the insurrectionary tactics of the Salvadoran workers facing the same crisis, the Costa Rican small coffee producers worked through civil society, holding public meetings, lobbying legislators, publicizing their views in sympathetic newspapers, and in general working within the democratic rules of the game (Paige 1997, 129). As with all class compromises, this one was a complex web of alignments and bargains through which various class interests were coordinated and the role of the state was expanded. Thus, if small producers were pitted against processors over issues of price and credit terms, the two joined forces in opposing a state that wanted to impose new taxes. One conflict between the two groups led to arbitration mechanisms for fixing prices, new sources of public-sector credit, and the formation of coffee cooperatives (production and credit). Small producers initially opposed key welfare-state initiatives (e.g., extending the Labor Code to coffee peons and new taxes). What won them over politically was the nationalized banking system and subsidized production credit, as well as other state welfare provisions (Acuña 1987).

Accounts of this tumultuous period of Costa Rican history tend to emphasize complex and constantly shifting political alignments, the role of political figures, and the overall messiness of the political process. But if this period did ultimately mark a critical juncture, setting Costa Rica down the path of agrarian social democracy, it is because, below the surface of politics, were well-organized class interests that were slowly but surely forging compromises. The first came in the form of the 1933 "coffee pact" which, in effect, regulated the relation between producers and processors. The coordination of class interests was further deepened through the reforms of Calderón and Figueres. These have been described at length in chapter 4, but four general points need to be reiterated. First, in each episode of the political upheavals that eventually produced the 1948 civil war, the fluctuating alliances were led by reformist elites. The basic interdependency of class interests (rooted in the producer–processor axis) and the moderation of the Communist Party muted the class-polarized rhetoric of anti-communism so typical of political elites in the rest of Central America. Second, subordinate class interests were sufficiently well organized that political elites had to compete for their support (Mahoney 2001). Third, the overall strength of civil society provided an open playing field in which to test new ideas and initiatives and to seek accommodations. Fourth, the presence of a well-organized, programmatic, but reformist Communist Party (*'comunismo a la tica'*) that could operate openly during the critical juncture period ensured continuous pressure for social reform. The Communists formed part of Calderón's alliance and informed much of his social agenda. Though the Communists were banned and repressed by Figueres, his own impeccable credentials as an anti-communist allowed him to actually extend and radicalize the Calderón agenda (see Paige 1997, 148–50).

Mauritius: societal demands and a reformist colonial state

The state was central to the configuration of social forces that paved the way for social democracy in Mauritius. The fusion of political and economic power, so fateful for democracy, did not transpire in the country. To contain the power of the Franco-Mauritian oligarchy, the British colonial state aligned itself with the Hindu majority. Market-based land transfers that began in the nineteenth century and the extension of public legality created an independent Hindu peasantry with significant associational capacity.[10] Beginning in the early 1900s, educated urban dwellers, mainly Creoles, demanded inclusion in the state. These agitations were followed up by a popular movement of Indian-Mauritian agricultural laborers in the 1930s and 1940s who then joined, and later dominated, the Mauritian Labour Party (MLP). This movement used strikes, marches, sit-ins, and petition drives to demand political changes. Riding this wave of pressure from below, the MLP dominated the Assembly from 1947 to independence, exerting continuous pressure on the state for reform. But as Lange (2003) argues, if demand-side pressures were important, so was the reform predisposition of the colonial state. Following World War II, the colonial office adopted a more labor-friendly policy. Reforms included decentralization of administration and services, expansion of representation in the legislature, the direct incorporation of labor through a newly constituted labor department (which included aggressive efforts to organize unions), and a range of social-welfare measures. A labor-friendly and interventionist colonial state, prodded by societal demands, implanted the institutional basis of social democracy.

The basic terms of Mauritius's social democracy were expressed soon after independence in a tacit class compromise. The plantocracy and Creole elite had opposed independence because they feared that the Hindu majority would use its political advantage, including its control of the state bureaucracy, to challenge their economic dominance. They also feared the revolutionary-socialist rhetoric of the trans-ethnic MMM in the early 1970s. Reform was preferable, and they yielded when offered the compromise solution of a modest social-democratic state that would forgo asset redistribution in favor of progressive taxation and social policies (chapter 5). This compromise reflected the Fabian-socialist ideology of the MLP. But it was also made possible by the balance of class forces that had emerged from Mauritius's gradual and incorporating agrarian transition. The white and Creole landed elite was politically too weak to block independence and democracy, but economically significant enough to pose a viable exit threat, whereas the Hindu middle class, including a significant base of smallholders, was politically powerful enough to push for democracy, but enjoyed enough economic security (land and state employment) to forgo a radical redistributive agenda.

In the postcolonial period, competitive mobilization, fueled both by the three dominant parties and a multiethnic society, has played a critical role in maintaining a balance between the state's market-enhancing policies and commitments to promoting equity. Mauritius, as a small

---

[10] Between 1910 and 1921, the sugarcane area controlled by Indo-Mauritians nearly doubled, resulting in the formation of 150 villages of small landowners (Lange 2003, 407).

and highly exposed island economy, has had to be innovative to meet the challenges of globalization. Reformist center-left governments have introduced an Export-Processing Zone, bargained for preferential trading agreements, and provided significant incentives to investors in targeted sectors. Closely contested elections, pitting ideologically similar coalitions against each other, have accentuated governmental responsiveness to social needs. The result is the proactive social policies described in chapter 5.

Kerala and reformist mass mobilization

Surveying the political and social field in Kerala in the 1940s, one might wonder why Kerala did not follow the Chilean route of hyper-mobilization. On the one hand, landed elites were still extremely powerful, in no small part because of the deep roots of the caste system. On the other hand, mass-based mobilization was spreading and becoming increasingly militant. Anti-caste reformist movements had given way to confrontational strikes and land agitations. The countryside was in a state of constant ferment, with the CPI openly espousing revolutionary ideologies. In 1946, on the eve of independence, the Communists even staged an insurrection against the Dewan of Travancore. The Punnapra-Vayalar insurrection that began as a strike of 17,000 coir workers but quickly escalated into an anti-absolutist movement – thereby securing the CPI's pro-democracy credentials – was poorly organized and quickly repressed, but nonetheless polarized class positions. When the Communists came to power in 1957, tensions escalated further, especially when the Communist government introduced land-reform legislation and extended government control over parochial schools, thus directly challenging the small, but powerful Christian community. A coalition of the Church and landed elites organized by the Congress Party mobilized against the government, organizing strikes and protests in an attempt to make the state ungovernable. When order deteriorated, the center stepped in, invoking the presidential-rule provision of the Indian constitution.

The dismissal of the CPI government was a setback, but it also reinvigorated the organizational wing of the party. The party handily won the next elections, securing 44 percent of the popular vote. The sharp contrast here with Chile raises a critical question: how did newly minted parliamentary institutions absorb very high levels of mobilization and counter-mobilization, including a Communist Party that directly threatened the social and economic base of dominant interests?

This absorptive capacity can be explained by three factors. First, the social base of the Communist Party spanned the urban–rural divide and brought together subordinate classes with a wide range of material interests. The coalition was held together more by successful appeals to anti-castism and general calls for social justice than a dogmatic class-based ideology. The biggest and most influential segment of this alliance was a middle peasantry that was more interested in securing property rights, basic welfare reforms, and support for agriculture than socialization of the economy. Indeed, though the party was Marxist-Leninist in its ideology, circumstances dictated that the CPI was first and foremost a party that promoted democracy and social citizenship rather than socialism. Second, the party was not only basically reformist, but also eminently pragmatic. On the one hand, it could hardly go it alone. Kerala society was so diverse and divided by caste, community, and class that no party could aspire to electoral hegemony. Even at its electoral height in 1957, the CPI received less than majority support, and the two communist parties – the CPI and larger CPI(M) – have always needed coalition partners to form governments. On the other hand, the party quickly learned that the insurrectionary route was not viable – the violently repressed Telengana uprising completely destroyed the CPI in Andhra Pradesh – and that the parliamentary route was more useful than the Leninist line suggested. In the last decade before independence, the CPI had achieved some notable electoral gains in regional elections. It even pushed through some reforms, learning en route how to use legislative proposals to rally the masses and parliamentary procedure to publicize concrete grievances (Nossiter 1982). By 1953, the party had decided to use parliamentary struggle as a means for mobilizing the masses. Third, elite opposition in Kerala could not coalesce into an authoritarian reaction because of its own internal divisions, its comparatively weak economic basis, and the larger national democratic context. Indeed, dominant groups even failed ultimately to stem the tide of social and economic reform through parliamentary means. The momentum of the left's social revolution, combined with parliamentary reformism, paved the way for gradual but deep transformations.

Political parties and ideology

These accounts of the dynamics of mobilization during critical junctures underline the role that parties and ideologies played in shaping social-democratic outcomes. A precondition for social democracy is the existence of a party that can articulate a coherent vision of social transformation. For such a party or parties to take root, a discourse of social rights and equity has to resonate in society. Kerala and Mauritius present the most clear-cut pattern: anti-colonial parties, built in large part on the strength of lower-class mobilization, developed a significant organizational presence in the colonial period and moved to implement their programs when voted into power. Social-democratic parties have had to contend with significant organized opposition from the left in Mauritius (the early MMM) and from the center-right in Kerala (the Congress). In Costa Rica, the parties of reform have been more elite dominated; nevertheless, in the context of a much more egalitarian and homogeneous society, elites had to be responsive to a large and independent rural popular sector. A reformist Communist Party that was tied to a small proletarianized workforce provided pressures from the left and important ideological repertories. In all three cases, social democracy was the result of a continuous and gradual ratcheting-up effect created by a political playing field that had four characteristics: (1) competitive party politics, (2) organized subordinate groups, (3) weak traditional elites who were politically delegitimated or divided elites who needed to appeal to organized subordinate groups, and (4) the ideological preeminence of a social-rights discourse.

Under highly competitive conditions, Chilean politics in the 1960s and early 1970s also produced a leftist transformative project. But it was a project that left little room for negotiated compromises. The immediate problem was the revolutionary demands and agitations of supporters of Allende's Popular Unity government. But this ideological intransigence was itself the result of the circumstances of the entry of the masses into politics. Working-class politics developed in an enclave economy, and in direct confrontation with capital. Two failed episodes of state-led compromise (the incorporation of the 1920s and the Popular Front period) had polarized and radicalized politics.[11] When the rural sector was belatedly mobilized in the 1960s, its sudden turn to the left not only marked the end of the traditional rural order but also effectively ruled out elite-led reformism (as in the case of Costa Rica). But if the dominant class could no longer secure its interests politically, it was cohesive and powerful enough to react when threatened – in contrast to Kerala and Mauritius. A Bonapartist solution was made more likely owing to the military's penchant for intervening to resolve class stalemates. But, this time, there was no room for selective incorporation.

State and civil society in social democracy

A peculiar interplay of the state and civil society was central not only to the historical trajectory of our cases, but also to the manner in which

---

[11] By 1965, the Socialist Party had embraced Leninism and rejected the electoral road to socialism (Roberts 1998, 92).

they negotiate the challenges of neoliberal globalization (chapter 8). The literature on social democracy emphasizes the central role of the state in coordinating class compromise and providing social welfare. A strong cohesive state, one that is linked to subordinate class interests and can manage the delicate balance between equity and growth, is indeed the sine qua non of social democracy. But this form of embeddedness is rare; it is the product of specific patterns of class mobilization. Explaining such patterns requires close attention to the constitution and role of civil society.

Just how central civil society is to our explanations becomes clear when we compare our findings to Atul Kohli's (2004) historical explanation of the rise of pro-growth developmental states in the global periphery. Through a detailed comparison of South Korea, India, Brazil, and Nigeria, Kohli argues that states that have successfully directed industrialization in the global periphery have benefited from building significant political authority, specifically the capacity to formulate and pursue pro-growth policies with single-minded determination. He labels such states, of which South Korea is the prototype, *cohesive-capitalist*, emphasizing both their institutional coherence and their close ties to business elites, and contrasts them with *fragmented-multiclass* states (India and Brazil). The latter have had to answer to an array of distributional demands, thus failing to single-mindedly pursue pro-growth policies. Kohli's claim that effective management of the economy requires, especially in the early industrial stages, a state that is insulated from popular pressures, is widely accepted. In the introductory chapter, we recognized this imperative as posing a fundamental dilemma in the global periphery. Because the advent of popular power has often *preceded* sustained industrialization (unlike in South Korea or other industrial countries), states in developing countries have usually failed to rise above the logic of populism and rent-seeking in mobilized but fragmented polities. How then have our cases escaped this trap?

The answer, as we have emphasized, lies in the dynamics of class formation and resulting configurations of power. Lower-class mobilization in all of our cases produced multiclass political movements making encompassing demands; such demands, by their very nature, conduce to the formation of cohesive states.[12] Although structural factors (particularly the timing and modality of integration into the world economy) created certain *possibilities* of class formation and coalitions, the realization of these possibilities depended on political organization and political

---

[12] Kohli recognizes the possibility of a "cohesive-multiclass" state by pointing to well-organized social democracies such as Sweden (2004, 10 fn. 13).

strategies. A robust civil society, in turn, provided the optimal milieu for these strategies and organizations to favor social-democratic outcomes. Vibrant civil society enhanced both the ability of subordinate groups to organize and demand political and social rights and the likelihood that distributional conflicts would be peacefully mediated. Even today, chapter 8 argues, strong civil societies in Costa Rica, Kerala, and Mauritius act as effective countervailing forces to neoliberal globalization, allowing for more socially mediated and equitable transitions to competitive, export-oriented economies.

The positive role of civil society in paving the way for social democracy is probably most clear in the case of Costa Rica. Much as in Tocqueville's America, an abundance of land and the absence of feudal vestiges proved to be fertile ground for the expansion of democratic civil society. The class structure reinforced this trend. Though coffee barons did exert considerable control over politics well into the twentieth century, their dominance, as Sheahan notes, "was exercised in classic nineteenth-century liberal style: they emphasized private property with protection of individuals from arbitrary government, nationwide education, and an orientation toward free trade" (1987, 289). They also favored modernizing society through the expansion of mass education as early as the 1880s, which, as we noted in chapter 4, not only universalized access to primary education but also contributed to consolidating notions of nation, citizenship, entitlement, and rights. Thus, even during the period of upper-class dominance preceding the first major reformist administrations (1870–1941), middle and popular sectors created a range of civic associations, including trade unions and a communist party in the 1930s (Yashar 1997, 34).

In Kerala and Mauritius, colonial states that were more rational-legal than repressive invigorated associational life. They allowed subordinate classes and ethnic/caste groups to organize well before the advent of formal democracy. Subordinate groups in these cases, as in Costa Rica, resorted to social-movement repertoires of strikes, protests, and petitions to press for political inclusion and social protection; instances of state repression were rare. Most strikingly, the ethnic heterogeneity of these two territories did not lead to the common curse of chronic communal conflicts. Both civil societies evolved institutions capable of mediating communal tensions and focusing politics on equitable treatment and common goals of generalized prosperity. In all three cases, therefore, a robust and inclusive public sphere nurtured political discourses of social rights over group rights, and the state's role in promoting equity.

Civil society in Chile evolved very differently, and this difference is central to explaining the rise of bourgeois authoritarianism and the diluted social democracy of the contemporary period. Chile's civil society in the

1920s was highly bifurcated, with a vibrant and autonomous working-class movement in the mining sector, and dependent clientelism in the countryside. The mining workforce, especially in the nitrate sector, was highly mobile and independent, moving from one job to another in response to the boom-and-bust cycles of global demand (Bergquist 1986, 54). This independence, coupled with insecurity, produced a solidaristic and militant working class, whose ties included mutual-aid societies serving both cultural and welfare functions (Bergquist 1986, 54–55). Under the influence of anarchists and socialist organizers, the nitrate workers developed political alliances with other workers and became an effective political force early in the twentieth century. The militancy of this sector, and the fact that it was located at such a critical node in the dependent capitalist economy, produced highly conflictual labor–capital relations. In contrast to the fairly stable and continuous process by which subordinate groups entered the political field in Costa Rica, Kerala, and Mauritius, the Chilean working class evolved politically through cycles of militancy, repression, and incorporation. This pattern had two effects. On the one hand, as the urban working class had developed significant capacity for autonomous organization, it remained ideologically autonomous and radical, supporting Marxist parties. On the other hand, the form of state incorporation that characterized Chile (Collier and Collier 1991) was top-down and selective, with benefits limited to highly organized working- and middle-class segments. This arrangement rested on an agreement not to interfere in class relations in the countryside. In 1939, the Marxist parties cut short a major organizational drive of rural workers (the largest segment of the Chilean working class), under pressure from conservative coalitional partners (Bergquist 1986, 73).

Hence, the most notable difference between Chile, on the one hand, and Costa Rica, Mauritius, and Kerala, on the other, is that the rural areas in Chile remained under the political control of landlords well into the mid-twentieth century. When peasants were mobilized in the 1960s, it was by political parties whose intent was to win elections. The peasantry rapidly organized its own associations, but within a context that was already highly politicized. A thinly developed civil society left little room for mediating the class conflicts that rapidly escalated. The left's tenuous hold over the peasantry could not, moreover, counter important redoubts of authoritarian ideology.[13] Chile thus illustrates Yashar's argument that

[13] The similarity here with the state of civil society in pre-Nazi Germany is striking. Though the workers' movement had developed an extensive network of associational groups, the peasantry remained largely unorganized until the 1920s. But its limited associational experience and autonomy made it particularly susceptible to the authoritarian appeals of the traditional hierarchical rural order.

"when civil society is shallow, old elites are less likely to identify coalitional partners and more likely to identify an emerging civil society as a threat; in this setting, old elites are more likely to support if not engineer democracy's overthrow" (1997, 19). When left-wing mobilization threatened private property, Chile's industrial/landed elite abandoned consent in favor of force, and the state crushed civil society. The rapidity with which peasant organizations were thoroughly dismantled in the Pinochet period testifies not only to the ferocity of repression, but also to the shallow roots of civil society.

In all of our cases, the relationship between the state and civil society continues to have important effects. In Kerala, and Costa Rica, where the pressure to embrace neoliberal reforms has been great, an autonomous and mobilized civil society has been (as Karl Polanyi [2001] might have predicted) a powerful countervailing movement. In both cases, widespread resistance to reforms, as well as counterprojects, explains not only the half-hearted nature of the measures that have actually been adopted, but also the extent to which the more polarizing effects witnessed in their respective regions have been checked. In Mauritius, the pressure to reform has been less acute, but the degree to which the market has been embedded in civil society is nonetheless reflected in the extent to which the state's proactive economic policies have been subject to the political imperative of ensuring that the benefits of growth be widely shared. It is notable that in all three cases the countervailing force to neoliberal globalization has not been a cohesive, militant working class, but rather an inclusive and activated civil society united around the implicit idea of socially embedded markets.

In Chile, the historical imbalance between political and civil society continues to have a profound effect on the capacity of subordinate groups to engage the state effectively. Though resistance to authoritarianism gave birth to vibrant and autonomous popular movements in the early 1980s, especially in the *poblaciones* of Santiago, political parties have taken center stage with the advent of political democracy. There has been a sharp decrease in the activities of popular organizations (Oxhorn 1995). The Concertación has kept civil society at arm's length (chapter 6), a posture more consistent with the Third-Way regime than classic or radical social democracy. Thus, even though the Concertación has been responsive to the legacies of class politics and has sought to counteract the socially disruptive effects of its pro-market strategies, the response has largely been top-down, driven by a technocratic political elite. In contrast to Costa Rica, Kerala, and Mauritius, this combination of a strong state with a weak civil society underscores the continuing challenge of lower-class incorporation in Chile.

Conclusion

This comparative analysis suggests that, though there are multiple paths to social democracy in the periphery, certain historical conditions favor such an outcome. The absence or demise of landlords and the formation of an independent peasantry promote democratization and demands to regulate the market in the public interest. In the three more successful cases, a smallholding rural class played a particularly important role. This class ensured that the transition to a market economy did not marginalize the rural poor, thus laying the foundation for an inclusive social democracy. The conditions under which this reconfiguration of class relations has emerged have varied, depending on the class structure prior to commercialization, the precise pattern of commercialization, and the nature of the colonial state. But what was critical in all cases was (a) a civil society that provided spaces in which subordinate class interests could self-organize, and (b) a state that had sufficient autonomy from dominant interests to respond to societal pressures and enough capacity to do so effectively.

Chile's discontinuous and arrested path to social democracy is a salutary reminder of just how delicate the balance of class power must be to keep that path open. This observation allows us to conclude by highlighting the importance of politics. To borrow from Gramsci, the organic moments of transformation were structured by long-term processes of class formation and state building that produced configurations of class forces conducive to social democracy. But the final act, the conjunctural moment that produced, or failed to produce, social-democratic trajectories, was the stuff of politics – shaped most notably by political parties and their various organizational strategies, ideologies, and situational logics.

8   Challenges of globalization

"Globalisation has so far provided only a Disneyesque beacon of light and a fake optimism to the poor," declares Ash Narain Roy in a comment typical of critics of contemporary neoliberalism (1999, 118). Yet our four cases suggest – globalization notwithstanding – that it is still possible in the global periphery to attain unusually high levels of well-being for the majorities, while preserving and in some cases extending (Costa Rica, Mauritius) many earlier gains in the areas of health, education, and social protections.[1] In three of the cases (Costa Rica, Mauritius, and Chile), it has been possible to do so while becoming vigorously competitive and attracting significant capital investments. Kerala, while hardly a magnet for foreign or even domestic Indian capital, has largely succeeded in conserving its extensive social-welfare apparatus through a particular kind of class politics that has attenuated otherwise deleterious impacts of economic liberalization. Despite the overwhelmingly negative context of the post-1980 world economy, and continuing problems with clientelism and bureaucratic inefficiencies, some countries and regions in the global south have managed to adapt in remarkable, if unheroic, ways and to live and even prosper with globalization.

This chapter aims: (1) to examine the impacts of the liberalized trade regime for social-democratic projects in developing countries; (2) to analyze how the policies of social-democratic regimes may complement the needs of capital and thus permit a viable insertion of a country in the globalized economy; and (3) to consider whether the pressures of neoliberal globalization are eroding the more egalitarian and participatory models of social democracy, moving them in the direction of Third-Way policies. Though questioning the conventional claim that neoliberal economic policies and the more radical forms of social democracy are incompatible, we conclude that the complementarities between the two are greater

---

[1] In Chile, social spending as a percentage of GDP and social security coverage as a percentage of population were higher during the 1970–1973 Popular Unity government than today. The post-1990 Concertación governments have, however, achieved gains in both areas as compared with the situation under the Pinochet dictatorship.

in developed than in less-developed countries. However, countries that consolidate welfare-state institutions and a social-democratic consensus prior to market opening are more favorably situated to successfully adapt social-democratic principles to the exigencies of globalization. This adaptation, furthermore, does not necessarily require an embrace of the Third Way.

Although Costa Rica, Mauritius, Chile, and Kerala have followed diverse routes and developed different varieties of social democracy, all have weathered globalization with considerable success – at least as compared with most societies in the global periphery. Understanding this success requires an historical analysis of the specific kinds of class compromises, conjunctures, and leadership choices that characterize the paths toward social democracy. We have undertaken this analysis in Part II and chapter 7, and this chapter builds on that foundation.

Neoliberal globalization in the post-Bretton Woods period

The expression "globalization" was largely unknown before the 1970s when, according to David Harvey (2000, 12–13), it "spread like wildfire" as American Express used it to advertise the global reach of its credit card.[2] In addition to the economic correlates of this shift, outlined in chapter 2, a political and ideological displacement was also underway. The elections of Margaret Thatcher in 1979, Ronald Reagan in 1980, and Brian Mulroney in 1984 signaled that free-market ideas had a heretofore unprecedented resonance among elites and electorates in Britain, the United States, and Canada. In the area of economic doctrine, free-market fundamentalists such as Milton Friedman and Friedrich von Hayek (and their followers), who for decades had been widely regarded as outlandish zealots, suddenly had access to the highest policymaking circles.[3]

The collapse of the Bretton Woods system of fixed exchange rates introduced a period of volatility and instability in the world economy, particularly after 1980. Previously insulated national economies suffered

---

[2] Held and McGrew (2003, 1) date the use of the term to the "1960s and early 1970s."
[3] It is not hard to grasp why many had long seen these liberal theorists as cranks. Hayek, for example, suggested that the election of the Labour Party would start Britain down a slippery slope to the end of democracy and, possibly, to totalitarianism (Hayek 1944, 63, 200). Among the US government activities that Friedman believed could not "validly be justified" in relation to liberal principles were the regulation of transportation by the Interstate Commerce Commission, of broadcast media by the Federal Communications Commission, the provision of pensions, and "licensure provisions . . . which restrict particular enterprises or occupations or professions to people who have a license" (Friedman 1962, 35).

brusque openings that undermined uncompetitive sectors of domestic agriculture and industry; accumulated debts from soaring petroleum prices and interest rates in the 1970s made government and public-sector deficits balloon out of control; inflation and currency devaluations impoverished developing-country middle classes and threatened the physical survival of the poor; unemployment rose rapidly, and massive tax evasion and capital flight complicated recovery efforts (except, of course, in the small number of cases where net flows were positive or in the burgeoning offshore tax havens). Probably the most dramatic example of this broad downward trend was the Latin American debt crisis that began in the early 1980s and led several countries to default (or at least to postpone payment of their foreign obligations), sending ripples of anxiety coursing through the international financial system.

In this atmosphere of crisis, the IMF, as the institution charged with resolving short-term disequilibria, first broadened its role as a source of information on member countries' economic performance ("surveillance," as some internal reports termed it) and then became increasingly involved in debt restructuring (Dominguez 1993, 358; Harper 2000). In addition, for any given country, certification that it was in compliance with IMF guidelines and macroeconomic targets frequently became a requirement – formal or informal – for obtaining loan rollovers or short- or long-term credit from other sources, private or multilateral, as well as bilateral aid. Because member countries' votes within the IMF were in proportion to their capital contributions, the United States, as the largest contributor, exercised an outsized influence on all aspects of IMF policy (along with the other G7 countries).[4] With neoliberal doctrine ascendant in the economics profession and an administration in Washington that was strongly committed to what Ronald Reagan had termed "the magic of the marketplace," US influence in the IMF strengthened already existing biases within the institution in favor of orthodox recipes for restructuring (see chapter 2).

While IMF officials have adamantly denied that they apply a single "blueprint" to different countries with distinct macroeconomic problems (IMF Assessment Project 1992, 15–16), it is nonetheless possible to outline some general features of the stabilization and structural adjustment agreements that, beginning in the 1980s, radically reshaped economies and societies throughout the developing world. The specifics,

---

[4] In the 1970s, for the first time, the IMF's primary clients were no longer the developed countries whose capital contributions had given them voting power in the IMF. "The Fund thus changed," as John Toye points out, "from an institution of collective action into an instrument to discipline others" (2003, 359).

of course, varied from case to case. The IMF's role was sometimes limited to an initial stabilization phase (usually intended to quell hyperinflation), followed by a structural (or sometimes, sectoral) adjustment program designed and supervised primarily by the World Bank and/or one of the regional multilateral development banks (e.g., the Inter-American Development Bank). At other times, the IMF was also closely involved in the structural adjustment phase.[5] We should also acknowledge that both stabilization and structural adjustment programs were the product of negotiations and agreements between the international financial institutions (IFIs) and individual member countries. That said, it should be obvious that such negotiations were hardly between equal parties. Rather, economically prostrated countries, often with limited technocratic expertise and few experienced negotiators, had to face powerful international institutions backed with abundant human and other resources. This skewed configuration – and the increasing international hegemony of the Washington Consensus – often shifted balances of power within the affected countries in favor of elite sectors who were both hostile to welfare statism and sympathetic to, and with a material interest in, neoliberal "solutions."

Neoliberal globalization is usefully conceived as entailing the reform of both state policies and institutions, typically under the supervision of the international financial institutions, and as reshaping the rules and practices governing world trade, foreign investment, and financial flows. State reform usually emphasized measures described in chapter 2: reducing budget deficits and public-sector payrolls, devaluing currencies and "flattening" tax regimes to encourage export-oriented investment, judicial reform to guarantee property rights and enforcement of contracts, and reducing or doing away with subsidies and non-tariff barriers to trade in order to eliminate distortions and "get the prices right." The reshaping of world trade and investment also had dramatic impacts on the social-democratic experiments in the global south.

The post-1980 emphasis on greater integration and liberalization of the world's economies involved the creation of a new trade regime, first under the General Agreement on Tariffs and Trade (GATT) and, after January 1, 1995, under the World Trade Organization (WTO). The remote origins of GATT are in a resolution of the Bretton Woods conference (1944) that called for founding an organization that would promote cooperation and create a code of conduct for nation-states engaging in international trade. Formed in 1947, with twenty-three participating

---

[5] See Toye (2003, 366–67) on the blurring of boundaries between IMF and World Bank lending practices in the 1980s and the conflicts that occurred as a result.

countries, GATT only became a permanent organization in the mid-1950s (Dominguez 1993, 368–69). Most GATT regulations concerned trade in goods and, especially, "at-the-border" restrictions on trade. The WTO, however, with nearly 150 member countries, moved far beyond the comparatively modest GATT agenda. WTO rules focus not just on tariffs but on many "behind-the-border" regulatory matters as well (e.g., non-tariff barriers to trade). Its jurisdiction covers not just trade in goods and discriminatory trade practices, but also intellectual property and patents, trade in services, technical, procurement, sanitary and phytosanitary standards, and measures of any kind that might be deemed as discriminating against, or unfairly limiting, foreign investors.[6] WTO rules ban policies that developmental states once utilized to improve well-being and to solidify horizontal linkages and fuel dynamism, notably export subsidies, domestic content and procurement requirements, and quantitative restrictions on imports. The General Agreement on Trade in Services complicates developing countries' efforts to protect public-sector service provision from foreign competition. The Trade-Related Aspects of Intellectual Property Rights accord raises the cost of medicines, technology, and scientific knowledge, and increases flows of rents from less-developed countries to northern patent and copyright holders. WTO provisions for "special and differential treatment" for developing countries permit longer phase-in periods for complying with some rules, but they aim mainly to foster administrative capacity rather than to allow incubation of new industries or other steps to heighten competitiveness (Hoekman 2004). The WTO dispute-resolution system is legally binding on member governments, with violators subject to penalties and retaliatory sanctions. Most importantly, the liberalization imposed on developing countries under the new trade regime stands in stark contrast to the protectionist policies historically employed in virtually all now-developed countries (Wade 2003).

In contrast to the international financial institutions, where US and G7 influence derives from the weight of their capital contributions, WTO governance supposedly operates through consensus. Nevertheless, unequal power relations shape its negotiations, too. This unequal power is reflected in informal "green room" negotiations involving just the key players – though minor players are expected to endorse the resulting agreements – in unofficial "mini-Ministerials," in General Council

[6] WTO consists of a number of binding agreements, the most important of which are on Trade-Related Aspects of Intellectual Property Rights (TRIPS), Agriculture (AoA), Trade in Services (GATS), Technical Barriers to Trade (TBT), Trade-Related Investment Measures (TRIMS), and Sanitary and Phytosanitary Standards (SPS) (Soros 2002, 49–51; Sinclair 2003, 347).

meetings closed to most poorer countries' representatives, and in persistent efforts to employ the vastly greater technical and legal resources of developed countries to obtain outcomes favorable to the latter's corporate interests. In addition, private-sector lobbyists – notably agribusiness, pharmaceutical, and financial-market interests – have had a conspicuous presence in and around WTO policy discussions.

The most striking handicap that less-developed countries face under the new trade regime is that the sectors in which they are most competitive – agriculture and textiles – are those where developed-country subsidies and import quotas limit their advantages (Watkins and Fowler 2002; Panic 2003, 376). Agricultural subsidies in the European Union and the United States, particularly after the mid- to late 1990s when supply management and land set-aside regulations were largely eliminated, have constituted a major drag on the farm sectors in less-developed countries, both by impeding market access and by depressing prices.[7] The WTO prohibits the sale of products abroad at less than their cost of production, but it employs very narrow definitions of what constitutes "trade-distorting" subsidies, particularly in the Agreement on Agriculture, and has consequently countenanced continued "dumping" of US and European surplus food that undermines producers in the global periphery. Moreover, the organization has been ineffective in preventing practices that rely on non-trade mechanisms, such as food aid, that sometimes constitute disguised forms of dumping farm products.

Competition in the textile sector, emblematic for many of the globalization-inspired "race to the bottom," is likely to intensify in coming years, presenting non-core countries with development policy dilemmas. Many countries that attracted garment assembly plants, including Costa Rica and Mauritius, enjoyed preferential access to the markets of their main trading partners, as well as export quotas established in the 1974 international Multifibre Agreement (MFA) (an accord that nonetheless aimed primarily at protecting developed-country industries). Quota-based MFA preferences were eliminated in 2005, although some developed countries will continue to permit duty-free imports of everything from blue jeans to brassieres under bilateral and regional trade pacts (e.g., the US Caribbean Basin Initiative [CBI], North American Free Trade Agreement [NAFTA], and African Growth and Opportunity Act

---

[7] Japan also heavily subsidizes its agricultural producers, but these participate little in foreign markets. Not all developed countries subsidize their farm sectors. The seventeen members of the Cairns Group (whose members include Argentina, Australia, Brazil, Canada, Chile, Costa Rica, New Zealand, and South Africa), which account for about one-third of global agricultural exports, generally have limited or no direct or indirect subsidies for farmers.

[AGOA], or, until 2007, the EU's Lomé Convention). Such preferences, however, are likely to come under increasing pressure in and outside of the WTO as the lowest-cost apparel producers, especially China and India, capture a rising proportion of world textile output and drain investment from higher-cost countries, such as Mexico, Costa Rica, and Mauritius. In addition, US trade negotiators have threatened to phase out CBI concessions in countries that fail to sign free-trade accords permitting greater access for US products and investors.

WTO rules have had an impact that is consonant – indeed, synergetic – with the objectives of the international financial institutions.[8] The latter, for example, often favor privatization of public-sector service provision, and state-owned enterprises in general, as a way of reducing fiscal deficits. Examples of services the IFIs target include postal services, electrical generation and transmission, railways, insurance, health care, higher education, water distribution, and sale of alcoholic beverages. Under the WTO, governments are encouraged or even forced to privatize services if they are to remain in compliance with GATS provisions that prohibit monopolies or that require exclusive providers to be competitive with foreign suppliers (Sinclair 2003, 353–54). Provisions such as these, along with the WTO's insistence on most-favored-nation treatment for foreign enterprises, have led critics to charge that facilitating investment is the hidden agenda behind the new global trade accords (whether WTO, NAFTA, or other regional and bilateral agreements). Indeed, bilateral trade agreements, particularly those the United States has signed or would like to sign, typically impose stricter disciplines than the WTO in areas such as investment, intellectual property, and the movement of funds into and out of a country (Rodrik 2004, 33).

Although this new trade regime may appear unstoppable, forms of protest and resistance have appeared. Oppositional tactics contributed to delaying the completion of GATT's Uruguay Round of negotiations (in the early 1990s) and shaping the outcome of two WTO ministerial meetings, in Seattle in 1999 and Cancún in 2003. At the Seattle meeting, street protests precipitated a veritable "revolt" of delegates from the global periphery who opposed further trade liberalization and their exclusion from closed "green room" negotiations (Sinai 2000). In Cancún, a G21 coalition of developing countries, led by Brazil, India, and China, halted the trade negotiations. At issue were the US and EU intransigence on agricultural subsidies and dumping, as well as developed-country efforts to expand the ambit of the WTO in the areas of investment, competition

---

[8] And with those of the regional and bilateral free trade pacts, such as NAFTA, that the United States and other developed countries initiated in the 1990s and after.

law, and government procurement. Developing countries are also increasingly uniting around common positions in the non-agricultural market access (NAMA) negotiations within WTO. These new groupings have produced what could be construed as a reprise of the demand in the 1970s for a "new international economic order." There is growing pressure for expanding the existing WTO "special and differential treatment" provisions that apply to developing countries, for conditioning the implementation of trade disciplines on the attainment of specified national development goals, and for establishing global funding mechanisms to address adjustment costs (Hoekman 2004).

Globalization and threats to social democracies

Conventional approaches to economic globalization assert that it undermines the autonomy of nation-states in policymaking areas that were the pillars of the social-democratic developmental state. These areas include the use of monetary tools to expand the economy, the channeling of tax-supported public investment to meet societal needs, the wielding of industrial strategies to orchestrate private investment, and the protection of national manufacturers through government procurement and domestic-content rules. This conventional wisdom, along with associated claims about "footloose capital" and the "race to the bottom," has received critical scrutiny in recent years.

Perhaps surprisingly, considerable evidence exists, particularly for developed countries, that globalization and welfare provision are intimately connected. On the one hand, interventionist welfare policies provide benefits to capital in a globalizing world. These benefits take the form of high productivity (a healthy, educated workforce, good infrastructure, an effective, legitimate state), and security of investment and profits owing to political stability. These benefits often blunt corporate "exit threats" (Pierson 2001a; Mosley 2005). On the other hand, increased exposure to global markets – again, especially in developed countries – is actually associated with *greater* government spending on redistributive programs that compensate for market-generated inequalities and insecurities (Garrett 2003). According to Dani Rodrik, there is "a striking correlation between an economy's exposure to foreign trade and the size of its welfare state. It is in the most open countries, such as Sweden, Denmark, and the Netherlands, that spending on income transfers has expanded the most" (2003, 380–81). In the World Economic Forum's Growth Competitiveness Index (GCI) rankings (based on the effectiveness of countries' public institutions, "technological readiness," and macroeconomic environment), developed-country welfare states are well represented at the top of the list (López-Claros 2005, xiii). However, Sweden, Denmark, the Netherlands, and other developed-country social democracies built their welfare states well before the post-1980 liberalization of capital markets.

Although much depends on state capabilities, democratic or authoritarian polities, and economic profiles, the general situation in the less-developed countries conforms more closely to the conventional view of globalization's negative impact on social policy (Rudra 2002). Some studies of developing countries indicate that welfare spending has expanded over the past quarter century, but they also reveal that greater trade openness is positively correlated with *smaller* increases in social spending (Yoon 2004). Thus, Latin America, with relatively low levels of trade exposure, has seen faster welfare-state growth since the early 1980s crisis than most of Asia, with Africa falling in between.

Yet our four case studies contradict this association of trade openness with lower social spending. Significantly, these cases, despite their high social spending, rank relatively high in their regions in competitiveness, according to the conventional criteria of the World Economic Forum's GCI. Mauritius, ranked 49th out of 104 countries worldwide, is nonetheless considered one of the most competitive places in Africa (after South Africa, Tunisia, and Botswana). Chile, ranked 22nd worldwide, is the first in Latin America, and Costa Rica, ranked 50th, third after Mexico (48th). While Kerala, as a sub-national polity, does not appear on the list, India is ranked 55th, exceeded in Asia only by Taiwan, Singapore, Korea, Malaysia, and China (López-Claros 2005, xiii). Within India, according to the Confederation of Indian Industry, Kerala ranked third out of eighteen states in an overall achievement measure that included investment climate, infrastructure penetration, performance of the financial sector, consumer purchases of goods and durables, expenditure on education and health, performance of the social sector, environment, law, order, and justice, level of affluence, and the penetration of mass media in the state. This is a remarkably high position given the perception of many investors that Kerala is a hotbed of labor militancy. So we cannot posit any inexorable logic of economic globalization that undermines social democracies, even in the global periphery.

How have the developed-country social democracies – and the few relatively successful developing-country ones – managed to maintain significant social-welfare apparatuses at the same time as they opened to global markets? To explore this question, we divide the potential "globalization constraints" into three: (1) trade competitiveness pressures, (2) the multinationalization of production and foreign direct investment, and (3) the integration of financial markets (Garrett 2003, 385).

Exposure to foreign trade competition, under certain conditions, spurs expansion – not contraction – of state welfare spending, as governments compensate people for the higher risks of volatile global markets (Garrett 2003; Rodrik 2003). Democratic governments, which are subject to popular pressures during contested elections, are more likely to respond with compensation than authoritarian governments (Mosley 2005, 356). Yoon (2004) suggests that welfare states have expanded, albeit more slowly than elsewhere, even in the developing regions of greatest trade openness, such as East Asia. Trade openness is likely to result in greater pressure on benefits (e.g., pensions, unemployment insurance) funded by direct employer and employee contributions, than on health and education spending, which are funded from tax revenue (Yoon 2004). Much of the latter derives from indirect and regressive taxation that only minimally affects capital. Hence, trade openness does not necessarily induce a "race to the bottom," even in developing countries.

Our four cases have adjusted to increased trade openness without jettisoning social programs. Mauritius (see chapter 5) obtained preferential sugar prices from the European Union, and imposed an export tax to finance social-welfare programs and diversify the economy. Although the tax was repealed in 1994, this two-pronged strategy raised revenue without devastating consequences for investment in other export sectors in which the country hoped to hone its competitive edge. Nonetheless, the Mauritian government, in moving to attract high-tech and other high-value-added activities, is experiencing setbacks from increased competition, particularly in garment assembly and sugar exports, as trade preferences are phased out. In Chile (see chapter 6), trade openness and a pro-business climate have been top priorities since the Pinochet dictatorship. The Concertación government, though sharing this export- and growth-oriented approach to augmenting welfare, has encountered difficulties in expanding social programs and placing them on a sounder fiscal footing. Concertación secured a temporary increase in the corporate tax rate in the early 1990s over strong right-wing opposition but also had to raise the regressive value-added tax in order to fund social spending. Some targeted anti-poverty efforts such as *Chile Solidario* are funded by the World Bank and foreign donors rather than the Chilean government. Costa Rica (see chapter 4) benefited from special access to the US market under the Caribbean Basin Initiative and, in anticipation of losing such preferences, sought high-technology investment. Like Chile, it actively sought to open markets by establishing bilateral free-trade treaties with regional partners, and it has also relied on regressive taxes to finance social programs. Costa Rica's more extensive social programs rest in part on this problematical revenue base, but also

significantly on rising indebtedness. This trend suggests that trade openness poses threats that are manageable but cannot be indefinitely contained without major productivity advances, steady growth, and fiscal
reform.

Of the four cases examined, Kerala (see chapter 3) has been most
impacted by trade competitiveness pressures, despite assets potentially
attractive to capital, such as its highly educated labor force, good communications infrastructure, and effective state institutions. Its overall low
level of development and largely rural population complicate the creation
of horizontal and vertical economic linkages. Also, its insertion within a
much larger polity means that its governments have fewer policy instruments for managing the opening to global markets.

The *multinationalization of production through foreign direct investment*
poses related, yet different challenges, mostly tied to the "exit threats"
that capital may use to discipline labor and national governments. Foreign investment may provide opportunities for backward and forward
linkages and "clusters" of related enterprises that generate more permanent, higher-quality jobs. The conventional argument is that high wages
and a high social wage (and, secondarily, strict environmental or other
regulations) will lead capital to seek more favorable conditions elsewhere,
in a "race to the bottom." This claim is clearly most valid for the exit of
labor-intensive, low-value-added kinds of manufacturing, such as textile producers (which in recent years have abandoned Mexico and other
Latin American and Caribbean countries in growing numbers). In more
high-technology export sectors, wage costs usually constitute only a small
proportion of total value added; they are not, therefore, the primary consideration in locational decisions by transnational corporations (Brosnan
2003, 187).

The "race-to-the-bottom" argument – while accurate for much low-
skill, labor-intensive, low-wage manufacturing – tends to oversimplify
the considerations that underlie many real-world decisions about foreign direct investment. Most foreign direct investment flows to OECD
countries, which implies that imperatives other than low wage levels are
involved. Transnational corporations vary widely in the proportions of
assets, sales, and employment situated in their "home" nations. Many
view having diversified production sites as part of a strategy to hedge
currency risks (Garrett 2003, 389–90). Corporate investors are often less
concerned with their tax rates than with labor productivity and political
stability, both of which are areas of historical strength in social-democratic
systems. While some scholars claim that global capital mobility is forcing
down taxes worldwide (Epstein 2003, 159), others note that tax policy is only one of various factors, and rarely the weightiest one, shaping

investment decisions (Swank 2003, 404). In a study of twelve developed-country welfare states, Fritz Scharpf (1999, 18), for example, found that employment in internationally exposed industrial and service sectors was barely affected by the overall tax burden or by personal and corporate income-tax levels. Negative impacts on jobs were associated instead with social security and consumption taxes, and were concentrated in locally produced and consumed services.

Indeed, important sectors of capital may be willing to pay a larger share of taxes in return for reaping the advantages of social expenditures, a phenomenon that in the context of neoliberal globalization potentially benefits nations with welfare states. Social spending may reduce uncertainty and enhance individuals' capacity to accept change, bear more risks, and acquire specialized skills, all of which potentially benefit investors (Hemerijck 2002, 174–75). As our case study chapters indicate, social-democratic regimes have a good track record of attracting poverty-reducing, "higher-end" forms of investment.

Yet the social outcome depends on political conditions. The viability of social-democratic models under neoliberalism is closely linked to strong labor movements or cross-class coalitions that act as a check on political elites' push for retrenchment of the welfare state (Pierson 2001a; Hemerijck 2002; Garrett 2003). Conversely, the absence of strong workers' movements, especially likely in less-developed countries with large surpluses of low-skilled labor, is associated with cuts in social-welfare spending (Rudra 2002). Certainly Kerala's radical mobilizational version of social democracy grows out of the impressive organizational capacity of the CPI(M) and its allies. While Costa Rica's left parties and labor unions have suffered many reverses since the early 1980s, welfare-state entitlements and public-sector provision of low-cost services have become naturalized as "rights," and are tenaciously defended by a broad range of civil-society actors. In Mauritius, similarly, pressure from below led to a system of tripartite wage negotiations and labor tribunals that institutionalizes protections for workers and for capital. Chile's Concertación government, in contrast, has been unable to mediate comparable class compromises, or to overcome the legacy of political demobilization bequeathed by the dictatorship. The relative "thinness" of Chile's welfare-state protections reflects, in part, this disadvantageous position of organized labor.

A more serious constraint on policy autonomy than the multinationalization of production is *the liberalization and integration of financial markets*. The conventional wisdom teaches that such liberalization forces governments to placate skittish bond and equity holders with conservative monetary, fiscal, trade, and social policies. But, again, this conventional wisdom needs to be subjected to empirical scrutiny. Swank claims, contrary to the globalization thesis, that "there is no evidence for the period from the 1960s through the mid-1990s that the economic and political pressures associated with international capital mobility have dramatically shifted tax burdens from capital to other factors of production or substantially undercut the general fiscal capacity of governments to raise revenues" (2003, 409). However, the four cases examined in this volume do not entirely support Swank's conclusion. In three cases, as David Held (2004, 15) remarks in connection with industrial countries, "there is increasingly a disjuncture between [social democracy's] proclaimed value orientations and the policy instruments available to realize them." In Chile and Costa Rica, the tax burden was always regressive and has become more so, while in Mauritius some progressive tax measures have been rescinded due to pressure from capital and tax concessions have been a major tool for attracting investment. Kerala's social spending relies heavily on sales-tax revenue (as a state it cannot levy income taxes), and it too has turned to tax holidays in order to draw investors, though with little success.

Nonetheless, though the reliance of social-democratic regimes on regressive taxes undoubtedly raises questions about distributive justice, it may constitute less of an issue than the conventional globalization narratives suggest. The multinationalization of production and the informalization of much high-income professional labor have surely complicated states' efforts to exact direct taxes on corporate and individual earnings. Where corporate earnings are largely inaccessible and income tax withholding is unevenly enforced, consumption levies may be one of the few practical, if unpalatable, alternatives.

Garrett, like Swank, is sanguine about financial-market integration, emphasizing that "unlike exporters and multinational producers, financial-market actors care much less about productivity and the real economy than they do about monetary phenomena that affect day-to-day returns on financial transactions" (2003, 391). Most importantly, if markets anticipate increases in inflation, they will pay less for the national currency and require higher interest rates in order to make loans, so as to make up for the anticipated depreciation. Much of the success or failure of government spending initiatives, then, hinges on how the revenues are raised. Programs financed through new taxes are likely to be of relatively little concern to financial-market actors, even if some of the burden falls on capital. Borrowed funds, on the other hand, raise the specter of inflation, since the markets understand that governments will have an incentive to reduce the real cost of their debts via inflationary monetary policies. Thus, according to Garrett, "the financial markets care much less about the size and scope of government interventions than about how they are paid for" (2003, 392). If this is true, prudent social-democratic regimes may continue with their interventionist policies despite financial integration.

A crucial piece of the "footloose capital" argument concerns the growing importance of offshore tax havens in the world economy. Clearly, financial institutions located in politically independent microstates with bank secrecy laws are an inviting place for the ultra-rich and corporate investors to stash funds. Since the mid-1970s, the G7 central banks, working through the Zurich-based Bank for International Settlements (BIS), have spearheaded a persistent effort to regain some regulatory authority over the post-Bretton Woods world economy. By 1988, they had managed to establish the BIS's uniform capital adequacy requirements for international banks and, most importantly, to extend this regulatory and supervisory regime to the offshore financial centers (Helleiner 2000, 18–20). In 2000, the G7-supported Financial Stability Forum, the OECD, and the European Union stepped up pressure on the tax havens, especially those that failed to meet international standards in their supervisory, regulatory, information sharing, and cooperation practices. Jurisdictions that refused to make certain kinds of information about financial activities and ownership structures available to outside authorities were threatened with sanctions that could include a ban on banking transactions and a cut off of development aid (Patomäki 2001, 154; FSF 2002). Following the September 11, 2001 terror attacks in the United States, offshore banks came under increasing scrutiny for their actual or potential role in facilitating terrorism. These measures indicate that it is possible – albeit hardly an easy matter – to reassert some control over the money laundering and tax evasion that keep tax havens in business and that contribute to fiscal crises of nation-states worldwide.

Costa Rica and Mauritius, rather than simply watch capital flee to foreign tax havens, have chosen to enter offshore banking directly. Neither has met with dramatic success. In Costa Rica – adjacent to the major regional banking center in Panama – the collapse of several private investment firms, some of which were little more than pyramid or money-laundering schemes, has dampened confidence. For Mauritius – located in one of the world's least economically dynamic regions – the offshore sector has generated some high-wage employment and some business links to neighboring countries but is unlikely to become a real engine of growth. The offshore strategy, moreover, caters to tax-averse investors, one of the least desirable sources of capital for a social-democratic state.

Despite these several challenges, our four cases have learned to live – and even prosper – with globalization. For the classic social-democratic developmental states, the key challenge has been to sustain expensive systems of universal entitlements and encourage administrative efficiency while stimulating innovation and increasing competitiveness in selected (preferably high-productivity, high-value-added) exports. Mauritius and Costa Rica both employed a multi-strand strategy that emphasized tourism, textile and agricultural exports, and – eventually – offshore banking and high-technology sectors. Importantly, both Mauritius and Costa Rica benefited from preferential trade arrangements with their main commercial partners and received lenient treatment from the international financial institutions, which were likely fearful of the potential radicalizing impact of orthodox adjustment policies. In both countries, high levels of public support for the main welfare-state institutions meant that the beneficiaries of such measures must extend beyond small elites to the broader population. Also, politicians have limited room for implementing unpopular neoliberal measures (such as privatization or making labor markets more flexible), if their parties hope to win reelection. Both countries demonstrate that it is possible, at least in the medium term, to liberalize trade and financial flows with only minimal downsizing of the public sector.

Yet the tendencies in these countries are not unequivocally auspicious. A rapidly shifting international environment – with the phasing out of preferential trade arrangements, competitive pressures from developing-nation competitors, and demands for further liberalization and privatization on the part of the international financial institutions and trading partners – might push these "classic" regimes toward a less inclusive Third-Way model. It is here that both state capacity and grass-roots pressure become essential for preserving social conquests: the former as the locus of strategic innovation and planning, and the latter as a constant political counterbalance to the pressures of globalization.

The radical social-democratic type, represented by Kerala, has delivered some kinds of social protections beyond those offered by the classic social-democratic developmental regimes (or by other Indian states). These include more profound processes of agrarian reform, the extension of the labor code to almost all informal-sector and rural laborers, and the provision of subsidized foods through state-run retail outlets (a benefit that existed in Costa Rica in the "golden age" of the welfare state). As noted in chapter 3, each of these gains resulted from sustained mass mobilizations. More generally, the destruction of traditional caste-, class-, and communal-based forms of patrimonialism and a continuing hyper-mobilization of the citizenry made possible a style of democratic politics that provided a check on liberalizing pressures emanating from the national government in New Delhi or from abroad.

Finally, the Chilean model, a variant of the Third Way that is frequently hailed in World Bank reports, has delivered impressive economic-growth rates and significant reductions in poverty. It has achieved these goals through an export-oriented market economy and a lean, technocratic state, and through mainly targeted social programs rather than universal entitlements. While the Socialist Party has been a key player in the post-1990 Concertación governments, its room for maneuver is limited by several legacies of the dictatorship, notably a flexible labor regime, a largely demobilized working class, and the military's appointment of nine "designated senators" (a practice that ceased in 2006) capable of blocking progressive legislation. The lack of protection, especially for rural workers, and a minimal social pact mean that the labor market itself reproduces inequality and near-poverty living standards for many (Frank 2004).

Do social-democratic legacies generate competitive advantages?

The formidable challenges globalization poses to social-democratic development models need to be considered as one pole of a dynamic tension that also includes significant complementarities at the other. The actual or potential erosion of safety nets, subsidies, trade protections, and the public sector exists alongside demands from capital – at least from those firms engaged in producing high-technology products and services – for a healthy, educated, and therefore productive workforce, for reliable and inexpensive infrastructure, and for legitimate government capable of maintaining political stability and mediating societal disputes.

Some sectors of capital pursue not simply the lowest wages or the most lax environmental standards – instigating a "race to the bottom" – but the potential profits to be derived from *high labor productivity*.[9] High productivity is particularly salient for more sophisticated or higher-technology goods and services. It derives from several sources. First, of course, are education and related human-capital investment – the inculcation in the population of the literacy and analytical skills required to master complex production processes and creatively innovate, as well as the disposition to submit to the necessary forms of workplace discipline. Second, human health is of interest to capital for narrowly instrumental reasons (reduced absenteeism, greater ability to concentrate on learning or on complicated

---

[9] According to Garrett, who argues that productivity is an important part of foreign direct investment decisions, small-government-low-wage economies tend to be less productive than welfare states (2003, 389–90).

or repetitive tasks), but also for its broader relation to social stability (and to quality of life in places where high-ranking executives may be posted). Health care, along with other "non-productive" components of social expenditure (disability, old-age, and unemployment transfers), mitigate income inequalities and fortify the social cohesion and sense of trust that facilitate high productivity (Pierson 2001b, 463; Garrett 2003). And third, state action to buttress competitiveness – what elsewhere in this volume we term "picking winners" – may prove highly attractive to specific sectors of capital.[10] A country may develop advantages in activities in which a deliberate state effort is made to reinforce efficiency and attention to market opportunities (India's or Brazil's competitiveness in certain aspects of computing, for example) (Solís 1992, 177).

State provision of infrastructure and services constitutes a major subsidy to capital that is sometimes insufficiently appreciated in discussions of globalization. While the tax holidays and giveaways associated with Export-Processing Zones have received considerable critical attention, less notice has been given to how state investment has contributed to competitiveness. State construction and maintenance of roads, railways, airports, and seaports, even when these have subsequently undergone partial or total privatization, constitute a legacy that is attractive to private capital. Similarly, state provision of reliable electricity, water, and telephone and Internet communications, sometimes at preferential or artificially low rates, is a major factor in luring investment. While contradictory pressures to privatize utilities and other public-sector entities frequently arise, especially when they are overly bureaucratic or fail to provide adequate service, the synergy between the interventionist state and private capital is quite considerable and is hardly lost on the latter.[11]

This last observation may appear as a page taken from Anthony Giddens, but we part company with the author of *The Third Way* in insisting on the desirability – indeed, the necessity – of state-led service provision in any viable developing-country social-democratic project that hopes to enjoy *political stability*. Little evidence exists that in developing countries the market alone will provide adequate health care and education, much

---

[10] "Picking winners" is, as Rodrik (2004, 37) notes, difficult in a world characterized by imperfect information, especially about the future. Successful "picking winners" strategies, then, actually involve both uncertainty and a willingness to jettison "losers" in a timely way.

[11] It should be emphasized, however, that public-sector inefficiencies are not the only source of such pressure. The case of the Costa Rican Electrical Institute (ICE), discussed in chapter 4, indicates that campaigns to privatize may originate primarily in neoliberal zeal and private-sector greed and may have scant relation to the efficiency or lack of it of the targeted enterprises.

less universal access to potable water, electricity, or telephone lines.[12] Giddens is adamant in maintaining that social democrats "should move away from what has sometimes been in the past an obsession with inequality" (1998, 100). But economic adjustment programs have usually exacerbated rather than ameliorated inequalities in less-developed countries, with privatization in particular frequently raising the cost of basic services. As the global and national gaps between rich and poor widen, existing patterns of inclusion and exclusion are exacerbated, which ultimately complicates any effort to empower the disempowered (Held 2004, 45).

It is hardly "obsessive" to observe that this rising inequality has often had profoundly destabilizing effects (UNDP 2004, 41).[13] The sources of these are varied, but it is worth observing that in addition to the criminality of the desperately hungry that has long characterized the countries of the south, new kinds of violence and anomie are emerging that are directly linked to the globalization of consumerism and media imagery of "the good life." As Eduardo Galeano points out, "Advertising enjoins everyone to consume, while the economy prohibits the vast majority of humanity from doing so. The command that everybody do what so many cannot, becomes an invitation to crime" (2000, 25).

Stability-seeking investors have, of course, to weigh the very substantial direct and indirect costs of locating in places where crime, generalized violence, and possibly civil conflict affect business and the lives of executives and employees. Inequality and poverty have a price, as well as obvious benefits, for capital, and not all sectors of capital will compute the trade-offs in the same way. Moreover, the more far-sighted sectors may also recognize that government spending on policies that reduce inequality by redistributing income and socializing risks not only increases stability, but also contributes to shoring up political support for market openness (Epstein 2003, 161; Garrett 2003, 385, 388; Rodrik 2003, 381). This has become a crucial consideration for capital in recent years, as the neoliberal elite consensus has fractured.

In Chile, Costa Rica, and Mauritius, a high social wage and extensive investment in human capital (education and health care, in particular) have proven attractive to capital, despite their high costs, at least some of which are inevitably borne by business. This is true in Kerala as well, though the largely mistaken perception of conflictual labor relations

---

[12] In contrast, provision based on a public-sector "solidary model" can attempt to maximize a collective good, such as universalizing coverage of a low-cost basic telephone service, through redistributive subsidies charged to less essential services, such as international or cellular calling (Fumero Paniagua 2004, 210–11).

[13] Conversely, as we argue above, even limited economic growth tends to have a more positive social impact in a situation of greater equality.

has produced less investment than would otherwise be expected, given the state's human resources and infrastructure. Conflict-management mechanisms, epitomized in Costa Rica and Mauritius by the state's continuing – if at times, uneven – involvement in labor-market regulation, contribute both to creating the long-term political stability sought by some sectors of capital and to mitigating the negative distributional impact of increased market openness. *Government mediation of inherently adversarial class relations has a circular effect; it enhances the political legitimacy of the mediating institutions and of the state's broader role in managing the market opening.* Chile, where the state is only minimally involved in the highly flexible labor regime, is a negative case that nonetheless would tend to confirm the latter point. Labor flexibility is attractive to capital, but it has actual and potential political costs: antagonistic class relations and diminished popular support for economic liberalization.

Conclusion

Despite the potential complementarities between a globalization based on open markets and the social-democratic project of investing in human needs and reducing inequality, few countries in the global periphery have so far realized these complementarities. The strategy of high-tech development may work for a select few countries, creating positive multiplier effects and generating revenue to fund social programs; but is it possible to "scale-up" this experiment so that many more countries can participate in what is, in effect, an informatics niche in the global economy? That remains the key question. Meanwhile, the harsh reality in most developing countries is low average-skill levels, high unemployment, restrictive labor codes, and a burgeoning informal sector. Together, these features weaken workers' organizations that, in the industrial countries, have championed welfare states.

Nonetheless, the four social-democratic experiments considered in this volume stand in contrast to the overall pattern. They have, with varying degrees of success, managed the transition to market openness while maintaining vastly more social protections than neighboring societies. Furthermore, despite high levels of public-welfare expenditures and, with the exception of Chile, despite significant state intervention in labor markets, they rank high on conventional competitiveness measures. Yet, in all four cases, substantial progress in human capital, infrastructural development, and state capacity-building *preceded* rather than accompanied the market opening. The same, of course, is true of Taiwan and South Korea, both of which have achieved impressive levels of human development. Policy legacies, together with citizens' attachment to welfare-state institutions, constrain the erosion of democratic developmental states.

Chile, Costa Rica, Kerala, and Mauritius have managed to survive, and even prosper, in a global context fraught with dangers. The last three cases suggest, moreover, that the Blairite or Chilean-style Third Way is not the sole positive alternative to the bureaucratism and authoritarianism of what used to be called "actually existing socialism," on the one hand, and the inequalities and insecurities of untrammeled "savage capitalism," on the other. Proponents of the Third Way, as Cristovam Buarque (2000, 49–50) notes, "consider capitalism the ultimate civilizing project," failing to acknowledge its ethical and technical frailties. Full social democracy, in contrast, starts from the premise that unregulated markets generate unacceptable levels of inequality and injustice and that state action, especially in the area of redistribution, is required to achieve a minimally humane society. Globalization has not rendered this system obsolete in the global periphery.

9   Prospects

To succeed, social-democratic movements in the global periphery steer a course toward a society without widespread poverty or social exclusion, avoiding the two current utopian projects. The first utopia is a neoliberal fantasy, the self-regulating market. In the prescient words of Karl Polanyi, this utopia "would result in the demolition of society" with humanity "robbed of the protective covering of social institutions" and perishing "from the effects of social exposure" (2001 [1944], 74). The second utopia, subscribed to by some tendencies in the global justice movement, advocates "delinking," "localization," and "post-growth" as related strategies to achieve ecological sustainability, grass-roots democracy, and genuine community (Hines 2000; Amin 2001, 16, 26; Cavanagh et al. 2002; Hamilton 2004).[1] In contrast, social democracy constitutes what the disillusioned Yugoslav communist, Milovan Djilas, approvingly called an "unperfect society" (1969). The pursuit of a perfect society leads to despotism, Djilas warned; far better, then, to opt for the perpetually "unperfect" society – such as those in Scandinavia – that pragmatically strive to reconcile liberty, equality, and community with the demands of a market economy.

Proponents of the self-regulating market utopia, though still highly influential, have recently seen their ideological hegemony eroded. This erosion was evident by the late 1990s in the increasingly heterodox declarations of its erstwhile architects (such as former World Bank chief economist Joseph Stiglitz and former "shock therapy" advocate Jeffrey Sachs);[2] in the oft-noted neoliberal "reform fatigue" in developing countries; and in the growing criticism of neoliberal prescriptions by

---

[1] A third utopia, communism, had been "unarmed" (to use Jorge Castañeda's term) by the economic and political shortcomings of "actually existing socialism" in the 1970s and 1980s and the collapse of the Soviet bloc.

[2] Stiglitz (2002) has vociferously denounced "market fundamentalism" and the power of financiers and commercial interests in the global economy (2002), while Sachs (2004) has declared that "a little less ideology, and a little more openness to the ideas adopted by the Nordic states, would do us all a world of good."

left-of-center governments and popular movements, especially in Latin America. This conjuncture may provide, as Dani Rodrik suggests, "a rare historic opportunity . . . to fashion an agenda for economic policies that takes an intelligent intermediate stand" between the extremes of "unbridled statism and unchecked laissez-faire" (2004, 2). In a few countries, this "intelligent intermediate stand" reflects monumental changes in elite sensibilities.[3] In many others, it grows out of pressure from below.

The second utopian project proposes "delinking" from global capitalism. Its proponents reject efforts to reform global governance, claiming that peoples in the global periphery cannot improve their welfare within global capitalism. "Post-growth" or "de-growth" advocates rightly point to the deleterious environmental impacts of exaggerated consumerism and unregulated economic expansion. Like "localization" supporters, however, they call for an unrealistic future: self-contained communities and reductions in production and long-distance trade. Rarely do they acknowledge that economic growth in poor countries can improve well-being (Hamilton 2004, 220). Moreover, "localization" and "post-growth" enthusiasts say little or nothing about how the funds needed to purchase goods undersupplied locally would be generated, or how communities could enforce limits on firm size and long-distance commerce (Robothan 2005).

Kerala, Costa Rica, Mauritius, and even Chile suggest, contrary to the latter utopia, that much can be achieved by middle- and low-income countries despite global capitalism. Their experience also suggests, contrary to neoliberal utopia, that regulated markets and developmental states can enhance, rather than impair, market functioning – when viewed from the perspective of societal well-being. By simultaneously engaging and taming global market forces and encouraging high productivity, high-value-added economies, the state can extend an impressive range of social protections.

Social democracy rests on the assumption that unregulated markets engender unacceptable levels of inequality, suffering, and injustice, and that democratically directed state action is therefore needed to counter these destructive tendencies. Without minimizing the obstacles, this book demonstrates the possibility of social-democratic routes in the global periphery. This possibility rests on two significant findings:

• Although the conditions that favor social democracy in the periphery are, in combination, found in few developing countries, political action

---

[3] "The Brazilian elite today," Buarque writes, "feels as much shame about the poverty disclosed in [publications of] world indicators as it felt in the last century about slavery" (2000, 70).

can create some of these conditions. Social democracies make themselves as much as they are made.

- Activist democratic regimes that orchestrate egalitarian capitalist development in a globalizing world are not doomed to self-destruction, contrary to much neoliberal and radical-left opinion. Although populism, a tendency to state degeneration, and neoliberal globalization present major challenges, they are challenges that have been, and therefore can be, creatively surmounted.

Making social democracies

Social democracy, as a general type, features a democratically controlled and proactive state that pursues equitable and broad-based development within a largely market economy. "Equitable development" refers to a pattern of growth that mitigates poverty and injustice by favoring disadvantaged groups, usually at the relative expense of the privileged. Depending on the circumstances, equity-promoting policies and initiatives include some combination of the following: accessible and good quality public education, health, and sanitation facilities; subsidies on necessities; tax-supported pensions; social insurance arrangements; labor-market regulations to enhance job security and wage levels; land redistribution; and industrial strategies to foster the creation of "good" jobs. The final aspect, arguably, has become increasingly important as global market integration advances.

Despite the scholarly skepticism regarding the applicability of social democracy in the global periphery, we hope to have persuaded the reader about its relevance in the cases of Kerala, Costa Rica, Mauritius, and Chile. Recent trends are expanding the list of potential cases. A widespread backlash against free-market prescriptions in Latin America since 2000, for instance, has brought the democratic or quasi-democratic left to power in countries accounting for three-quarters of the region's population: Brazil, Argentina, Venezuela, Ecuador, Uruguay, Bolivia, as well as Chile (since the election of a Socialist president in 2000). Uprisings in protest against neoliberal reforms have also occurred in Mexico (the Zapatistas), Bolivia (periodically since 2003, with so-called water and gas "wars" over privatization forcing the resignation of two presidents), Ecuador (in 2000, leading to the toppling of a government, and again in 2004–2005 as erstwhile supporters forced President Gutiérrez to resign for betraying his radical promises), and Nicaragua (where violent demonstrations in 2005 threatened to reduce the country to chaos). What united these leftist leaders and popular protest movements was not socialist doctrine, but an inchoate view that failed neoliberal prescriptions should be replaced with egalitarian and nationalist policies and a more central economic role for a democratized state. Meanwhile, in East Asia, free elections and economic crisis have combined to push governments in Taiwan, South Korea, and elsewhere in a social-democratic direction. Our four hopeful cases cannot, therefore, be construed as lonely exceptions within a neoliberal global south.

Yet our cases are exceptional in their sociopolitical development. They demonstrate, in their various ways, that relatively modest levels of economic development need not prevent developing countries from tackling some major problems. Exemplary social indicators set the four countries/states apart from their neighbors. They have eliminated adult illiteracy, instituted universal basic education, improved health and nutrition so that infant-mortality rates and life expectancy approximate those in industrial countries, and moved toward gender equity. Whereas the scope of social-security arrangements in other countries mirrors the existing social inequality, as chapter 2 shows, these arrangements in our exemplars are inclusive. Finally, the four social democracies have not only consolidated, but also deepened, democracy.[4] In regions wracked by conflict and breakdown, our cases represent models of stability.

Of course, such exemplary cases emerge from special socioeconomic and political conditions. Chapter 2 forewarned the reader against any romantic notions about social democracy in the global periphery. The challenges are many. Yet the prospects are not as bleak as they may appear. The 1920s and 1930s in Europe were also bleak decades; yet they saw the rise not only of fascism and Stalinism, but also of the first social-democratic governments. Politics matters in shaping outcomes (Glatzer and Rueschemeyer 2005): some of the principal conditions favoring social democracy are amenable to political intervention.

We explored these conditions in chapter 7. The fine-meshed analytical framework employed there moves from the most remote (structural/historical) causes to the more proximate (configurational and conjunctural) factors The former includes, in schematic terms, two historical developments:
- The extension of market relations into the periphery propels, in some cases, a pattern of dependent capitalist transformation that weakens the reactionary landlord class and/or dependent peasantry, and increases the size and leverage of classes that typically support social democracy, in particular the middle classes (especially small farmers) and

---

[4] Even Chile has deepened the deformed democracy bequeathed by Pinochet's 1980 constitution. Amendments passed by a joint session of Congress in August 2005 permit the president to fire and appoint senior military officers, abolished the military's right to appoint senators, and reduced the presidential term from six to four years.

the formal-sector working class. This transformation occurs within an increasingly integrated global economy where people are subjected to volatile and unpredictable market forces. Meanwhile, traditional norms of reciprocity and mutual support are eroding. These trends explain why vulnerable producers strongly demand social protections.

- A state-building process, impelled either by centralizing colonial or postcolonial elites or demands from below, leads to the emergence of an effective (that is, a relatively coherent, disciplined, and expert) state, one capable of designing and implementing complex economic and social policies and mediating class compromises.

Other important factors are of a more immediate – configurational and conjuctural – nature:

- The main configurational factor is the self-organization of classes, forged in capitalist transformation, whose structural position predisposes them to support equitable and socially protected development. A robust civil society emerges that gives impetus to democratization, forges political space for the autonomous organization of these subordinate classes and groups, and increases the likelihood of class coordination.
- More or less cohesive left-of-center or center-left parties or movements emerge that are capable of mobilizing or simply giving voice to subordinate classes or groups on a programmatic basis.
- At a critical juncture – usually involving a political and economic crisis – decisions are made as to coalitional partners and the distribution of the social product that amount to a social-democratic class compromise. The leverage of the subordinate, organized groups persuades the dominant class to accept a compromise involving democracy and the sharing of the economic surplus. However, such social compacts are possible only when a delicate balance has been achieved. On the one hand, radical popular movements are either defeated or moderate their demands by abandoning revolutionary goals (notably, the expropriation of property) and, on the other hand, dominant groups are constrained by either structural factors (the absence of sympathetic armed forces, for example) or their own political weakness from resorting to repression. Social democracy requires a disciplined respect for private property and strict limits to reform on the part of the left forces, or capital will not cooperate. Equally, it requires respect on the part of capital for the principle of social democracy, namely the political allocation of part of the economic surplus.
- A final, crucial, condition is the absence of a major foreign power that, perceiving an emergent social-democratic regime as a threat, intervenes to destabilize that regime.

In practice, structural, configurational, and conjunctural factors inter-twine to shape class compromises. On the one hand, social democracy requires a configuration of class forces that can induce a capitalist class to accept a smaller share of the surplus in exchange for legitimacy, political and social peace, and potentially high productivity. This configuration is facilitated by a particular pattern of capitalist transformation: one that increases the potential power of small farmers and middle sectors and/or a working class, while weakening (or avoiding the emergence of) classes with an interest in preserving pre-democratic and pre-capitalist institu-tions. However, the realization of this potential power demands political action – both self-organization and mobilizational activities by left-of-center parties – and astute leadership. On the other hand, the peak orga-nizations of the economic elites must be convinced that the subordinate classes will not threaten private property. Social pacts are therefore quite variable, depending not only on a balance of class forces, but also on both (a) the exigencies of a social and political crisis whose resolution demands political realignment and (b) the perceived reliability and organizational discipline of the social-democratic movement.

At the one extreme is the minimal social pact of post-1990 Chile. Here, a radicalized and highly mobilized socialist movement, spearheaded by the working class, was decisively and brutally defeated in the coup of 1973 and its aftermath. The Pinochet dictatorship eradicated the radical left, imposed stringent restrictions on unions, demobilized civil society, reasserted market relations, and bequeathed a constitutional system that buttressed the power of the right. With the return to civilian rule since 1990, the center-left coalition has been able to extract a series of only minor concessions from a rejuvenated business class. Agricultural work-ers remain poorly paid and marginalized. However, this Third Way is a work in progress: the election as president of the Socialist Party's Ricardo Lagos in 2000 and Michelle Bachelet in 2006 led to a deepening of social citizenship and constitutional reform. Popular sentiment has pushed the government, slowly and deliberately, to extend social protection (Cypher 2004, 531–32). This gradual movement reflects the continuing saliency of class politics, which arises from earlier cycles of class mobilization.

At the other extreme is the egalitarian class compromise in Kerala. Before independence, the states that amalgamated in 1956 to form Kerala featured strong caste divisions, quasi-feudal class relations in large areas of the countryside, and widespread poverty – apparently barren soil for social democracy. In the Princely states of Travancore and Cochin, how-ever, there was a history of political mobilization along class/caste lines dating from the late nineteenth century. Caste-based associations directly challenged the social inequalities of the caste system. Meanwhile, in the north (Malabar), peasant insurgencies challenged Brahmin landlordism. Socialists within the Indian Congress Party linked the nationalist and social reform movements within what became Kerala, thereby drawing on agrarian discontent in the anti-colonial struggle. Nationalism in this area thus became a lower-class movement against the colonial–feudal nexus. After the socialists broke with Congress in 1941 to form the Communist Party of India (CPI), they orchestrated and organized this lower-class protest. This protest channeled itself into a peaceful, democratic process because the colonial order was open enough to allow these tactics to succeed. Eventually, the CPI(M) (formed from a split in the CPI) built an alliance of the agrarian poor and the proto-proletariat that overturned the remaining pre-capitalist social structures and established a smallholder sector. Hence, political action helped forge the material and class basis for a class compromise that heavily favored the subordinate classes. That Kerala was a state within a federation that respected private property ensured that the CPI(M) would work within the capitalist system, irrespective of revolutionary rhetoric.

Brazil in recent years illustrates the important role of social-democratic *politics* even (or especially) in countries lacking a social-democratic *regime*. Brazil is not a promising candidate for social democracy. Not only is it one of the most inegalitarian countries in the world, with a powerful economic elite, but it also has a history of military interventions against redistributive regimes. Also, the country's low savings rate makes it dependent on attracting foreign investment (Kohli 2004, 188–90). Yet neither Mauritius nor Costa Rica appeared to be promising candidates either, as the relevant chapters in Part II attest. Politics can make a difference.

Admittedly, only limited distributional gains had been achieved by 2006. Under President Fernando Henrique Cardoso (1994–2002), the leader of the small Brazilian Social Democratic Party (PSDB), we may speak of a social-democratic president but not a social-democratic regime. There did not emerge a class compromise supportive of democratically controlled state interventions to enhance equality, solidarity, economic security, and job-creating investment. Rather, Cardoso allied his minority party with (among others) the powerful and conservative Party of the Liberal Front (PFL), thus moving his government to the free-market right. Nonetheless, Cardoso did achieve some social progress by taming inflation, improving access to education and health care, reducing levels of extreme poverty, and supporting an aggressive and highly successful response to the HIV/AIDS crisis (Cunningham 1999, 84; Encarnación 2002/2003).

Luiz Inácio "Lula" da Silva seemingly emerged in a stronger position than Cardoso following the election of October 2002. His Workers Party

(PT) was not only unusually cohesive, but also the largest party in the legislature. Although Lula sought to negotiate a broad social pact involving unions, employers, and opposition parties, he did not initially succeed and instead reassured investors through a range of market-friendly appointments and policies. Hence, Lula's social-democratic government has not implanted a social-democratic regime.[5] But the PT did overcome some of the hindrances to eventually achieving such a regime – hindrances that some scholars had earlier portrayed as virtually insurmountable.

Paul Cammack, Kurt Weyland, and others have highlighted the severe limits to egalitarian, social-democratic approaches in Brazil. Cammack (1997) explores why Cardoso failed to implement his 1994 program, which the latter portrayed as a "modernized" social-democratic project capable of coming to terms with globalization. One limitation was the priority the government assigned to neoliberal economic reforms, in an effort to stabilize the economy and enhance Brazil's competitiveness. Although Cardoso succeeded in economic stabilization, the achievement of this goal augmented the power of capital, ruling out any egalitarian policies that might lead to capital flight (Cammack 1997, 239). Secondly, Cardoso lacked the political base for social-democratic success: a disciplined party with a left-of-center cohesive ideology and extensive roots in the subordinate classes. Instead, his own PSDB, though ostensibly social-democratic, was a minority party of recent origin. It allied itself with right and center-right parties, and engaged in the traditional clientelistic practices of an unreconstructed, elite-dominated political process to gain power (Cammack 1997, 241; Smith and Messari 1998, 2; Cunningham 1999, 80–81). Not surprisingly, then, though some progress was made, tax reform was abandoned, social-security reform scaled down, and land reform neglected

Weyland, writing in the mid-1990s, focuses on the organizational hurdle to redistributive reform – typified as "organizational fragmentation" – and elevates it into a nearly insurmountable obstacle:

Associations of narrow scope and personalist links to people of higher status have kept the poor divided and separated them from potential allies. Few, if any, encompassing interest associations and social movements or broad-based political parties have emerged through which the poor could successfully advance their interest in redistribution. Personalistic networks and narrow associations have also helped corrode the internal unity of the state. (1996, 4)

---

[5] But note that social pacts usually arise in times of economic or political crisis. To persuade privileged classes to yield some of their power and privileges, leaders need to identify a demonstrable, though containable, threat to propertied interests.

The "only hope" for "reducing inequality while maintaining liberty," he says, lies in patient efforts to "deepen democracy" and hence reduce fragmentation and personalism (Weyland 1996, 224). The prognosis, however, is gloomy: "Given the self-perpetuating and mutually reinforcing tendencies of personalism, segmentation, and state fragmentation, it will take a long time to defeat these obstacles to redistribution" (Weyland 1996, 224).

Yet, contrary to this prognosis, the PT has made substantial progress in overcoming these obstacles since Weyland completed his research in the early 1990s. It has forged a left-of-center mass party with a cohesive social-democratic ideology, with an extensive programmatic base encompassing unions and new social movements, and with an internally democratic structure that holds leaders accountable to the rank and file. Despite scandals at the top echelons of the party, the PT remains a formidable organization.

Overall, the PT has established a basis for class compromise by delineating the limits of social reform and exercising discipline upon its militants. The party has moved from an initially radical-socialist position – summed up in a resolution in 1993 that "capitalism and private property cannot provide a future for humanity" (quoted in Samuels 2004, 1003) – to a reformist position that accepts private property and the capitalist system, provided the fruits are shared. The PT's 2002 campaign dropped any reference to socialism, while calling for tax and social-security reform, deepening democracy, and a moderate land-reform program. Moreover, this pragmatic shift was not just an opportunistic move on the part of the top leadership; it reflected the posture of leading constituencies in the party (Samuels 2004, 1006–14). Certain trends pushed the party toward the political center: a decline of the traditional industrial unions and rise of public-sector unions, the emergence of a "pragmatic and instrumental approach" within the new social movements affiliated to the PT, and the increasing number of PT delegates concerned with broadening the party's appeal so they could maintain or win power at the state or municipal levels. Internal democracy has insured that the PT's policies and leaders reflect the preferences of the rank and file.

Not only is the party cohesively social-democratic and internally democratic, but it is also well organized and programmatic in its politics. The PT has largely overcome the fragmentation that Weyland lamented. It has a relatively extensive membership in Brazilian terms; it depends mainly upon volunteers and members' contributions in its campaigns; it avoids personalism through an "institutionalized, hierarchical structure linking local to state to national organizations"; and it can and does discipline its members and legislators (Samuels 2004, 1001). The PT has adopted a largely programmatic approach to politics. Although it has not abandoned old-style clientelism – as the party scandals of 2005 involving bribes and kickbacks revealed[6] – the rank and file have held the tainted officials accountable for their actions.

A prime PT goal is to deepen democracy by empowering ordinary people to participate in political decision making.[7] For instance, the party is noted for introducing "participatory budgeting" in the municipalities it controls. Participatory budgeting involves the creation of forums where citizens, including the socially disadvantaged, select infrastructural priorities, allocate public resources to priority projects, and monitor public spending (see Baiocchi 2003 for several case studies). The experiment in Porto Alegre, the capital city of Rio Grande do Sul, is the most widely recognized. This city, like others in Brazil, was characterized by clientelism, social exclusion, and corruption during the military dictatorship (1964–1984) and the redemocratization that followed. In 1989, after the PT won the election, participatory budgeting was introduced and transformed clientelistic budgeting into an accountable, bottom-up, and deliberative system (Baiocchi 2005). More broadly, a 2005 study of five selected pairs of Brazilian municipalities found that, in the municipality in each pair that adopted participatory budgeting, the organized presence of the PT had broken the traditional hold of clientelistic politics. PT had significantly improved the access of people to participate in local-government decision making (Baiocchi, Chaudhuri, and Heller 2005).

So, despite the failure of Lula's administration to install a social-democratic regime, avoid party scandals, or even win substantial benefits for the poor, the PT has, nevertheless, demonstrated that the obstacles to an effective social-democratic politics are not insurmountable. Brazil is a highly inegalitarian country, with a history of authoritarian regimes alternating with populist regimes that direct benefits to narrow urban constituencies (Kohli 2004, chs. 4 and 5). But by building a less clientelistic,

---

[6] After two leftist parties deserted the PT coalition, the PT purportedly resorted to bribing MPs from two minor parties to maintain its majority. Kickbacks from firms receiving government contracts and from state corporations apparently provided the funds, according to testimony at a public inquiry (*BBC News*, May 17, 2005 and July 11, 2005 and *New York Times*, July 18, 2005). But Lula's supporters seemed unperturbed by these revelations. The President's approval rating rose even higher while the scandal unfolded.

[7] This was also Cardoso's goal. He encouraged the formation of Management Councils to enhance governmental accountability from the municipal to the federal level in such social policy fields as health and education. These councils were composed equally of representatives of citizens, relevant NGOs, and government. Five thousand health councils had been established by 2002. The more powerful of these councils, such as the São Paulo Municipal Health Council, have pressed for the recognition of universal health care as a right of citizenship (Coelho, de Andrade, and Montoya 2002).

more programmatic, mass-based, and cohesive left-of center party, the PT is changing the face of Brazilian politics.

The essence of this transformation is, as Jorge Castañeda phrases it, to "democratize democracy" (Castañeda 1993). Broadening civil and political rights opens prospects for future social reform. Patient efforts to organize a class constituency, involve citizens in governmental decision making, and strengthen democratic institutions – especially left-of-center parties but also the judicial and legislative institutions that enforce governmental accountability and transparency – will reduce the capacity of private interests to manipulate politicians and bureaucrats, or intimidate the poor and their organizations. The proactive political stance of social democracy – that activists need not wait for conditions to mature but could actively foster them – is as relevant in the periphery today as in Western Europe in the first decades of the twentieth century.

Social democracies can surmount generic challenges

Our four hopeful cases have not only emerged as social democracies in diverse circumstances, but also survived over many years. Their survival – indeed, success – contradicts the prevailing gloom about the viability of social democracy in the context of globalization. Skeptics have identified ineluctable dilemmas and destructive tendencies that purportedly afflict all experiments in egalitarian development. On closer examination, however, these dilemmas and tendencies more closely resemble avoidable pitfalls than intrinsic and deadly pathologies.

In particular, skeptics focus on one or more of three allegedly self-destructive tendencies in social democracy in the periphery. Their overlapping claims are these:

- Electoral competition impels social-democratic parties to resort to unsustainable populism and clientelism to buttress support among well-organized and rights-conscious constituencies. This politics provokes inflation and an economic crisis, which leaves the poor worse off than before.
- Social-democratic regimes steer market forces in order to minimize unjust outcomes and provide good jobs. This strategy will fail, producing economic stagnation, because states lack the capacity to govern the market effectively.
- Global market integration has enhanced the power of capital and neoliberal agencies to the point where proactive, equity-enhancing, and high-cost regimes cannot survive.

Although all these theses identify genuine dilemmas and tensions, none of them need be fatal to social democracy in the periphery. The possibility of such regimes remains open.

Avoiding unsustainable populism

One neoliberal argument – a "perversity thesis" (Hirschman 1991, 11) – contends that, albeit desirable in principle, social democracy in the periphery will produce just the opposite results from those intended. Heavily participatory and equity-oriented politics will harm, rather than assist, poor and excluded citizens. How does this happen? Closely contested elections tempt reformers to yield to the redistributive pressures from well-organized unionized workers, peasant and farmers' associations, neighborhood associations, and so on, leading to a destructive "macroeconomic populism" (Dornbusch and Edwards 1990). The resulting budget and trade deficits fuel inflation and capital flight, threatening economic collapse. To arrest the economic decline, governments will adopt stabilization programs under IMF auspices. The austerity measures needed to curb inflation then reduce real wages and social benefits to levels below those which obtained before the populist measures. In less extreme instances, generous social protection and poverty-reduction programs will require relatively high taxes and labor-market regulations to protect job security and raise minimum wages. The high costs and extensive regulations will discourage investment or lead to costs being passed on to consumers in the form of higher prices. Either way, production suffers – thus unnecessarily curtailing a society's capacity to reduce poverty. It is therefore better to rely on liberalized markets to spur the economic growth that will, in time, spontaneously resolve the problems of destitution and unemployment. Growth is good for the poor.[8]

This thesis identifies a genuine pitfall of egalitarian and democratic development strategies. In the era of highly regulated import-substitution industrialization (1950–1980s), several promising social-democratic experiments collapsed as incipient democratic-developmental states succumbed to populism and corruption. However, subsequent market-oriented reform programs have not yielded the hoped-for prosperity either, prompting later political attempts to reinstitute social entitlements.

---

[8] Dollar and Kraay (2002) argue, in a much-cited article, that the income per capita in the poorest quintile rises one-for-one with overall per capita growth, and that the standard policies advocated by the IMF and World Bank promote the growth that is good for the poor.

Venezuela is a case in point. What began as a democratic-developmental state soon degenerated into a corrupt, populist system designed to buy off workers and the poor. Royalties and taxes from the country's massive oil exports sabotaged this social-democratic experiment. Plentiful revenues attracted opportunists to political life and tempted parties to curry public favor via populist appeals rather than deepening democracy. When world oil prices tumbled, economic and political disaster soon followed.

Acción Democrática (AD) was the main social-democratic party; it emerged as a socially reformist opposition during the dictatorship of Juan Vicente Gómez (1905–1935). As in Costa Rica, the first AD government under Rómulo Betancourt arrived in power through undemocratic means – a military coup in 1945. Like the PLN (National Liberation Party) in Costa Rica, the AD repressed the radical unions and Communists while instituting redistributive policies. Although this reformist administration was terminated by another coup in 1948, a moderate AD returned to power in a democratic transition in 1958 engineered through a social pact. This pact, or class compromise, involved the military, in addition to capital, the workers, and the poor (Gómez Calcano 1993, 189–90). The army agreed to submit to civilian rule, in exchange for the preservation of certain privileges and autonomy. The business associations traded state-directed development, together with a redistribution of a share of the surplus to workers and the poor, to gain the profits deriving from a protected and subsidized import-substitution industrial strategy. The popular sectors, finally, were to receive their share of the surplus in the form of decent wages and a modern welfare state. Oil revenues would fund both industrialization and the welfare state.

This compromise survived until the collapse of oil prices in the 1980s. Buttressed by flush revenues in a highly centralized state in the 1960s, the AD and the Christian Socialists (COPEI) evolved into political machines, shoring up their electoral support through populist redistribution and clientelistic relations. Public employment, in particular, expanded in response to the exigencies of clientelism. The sharp decline of oil revenues led to heavy public borrowing in the early 1980s to maintain an advanced welfare state, a bloated public sector, and subsidies to industries. High inflation and capital flight brought on an economic crisis. Economic problems induced the government to adopt an IMF-style stabilization program and, when this failed, approach the IMF directly. The IMF stabilization and adjustment program, introduced in 1989, in turn led to urban riots and political turmoil (including two attempted coups). The experiment ended in the early 1990s, amidst popular disillusionment with the broken promises of the two main parties, including the social-democratic AD (Ellner 2003, 10–11; Lombardi 2003, 4).

This cycle of rent-fueled populism appears to be repeating itself. A left-wing populist, Hugo Chávez, won a landslide electoral victory in 1998, in the midst of chaos and popular rejection of the old-line parties and neoliberal policies. Chávez has employed the same populist mechanisms as the AD and COPEI in earlier days – using the country's newly burgeoning oil revenues to create jobs, generous social programs, and accessible health services for workers and the poor (Naim 2001). The absence of a class compromise, and indeed the striking polarization of the population, underlines that this experiment is not a social-democratic one. The hostility of the US government toward Chávez further inflamed the political situation. Indeed, Chávez has repressed the non-*chavista* labor unions, as well as the AD and COPEI. Nevertheless, flush oil revenues and radical rhetoric have permitted Chávez to hold the support of the workers and poorer citizens, and thus survive a well-organized campaign in 2004 to force a recall vote.

Sri Lanka is another example of a promising democratic-developmental state that fell prey to bureaucratic sclerosis and populist pressures. Between gaining independence in 1948 and the late 1970s, Sri Lanka registered the most advanced social indicators of any low-income developing country. The origins of this social democracy, like those in Kerala, can be traced to an unusual colonial history. Regular elections based on universal adult suffrage since 1931 entrenched democratic politics. This favorable political environment also permitted the formation of leftist organizations, including the Communist Party, unions, and other popular movements from the late 1930s (Uyangoda 2000). Indeed, socialist parties have played an important role in governing coalitions from independence until 1977. The long experience of democratic politics, together with a vibrant civil society and radical parties, generated strong public demand for extending social citizenship.

The social-democratic developmental state, after independence, undertook extensive land reform, implemented a heavily protected import-substitution industrialization (ISI), expanded the number of state-owned enterprises, instituted subsidies and price controls, entrenched workers' rights, and built a welfare state featuring free education and health care, public pensions, and workman's compensation (Lakshman 1997, 4–8). As in Kerala, smallholders formed a key constituency of leftist parties. The success of the Sri Lankan strategy demanded an expert, disciplined, and highly motivated public service; however, by the 1960s, clientelism had weakened the public sector while competitive populist appeals during election campaigns had overextended demands on the state. The outcome was tragic: an advanced welfare state produced a well-educated, youthful population, but heavy-handed and extensive regulations and protectionism wrought economic stagnation and high unemployment (Bhalla and Glewwe 1987, 51). The result was frustrated career expectations and political disaffection (Abeyratne 2004, 1301–02).

In 1977, the conservative United National Party interpreted its sweeping electoral victory as a mandate to recast the crisis-ridden economy in a neoliberal direction. But liberalization did not promote broad-based prosperity. The new strategy – featuring an open economy and export-oriented industrialization – met with early economic success. The market reforms, however, raised political tensions by fostering regional inequalities that favored the Sinhalese majority and by curtailing entitlements and public employment (Lakshman 1997, 9). These trends exacerbated long-standing ethnic divisions, thus contributing to the civil war that erupted in 1983 (Dunham and Jayasuriya 2000). Tamil separatists successfully framed the issue of shattered aspirations as a Sinhalese plot to favor their own people (Abeyratne 2004, 1313).

In 1994, a center-left government returned to power. Despite pressures from the IMF and donors, certain features of the welfare state survive in the twenty-first century, along with an open economy: "rigidities" in labor markets to protect job security, a relatively large public sector (including state-owned enterprises), and free public schools and health facilities (World Bank 2000). Entitlements, once won, cannot long be withheld.

Although these, and other, cautionary tales can be told, they indicate not an inevitable perversity in which social democracy breeds populist excess and economic decline, but a pitfall to be avoided. Our four cases indicate that social-democratic movements do not necessarily succumb to these populist temptations and economic dead-ends. The real culprits responsible for populism are twofold: (1) leftist parties that are too weak to set firm parameters to redistributive politics, and (2) an inwardly oriented ISI model of the developmental state that involves such heavy regulation and subsidization that it suffocates market forces. Ironically, global neoliberalism, which has often been blamed for the demise of social democracy, has provided an antidote to these destructive tendencies. By requiring fiscal and monetary discipline and external openness, the international financial institutions have saved some progressive regimes from the downward spirals to which they were earlier prone.

Maintaining uncaptured industrial policies

In addition to this perversity thesis, a "futility thesis" (Hirschman 1991, 75–76) takes aim at proactive social-democratic regimes that, constrained by open economies in using demand-management to foster equity, focus on the supply side, specifically by guiding private investment into activities that generate good jobs. The futility thesis contends that governments should exercise the utmost restraint in industrial policy. Attempts to steer the economy will allegedly not succeed. Sanjaya Lall (2003, 2) succinctly summarizes the neoliberal argument:

The best strategy for all countries and in all situations is to liberalize – and not do much else. Integration into the international economy, with resource allocation driven by free markets, will let them realize their 'natural' comparative advantage. This will in turn optimize dynamic advantage and so yield the highest rate of sustainable growth attainable – no government intervention can improve upon this but will only serve to reduce welfare.

A more "permissive" neoliberal statement on activist states is found in the World Bank's *World Development Report 1997: The State in a Changing World*. Here, the World Bank is ready to accept, in principle, that governments might go so far as to foster private networks supporting complex economic activities, or even coordinate investment in new activities (World Bank 1997, 72–73). This report also contends, however, that in practice, governments in the developing world should engage only in "initiatives that require . . . a light touch." They should eschew "high-intensity" activities (such as coordinating investment) because states lack the institutional capacity to carry off such activities successfully (World Bank 1997, 74–75). And states should never yield to the temptation to "supplant market judgments with information and judgments generated in the public sector" (World Bank 1997, 74) – that is, states should not adopt industrial strategies that involve picking winners. That road can lead to "disaster." Most states, with their typically low capabilities, are advised to restrict themselves to providing macroeconomic stability, setting clear rules, maintaining order, and ensuring high-quality education, health facilities, and infrastructure.

The main problem with even this nuanced futility thesis is that the evidence does not support it. As Lall observes (2003, 7–10), "the region that liberalized the most, the earliest and the fastest" – Latin America and the Caribbean – has been the worst performer in terms of world market share in manufacturing value-added since 1980. In contrast, the best-performing region in the global south during this period – East Asia (including China) – did not adhere to the Washington Consensus. Instead, these industrializing countries typically featured an interventionist state pursuing well-developed industrial strategies.

Social-democratic regimes are, by definition, activist regimes that intervene in markets to improve their outcomes. If they aim to enhance equity by creating good jobs, governments have a strong rationale for adopting an industrial strategy: competitive pressures impel firms to seek out the lowest-cost location for each of its manufacturing processes or business functions. To shift their economies to a higher technological trajectory, developing-country governments need to develop new industrial capabilities (Lall 2003, 5; Rodrik 2004, 5, 8). Otherwise, foreign direct investment will flow only to those few countries with established capabilities. These capabilities include: a labor force with the skills to manage higher-technology operations, an advanced infrastructure to support information and communication technology, legal systems and rules that allow knowledge to flow across borders, and social programs to preserve social cohesion by buffering the living standards of the poor and those in declining economic sectors (Lall 2003, 5). Finally, the government needs to orchestrate assistance and incentives (targeted credits, subsidies, and tax concessions) to encourage firms to enter competitive global markets.[9] All this adds up to a sophisticated industrial strategy that does, indeed, pick winners (albeit in terms of sectors, not firms).

An activist state operates in all four of our cases, generally with considerable success. The judgment applies even to Chile, which represents the minimally social-democratic Third-Way regime. Often touted as a free-market success story, Chile does not exemplify laissez-faire. For example, the government until the late 1990s channeled large surpluses from CODELCO, a nationalized copper company, into social programs and other state-led projects. CORFO, a state development agency created in the 1930s, continued to build new industries and introduce new technologies during the dictatorship and after (Cypher 2004, 529–30). In addition, post-1990 governments built export markets by providing private firms with specialized information on foreign market conditions, supplying cheap credit to exporters, furnishing the necessary infrastructure (for example, irrigation for certain export crops), and insuring firms against the major risks entailed in entering new markets – volatile prices, weather shocks, and crop infestations (Kurtz 2002). Costa Rica and Mauritius have operated developmental states throughout their histories as social democracies. Astute industrial strategies in Mauritius have moved the economy up the technological ladder from its original dependence on sugar exports into, first, tourism and textiles manufacture, second, offshore financial and business services, and third and most recently, into ICT industries. Although the success of the most recent venture remains to be seen, the country's impressive track record thus far inspires confidence. Costa Rica has similarly pursued industrial strategies to diversify

---

[9] The new trade and investment rules administered by the WTO permit only general subsidies not linked to trade performance.

its economy according to a very similar pattern to that in Mauritius. A major investment in the country by INTEL attests to Costa Rica's success in shifting the economy into a higher technological trajectory, with the superior jobs that such a shift entails.[10] Kerala, as a state within India, does not have the legislative powers to mount a full-fledged industrial strategy. However, it too has sought to attract investment through state policies to build on Kerala's human resources, though regional dynamics have limited the success of these policies in attracting investment (see chapter 3).

Although the futility thesis is wrong in positing the inevitable failure of industrial strategies, it does pinpoint a genuine pitfall of state-intensive, social-democratic development. Peter Evans suggests that developmental states are "inherently degenerative" (Evans 1997). When political and bureaucratic elites are heavily involved in channeling incentives to private firms, the former will be tempted to engage in collusive rent-seeking. The initially productive cooperation between state officials and business ("embedded autonomy," in Evans's [1995] terms) will then degenerate into "crony capitalism" (as in East Asia by 1997). To be sure, corruption scandals periodically surface in Costa Rica, Mauritius, and Kerala – these cases vividly publicized in the pages of local newspapers. Even Chile, with its reputation for unusual state capacity and rectitude, experienced egregious corruption in the privatization of state corporations under Pinochet. The antidote to this degenerative tendency is twofold: (1) a vigilant and assertive civil society, including an independent press; and (2) well-articulated and accountable bureaucratic state apparatuses in which rent-seeking is minimal. Both aspects obtain, to a greater or lesser extent, in our cases.

Living with globalization

Globalization is another obstacle to social democracy in the periphery that skeptics identify, a debate that chapter 8 engages in detail. According to these skeptics, freeing the cross-border movement of capital, goods, services, and skills augments the leverage of capital vis-à-vis national governments, local communities, and employees, and thus weakens the national capacity to impose equity-related costs upon business. Capital mobility renders credible the investors' threat to bypass, or exit from, jurisdictions with high costs in the form of taxes and employee benefits or "excessive" regulations. Also, such powerful institutions of international

---

[10] A major problem associated with technological upgrading is growing inequality, associated in particular with the high salaries that ICT professionals command.

economic governance as the IMF, the World Bank, and the WTO press their neoliberal agenda upon less-developed members. These pressures, so the argument goes, undercut social democracy by requiring progressive market liberalization (including flexible labor markets), shrinking the public sector, and reversing the comprehensiveness and universality of tax-supported social programs.

Yet, contrary to this thesis, our four cases have not only preserved or improved their social achievements during the era of globalization but have also advanced their competitive position by diversifying their exports.[11] They have achieved this feat by adapting to globalization through a gradual and selective liberalization. There is therefore no necessary trade-off between selective liberalization and the maintenance or promotion of social equity, provided a well-organized leftist party/coalition holds democratically attained power, or popular movements remain vigorous in defense of social programs.[12] Social democracies may have higher costs than other countries; but prospective investors weigh these costs against productivity-enhancing human capital, good infrastructure, and superior conflict-management institutions that safeguard social cohesion and industrial peace. These advantages will not persuade export-oriented producers of labor-intensive and low-skilled goods, such as textiles, to continue manufacturing activities in high-cost locations. However, state-supported efforts to increase productivity and diversify to more technology-intensive exports can compensate for rising labor costs. High-quality human capital and public infrastructure (especially in communications) are attractive to investors in an increasingly knowledge-based global economy. Social democracy in the periphery can therefore adjust to global market integration through astute industrial and labor policies.

Does this adjustment involve movement toward the Third Way? The vagueness of this model, not to mention the emotional response it evokes in those on the ideological left, makes the question a difficult one to answer. Many writers have used the term to describe the myriad ways in which "old-style" or "traditional" European social democracies have adapted to certain new realities since the late 1970s (Driver and Martell 2000; De Beuss and Koelble 2001). These realities include not just closer

[11] Again, this is less true of Kerala than the others, for reasons discussed below.

[12] There is further support for this proposition in a cross-national study that found that, for developing countries as a whole, social spending (welfare, public health, and education) increased between 1980 and 1997 (the era of globalization) as a proportion of GDP. Not surprisingly, this study discovered that social spending is higher in those countries in which (a) a well-organized working class is integrated with a leftist party, (b) there is a greater degree of democracy, and (c) there is a recent history of political instability (Yoon 2004).

global economic integration and the hegemony of neoliberal ideas, but also the transition to post-industrial economies with diminished industrial working classes, the growth of individualism, and aging populations that put stress on welfare states. Scholars now designate even such prototypes of social democracy as Sweden, Denmark, and the Netherlands as "Third Way" (Green-Pedersen and van Kersbergen 2002; Whyman 2003). Obviously, not one, but many, "Third Ways" exist, each one a particular synthesis of left and right. What all have in common is the surrender of the socialist vision in favor of humanizing capitalism, and concessions in the form of privatizations, public–private partnerships, and an emphasis on supply-side measures to enhance employment and increase productivity and equity. If this is what we mean by the Third Way, then Costa Rica, Mauritius, and Chile have certainly moved in that direction.

However, in chapter 1, we defined the Third Way more specifically to approximate the reality of New Labour in Britain since 1997 and Chile since 1990. Both New Labour and Concertación represent social-democratic governments governing primarily in a neoliberal direction while trying to maintain their traditional working-class and public-sector middle-class support, with all the compromises and confusion that such a strategy entails (on New Labour, cf. Hall 2003, 3). In these terms, the Third Way includes: equality of opportunity, not results, as manifest primarily in the public provision of education, training, and health facilities, albeit within a "two-tier" system; fiscal and monetary discipline; a minimum safety net for those who cannot compete; targeting of some social benefits and protections; private delivery of some public services; extensive privatization; and industrial policies to diversify exports and attract investment.

If we conceive of the Third Way in this restrictive sense, our cases suggest only a weak tendency in this direction. Kerala remains a radical social democracy. The Left Democratic Front government (1996–2001) responded to the challenges posed by the bureaucratic rigidities of a dirigiste state and by India's neoliberal reforms (since 1991) by simultaneously adopting policies to attract private investment and deepening participatory democracy. Chapter 3 records how the LDF reasserted popular power by launching the People's Campaign for Decentralized Planning in 1996. This campaign involved transferring more authority and resources (33–40 percent of the state's planning budget) to local governments, while enhancing their participatory structures. Many development projects – roads, housing estates, water services, child care, and the promotion of local agriculture – are now planned and implemented at the local level. Attesting to this program's popularity, the Congress-led state government (2001–2006) adjusted, but did not fundamentally alter, this initiative. Kerala, therefore, does not fit the pattern of the Third Way – but Kerala, as a state within a federation, does not exercise the same policy levers or face the same exigencies as our other cases.

Chile is a pioneer of the minimal Third Way in the developing world. This limited outcome reflects the demobilization of popular movements under Pinochet and their continuing weakness under subsequent governments, the severe limitations imposed by the 1980 Pinochet constitution (amended only in July 2005), the power of an intransigent and cohesive corporate elite, and the Concertación's concern not to sabotage a successful economic model. Nonetheless, the 2000 and 2006 elections of Socialist presidents may herald, not a continued social-democratic route to neoliberalism, but a neoliberal route to social democracy. Since 2000, the government has undertaken constitutional reform, prosecuted human-rights offenders from the Pinochet era, enhanced public health and education by channeling increased resources into the public system, and initiated an unemployment insurance scheme. A high-growth economy also generated abundant new jobs that lifted many Chileans out of poverty. Nevertheless, poorer Chileans share the general Latin American disillusion with neoliberalism (Agacino 2003, 65–67); therefore, the governing coalition remains under strong grass-roots pressure to tackle the many entrenched social inequities.

Of the remaining two cases, Costa Rica in certain respects had moved towards the Third Way in the 1990s. Costa Rica and Mauritius initially had a fairly similar array of state-owned enterprises, import-substitution measures, subsidies, incentives to investors who engaged in mandated activities, and superior public services and social-security arrangements (see chapters 4 and 5 for details). But Costa Rica's severe economic difficulties in the 1980s, combined with the evaporation of a benign US attitude (coincident with the defeat of the Sandinistas in nearby Nicaragua), heightened pressures to conform to neoliberal ideology. President José Maria Figueres Olsen publicly endorsed a "Third Way" in the mid-1990s (defined as lying between old-style statism and the current Chilean model) (Clark 2001, 103). This approach has, in practice, entailed half-hearted market-friendly reforms: conservative fiscal and monetary policies, financial and trade liberalization, some privatizations, and efficiency-enhancing market mechanisms introduced into public pensions, education, and health care. However, the level of public investment in these central pillars of the welfare state has not fallen – nor is it likely to, in light of the public's attachment to these programs. And a democratic developmental state continues to orchestrate a diversification of the economy. It is therefore premature to classify Costa Rica as Third

Way. More accurately, we can speak of a system reinventing itself while maintaining universal entitlements and social spending levels, and while remaining publicly committed to reducing exclusion and inequality. A creative synthesis – a Third Way in the broader sense – may result.

Mauritius has experienced less change in its classic social-democratic regime. That its economic difficulties in 1979–1980 were quickly rectified, and not repeated, accounts in part for this continuity. The country has not had to return to IMF tutelage since the early 1980s. Mauritius has diversified its economy from its initial dependence on sugar exports to now encompass tourism, textile manufactures, financial and business services, and most recently (and ambitiously) ICT services. However, preferential trade arrangements involving sugar and textiles contributed heavily to this success. The current phasing out of these arrangements may augment pressures on the government to move further in deregulating labor markets and paring the size and role of the public sector – that is, to move further toward the Third Way. Small economies lacking trade preferences are highly vulnerable to shifting global market conditions (Read 2004, 48–49).

In sum, globalization and social democracy in the periphery may be more compatible than is commonly thought. The pragmatism and adaptability of our cases to external economic circumstances is apparent. It is not inevitable that this adaptation will take the form of a diluted Third Way. Politics continues to shape this adaptation, its impact determined by the degree of popular mobilization, the extent of inequality occasioned by neoliberal policies, and regional shifts in popular attitudes toward neoliberalism. To transform the capitalist market from society's tyrant to its helpful servant, therefore, remains a project for the global south, as well as the north.

* * *

The precise policy instruments for realizing this project will necessarily vary, depending on the challenges of the age. A proactive state and an international strategy will, however, be fundamental. The state remains the only entity with the legitimacy and capacity to capture and redirect the wealth that society produces, despite the immense challenges that globalized capital flows pose to its autonomy and robustness. Yet the reality and promise of a global market economy demands, in addition, an international strategy in which state-level progressive regimes press for a social-democratic globalization. Global levies on capital flows (such as the proposed Tobin tax), and on carbon emissions, are two measures that could contribute to "civilizing" savage capitalism. Subordinating trade agreements to international charters of human rights and to minimum health and environmental standards would also serve this end. Finally, global movements that champion democratic reform of supranational institutions are another essential dimension of any viable project for social inclusion and genuine democracy (see Sandbrook 2003; Held 2004).

The challenges of globalization to social-democratic experiments exist alongside the complementarities that have given some of these experiments a provisional lease on life. Making progress in this difficult context – as Kerala, Costa Rica, Mauritius, and Chile have managed to do – requires state capacity, constant innovation, and an informed and mobilized citizenry. Efforts to extend their social conquests elsewhere will no doubt be one of the central dramas in the unfolding history of the twenty-first century.

References

Abernathy, David B. 2000. *The Dynamics of Global Dominance: European Overseas Empires, 1415–1980.* New Haven: Yale University Press.

Abers, Rebecca. 1998. "From Clientelism to Co-operation: Local Government Participatory Organizing in Porto Alegre Brazil." *Politics and Society* 26 (4): 511–37.

Abeyratne, Sirimal. 2004. "Economic Roots of Political Conflict: The Case of Sri Lanka." *World Economy* 27 (8): 1295–314.

Acuña, Víctor Hugo. 1987. "La ideologia de los pequeños y medianos productores cafetaleros costarricenses (1900–1961)." *Revista de Historia* 16: 13–159.

Adler, Glenn, and Eddie Webster. 1995. "Challenging Transition Theory: The Labor Movement, Radical Reform, and Transition to Democracy in South Africa." *Politics and Society* 23 (1): 75–106.

Agacino, Rafael. 2003. "Chile Thirty Years after the Coup: Chiaroscuro, Illusions, and Cracks in the Mature Counterrevolution." *Latin American Perspectives* 30 (5): 41–69.

Aggarwal, Vinod K. 1996. *Debt Games: Strategic Interaction in International Debt Rescheduling.* Cambridge: Cambridge University Press.

Agosín, Manuel R. 1999. "Comercio y crecimiento en Chile." *Revista de la CEPAL* (August): 79–100.

Aguilera Reyes, Máximo. 1994. "La economía chilena en el período 1974–1993." Documentos Docentes. Universidad Central, Facultad de Ciencias Económicas.

Ahluwalia, Montek S. 2002. "The Economic Performance of the States in the Post-Reforms Period." In *Facets of the Indian Economy*, ed. R. Mohan. Oxford: Oxford University Press.

Alarcón, Celia, and Giovanni Stumpo. 2001. "Políticas para pequeñas y medianas empresas en Chile." *Revista de Cepal* (August).

Alavi, Hamza. 1982. "The State and Class under Peripheral Capitalism." In *Sociology of "Developing Societies,"* ed. Hamza Alavi and Theodor Shanin. New York: Monthly Review Press.

Allen, Chris. 1999. "Warfare, Endemic Violence and State Collapse in Africa." *Review of African Political Economy* 81 (26): 367–85.

Allen, Richard B. 1999. *Slaves, Freedmen, and Indentured Laborers in Colonial Mauritius.* New York: Cambridge University Press.

Alvarenga Venutolo, Patricia. 2003. "La historia social en la Costa Rica con-temporánea." In *Entre dos siglos: La investigación histórica costarricense (1992–2002)*, I. Molina Jiménez, F. Enríquez Solano y J. M. Cerdas Albertazzi. Alajuela. Museo Histórico Cultural Juan Santamaría.

Amin, Samir. 2001. "Capitalismo, imperialismo, mundialización." In *Resistencias mundiales: de Seattle a Porto Alegre*, ed. José Seoane and Emilio Taddei. Buenos Aires: CLACSO.

Andreasson, Stefan. 2003. "Economic Reforms and 'Virtual Democracy' in South Africa and Zimbabwe: The Incompatibility of Liberalization, Inclusion and Development." *Journal of Contemporary African Studies* 21 (3): 383–406.

Angell, Alan. 1972. *Politics and the Labor Movement in Chile*. London: Oxford University Press.

Anker, Richard, Rajendra Paratian, and Raymond Torres. 2001. *Mauritius: Studies on the Social Dimensions of Globalization*. Geneva: International Labour Office.

Arunasalon, José. 1997. "Balanced Approach: Challenges Facing Tourism." In *Mauritius: The Democratic Road to Development*. London.

Azam, Jean Paul. 2001. "The Redistributive State and Conflicts in Africa." *Journal of Peace Research* 38 (4): 429–44.

Baiocchi, Gianpaolo, ed. 2003. *Radicals in Power: The Workers Party and Experiments in Urban Democracy in Brazil*. London: Zed Books.

    2005. *Militants and Citizens: The Politics of Participatory Democracy in Porto Alegre*. Stanford: Stanford University Press.

Baiocchi, Gianpaolo, Shubham Chaudhuri, and Patrick Heller. 2005. "Evaluating Empowerment: Participatory Budgeting in Brazil." Policy Research Working Paper, World Bank, Washington, DC.

Baldwin, Peter. 1990. *The Politics of Social Solidarity: Class Bases of the European Welfare State 1875–1975*. Cambridge: Cambridge University Press.

Barahona Montero, Manuel Antonio. 1999. "El desarrollo social." In *Costa Rica contemporánea: Raíces del estado de la nación*, ed. Juan Rafael Quesada Camacho et al. San José: Editorial de la Universidad de Costa Rica.

Barrientos, Stephanie. 1997. "The Hidden Ingredient: Female Labour in Chilean Fruit Exports." *Bulletin of Latin American Research* 15 (1): 70–81.

Bauer, Arnold J. 1995. "Landlord and Campesino in the Chilean Road to Democracy." In *Agrarian Structure and Political Power: Landlord and Peasant in the Making of Latin America*, ed. Evelyne Huber and Frank Safford, 183–232. Pittsburgh: University of Pittsburgh Press.

Bello, Walden. 2003. "International Organizations and the Architecture of World Power." In *Another World is Possible: Popular Alternatives to Globalization at the World Social Forum*, ed. W. F. Fisher and T. Ponniah, 285–89. London: Zed Books.

Bergquist, Charles W. 1986. *Labor in Latin America: Comparative Essays on Chile, Argentina, Venezuela, and Colombia*. Stanford: Stanford University Press.

Berman, Sheri. 1997. "Civil Society and the Collapse of the Weimar Republic." *World Politics* 49: 401–29.

    2003. "The Roots and Rationale of Social Democracy." Social Philosophy and Policy 29 (1): 113–44.

Bernstein, Eduard. [1909] 1961. *Evolutionary Socialism: A Criticism and Affirmation.* Reprint, New York: Schocken Books.

Berry, Albert, and John Serieux. 2004. "All About the Giants: Probing the Influence on World Growth and Income Inequality at the End of the 20th Century." *CESifo Economic Studies* 50 (1): 133–70.

Betcherman, Gordon. 2002. "An Overview of Labor Markets Worldwide: Key Trends and Major Policy Issues." Social Protection Discussion Paper, World Bank, Social Protection Unit, Washington, DC.

Beyer, Harald. 1995. "Logros en pobreza. Frustración en la igualdad." *Estudios Públicos* 60: 16–31.

Bhalla, S. S., and P. Glewwe. 1987. "Growth and Equity in Developing Countries: A Reinterpretation of the Sri Lanka Experience." *World Bank Economic Review* 1 (1): 35–63.

Bianchi, Robert. 1986. "The Corporatization of the Egyptian Labor Movement." *Middle East Journal* 40 (3): 429–44.

BID [Banco Interamericano de Desarrollo]. 1996. *A la búsqueda del siglo XXI: Nuevos caminos de desarrollo en Costa Rica.* San José: Editorial de la Universidad de Costa Rica.

Bird, Graham. 1995. *IMF Lending to Developing Countries: Issues and Evidence.* London: Routledge.

Blair, Tony. 1996. *New Britain.* Boulder: Westview.

Blanton, Robert, T. David Mason, and Brian Athow. 2001. "Colonial Style and Post-Colonial Conflict in Africa." *Journal of Peace Research* 38 (4): 473–91.

Bob, Clifford. 2001. "Marketing Rebellion: Insurgent Groups, International Media and NGO Support." *International Politics* 38 (3): 311–34.

Borzutsky, Silvia. 2002. *Vital Connections. Politics, Social Security and Inequality in Chile.* Notre Dame: University of Notre Dame Press.

Botey, Ana María, and Rodolfo Cisneros. 1984. *La crisis de 1929 y la fundación del Partido Comunista de Costa Rica.* San José: Editorial Costa Rica.

Boylan, Delia M. 1996. "Taxation and Transition. The Politics of the 1990 Chilean Tax Reform." *Latin American Research Review* 31 (1): 7–31.

Brautigam, Deborah. 1999. "The 'Mauritius Miracle': Democracy, Institutions, and Economic Policy." In *State, Conflict, and Democracy in Africa*, ed. Richard Joseph, 137–62. Boulder: Lynne Rienner.

———. 2004. "The People's Budget? Politics, Participation and Pro-Poor Policy." *Development Policy Review* 22 (6): 653–68.

Brenes, Adrián. 2001. "¿Qué es el 'efecto Intel'?" *Actualidad Económica* 15 (239): 54–59.

Brenes, Lidiette. 1990. *La nacionalización bancaria en Costa Rica: Un juicio histórico.* San José: Facultad Latinoamericana de Ciencias Sociales.

Brenner, Robert. 1985. "Agrarian Class Structure and Economic Development in Pre-Industrial Europe." In *The Brenner Debate*, ed. T. H. Aston and C. H. E. Philipin. Cambridge: Cambridge University Press.

Brooks, Risa A. 2002. "Liberalization and Militancy in the Arab World." *Orbis* (Fall): 611–21.

Brosnan, Peter. 2003. "The Minimum Wage in a Global Context." In *The Handbook of Globalisation*, ed. Jonathan Michie. Cheltenham, UK: Edward Elgar.

Brumberg, Daniel. 1995. "Authoritarian Legacies and Reform Strategies in the Arab World." In *Political Liberalization and Democratization in the Arab World*, Vol. I, ed. Rex Brynen, Bahgat Korany, and Paul Noble. Boulder: Lynne Rienner.

Buarque, Cristovam. 2000. "El camino provisional." In *La tercera vía: ¿es posible en nuestra América?* ed. Rodrigo Carazo Odio. Cartago, Costa Rica: Libro Universitario Regional.

Buitelaar, Rudolf, Ramón Padilla, and Ruth Urrutia-Álvarez. 2000. "Costa Rica: sistema nacional de innovación." In *Empleo, crecimiento y equidad: Los retos de las reformas económicas de finales del siglo XX en Costa Rica*, ed. Anabelle Ulate Quirós. San José: Editorial de la Universidad de Costa Rica.

Bulmer-Thomas, Victor. 1987. *The Political Economy of Central America Since 1920*. Cambridge: Cambridge University Press.

Bunwaree, Sheila. 1999. "Gender Inequality: The Mauritian Experience." In *Gender, Education and Development*, ed. C. Heward and S. Bunwaree. London: Zed Books.

——— 2001. "The Marginal in the Miracle: Human Capital in Mauritius." *International Journal of Education and Development* 21: 257–71.

Burgat, François. 2003. *Face to Face with Political Islam*. London: I. B. Tauris and Co.

Cademartori, José. 2003. "The Chilean Neoliberal Model Enters into Crisis." *Latin American Perspectives* 30 (5): 79–88.

Cameron, David. 1984. "Social Democracy, Corporatism, Labor Quiescence, and the Representation of Economic Interests in Advanced Capitalist Democracies." In *Order and Conflict in Contemporary Capitalism*, ed. John Goldthorpe, 143–80. Oxford: Oxford University Press.

Cammack, Paul. 1997. "Cardoso's Political Project in Brazil: The Limits of Social Democracy." In *The Socialist Register 1997*, ed. Leo Panitch. New Jersey: Humanities Press.

Cardoso, Fernando H. 1993. "The Challenges of Social Democracy in Latin America." In *Social Democracy in Latin America: Prospects for Change*, ed. Menno Vellinga, 273–96. Boulder: Westview.

Cardozo Rodas, Victorino. 1990. *Política salarial del Estado costarricense*. Heredia, Costa Rica: Editorial de la Universidad Nacional.

Carrera, Silvia. 1997. "Cambios en la planificación de los servicios de salud promovidos por la reforma del sector salud." In *Costa Rica: Las políticas de salud en el umbral de la reforma*, ed. Ludwig Güendel. San José: UNICEF and Ministerio de Salud.

Carroll, B. W., and T. Carroll. 1999a. "The Consolidation of Democracy in Mauritius." *Democratization* 6 (1): 179–97.

——— 1999b. "Civic Networks, Legitimacy and the Policy Process." *Governance* 12 (1): 1–28.

——— 2000. "Accommodating Ethnic Diversity in the Modernizing Democratic State: Theory and Practice in the Case of Mauritius." *Ethnic and Racial Studies* 23 (1): 120–42.

Carroll, B. W., and S. K. Joypaul. 1993. "The Mauritian Senior Public Service since Independence." *International Review of Administrative Sciences* 59 (3): 423–40.

Castañeda, Jorge. 1993. *Utopia Unarmed: The Latin American Left after the Cold War*. New York: Alfred A. Knopf.

Castells, Manuel. 1974. *La lucha de classes en Chile*. Buenos Aires: Siglo XXI.

Castiglioni, Rossana. 2001. "The Politics of Retrenchment: The Quandaries of Social Protection Under Military Rule in Chile, 1973–1990." *Latin American Politics and Society* 43 (4): 37–66.

Castro Valverde, Carlos. 1998. "La reforma del sector salud y el modelo de atención integral." In *La reforma del sistema nacional de salud: Estrategias, avances, perspectivas*, ed. Carlos Castro Valverde and Luis Bernardo Sáenz. San José: Ministerio de Planificación Nacional y Política Económica.

Cavanagh, John et al. 2002. *Alternatives to Economic Globalization: A Better World is Possible*. San Francisco: Berrett-Koehler.

CCSS [Caja Costarricense de Seguro Social]. 2004. "Cuadro No. 1 cobertura de seguro de salud." Available from: http://www.info.ccss.sa.cr/actuarial/indicobe.html.

Centre for Applied Social Research. 2003. *Mauritian Social Attitudes Survey 2002: Report*. Réduit: University of Mauritius.

CEPAL. 2002. *Panorama social de América Latina, 2001–2002*. Santiago: CEPAL. 2003. *Panorama social de América Latina, 2002–2003*. Santiago: CEPAL.

Cerdas, Rodolfo. 1978. "Costa Rica: Problemas actuales de una revolución democrática." In *¿Democracia en Costa Rica? Cinco opiniones polémicas*, ed. Chester Zelaya. San José: Editorial Universidad Estatal a Distancia.

Chalmers, D. A., S. B. Martin, and K. Piester. 1997. "Associative Networks: New Structures of Representation for the Popular Sectors?" In *The New Politics of Inequality in Latin America*, ed. D. A. Chalmers, S. B. Martin, and K. Piester. New York: Oxford University Press.

Chatterjee, Partha. 2001. "Democracy and the Violence of the State: A Political Negotiation of Death." *Inter-Asian Cultural Studies* 2: 7–21.

Chaudhuri, Shubham, K. N. Harilal, and Patrick Heller. 2004. "Does Decentralization Make a Difference? A Study of the People's Campaign for Decentralized Planning in the Indian State of Kerala." Thiruvananthapuram: Centre for Development Studies.

Chibber, Vivek. 2003. *Locked in Place: State-Building and Late Industrialization in India*. Princeton: Princeton University Press.

Clark, Mary A. 2001. *Gradual Economic Reform in Latin America: The Costa Rican Experience*. Albany: State University of New York Press.

Coelho, V. S. P., A. L. Andrade, and M. C. Montoya. 2002. "Deliberative Fora and the Democratisation of Social Policies in Brazil." *Institute of Development Studies Bulletin* 33 (2): 65–73.

Collier, David, ed. 1979. *The New Authoritarianism in Latin America*. Princeton: Princeton University Press.

Collier, Ruth Berins, and David Collier. 1991. *Shaping the Political Arena: Critical Junctures, the Labor Movement, and Regime Dynamics in Latin America*. Princeton: Princeton University Press.

Communist Party of India, Marxist (CPI(M)). 2000. "Programme: Updated at Special Conference at Thiruvananthapuram in October 2000."

Conaghan, Catherine, James A. Malloy, and Luis A. Abugattas. 1990. "Business and the Boys: The Politics of Neoliberalism in the Central Andes." *Latin American Research Review* 25 (2): 3–30.

Cordero Pérez, Carlos. 2002. "Intel invertirá en empresas ticas." *El Financiero* 7 (378): 30.

  2003. "Intel a punto de invertir en otra empresa tica." *El Financiero* 7 (397): 27.

CORFO. 2001. *Memoria. Actividad 2001.* Available from: http://www.corfo.cl.

  2003. *High Technology Investment Program.* Available from: http://www.hightechchile.com.

Cornia, Giovanni Andrea, Tony Addison, and Sampsa Kushi. 2004. "Income Distribution Changes and Their Impact in the Post-Second World War Period." In *Inequality, Growth and Poverty in an Era of Liberalization and Globalization,* ed. Giovanni Andrea Cornia. Oxford: Oxford University Press.

Cunningham, S. M. 1999. "Made in Brazil: Cardoso's Critical Path from Dependency via Neoliberal Options and the Third Way in the 1990s." *European Review of Latin American and Caribbean Studies* 67: 75–86.

Cypher, James M. 2004. "Pinochet Meets Polanyi? The Curious Case of the Chilean Embrace of 'Free' Market Economics." *Journal of Economic Issues* 38 (2): 527–35.

Darga, A. 1996. "Autonomous Economic and Social Development in Democracy: An Appreciation of the Mauritian 'Miracle.'" *African Development* 21 (2/3): 79–88.

  1998. "A Comparative Analysis of the Accumulation Process and Capital Mobilization in Mauritius, Tanzania and Zimbabwe." UNCTAD Report, Geneva, September.

Datt, Guarav, and Martin Ravallion. 1996. "Why Have Some Indian States Done Better than Others?" Policy Research Working Paper no. 1594, World Bank, Washington, DC.

De Beuss, J., and T. Koelble. 2001. "The Third Way Diffusion of Social Democracy: Western Europe and South Africa Compared." *Politikon* 28 (2): 181–94.

De Mesa, Alberto Arenas, and Paula Benavides Salazar. 2003. *Protección social en Chile. Financiamiento, cobertura y desempeño, 1990–2000.* Santiago: Oficina Internacional de Trabajo.

Debroy, Bibek, Laveesh Bhandari, and Nilanjan Banik. 2003. "How Are the States Doing?" New Delhi Rajiv Gandhi Institute for Contemporary Studies.

DeMartino, George. 1999. "Global Neoliberalism, Policy Autonomy and International Competitive Dynamics." *Journal of Economic Issues* 23 (2): 343–49.

Desai, Menali. 2001. "Party Formation, Political Power, and the Capacity for Reform: Comparing Left Parties in Kerala and West Bengal, India." *Social Forces* 80: 37–60.

  2002. "The Autonomy of Party Practices in India, 1934–1940." *American Journal of Sociology* 108: 616–57.

Deyo, Frederic C. 1987. *The Political Economy of the New Asian Industrialism.* Ithaca: Cornell University Press.

Diamond, Larry. 1988. "Introduction." In *Democracy in Developing Countries*, Vol. II: *Africa*, ed. L. Diamond, J. J. Linz, and S. M. Lipset. Boulder: Lynne Rienner.

Díaz, Alvaro. 1997. "Chile: Neoliberal Policy, Socioeconomic Reorganization, and Urban Labor Markets." In *Global Restructuring, Employment, and Social Inequality in Urban Latin America*, ed. Richard Tardanico and Rafael Menjívar. Miami: University of Miami Press.

Djilas, Milovan. 1969. *Unperfect Society: Beyond the New Class*. New York: Harcourt, Brace and World.

Dollar, David, and Aart Kraay. 2002. "Growth is Good for the Poor." *Journal of Economic Growth* 7: 195–225.

Dominguez, Kathryn M. 1993. "The Role of International Organizations in the Bretton Woods System." In *A Retrospective on the Bretton Woods System: Lessons for International Monetary Reform*, ed. Michael D. Bordo and Barry Eichengreen. Chicago: University of Chicago Press.

Dornbusch, R., and S. Edwards. 1990. "Macroeconomic Populism." *Journal of Development Economics* 32 (2): 247–77.

Drake, Paul W. 1978. *Socialism and Populism in Chile, 1932–52*. Urbana: University of Illinois Press.

Drèze, Jean, and Haris Gazdar. 1996. "Uttar Pradesh: The Burden of Inertia." In *Indian Development*, ed. Jean Drèze and Amartya Sen, 33–128. Delhi: Oxford University Press.

Drèze, Jean, and A. K. Sen. 1989. *Hunger and Public Action*. Oxford: Oxford University Press.

  1991. "Public Action for Social Security: Foundations and Strategy." In *Social Security in Developing Countries*, ed. Echtisham Ahmad, Jean Drèze, John Hills, and Amartya Sen. Oxford: Clarendon Press.

  1995. *India: Economic Development and Social Opportunity*. Delhi: Oxford University Press.

Driver, S., and L. Martell. 2000. "Left, Right and the Third Way." *Policy and Politics* 28 (2): 47–61.

Dukhira, Chit. 2002. *History of Mauritius: Experiments in Democracy*. Quatre-Bornes, Mauritius: Dukhira.

Dunham, D., and S. Jayasuriya. 2000. "Equity, Growth and Insurrection: Liberalization and the Welfare Debate in Contemporary Sri Lanka." *Oxford Development Studies* 28 (1): 97–110.

Easterly, William. 2001. "The Lost Decades: Developing Countries' Stagnation in Spite of Policy Reform 1980–98." *Journal of Economic Growth* 6: 135–57.

Easterly, William, and Ross Levine. 2002. "Tropics, Germs, and Crops: How Endowments Influence Economic Development." National Bureau for Economic Research Working Paper 9106, Washington, DC, August.

Edelman, Marc. 1999. *Peasants against Globalization: Rural Social Movements in Costa Rica*. Stanford: Stanford University Press.

Edwards, Sebastian. 1985. "Economic Policy and the Record of Economic Growth in Chile, 1973–1982." In *The National Economic Policies of Chile*, ed. Gary M. Walton. Greenwich: Lai Press Inc.

Edwards, Sebastian, and Alejandra Cox Edwards. 1987. *Monetarism and Liberalization: The Chilean Experiment*. Cambridge, MA: Ballinger Publishing Co.

Ehteshami, Anoushiravan, and Emma C. Murphy. 1996. "Transformation of the Corporatist State in the Middle East." *Third World Quarterly* 17 (4): 753–772.

Ellis, Stephen. 2003. "The Old Roots of Africa's New Wars." *Internationale Politik und Gersellschaft* 2: 29–43.

Ellner, S. 2003. "Introduction: The Search for Explanations." In *Venezuelan Politics in the Chávez Period*, ed. S. Ellner. Boulder: Lynne Rienner.

Elster, Jon. 1999. *Strong Feelings: Emotion, Addiction, and Human Behavior, The Jean Nicod Lectures, 1997*. Cambridge, MA: MIT Press.

Encarnación, Omar. 2002/2003. "Lula's Big Win." *World Policy Journal* 19 (11).

Epstein, Gerald. 2003. "The Role and Control of Multinational Corporations in the World Economy." In *The Handbook of Globalisation*, ed. Jonathan Michie. Cheltenham, UK: Edward Elgar.

Escobar, Patricio. 2003. "The New Labor Market: The Effects of the Neoliberal Experiment in Chile." *Latin American Perspectives* 30 (5): 70–78.

Esping-Andersen, Gøsta. 1985. *Politics against Markets: The Social Democratic Road to Power*. Princeton: Princeton University Press.

1999. *Social Foundations of Postindustrial Economies*. New York: Oxford University Press.

Evans, Peter B. 1995. *Embedded Autonomy: States and Industrial Transformation*. Princeton: Princeton University Press.

1997. "State Structure, Government–Business Relations, and Economic Transformation." In *Business and the State in Developing Countries*, ed. S. Maxfield and B. R. Schneider. Ithaca: Cornell University Press.

2005. "Neo-Liberalism as an Opportunity: Constraints and Innovations in Contemporary Development Strategy." In *The Case for Policy Space: Reasserting Development in a Globalizing World*, ed. Kevin Gallagher. London: Zed Books.

Evans, Peter, and John D. Stephens. 1988. "Development and the World Economy," in *Handbook of Sociology*, ed. Neil Smelser, 739–73. London: Sage Publications.

Evans, Sterling. 1999. *The Green Republic: A Conservation History of Costa Rica*. Austin: University of Texas Press.

Faux, Jeff. 2004. "Without Consent: Global Capital Mobility and Democracy." *Dissent* (Winter): 43–50.

Feres, Juan Carlos. 2001. "La pobreza en Chile en el año 2000." Santiago: CEPAL.

Ffrench-Davis, Ricardo. 2002. "El Impacto de las exportaciones sobre el crecimiento en Chile." *Revista de la CEPAL* (April): 143–60.

FIAS [Foreign Investment Advisory Service]. 1996. *Costa Rica: A Strategy for Foreign Investment in Costa Rica's Electronics Industry*. FIAS – A Joint Service of the International Finance Corporation and the World Bank. Washington, DC: FIAS.

Fox, James W. 1998. *Real Progress: Fifty Years of USAID in Costa Rica*. USAID Program and Operations Assessment Report, Vol. 23. Washington, DC: Center for Development Information and Evaluation, USAID.

Fox, Jonathan. 1996. "How Does Civil Society Thicken? The Political Construction of Social Capital in Rural Mexico." *World Development* 24 (6): 1089–103.

Foxley, Alejandro, Eduardo Aninat, and J. P. Arellano. 1979. *Redistributive Effects of Government Programs: The Chilean Case.* Oxford: Pergamon Press.

Frank, Volker. 2004. "Politics Without Policy: The Failure of Social Concertación in Democratic Chile, 1990–2000." In *Victims of the Chilean Miracle: Workers and Neoliberalism in the Pinochet Era, 1973–2002,* ed. Peter Winn. Durham: Duke University Press.

Friedman, Milton. 1962. *Capitalism and Freedom.* Chicago: University of Chicago Press.

FSF [Financial Stability Forum]. 2002. "Financial Stability Forum Reviews Vulnerabilities and Efforts to Strengthen the International Financial System." Available from: http://www.fsforum.org/publications/PR_Toronto02.pdf.

Fuller, Graham E. 2003. *The Future of Political Islam.* New York: Palgrave.

Fumero Paniagua, Gerardo. 2004. "Costa en el marco del TLC y sus consecuencias en el área de la telecomunicaciones." In *¿Debe Costa Rica aprobarlo? LTC con Estados Unidos: Contribuciones para el debate,* ed. María Florez-Estrada and Gerardo Hernández. San José: Instituto de Investigaciones Sociales, Universidad de Costa Rica.

Galeano, Eduardo. 2000. *Upside Down: A Primer for the Looking-Glass World.* New York: Metropolitan Books.

García Argañarás, Fernando. 1997. "The Drug War at the Supply End: The Case of Bolivia." *Latin American Perspectives* 24 (5): 59–80.

Garnier, Leonardo, and Roberto Hidalgo. 1998. "El Estado necesario y la política de desarrollo." In *Costa Rica entre la ilusión y la desesperanza (una alternativa para el desarrollo),* ed. Jorge Corni. San José: Editorial Guayacán.

Garrett, Geoffrey. 1998. *Partisan Politics in the Global Economy.* Cambridge: Cambridge University Press.

——— 2003. "Global Markets and National Politics." In *The Global Transformations Reader,* 2nd edition, ed. David Held and Anthony McGrew. Cambridge: Polity Press.

Ghabra, Shafeeq. 2003. "Balancing State and Society: The Islamic Movement in Kuwait." In *Revolutionaries and Reformers: Contemporary Islamic Movements in the Middle East,* ed. Barry Rubin. Albany: State University of New York Press.

Gibbon, Peter. 2000. "'Back to the Basics' through Delocalisation: The Mauritian Garment Industry at the End of the Twentieth Century." Centre for Development Research, Working Paper X.00.7, Copenhagen, October.

Giddens, Anthony. 1998. *The Third Way: The Renewal of Social Democracy.* Cambridge: Polity Press.

——— 2000. *The Third Way and Its Critics.* Cambridge: Polity Press.

Glatzer, Miguel and Dietrich Rueschemeyer. 2005. "Conclusion: Globalization and Social Welfare Policy." In *Globalization and the Future of the Welfare State,* ed. M. Glatzer and D. Rueschemeyer. Pittsburgh: University of Pittsburgh Press.

Global News Bank. Available from: http://infoweb1.newsbank.com.

Gokhool, P. A. 1999. "The Trade Union Situation in Mauritius at the Eve of the Third Millennium." B.Sc. dissertation, Social Studies, University of Mauritius, April.

Gómez Calcano, Luis. 1993. "Venezuelan Social Democracy: From Populism to Pragmatism." In *Social Democracy in Latin America*, ed. Menno Vellinga. Boulder: Westview.

González Ortega, Alfonso, and Manuel Solís Avendaño. 2001. *Entre el desarraigo y el despojo: Costa Rica en el fin de siglo*. San José: Editorial de la Universidad de Costa Rica.

González-Vega, Claudio. 1984. "Fear of Adjusting: The Social Costs of Economic Policies in Costa Rica in the 1970s." In *Revolution and Counterrevolution in Central America and the Caribbean*, ed. Donald E. Schultz and Douglas H. Graham. Boulder: Westview.

Gough, Ian, and Geoff Wood et al. 2004. *Insecurity and Welfare Regimes in Asia, Africa and Latin America*. Cambridge: Cambridge University Press.

Government of Kerala. 2003. *Budget in Brief, 2003–2004*. Thiruvananthapuram.

Gramsci, Antonio. 1972. *Selections from the Prison Notebooks of Antonio Gramsci*, ed. and trans. Quinton Hoare and Geoffrey Nowell-Smith. New York: International Publishers.

Gray, John. 1998. *False Dawn: The Delusions of Global Capitalism*. London: Granta.

Green, Duncan. 1996. "Latin America: Neoliberal Failure and the Search for Alternatives." *Third World Quarterly* 17 (1): 109–22.

Green-Pedersen, C., and K. van Kersbergen. 2002. "The Politics of the Third Way: The Transformation of Social Democracy in Denmark and the Netherlands." *Party Politics* 8 (5): 507–24.

Griffith-Jones, Stephany. 1991. *Chile to 1991: The End of an Era?* Special Report No. 1073, The Economic Intelligence Unit.

———. 1992. "Cross Conditionality or the Spread of Obligatory Adjustment: A Review of the Issues and Questions for Research." In *Cross Conditionality, Banking Regulation and Third World Debt*, ed. Emilio Rodríguez and Stephany Griffith-Jones. Houndmills, Basingstoke, Hampshire: Macmillan.

Grindle, Merilee S. 1996. *Challenging the State: Crisis and Innovation in Latin America and Africa*. Cambridge: Cambridge University Press.

Gudmundson, Lowell. 1986. *Costa Rica before Coffee: Society and Economy on the Eve of the Export Boom*. Baton Rouge: Louisiana State University Press.

———. 1995. "Lord and Peasant in the Making of Modern Central America." In *Agrarian Structure and Political Power: Landlord and Peasant in the Making of Latin America*, ed. Evelyne Huber and Frank Safford. Pittsburgh: University of Pittsburgh Press.

Gulhati, Ravi, and Raj Nallari. 1990. *Successful Stabilization and Recovery in Mauritius*, Economic Development Institute Policy Case Series #5, World Bank, Washington, DC.

———. 2000. "Views from the Periphery: Future of Neoliberalism in Latin America." *Third World Quarterly* 21 (1): 141–56.

Haagh, Louise. 2002. *Citizenship, Labor Markets and Democratization*. New York: Palgrave.

Habermas, Jürgen. 1989. *The Structural Transformation of the Public Sphere: An Inquiry into a Category of Bourgeois Society*. Cambridge, MA: MIT Press.

1996. *Between Facts and Norms: Contributions to a Discourse Theory of Law and Democracy*, Studies in Contemporary German Social Thought. Cambridge, MA: MIT Press.

Hadiz, Vedi R. 1997. "State and Labor in the Early New Order." In *State and Labor in New Order Indonesia*, ed. Rob Lamber. Asia Papers No. 6. Nedlands, Western Australia: University of Western Australia Press.

Hall, Stuart. 2003. "New Labour's Double Shuffle." *Soundings* 24 (November): 10–24.

Hamilton, Clive. 2004. *Growth Fetish*. London: Pluto Press.

Hansen, Thomas Blom. 1999. *The Saffron Wave: Democracy and Hindu Nationalism in Modern India*. Princeton: Princeton University Press.

Harilal, K. N., and K. J. Joseph. 2000. "Stagnation and Revival of the Kerala Economy: An Open Economy Perspective." Working Paper no. 305, Center for Development Studies, Thiruvananthapuram.

Harper, Richard. 2000. "The Social Organization of the IMF's Mission Work." In *Audit Cultures: Anthropological Studies in Accountability, Ethics and the Academy*, ed. Marilyn Strathern. London: Routledge.

Harvey, David. 2000. *Spaces of Hope*. Berkeley: University of California Press.

Havnevik, Kjell J. 1987. "Introduction." In *The IMF and the World Bank in Africa*, ed. Kjell J. Havnevik. Uppsala: Institute of African Studies.

Hay, C. 1998. "Globalisation, Welfare Retrenchment, and 'the Logic of No Alternative.'" *Journal of Social Policy* 27 (2): 525–32.

Hayek, Friedrich A. von. 1944. *The Road to Serfdom*. Chicago: University of Chicago Press.

Held, David. 2004. *Global Covenant: The Social-Democratic Alternative to the Washington Consensus*. Cambridge: Polity Press.

Held, David, and Anthony McGrew. 2003. "The Great Globalisation Debate: An Introduction." In *The Global Transformations Reader*, 2nd edition, ed. David Held and Anthony McGrew. Cambridge: Polity Press.

Helleiner, Eric. 2000. "Globalization and Haute Finance – Déja Vu?" In *Karl Polanyi in Vienna: The Contemporary Significance of The Great Transformation*, ed. Kenneth McRobbie and Kari Polanyi Levitt. Montreal: Black Rose Books.

Heller, Patrick. 1999. *The Labor of Development: Workers and the Transformation of Capitalism in Kerala, India*. Ithaca: Cornell University Press.

2000. "Degrees of Democracy: Some Comparative Lessons from India." *World Politics* 52: 484–519.

2005. "Reinventing Public Power in the Age of Globalization: The Transformation of Movement Politics in Kerala." In *Social Movements in India: Poverty, Power, and Politics*, ed. Raka Ray and Mary Katzenstein. New York: Rowan and Littlefield.

Hemerijck, Anton. 2002. "The Self-Transformation of the European Social Model(s)." In *Why We Need a New Welfare State*, ed. Gøsta Esping-Andersen. London: Oxford University Press.

Henderson, Errol A. 2000. "When States Implode: The Correlates of Africa's Civil Wars, 1950–92." *Studies in Comparative International Development* 35 (2): 28–47

Hernández, Silvia. 1973. "El desarrollo capitalista del campo chileno." In *Chile: Reforma agraria y gobierno popular*, ed. Solon Barraclough, Almino

Affonso, Silvia Hernández, Hugo Zemelman, Sergio Gómez, and José Bengoa. Buenos Aires: Ediciones Periferia S.R.L.

Herring, Ronald J. 1983. *Land to the Tiller: The Political Economy of Agrarian Reform in South Asia*. New Haven: Yale University Press.

1996. "From Fanaticism to Power: Ratchet Politics and Peasant Mobilization in South India, 1836–1956." Paper presented for the Association of Asian Studies, Annual Meetings, Honolulu, April 11–14.

Hidalgo Capitán, Antonio Luis. 2003. *Costa Rica en evolución: Política económica, desarrollo y cambio estructural del sistema socioeconómico costarricense (1980–2002)*. San José: Editorial de la Universidad de Costa Rica and Servicio de Publicaciones de la Universidad de Huelva.

Hines, Colin. 2000. *Localization: A Global Manifesto*. London: Earthscan.

Hirschman, Albert O. 1968. "Political Economy of Import-Substituting Industrialization in Latin America." *Quarterly Journal of Economics* 82 (1): 2–32.

1971. *A Bias for Hope*. New Haven: Yale University Press.

1991. *The Rhetoric of Reaction: Perversity, Futility, Jeopardy*. Cambridge: Belknap Press.

Hirst, Paul. 1999. "Has Globalization Killed Social Democracy?" In *The New Social Democracy*, ed. A. Gamble and T. Wright, 84–96. Oxford: Blackwell.

Hirst, Paul, and Grahame Thompson. 1996. *Globalization in Question*. Cambridge: Polity Press.

2000. *Globalization in Question*. 2nd edition. Cambridge: Polity Press.

Hoekman, Bernard. 2004. "Operationalizing the Concept of Policy Space in the WTO: Beyond Special and Differential Treatment." Policy Brief #4, The William Davidson Institute, University of Michigan Business School. Available from: http://www.wdi.bus.umich.edu/publications/policy_brief/brief_04.pdf.

Honey, Martha. 1994. *Hostile Acts: US Policy in Costa Rica in the 1980s*. Gainesville: University Press of Florida.

2003. "Giving a Grade to Costa Rica's Green Tourism." *NACLA Report on the Americas* 36 (6): 39–46.

Hoogvelt, Angie. 1997. *Globalization and the Post-Colonial World*. Baltimore: Johns Hopkins University Press.

Hopkin, Jonathan, and Alfio Mastropaolo. 2001. "From Patronage to Clientelism: Comparing the Italian and Spanish Experiences." In *Clientelism, Interests and Democratic Representation*, ed. Simona Piattoni. Cambridge: Cambridge University Press.

Houbert, Jean. 1982–1983. "Mauritius: Politics and Pluralism at the Periphery." *Annuaire des Pays de l'Océan Indien* 9: 225–65.

Huber, Evelyne, and Frank Safford, eds. 1995. *Agrarian Structure and Political Power: Landlord and Peasant in the Making of Latin America*. Pittsburgh: University of Pittsburgh Press.

Huber, Evelyne, and John D. Stephens. 1998. "Internationalization and the Social Democratic Model: Crisis and Future Prospects." *Comparative Political Studies* 31 (3): 353–97.

2001. *Development and the Crisis of the Welfare State: Parties and Politics in Global Markets*. Chicago: University of Chicago Press.

Huff. W. G. 1994. *The Economic Growth of Singapore: Trade and Development in the Twentieth Century*. New York: Cambridge University Press.

ILO [International Labor Organization]. 2002. *Decent Work and the Informal Economy*. Report VI. Geneva: International Labor Office.

IMF Assessment Project. 1992. *IMF Conditionality 1980–1991*. Arlington: Alexis de Tocqueville Institution.

International Monetary Fund. 2002. *Staff Report for 2002 Article IV Consultation: Mauritius*. IMF Country Report #01/77, April 22.

Isamah, Austin N. 1995 "Labor Response to Structural Adjustment in Nigeria and Zambia." In *Between Liberalization and Repression: The Politics of Structural Adjustment*, ed. Thandnika Mkandawire and Adebayo Olukoshi. Oxford: CODESRIA.

Itzigsohn, José. 2000. *Developing Poverty: The State, Labor Market Deregulation, and the Informal Economy in Costa Rica and the Dominican Republic*. University Park: Pennsylvania State University Press.

Jaffrelot, Christophe. 1996. *The Hindu Nationalist Movement in India*. New York: Columbia University Press.

James, Harold. 1996. *International Monetary Cooperation since Bretton Woods*. Washington, DC and Oxford: International Monetary Fund and Oxford University Press.

Jeffrey, Robin. 1992. *Politics, Women and Well-Being: How Kerala Became a Model*. Houndmills, Basingstoke, Hampshire: Macmillan.

Jeromi, P. D. 2003. "What Ails Kerala's Economy: A Sectoral Explanation." *Economic and Political Weekly* (April): 1584–600.

Johnson, Chalmers. 1987. "Political Institutions and Economic Performance: The Government–Business Relationship in Japan, South Korea and Taiwan." In *The Political Economy of the New Asian Industrialism*, ed. F. C. Deyo, 136–64. Ithaca: Cornell University Press.

Joseph, Bright, and K. J. Joseph. 2005, "Commercial Agriculture in Kerala after the WTO." *South Asian Economic Journal* 6: 37–57.

Kannan, K. P. 2000. "Poverty Alleviation as Advancing Basic Human Capabilities: Kerala's Achievements Compared." In *Kerala: The Development Experience: Reflections on Sustainability and Replicability*, ed. Govindan Parayil, 40–65. London: Zed Books.

2003. "Food Security in Kerala." In *Towards a Food Secure India: Issues and Policies*, ed. S. Mahendra Dev, K. P. Kannan, and Nira Ramachandran, 186–206. New Dehli: Institute for Human Development.

Kannan, K. P., and V. N. Pillai. 2004. "Development as Freedom: An Interpretation of the 'Kerala Model.'" Working Paper no. 361, Center for Development Studies, Thiruvananthapuram.

Kapur, Devish, John P. Lewis, and Richard Webb. 1997. *The World Bank, Its First Half Century*, Vol. I: *History*. Washington, DC: Brookings Institution Press.

Katzenstein, Peter J. 1984. *Corporatism and Change: Austria, Switzerland, and the Politics of Industry, Cornell Studies in Political Economy*. Ithaca: Cornell University Press.

Kay, Cristóbal. 1981. "Political Economy, Class Alliances and Agrarian Change in Chile." *Journal of Peasant Studies* 8 (4): 485–513.

1997. "Globalization, Peasant Agriculture and Reconversion." *Bulletin of Latin American Studies* 6 (1): 11–24.

2002. "Chile's Neoliberal Agrarian Transformation and the Peasantry." *Journal of Agrarian Change* 2 (4): 464–501.

Kaztman, R., F. Fligueira, and M. Furtado. 2000. "New Challenges for Equity in Uruguay." *CEPAL Review* 72: 79–97.

Khoodabux, Ismael. 2000. *The Anatomy of Mauritius.* Port-Louis: Mauritius Printers.

Kieley, 2004. "The World Bank and Global Poverty Reduction: Good Policies or Bad Data?" *Journal of Contemporary Asia* 34 (1): 3–20.

Kline, Harvey F., and Vanessa Gray. 2000. "Colombia, Drugs, Guerrillas, Death Squads and US Aid." In *Latin American Politics and Development*, ed. Howard J. Wiarda and Harvey F. Kline. Boulder: Westview.

Kohli, Atul. 1987. *The State and Poverty in India: The Politics of Reform.* Cambridge: Cambridge University Press.

1990. *Democracy and Discontent: India's Growing Crisis of Governability.* Cambridge: Cambridge University Press.

2004. *State-Directed Development: Political Power and Industrialization in the Global Periphery.* Cambridge: Cambridge University Press.

Koo, Hagen. 2001. *Korean Workers: The Culture and Politics of Class Formation.* Ithaca: Cornell University Press.

Krishnan, T. N., and M. Kabir. 1992. "Social Intermediation and Health Transition: Lessons from Kerala." Working Paper no. 251, Center for Development Studies, Trivandrum.

Kurth, James. 1979. "Industrial Change and Political Change: A European Perspective." In *The New Authoritarianism in Latin America,* ed. David Collier, 319–62. Princeton: Princeton University Press.

Kurtz, Geoffrey. 2002. "Anthony Giddens's Third Way: A Critique." *Logos* 1 (3): 88–106.

Kurtz, Marcus J. 2001. "State Developmentalism without a Developmental State: The Public Foundations of the 'Free Market' Miracle in Chile." *Latin American Politics and Society* 43 (2): 1–25.

2004. *Free Market Democracy and the Chilean and Mexican Countryside.* Cambridge: Cambridge University Press.

Kurtz, Marcus J., and Peter Houtzager. 2000. "The Institutional Roots of Popular Mobilization: State Transformation and Rural Politics in Chile and Brazil." *Comparative Studies in Society and History* 42 (2): 394–425.

La Botz, Dan. 1988. *The Crisis of Mexican Labor.* New York: Praeger.

Lagos, Ricardo. 2001. "Building on a Successful Investment Strategy." Available from: http://www.foreigninvestment.cl/s.

Lakshman, W. D. 1997. "Introduction." In *Dilemmas of Development: Fifty Years of Economic Change in Sri Lanka*, ed. W. D. Lakshman, 1–27. Colombo: Sri Lanka Association of Economists.

Lall, Sanjaya. 2003. "Reinventing Industrial Strategy: The Role of Government Policy in Building Industrial Competitiveness." Working Paper 111, Queen Elizabeth House, University of Oxford, Oxford, October.

Landau, Alice. 2001. *Redrawing the Global Economy: Elements of Integration and Fragmentation.* New York: Palgrave.

Lange, M. 2003. "Embedding the Colonial State: A Comparative-Historical Analysis of State-Building and Broad-based Development in Mauritius." *Social Science History* 27 (3): 397–423.

———. 2004. "The British Colonial Lineages of Despotism and Development." Ph.D. dissertation, Department of Sociology, Brown University.

Larrañaga, Osvaldo. 1992. "Microeconomics, Income Distribution and Social Services: Chile During the 80s." Programa de Post-grado en Economía ILADES, Georgetown University, I-48 (September).

Laville, Rosabelle. 2000. "In the Politics of the Rainbow: Creoles and Civil Society in Mauritius." *Journal of Comtemporary African Studies* 18 (2): 277–94.

Lehoucq, Fabrice E. 1990. "Explicando los orígenes de los regímenes democráticos: Costa Rica bajo una perspectiva teórica." *Anuario de Estudios Centroamericanos* 16 (1): 7–29.

———. 1997. *Lucha electoral y sistema político en Costa Rica 1948–1998*. San José: Editorial Porvenir.

Lehoucq, Fabrice E., and Iván Molina. 2002. *Stuffing the Ballot Box: Fraud, Electoral Reform, and Democratization in Costa Rica*. Cambridge: Cambridge University Press.

Liang Lung Chong, J. 1998. "Globalisation and Female Workers in the Textiles and Clothing Industry." B.Sc. dissertation, Social Studies, University of Mauritius.

Lipsit, S. M., K. Seong, and J. C. Torres. 1993. "A Comparative Analysis of the Social Requisites of Democracy." *International Social Science Journal* 136: 155–75.

Lipton, Michael. 1977. *Why Poor People Stay Poor*. London: Temple Smith.

Lombardi, John V. 2003. "Prologue: Venezeula's Permanent Dilemma." In *Venezuelan Politics in the Chávez Period*, ed. S. Ellner, 1–6. Boulder: Lynne Rienner.

López-Claros, Augusto. 2005. "Executive Summary." In *The Global Competitiveness Report 2004–2005*, ed. Klaus Schwab, Michael E. Porter, and Xavier Sala-I-Martín. New York: World Economic Forum-Palgrave Macmillan.

Loveman, Brian. 1988. *The Legacy of Hispanic Capitalism*, 2nd edition. Oxford: Oxford University Press.

Loxley, John. 1986. *Debt and Disorder: External Financing for Development*. Boulder: Westview.

Luebbert, Gregory M. 1991. *Liberalism, Fascism, or Social Democracy: Social Classes and the Political Origins of Regimes in Interwar Europe*. New York: Oxford University Press.

Lustig, Nora. 1991. "From Structuralism to Neostructuralism: The Search for a Heterodox Paradigm." In *The Latin American Development Debate: Neostructuralism, Neomonetarism and Adjustment Processes*, ed. P. Meller, 27–42. Boulder: Westview.

MacPherson, S. 1987. "Theoretical Implications of Third World Social Policy Research." In *Comparative Social Policy and the Third World*, ed. Stewart MacPherson and James Midgley. New York: St. Martin's Press.

Mahajan, Gurpreet. 1999. "Civil Society and its Avtars: What Happened to Freedom and Democracy." *Economic and Political Weekly* 34: 1188–96.

Mahoney, James. 2000. "Path Dependency in Historical Sociology." *Theory and Society* 29 (4): 507–48.

2001. *The Legacies of Liberalism: Path Dependence and Political Regimes in Central America*. Baltimore: Johns Hopkins University Press.

Mair, Stefan. 2003. "The New World of Privatized Violence." *Internationale Politik and Gesellschaft* 2: 11–28.

Malloy, James. 1979. *The Politics of Social Security in Brazil*. Pittsburgh: University of Pittsburgh Press.

Mamalakis, Markos J. 1976. *The Growth and Structure of the Chilean Economy: From Independence to Allende*. New Haven: Yale University Press.

Marshall, T. H. 1950. *Citizenship and Social Class*. Cambridge: Cambridge University Press.

Martínez, Javier, and Alvaro Díaz. 1996. *Chile: The Great Transformation*. Washington, DC: Brookings Institution Press.

Martínez, Javier and Eugenio Tironi. 1985. "La clase obrera en el nuevo estilo de desarrollo: un unfoque estructural." In *Chile, 1973–1983*, ed. Revista Mexicana de Sociologia. Santiago, Chile: FLASCO.

Martinez, Luis. 2000. *The Algerian Civil War*. New York: Columbia University Press.

Martínez Franzoni, Juliana, and Carmelo Mesa-Lago. 2003. *La reforma de la seguridad social en Costa Rica en pensiones y salud: Avances, problemas pendientes y recomendaciones*. San José: Fundación Friedrich Ebert.

Martner, Gonzalo. 1988. *El gobierno del presidente Salvador Allende, 1970–1973: Una evaluación*. Santiago: Ediciones Literatura Americana Reunida.

Masís Iverson, Daniel. 1999. "Poder político y sociedad." In *Costa Rica contemporánea: Raíces del Estado de la nación*, ed. Juan Rafael Quesada Camacho et al. San José: Editorial de la Universidad de Costa Rica.

Mathur, Raj. 1997. "Parliamentary Representation of Minority Communities." *Africa Today* 44 (1): 61–82.

Mauritius, Central Statistics Office (CSO). 2002a. *Annual Digest of Statistics 2001*. Port-Louis: Government Printer, August.

2002b. *Economic and Social Indicators: Household Budget Survey*, no. 394. Port-Louis, Government Printer, November 5.

2003. *Economic and Social Indicators: Labour Force, Employment and Unemployment*, no. 402. Port-Louis: Government Printer, March 10.

Mauritius, Chamber of Commerce and Industry. 2006. *Economic Indicators, 2003–2006*. http://www.mcci.org/E_economy.htm.

Mauritius, Ministry of Commerce and Co-operatives. 2003. *Co-operatives: Road to Prosperity*. Port-Louis: Government Printer.

Mauritius, Ministry of the Environment. 2002. *Meeting the Challenges of Sustainable Development*. Port-Louis: Government Printer.

Mauritius, Ministry of Health and Quality of Life. 2001. *Health Statistics 2001*. Port-Louis: Government Printer.

Mauritius Research Council (MRC). 1999. *New Industrial Strategies: A Study of Gender, Migration, Labour and the EPZ in Mauritius*. Quatre Bornes: MRC, August.

McElhinny, Vince, Juliana Martínez Franzoni, Seth Nickinson, and Katherine Reilly. 2004. *'El Empaquetazo': IDB Competitiveness Loans, CAFTA and the*

Future of Political Consensus in Costa Rica. Washington, DC: Inter-American Development Bank Civil Society Initiative.

Mehta, Pratap. 1997. "India: Fragmentation amid Consensus." *Journal of Democracy* 8 (1): 56–69.

Meisenhelder, Thomas. 1999. "The Developmental State in Mauritius." *Journal of Modern African Studies* 35 (2): 279–97.

Meller, Patricio. 2000. "Pobreza y distribución del ingreso en Chile (Década del 90)." Working Paper no. 69, Departamento de Ingeniería Industrial, Universidad de Chile, Santiago.

Menon, Dilip. 1994. *Caste, Nationalism and Communism in South India: Malabar 1900–1948.* New Delhi: Cambridge University Press.

Mesa-Lago, Carmelo. 1978. *Social Security in Latin America.* Pittsburgh: University of Pittsburgh Press.

——— 1994. "Expansion of Social Security Protection to the Rural Populations of Latin America." In *Social Security in Developing Countries,* ed. T. S. Sankaran, R. K. A. Subrahmanya, and S. K. Wadhawan. New Delhi: Har-Anand Publications.

——— 2000. "Achieving and Sustaining Social Development with Limited Resources: The Experience of Costa Rica." In *Social Development and Public Policy: A Study of Some Successful Experiences,* ed. Dharam Ghai. London and New York: Macmillan and St. Martin's Press.

——— 2002. *Buscando un modelo económico en América Latina: ¿Mercado, socialista o mixto? Chile, Cuba y Costa Rica.* Caracas: Nueva Sociedad.

Micco, Alejandro J., and Ugo Parizza. 2005. "Should the Government Be in the Banking Business?" In *Economic and Social Progress in Latin America 2005 Report.* Washington: Inter-American Development Bank.

Midgley, James. 1984. *Social Security, Inequality and the Third World.* New York: John Wiley and Sons.

——— 1987. "Need and Deprivation in Developing Societies: A Profile." In *Comparative Social Policy and the Third World,* ed. Stewart MacPherson and James Midgley. New York: St. Martin's Press.

Migdal, Joel S. 1988. *Strong Societies and Weak States.* Princeton: Princeton University Press.

Milanovic, Branko. 2003. "The Two Faces of Globalization: Against Globalization as We Know It." *World Development* 31 (4): 667–83.

Miles, W. F. S. 1999. "The Mauritius Enigma." *Journal of Democracy* 10 (2): 91–104.

Mistry, Percy. 1999. "Mauritius: Quo Vadis?" *African Affairs* 98 (393): 551–69.

Molina Jiménez, Iván. 1991. *Costa Rica (1800–1850). El legado colonial y la génesis del capitalismo.* San José: Editorial de la Universidad de Costa Rica.

——— 2002. *Costarricense por dicha: Identidad nacional y cambio cultural en Costa Rica durante los siglos XIX y XX.* San José: Editorial de la Universidad de Costa Rica.

Molina Jiménez, Iván, and Steven Palmer. 1997. *Costa Rica 1930–1996: Historia de una Sociedad.* San José: Editorial Porvenir.

——— 1998. *The History of Costa Rica.* San José: Editorial de la Universidad de Costa Rica.

Monge Alfaro, Carlos. 1980. *Historia de Costa Rica.* San José: Trejos Hermanos.

Montecinos, Veronica. 1997. "Economic Policy, Social Policy and Family Economy in Chile." *Review of Social Economy* 55 (2): 224–33.

Moore, Barrington. 1966. *Social Origins of Dictatorship and Democracy: Lord and Peasant in the Making of the Modern World.* Boston: Beacon Press.

Moore, Mick. 2000. "States, Social Policies and Globalisation: Arguing on the Right Terrain?" *Institute of Development Studies Bulletin* 31 (4): 21–31.

——— 2003. "Polity Qualities: How Governance Affects Poverty." In *Changing Paths: International Development and the New Politics of Inclusion*, ed. P. Houtzager and M. Moore. Ann Arbor: University of Michigan Press.

Morales, Abelardo, and Carlos Castro. 2002. *Redes transfronterizas: Sociedad, empleo y migración entre Nicaragua y Costa Rica.* San José: FLACSO.

Morley, Samuel. 2001. "The Income Distribution Problem in Latin America and the Caribbean." Santiago: CEPAL.

Mosley, Layna. 2005. "Globalisation and the State: Still Room to Move?" *New Political Economy* 10 (3): 355–62.

Mujica Ateaga, Rodrigo. 1992. "La modernización agrícola entre 1974 y 1987." In *El modelo económico chileno*, 2nd edition, ed. Daniel L. Wisecarver. Santiago: Instituto de Economía de la Pontificia Universidad Católica de Chile y Centro Internacional para el Desarrollo Económico.

Mukhopadhyay, S. C. 2000. "CPI(M) in West Bengal: Woes of the Parliamentary Left." *Economic and Political Weekly*, June 10–16.

Muñoz Gomá, Oscar, and Carmen Celedón. 1996. "Chile in Transition: Economic and Political Strategies." In *Economic Policy and the Transition to Democracy: The Latin American Experience*, ed. Juan Antonio Morales and Gary McMahon. New York: St. Martin's Press.

Muñoz Guillén, Mercedes. 1990. *El Estado y la abolición del ejército 1914–1949.* San José: Editorial Porvenir.

Naim, Moisés. 2001. "The Real Story behind Venezuela's Woes." *Journal of Democracy* 12 (2): 17–31.

Nelson, Joan M. 1990. "Introduction." In *Economic Crisis and Policy Choice*, ed. Joan M. Nelson. Princeton: Princeton University Press.

Nossiter, T. J. 1982. *Communism in Kerala: A Study in Political Adaptation.* Berkeley: University of California Press for the Royal Institute of International Affairs.

Nyang'oro, Julius. 1989. *Corporatism in Africa: Comparative Analysis and Practice.* Boulder: Westview.

O'Donnell, Guillermo. 1994. "Delegative Democracy." *Journal of Democracy* 5 (1): 55–69.

Olivarría-Gambi, Mauricio. 2003 "Poverty Reduction in Chile: Has Economic Growth been Enough?" *Journal of Human Development* 4 (1): 103–23.

Oodiah, Malenn. 1991. *Mouvement Militant Mauricien: 20 Ans d'Histoire.* Port-Louis: Electronic Graphic Systems.

Ortega R. Eugenio. 1988. "Los pobres y la sobrevivencia." In *Pobreza en Chile*, ed. Eugenio Ortega R. and Ernesto Tironi B. Santiago: Centro de Estudios del Desarrollo.

Ortiz, Guillermo. 2003. "Latin America: Overcoming the Reform Fatigue." *Finance and Development* 40 (3): 14–17.

Osmani, S. R. 2001. "Growth and Poverty during Adjustment: Lessons from Sub Saharan Africa." In *Adjustment and Beyond: The Reform Experience in South Asia*, ed. Wahiduddin Mahmud. Houndmills, Basingstoke, Hampshire: Palgrave.

Ossa S., Fernando. 1992. "Políticas de fomento al sector exportador chileno." In *El modelo chileno*, 2nd edition, ed. Daniel L Wisecarver, 359–400. Santiago: Instituto de Economia de la Pontificia Universidad Católica de Chiley Centro Internacional para el Desarrollo Económics.

Oxhorn, Philip. 1995. *Organizing Civil Society: The Popular Sectors and the Struggle for Democracy in Chile*. University Park: Pennsylvania State University Press.

Paige, Jeffery M. 1997. *Coffee and Power: Revolution and the Rise of Democracy in Central America*. Cambridge: Harvard University Press.

Palan, R. 2000. "Recasting Political Authority: Globalization and the State." In *Globalization and its Critics*, ed. R. D. Germain, 139–63. New York: St. Martin's Press.

Paley, Julia. 2001. *Marketing Democracy: Power and Social Movements in Post-Dictatorship Chile*. Berkeley: University of California Press.

Palmer, Steven. 2003. *From Popular Medicine to Medical Populism: Doctors, Healers, and Public Power in Costa Rica, 1800–1940*. Durham: Duke University Press.

Panić, Mića. 2003. "A New Bretton Woods?" In *The Handbook of Globalisation*, ed. Jonathan Michie. Cheltenham, UK: Edward Elgar.

Panikkar, K. N. 1989. *Against Lord and State: Religious and Peasant Uprisings in Malabar 1836–1921*. Delhi: Oxford University Press.

Parayil, Govindan, and T. T Sreekumar. 2003. "Kerala's Experience of Development and Change." *Journal of Contemporary Asia* 33: 465–92.

Patomäki, Heikki. 2001. *Democratising Globalisation: The Leverage of the Tobin Tax*. London: Zed Books.

Pérez-Alemán, Paola. 2000. "Learning, Adjustment and Economic Development: Transforming Firms, the State and Associations in Chile." *World Development* 28 (1): 41–55.

Petras, James. 1969. *Politics and Social Forces in Chilean Development*. Berkeley: University of California Press.

Petras, James, and Fernando Ignacio Leiva. 1994. *Democracy and Poverty in Chile*. Boulder: Westview.

Petras, James, and Morris Morley. 1975. *The United States and Chile: Imperialism and the Overthrow of the Allende Government*. New York and London: Monthly Review Press.

Piattoni, Simona. 2001. "Clientelism, Interests and Democratic Representation." In *Clientelism, Interests and Democratic Representation*, ed. Simona Piattoni. Cambridge: Cambridge University Press.

Pierson, Chris. 2001a. "Globalisation and the End of Social Democracy." *Australian Journal of Politics and History* 47 (4): 459–74.

2001b. *Hard Choices: Social Democracy in the Twenty-first Century*. Cambridge: Polity Press.

Pillai, V. N. 2004. "Liberalisation of Rural Poverty: The Indian Experience." Working Paper 356, Center for Development Studies, Thiruvananthapuram.

Planning Commission. 2001. *National Human Development Report 2001*. New Delhi: Government of India.

Polanyi, Karl. 2001 [1944]. *The Great Transformation: The Political and Economic Origins of Our Time*. Boston: Beacon Press.

Powell, John Duncan. 1970. "Peasant Society and Clientelistic Politics." *American Political Science Review* 64: 411–25.

Prakash, B. A. 2004. "Economic Reforms and the Performance of Kerala's Economy." In *Kerala's Economic Development: Performance and Problems in the Post-Liberalisation Period*, ed. B. A. Prakash, 27–46. New Delhi: Sage Publications.

Proyecto Estado de la Nación. 2000. *Estado de la nación en desarrollo humano sostenible: Un análisis amplio y objetivo sobre la Costa Rica que tenemos a partir de los indicadores más actuales (1999)*. Pavas, Costa Rica: Proyecto Estado de la Nación en Desarrollo Humano Sostenible.

——— 2002. "Equidad e integración social." Available from: http://www.estadonacion.or.cr/Info2001/nacion7/equidad01.html.

——— 2005. "Estadísticas sociales (2001–2003). Pobreza." Available from: http://www.estadonacion.or.cr/Compendio/soc_pobreza01_03.htm.

Przeworski, Adam. 1985. *Capitalism and Social Democracy*. Cambridge: Cambridge University Press.

——— 1992. "The Neoliberal Fallacy." *Journal of Democracy* 3 (3): 45–59.

Puryear, Jeffery. 1996. *Thinking Politics: Intellectuals and Democracy in Chile*. Baltimore: Johns Hopkins University Press.

Raczynski, Dagmar. 1998. "The Crisis of Old Models of Social Protection in Latin America: New Alternatives for Dealing with Poverty." In *Poverty and Inequality in Latin America*, ed. Victor E. Tokman and Guillermo O'Donnell. Notre Dame: University of Notre Dame Press.

Ramachandran, V. K. 1997. "On Kerala's Development Achievements." In *Indian Development*, ed. Jean Drèze and Amartya Sen, 205–356. Delhi: Oxford University Press.

Ramakumar, R. 2004. "Socio-Economic Characteristics of Agricultural Workers: A Case Study of a Village in the Malabar Region of Kerala." Ph.D. dissertation, Indian Statistical Institute.

Raman, R. K. 2004. "The Asian Development Bank Loan for Kerala (India): The Adverse Implications and Search for Alternatives." Working Paper 357, Center for Development Studies, Thiruvananthapuram.

Raventós Vorst, Ciska. 2001. "Democracia y proceso de aprobación de las políticas de ajuste en Costa Rica (1980–1995)." In *La democracia de Costa Rica ante el siglo XXI*, ed. Jorge Rovira Mas. San José: Editorial de la Universidad de Costa Rica.

Read, R. 2004. "The Implications of Increasing Globalization and Regionalization for the Economic Growth of Small Island States." *World Development* 32 (2): 365–78.

Reddi, S. J. 1989. "The Development of Political Consciousness among Indians, 1870–1930." *Journal of Mauritian Studies* 3 (1): 1–15.

——— 1997. "The Making of a British Colonial State in Nineteenth Century Mauritius." Paper Presented to the "British Legacy" Conference, Mahatma Gandhi Institute, Réduit, May 6–9.

Remmer, Karen. 1984. *Party Competition in Argentina and Chile: Political Recruitment and Public Policy*. Lincoln: University of Nebraska Press.

Reno, William. 1995. "Markets, War and the Reconfiguration of Political Authority." *Canadian Journal of African Studies* 29 (2): 203–21.

——— 2003. "Political Networks in a Failing State: The Roots and Future of Violent Conflict in Sierra Leone." *Internationale Politik und Gesellschaft* 2: 45–66.

Rieger, E., and S. Leibfried. 1998. "Welfare State Limits to Globalization." *Politics and Society* 26 (3): 363–90.

Riley, Dylan. 2005. "Civic Associations and Authoritarian Regimes in Interwar Europe: Italy and Spain in Comparative Perspective." *American Journal of Sociology* 70: 288–310.

Roberts, Kenneth M. 1998. *Deepening Democracy? The Modern Left and Social Movements in Chile and Peru*. Stanford: Stanford University Press.

Robothan, Don. 2005. *Culture, Society, Economy: Globalization and Its Alternatives*. Thousand Oaks: Sage Publications.

Rodríguez-Clare, Andrés. 2001. "Costa Rica's Development Strategy Based on Human Capital and Technology: How It Got There, the Impact of Intel, and Lessons for Other Countries." *Journal of Human Development* 2(2):311–24.

Rodrik, Dani. 1997. *Has Globalization Gone Too Far?* Washington, DC: Institute of International Economics.

——— 2003. "Has Globalization Gone Too Far?" In *The Global Transformations Reader*, 2nd edition, ed. David Held and Anthony McGrew. Cambridge: Polity Press.

——— 2004. "Industrial Policy for the Twenty-First Century." Available from: http://ksghome.harvard.edu/~drodrik/UNIDOSep.pdf.

Román Vega, Isabel, and Roy Rivera Araya. 1990. *Tierra con fronteras: Treinta años de política de distribución de tierras en Costa Rica*. San José: Centro de Estudios para la Acción Social.

Rothstein, B. 2001. "Social Capital in the Social Democratic Welfare State." *Politics and Society* 29 (2): 207–41.

Rovira Mas, Jorge. 2000. "Comentarios a la reforma económica y los problemas sociales." In *Reforma económica y cambio social en América Latina y el Caribe*, ed. Mauricio de Miranda. Bogotá: Tercer Mundo Editores-Pontificia Universidad Javeriana de Cali.

——— 2001. "¿Se debilita el bipartidismo?" In *La democracia de Costa Rica ante el siglo XXI*, ed. Jorge Rovira Mas. San José: Editorial de la Universidad de Costa Rica.

Roy, Ash Narain. 1999. *The Third World in the Age of Globalisation: Requiem or New Agenda?* London: Zed Books.

Rudra, Nita. 2002. "Globalization and the Decline of the Welfare State in Less Developed Countries." *International Organization* 56 (2): 411–45.

Rueschemeyer, Dietrich, Evelyne H. Stephens, and John D. Stephens. 1992. *Capitalist Development and Democracy*. Chicago: University of Chicago Press.

Ruiz-Tagle, Jaime. 1991. *Trabajo y economía: Chile 1985–1991*. Santiago: Programa de Economía del Trabajo.

Ryan, Jeffrey J. 2004. "Decentralization and Democratic Instability: The Case of Costa Rica." *Public Administration Review* 64 (1): 81–91.

Saca, Nolvia Nery. 1999. "Desarrollo de Clusters en componentes electrónicos en Centro América." Documentos en Proceso – Working Papers Agenda Centroamericana para el Siglo XXI, Centro Latinoamericano de Competitividad y Desarrollo Sostenible, Instituto Centroamericano de Administración de Empresas, San José.

Sachs, Jeffrey. 2004. "The Best Countries in the World." Newsweek (July 26): 28.

Sader, Emir. 2003. "PT É Vítima de Blairismo Tropical." O Globo (December 21).

Sáenz, Luis Bernardo. 1998. "La modernización de la Caja Costarricense de Seguro Social." In La reforma del sistema nacional de salud: Estrategias, avances, perspectivas, ed. Carlos Castro Valverde and Luis Bernardo Sáenz. San José: Ministerio de Planificación Nacional y Política Económica.

Salazar, Jorge Mario. 1981. Política y reforma en Costa Rica, 1914–1958. San José: Editorial Porvenir.

Samuels, David. 2004. "From Socialism to Social Democracy: Party Organization in the Transformation of the Workers Party in Brazil." Comparative Political Studies 37 (9): 999–1024.

Sánchez-Acochea, Diego. 2006. "Development Trajectories and New Comparative Advantages: Costa Rica and the Dominican Republic under Globalization." World Development 34 (6): 996–1015.

Sandbrook, Richard. 1985. The Politics of Africa's Economic Stagnation. Cambridge: Cambridge University Press.

    2000. Closing the Circle: Democratization and Development in Africa. Toronto, London, and New York: Between the Lines and Zed Books.

    ed. 2003. Civilizing Globalization: A Survival Guide. Albany: State University of New York Press.

Sandbrook, Richard, and David Romano. 2004. "Globalization, Extremism and Violence in Poor Countries." Third World Quarterly 25 (5): 1007–31.

Sandoval García, Carlos. 2002. Otros amenazantes: Los nicaragüenses y la formación de identidades nacionales en Costa Rica. San José: Editorial de la Universidad de Costa Rica.

Santiso, Carlos. 2004. "The Contentious Washington Consensus: Reforming the Reforms in Emerging Markets." Review of International Political Economy 11 (2): 828–44.

Sassoon, Donald. 1997. One Hundred Years of Socialism: The West European Left in the Twentieth Century. London: Fontana.

Scharpf, Fritz W. 1999. "The Viability of Advanced Welfare States in the International Economy: Vulnerabilities and Options." MPIfG Working Paper, Max Planck Institute for the Study of Societies, September. Available from: http://www.mpi-fg-koeln.mpg.de/pu/workpap/wp99-9/wp99-9.html.

Schiefelbein, Ernesto. 2003. "Uso de la información generada por la evaluación del aprendizaje para proponer políticas educativas pertinentes." CIDE, Mexico City (February 16).

Schifter, Jacobo. 1978. "La democracia en Costa Rica como producto de la neutralización de clases." In ¿Democracia en Costa Rica? Cinco opiniones polémicas, ed. Chester Zelaya. San José: Editorial Universidad Estatal a Distancia.

Schmitter, Philip. 1974. "Still the Century of Corporatism." In *The New Corporatism*, ed. Fredrick B. Pike and Thomas Stritch. Notre Dame: University of Notre Dame Press.

Schwartz, Herman M. 1994. *States Versus Markets: The Emergence of the Global Economy*, 2nd edition. London: Macmillan.

Scott, Christopher. 1996. "The Distributive Impact of the New Economic Model in Chile." In *The New Economic Model in Latin America and its Impact on Income Distribution and Poverty*, ed. Victor Bulmer-Thomas. New York and London: St. Martin's Press and Institute of Latin American Studies.

Seegobin, R., and l. Collen. 1977. "Mauritius: Class Forces and Political Power." *Review of African Political Economy* 8: 109–18.

Seekings, Jeremy. 2004. "Trade Unions, Social Policy and Class Compromise in Post-Apartheid South Africa." *Review of African Political Economy* 100: 299–312.

Seligson, Mitchell A. 2002. "Trouble in Paradise? The Erosion of System Support in Costa Rica, 1978–1999." *Latin American Research Review* 37 (1): 160–85.

Sen, Gita. 1992. "Social Needs and Public Accountability." In *Development Policy and Public Action*, ed. Marc Wuyts, Maureen Mackintosh, and Tom Hewitt. Oxford: Oxford University Press.

Sheahan, John. 1987. *Patterns of Development in Latin America*. Princeton: Princeton University Press.

Short, R. P. 1984. "The Role of Public Enterprises: An International Statistical Comparison." In *Public Enterprise in Mixed Economies: Some Macroeconomic Aspects*, ed. Robert H. Floyd, Clive S. Gray, and R. P. Short. Washington, DC: IMF.

Silva, Eduardo. 1996. *The State and Capital in Chile: Business Elites, Technocrats and Market Economics*. Boulder: Westview.

Silva, Patricio. 1991. "Technocrats and Politics in Chile: from the Chicago Boys to the CIEPLAN Monks." *Journal of Latin American Studies* 23 (May): 385–410.

Sinai, Agnes. 2000. "Seattle Turning Point: The Day the South Cut Up Rough." *Le Monde Diplomatique* (January). Available from: http://www.monde-diplomatique.fr/en/2000/01/08sinai.

Sinclair, Scott. 2003. "The WTO and Its GATS." In *The Handbook of Globalisation*, ed. Jonathan Michie. Cheltenham, UK: Edward Elgar.

Singh, Har Mander. 1994. "ISSA Studies on the Extension of Social Security to Unprotected Groups in Asia and the Pacific." In *Social Security in Developing Countries*, ed. T. S. Sankaran, R. K. A. Subrahmanya, and S. K. Wadhawan. New Delhi: Har-Anand Publications.

Singh, Parduman. 1997. *Social Security Systems in Developing Countries: Asia, Africa and Latin America*. New Delhi: Friedrich Ebert Stiftung.

Skocpol, Theda. 1985. "Bringing the State Back In: Current Research." In *Bringing the State Back In*, ed. Peter Evans, Dietrich Rueschemeyer, and Theda Skocpol, 3–43. New York: Cambridge University Press.

Smith, W. C., and N. Messari. 1998. "Democracy and Reform in Cardoso's Brazil: Caught between Clientelism and Global Markets?" North–South Agendas, Paper 33, North–South Center, University of Miami, September.

Sojo, Ana. 1984. *Estado empresario y lucha política en Costa Rica*. San José: Editorial Universitaria Centroamericana.

———. 1998. "Los compromisos de gestión en salud de Costa Rica con una perspectiva comparativa." *Revista de la CEPAL* 68 (December): 73–103.

Solís, Manuel Antonio. 1992. *Costa Rica: ¿Reformismo socialdemócrata o liberal?* San José: FLACSO.

———. 2002. "Entre el cambio y la tradición: El fracaso de la privatización de la energía y las telecomunicaciones en Costa Rica." *Ciencias Sociales* 95: 33–47.

Soros, George. 2002. *On Globalization*. New York: Public Affairs.

Srebrnik, H. 2002. "'Full of Sound and Fury': Three Decades of Parliamentary Politics in Mauritius." *Journal of Southern African Studies* 28 (2): 277–89.

Stephens, E. H., and J. G. Stephens. 1983. "Democratic Socialism in Dependent Capitalism: An Analysis of the Manley Government in Jamaica." *Politics and Society* 12 (3): 373–411.

Stern, Robert W. 2001. *Democratization and Development in South Asia: Dominant Classes and Political Outcomes in India, Pakistan, and Bangladesh*. Westport: Praeger.

Stewart, Francis. 1987. "Should Conditionality Change?" In *The IMF and the World Bank in Africa*, ed. Kjell J. Havnevik. Uppsala: Institute of African Studies.

———. ed. 1995. *Adjustment and Poverty: Options and Choices*. London: Routledge.

———. 2001. "Adjustment and Poverty in Asia: Old Solutions and New Problems." In *Adjustment and Beyond: The Reform Experience in South Asia*, ed. Wahiduddin Mahmud. Houndmills, Basingstoke, Hampshire: Palgrave.

Stiglitz, Joseph E. 2002. *Globalization and Its Discontents*. New York: W. W. Norton.

Subramanian, A., and D. Roy. 2003. "Who Can Explain the Mauritian Miracle? Meade, Romer, Sachs, or Rodrik?" In *In Search of Prosperity*, ed. Dani Rodrik, 205–43. Princeton: Princeton University Press.

Sunkel, Osvaldo. 1965. "Change and Frustration in Chile." In *Obstacles to Change in Latin America*, ed. Claudio Veliz. Oxford: Oxford University Press.

———. ed. 1993. *Development from Within: Toward a Neostructuralist Approach for Latin America*. Boulder: Lynne Rienner.

Swank, Duane. 2003. "The Effect of Globalization on Taxation, Institutions, and Control of the Macroeconomy." In *The Global Transformations Reader*, 2nd edition, ed. David Held and Anthony McGrew. Cambridge: Polity Press.

Szeftel, Morris. 2000. "Clientelism, Corruption and Catastrophe." *Review of African Political Economy* 85 (27): 427–41.

Tangri, Roger. 1999. *The Politics of Patronage in Africa: Parastatals, Privatization and Private Enterprise*. Trenton: Africa World Press.

Tardanico, Richard, and Mario Lungo. 1995. "Local Dimensions of Global Restructuring: Changing Labour-Market Contours in Urban Costa Rica." *International Journal of Urban and Regional Research* 19 (2): 223–49.

Teelock, Vijayalakshmi. 2001. *Mauritian History: From its Beginnings to Modern Times*. Port-Louis: Mahatma Gandhi Institute.

Teeple, Gary. 1995. *Globalization and the Decline of Social Reform*. Toronto: Garamond Press.

Teichman, Judith. 1995. *Privatization and Political Change in Mexico*. Pittsburgh: University of Pittsburgh Press.

    2001. *The Politics of Freeing Markets in Latin America: Chile, Argentina and Mexico*. Chapel Hill: University of North Carolina Press.

    2002. "Private Sector Power and Market Reform: Exploring the Domestic Origins of Argentina's Meltdown and Mexico's Policy Failures." *Third World Quarterly* 23 (3): 491–528.

Teitelbaum, E. 2004. "Rethinking Repression: Political Unions and Economic Development in South Asia." Ph.D. dissertation, Cornell University.

Thacoor-Sidaya, Indira. 1998. "Women and Development in Mauritius." *Indian Quarterly* 54 (1/2).

Thampi, M. M. 2004. "Economic Liberalisation and Industrial Development in Kerala: Challenges to New Investments." In *Kerala's Economic Development: Performance and Problems in the Post-Liberalisation Period*, ed. B. A. Prakash, 245–62. New Delhi, Sage Publications.

Tharakan, Michael P. K. 1998. "Socio-religious Reform Movements, the Process of Democratization and Human Development: The Case of Kerala, South-West India." In *Democratization in the Third World: Concrete Cases in Comparative and Theoretical Perspective*, ed. Lars Rudebeck, Olle Törnquist, and Virgilio Rojas, 144–72. Houndmills, Basingstoke, Hampshire: Macmillan.

Therborn, Goran. 1977. "The Rule of Capital and the Rise of Democracy." *New Left Review* 103.

Thomas Isaac, T. M., and R. W. Franke. 2002. *Local Democracy and Development: The Kerala People's Campaign for Decentralized Planning*. Lanham: Rowman and Littlefield.

Thompson, E. P. 1964. *The Making of the English Working Class*. New York: Pantheon Books.

Thomson, Stuart. 2000. *The Social Democratic Dilemma: Ideology, Governance and Globalization*. London: Macmillan.

Thorp, Rosemary. 1998. *Progress, Poverty and Exclusion. An Economic History of Latin America in the Twentieth Century*. New York: Inter-American Development Bank.

Tibi, Bassam. 1998. *The Challenge of Fundamentalism: Political Islam and the New World Disorder*. Berkeley: University of California Press.

Tilly, Charles. 2000. "Processes and Mechanisms of Democratization." *Sociological Theory* 18: 1–16.

Tironi B., Ernesto. 1988. "Parte Tercera: Una evaluación de los programas de gasto social." In *Pobreza en Chile*, ed. Eugenio Ortega R. and Ernesto Tironi B. Santiago: Centro de Estudios del Desarrollo.

Tolnay, Adam. 2002. "Mauritius and the Internet Challenge." Unpublished Paper, George Washington University.

Törnquist, Olle. 1997. "Making Democratization Work: From Civil Society and Social Capital to Political Inclusion and Politicization. Theoretical Reflections on Concrete Cases in Indonesia, Kerala, and the Philippines." University of Oslo: Research Programme on Popular Movements, Development and Democratization.

Touraine, Alain. 1993. "Latin America: From Populism toward Social Democracy." In *Social Democracy in Latin America*, ed. Menno Vellinga, 297–309. Boulder: Westview.

Toye, John. 2003. "The International Monetary Fund (IMF) and the World Bank (WB)." In *The Handbook of Globalisation*, ed. Jonathan Michie. Cheltenham, UK: Edward Elgar.

Trejos París, María Eugenia. 1993. "Compensación social y desmovilización popular: La política social en el ajuste." In *Foro Costa Rica: Democracia económica y desarrollo social hacia el año 2000*, ed. Xabier Gorostiaga et al. San José: Asamblea Nacional de Trabajadores del Banco Popular (ATBP) and Centro de Estudios Para la Acción Social (CEPAS).

Trejos Solórzano, Juan Diego. 2000. *Reformas económicas y situación social en Costa Rica durante los años noventa*. Serie Divulgación Económica no. 32. San José: Instituto de Investigaciones en Ciencias Económicas, Universidad de Costa Rica.

Tussie, Diana. 1988. "The Coordination of Latin American Debtors: Is There a Logic behind the Story?" In *Managing World Debt*, ed. Stephany Griffith-Jones. New York: St. Martin's Press.

UN, Department of Economic and Social Affairs, Statistics Division. 2003. Available from: http://www.unstats.un.org.

UNCTAD. 2001. *Investment Policy Review: Mauritius*. Geneva and New York: United Nations.

UNDP [United Nations Development Programme]. 2001. *Human Development Report 2001: Making New Technologies Work for Human Development*. New York: Oxford University Press.

2002. *Desarrollo humano en Chile*. New York: UNDP.

2005. *Human Development Report 2005: International Cooperation at a Crossroads*. New York: UNDP.

Uppiah, S. L. D. 2000. "Impact of Retrenchment of Women Working in the EPZ Sector: Case Study of KFI Ltd." B.Sc. dissertation, Social Studies, University of Mauritius, May.

Uyangoda, J. 2000. "Post-Independence Social Movements." In *Sri Lanka's Development since Independence*, ed. W. D. Lakshman and C. A. Tisdall, 61–76. New York: Nova Science Publishers.

Valenzuela, J. Samuel. "Class Relations and Democratization: A Reassessment of Barrington Moore's Model." In *The Other Mirror: Grand Theory Through the Lens of Latin America*, ed. Miguel Angel Centeno and Fernando López-Alves. Princeton: Princeton University Press, 2001.

Valverde, José Manuel, Leda Marenco, and Carlos Sojo. 1985. *La lucha en contra del alza de las tarifas eléctricas: junio de 1983*. San José: CEPAS, Cuaderno de Estudio No. 2.

Vargas Solís, Luis Paulino. 2002. *Costa Rica, 1985–1997: Liberalización y ajuste estructural o la autodestrucción del neoliberalismo.* San José: Editorial Universidad Estatal a Distancia.

Varghese, T. C. 1970. *Agrarian Change and Economic Consequences: Land Tenures in Kerala 1850–1960.* Bombay: Allied Publishers.

Varshney, Ashutosh. 2002. *Ethnic Conflict and Civic Life: Hindus and Muslims in India.* New Haven: Yale University Press.

Varughese, Anil. 2003. "Globalization versus Cultural Authenticity? Valentine's Day and Hindu Values." In *Civilizing Globalization: A Survival Guide,* ed. Richard Sandbrook, 53–58. Albany: State University of New York Press.

Velasco, Andrés. 1994. "The State and Economic Policy: Chile 1952–1992." In *The Chilean Economy: Policy Lessons and Challenges,* ed. Barry P. Bosworth, Rudiger Dornbusch, and Raúl Labán. Washington, DC: Brookings Institution Press.

Vellinga, Menno, ed. 1993. *Social Democracy in Latin America.* Boulder: Westview.

Verba, Sidney. 1971. "Sequences and Development." Ch. 8 in *Crises and Sequences in Political Development.* Princeton: Princeton University Press.

von Braun, Joachim. 1991. "Social Security in Sub Saharan Africa: Reflections on Policy Challenges." In *Social Security in Developing Countries,* ed. Ehtisham Ahmad, Jean Drèze, John Hills, and Amartya Sen. Oxford: Clarendon Press.

Wade, Robert Hunter. 2003. "What Strategies Are Viable for Developing Countries Today? The World Trade Organization and the Shrinking of 'Development Space.'" *Review of International Political Economy* 10 (4): 621–44.

——— 2004a. "Is Globalization Reducing Poverty and Inequality?" *World Development* 32 (4): 567–89.

——— 2004b. "On the Causes of Increasing World Inequality, or Why the Matthew Effect Prevails." *New Political Economy* 9 (2): 163–89.

Wallerstein, Immanuel. 1982. "The Colonial Era in Africa: Changes in Social Structure." In *Colonialism in Africa, 1870–1960,* Vol. II: *The History and Politics of Colonialism, 1914–1960,* ed. L. H. Gann and Peter Duigan. Cambridge: Cambridge University Press.

Walzer, Michael. 2000. "The Idea of Civil Society: A Path to Social Reconstruction." In *Community Works: The Revival of Civil Society in America,* ed. E. J. Dionne, Jr. Washington, DC: Brookings Institution Press.

Watkins, Kevin, and Penny Fowler. 2002. *Rigged Rules and Double Standards: Trade, Globalisation and the Fight against Poverty.* Oxford: Oxfam International.

Weinstein, Martin. 1975. *Uruguay: The Politics of Failure.* Westport: Greenwood.

Weiss, Linda. 1998. *The Myth of the Powerless State: Governing the Economy in a Global Era.* New York: Cornell University Press.

West Bengal, Development and Planning Department. 2004. *West Bengal: Human Development Report.* West Bengal: Government Printer.

Weyland, Kurt. 1996. *Democracy without Equity: Failures of Reform in Brazil.* Pittsburgh: University of Pittsburgh Press.

White, Gordon. 1998. "Constructing a Democratic Developmental State." In *The Democratic Developmental State: Politics and Institutional Design*, ed. M. Robinson and G. White, 17–57. London: Oxford University Press.

Whyman, Philip. 2003. *Sweden and the 'Third Way': A Macroeconomic Evaluation*. Aldershot: Ashgate.

Williams, Robert G. 1994. *States and Social Evolution: Coffee and the Rise of National Governments in Central America*. Chapel Hill: University of North Carolina Press.

Williamson, John. 1990. "What Washington Means by Policy Reform." In *Latin American Adjustment: How Much Has Happened?*, ed. J. Williamson, 7–38. Washington, DC: Institute for International Economics.

Wisecarver, Daniel. 1992. "El sector forestal chileno: Políticas, desarrollo del recurso y exportaciones." In *El modelo económico chileno*, ed. Daniel L. Wisecarver, 481–516. Santiago: Instituto de Economía de la Pontificia Universidad Católica de Chile y Centro Internacional para el Desarrollo Económico.

Wong, Joseph. 2004a. "Democratization and the Left: Comparing East Asia and Latin America." *Comparative Political Studies* 37 (10): 1–24.

2004b. *Healthy Democracies: Welfare Politics in Taiwan and South Korea*. Ithaca: Cornell University Press.

World Bank. 1997. *World Development Report 1997: The State in a Changing World*. New York: Oxford University Press.

2000. *Sri Lanka: Recapturing Missed Opportunities*. Report #20430-CI. Washington, DC: World Bank.

2001. *World Development Report 2000/2001: Attacking Poverty*. New York: Oxford University Press.

2003a. *Global Economic Prospects and the Developing Countries*. Washington, DC: World Bank.

2003b. *Lifelong Learning in the Global Knowledge Economy: Challenges for Developing Countries*. Washington, DC: World Bank.

2004a. *African Development Indicators 2004*. Washington, DC: World Bank.

2004b. *2004 World Development Indicators*. Washington, DC: World Bank.

2004c. *World Development Report 2004: Making Services Work for People*. Washington, DC: World Bank.

World Bank, Operations Evaluation Department. 2002. *Chile: Country Assistance Evaluation*. Available from: http://www.worldbank.org/oed/.

Yashar, Deborah J. 1997. *Demanding Democracy: Reform and Reaction in Costa Rica and Guatemala, 1870s–1950s*. Stanford: Stanford University Press.

Yom, Sean L. 2002. "Islam and Globalization: Secularism, Religion and Radicalism." *Internationale Politik and Gesellschaft* 2: 84–109.

Yoon, Jungkeun. 2004. "Globalization and the Welfare State in Developing Countries." Paper prepared for delivery at the 2004 Annual Meeting, American Political Science Association, Chicago, September 2–5.

Young, Crawford. 2002. "Deciphering Disorder in Africa: Is Identity the Key?" *World Politics* 54: 532–37.

Zachariah, K. C., and I. S. R. Rajan. 2004. *Gulf Revisited: Economic Consequences of Emigration from Kerala*. Thiruvananthapuram: Centre for Development Studies.

Zeidan, David. 2003. "Radical Islam in Egypt. A Comparison of Two Groups." In *Revolutionaries and Reformers: Contemporary Islamic Movements in the Middle East*, ed. Barry Rubin. Albany: State University of New York Press.

Zeitlin, Maurice, and Richard Earl Ratcliff. 1988. *Landlords and Capitalists: The Dominant Class of Chile*. Princeton: Princeton University Press.

Zwanecki, Dunja. 2001. *Social Security Arrangements in Sub-Saharan Africa*. Regensburg: Transfer Verlag.

Index

CPSIA information can be obtained at www.ICGtesting.com
Printed in the USA
BVOW01s0924310514

355001BV00001B/3/P